The Law of International Organizations – Documents and Cases

The Law of International Organizations – Documents and Cases

Edited by

Snežana Trifunovska

eleven international publishing

Published, sold and distributed by Eleven International Publishing
P.O. Box 85576
2508 CG The Hague
The Netherlands
Tel.: + 31 70 33 070 33
Fax: + 31 70 33 070 30
e-mail: sales@budh.nl
www.elevenpub.com

Sold and distributed in USA and Canada
International Specialized Book Services
920 NE 58th Avenue, Suite 300
Portland, OR 97213-3786, USA
Tel: +1-800-944-6190 (toll-free)
Fax: +11-503-280-8832
orders@isbs.com
www.isbs.com

Eleven International Publishing is an imprint of Boom uitgevers Den Haag.

ISBN 978-94-6236-870-5

Printed in The Netherlands

Table of Contents

Foreword

This publication was prepared primarily with the purpose to provide students of the Law of International Organizations with an easy access to some of the basic documents and cases on the subject.

It reflects no attempt to be complete and to cover all international organizations, subject areas or case law. There is a great number and variety of international organizations created for virtually every field of human endeavour. Separate rules and practices apply to each of them and are determined by the needs and objectives for which the organization was created. The diversity exists, *inter alia*, with regard to objectives, fields of activity, internal structure, membership, powers, decision-making and financing. Though there are certainly similarities and common problems which made the development of the Law of International Organizations as a separate branch of International Public Law possible, there is still such a number and variety of documents and rules that compiling a systematic collection by including rules of all organizations and relevant case law would be an impossible task. Therefore, the publication includes a selection of documents and of (excerpts of) judicial cases which cover only few international organizations that are, in the view of the Editor, illustrative for various aspects of the Law of International Organizations discussed in her own introductory course. The significance of the organizations chosen, their influence in the field of activity, uniqueness and the representativeness of the methods adopted, played a role in making the selection. The collection also includes several documents of a general importance for international organizations such as the one on the law of treaties or responsibility. Each of the included materials is preceded by a note in order to provide brief additional information.

It is the hope of the Editor that this selection will be a useful tool to students and others studying and analysing various aspects of the Law of International Organizations.

PART ONE – DOCUMENTS

I. United Nations (UN)

Charter of the United Nations, 1945

[*Note:* The Charter was adopted on June 26, 1945 and entered into force on October 24, 1945 in accordance with Article 110.

Status since February 2018: 193 Members. The last admission to the UN membership took place in 2011 when the Republic of South Sudan became the UN member State.]

PREAMPLE

WE THE PEOPLES OF THE UNITED NATIONS DETERMINED
to save succeeding generations from the scourge of war, which twice in our lifetime has brought untold sorrow to mankind, and
to reaffirm faith in fundamental human rights, in the dignity and worth of the human person, in the equal rights of men and women and of nations large and small, and
to establish conditions under which justice and respect for the obligations arising from treaties and other sources of international law can be maintained, and
to promote social progress and better standards of life in larger freedom,
AND FOR THESE ENDS
to practice tolerance and live together in peace with one another as good neighbors, and
to unite our strength to maintain international peace and security, and
to ensure by the acceptance of principles and the institution of methods, that armed force shall not be used, save in the common interest, and
to employ international machinery for the promotion of the economic and social advancement of all peoples,
HAVE RESOLVED TO COMBINE OUR EFFORTS TO ACCOMPLISH THESE AIMS
Accordingly, our respective Governments, through representatives assembled in the city of San Francisco, who have exhibited their full powers found to be in good and due form, have agreed to the present Charter of the United Nations and do hereby establish an international organization to be known as the United Nations.

CHAPTER I – PURPOSES AND PRINCIPLES

Article 1
The Purposes of the United Nations are:
1. To maintain international peace and security, and to that end: to take effective collective measures for the prevention and removal of threats to the peace, and for the suppression of acts of aggression or other breaches of the peace, and to bring about by peaceful means, and in conformity with the prin-

ciples of justice and international law, adjustment or settlement of international disputes or situations which might lead to a breach of the peace;
2. To develop friendly relations among nations based on respect for the principle of equal rights and self-determination of peoples, and to take other appropriate measures to strengthen universal peace;
3. To achieve international cooperation in solving international problems of an economic, social, cultural, or humanitarian character, and in promoting and encouraging respect for human rights and for fundamental freedoms for all without distinction as to race, sex, language, or religion; and
4. To be a center for harmonizing the actions of nations in the attainment of these common ends.

Article 2
The Organization and its Members, in pursuit of the Purposes stated in Article 1, shall act in accordance with the following Principles.
1. The Organization is based on the principle of the sovereign equality of all its Members.
2. All Members, in order to ensure to all of them the rights and benefits resulting from membership, shall fulfil in good faith the obligations assumed by them in accordance with the present Charter.
3. All Members shall settle their international disputes by peaceful means in such a manner that international peace and security, and justice, are not endangered.
4. All Members shall refrain in their international relations from the threat or use of force against the territorial integrity or political independence of any state, or in any other manner inconsistent with the Purposes of the United Nations.
5. All Members shall give the United Nations every assistance in any action it takes in accordance with the present Charter, and shall refrain from giving assistance to any state against which the United Nations is taking preventive or enforcement action.
6. The Organization shall ensure that states which are not Members of the United Nations act in accordance with these Principles so far as may be necessary for the maintenance of international peace and security.
7. Nothing contained in the present Charter shall authorize the United Nations to intervene in matters which are essentially within the domestic jurisdiction of any state or shall require the Members to submit such matters to settlement under the present Charter; but this principle shall not prejudice the application of enforcement measures under Chapter VII.

CHAPTER II – MEMBERSHIP

Article 3
The original Members of the United Nations shall be the states which, having participated in the United Nations Conference on International Organization at San Francisco, or having previously signed the Declaration by United Nations of January 1, 1942, sign the present Charter and ratify it in accordance with Article 110.

Article 4
1. Membership in the United Nations is open to all other peace-loving states which accept the obligations contained in the present Charter and, in the judgment of the Organization, are able and willing to carry out these obligations.
2. The admission of any such state to membership in the United Nations will be effected by a decision of the General Assembly upon the recommendation of the Security Council.

Article 5
A member of the United Nations against which preventive or enforcement action has been taken by the Security Council may be suspended from the exercise of the rights and privileges of membership by the General Assembly upon the recommendation of the Security Council. The exercise of these rights and privileges may be restored by the Security Council.

Article 6
A Member of the United Nations which has persistently violated the Principles contained in the present Charter may be expelled from the Organization by the General Assembly upon the recommendation of the Security Council.

CHAPTER III – ORGANS

Article 7
1. There are established as the principal organs of the United Nations: a General Assembly, a Security Council, an Economic and Social Council, a Trusteeship Council, an International Court of Justice, and a Secretariat.
2. Such subsidiary organs as may be found necessary may be established in accordance with the present Charter.

Article 8
The United Nations shall place no restrictions on the eligibility of men and women to participate in any capacity and under conditions of equality in its principal and subsidiary organs.

CHAPTER IV – THE GENERAL ASSEMBLY

Composition

Article 9
1. The General Assembly shall consist of all the Members of the United Nations.
2. Each member shall have not more than five representatives in the General Assembly.

Functions and Powers

Article 10
The General Assembly may discuss any questions or any matters within the scope of the present Charter or relating to the powers and functions of any organs provided for in the present Charter, and, except as provided in Article 12, may make recommendations to the Members of the United Nations or to the Security Council or to both on any such questions or matters.

Article 11
1. The General Assembly may consider the general principles of cooperation in the maintenance of international peace and security, including the principles governing disarmament and the regulation of armaments, and may make recommendations with regard to such principles to the Members or to the Security Council or to both.
2. The General Assembly may discuss any questions relating to the maintenance of international peace and security brought before it by any Member of the United Nations, or by the Security Council,

or by a state which is not a Member of the United Nations in accordance with Article 35, paragraph 2, and, except as provided in Article 12, may make recommendations with regard to any such questions to the state or states concerned or to the Security Council or to both. Any such question on which action is necessary shall be referred to the Security Council by the General Assembly either before or after discussion.

3. The General Assembly may call the attention of the Security Council to situations which are likely to endanger international peace and security.

4. The powers of the General Assembly set forth in this Article shall not limit the general scope of Article 10.

Article 12

1. While the Security Council is exercising in respect of any dispute or situation the functions assigned to it in the present Charter, the General Assembly shall not make any recommendation with regard to that dispute or situation unless the Security Council so requests.

2. The Secretary-General, with the consent of the Security Council, shall notify the General Assembly at each session of any matters relative to the maintenance of international peace and security which are being dealt with by the Security Council and shall similarly notify the General Assembly, or the Members of the United Nations if the General Assembly is not in session, immediately the Security Council ceases to deal with such matters.

Article 13

1. The General Assembly shall initiate studies and make recommendations for the purpose of:

a. promoting international cooperation in the political field and encouraging the progressive development of international law and its codification;

b. promoting international cooperation in the economic, social, cultural, educational, and health fields, and assisting in the realization of human rights and fundamental freedoms for all without distinction as to race, sex, language, or religion.

2. The further responsibilities, functions and powers of the General Assembly with respect to matters mentioned in paragraph 1(b) above are set forth in Chapters IX and X.

Article 14

Subject to the provisions of Article 12, the General Assembly may recommend measures for the peaceful adjustment of any situation, regardless of origin, which it deems likely to impair the general welfare or friendly relations among nations, including situations resulting from a violation of the provisions of the present Charter setting forth the Purposes and Principles of the United Nations.

Article 15

1. The General Assembly shall receive and consider annual and special reports from the Security Council; these reports shall include an account of the measures that the Security Council has decided upon or taken to maintain international peace and security.

2. The General Assembly shall receive and consider reports from the other organs of the United Nations.

Article 16

The General Assembly shall perform such functions with respect to the international trusteeship system as are assigned to it under Chapters XII and XIII, including the approval of the trusteeship agreements for areas not designated as strategic.

Article 17

1. The General Assembly shall consider and approve the budget of the Organization.
2. The expenses of the Organization shall be borne by the Members as apportioned by the General Assembly.
3. The General Assembly shall consider and approve any financial and budgetary arrangements with specialized agencies referred to in Article 57 and shall examine the administrative budgets of such specialized agencies with a view to making recommendations to the agencies concerned.

Voting

Article 18

1. Each member of the General Assembly shall have one vote.
2. Decisions of the General Assembly on important questions shall be made by a two-thirds majority of the members present and voting. These questions shall include: recommendations with respect to the maintenance of international peace and security, the election of the non-permanent members of the Security Council, the election of the members of the Economic and Social Council, the election of members of the Trusteeship Council in accordance with paragraph 1(c) of Article 86, the admission of new Members to the United Nations, the suspension of the rights and privileges of membership, the expulsion of Members, questions relating to the operation of the trusteeship system, and budgetary questions.
3. Decisions on other questions, Composition including the determination of additional categories of questions to be decided by a two-thirds majority, shall be made by a majority of the members present and voting.

Article 19

A Member of the United Nations which is in arrears in the payment of its financial contributions to the Organization shall have no vote in the General Assembly if the amount of its arrears equals or exceeds the amount of the contributions due from it for the preceding two full years. The General Assembly may, nevertheless, permit such a Member to vote if it is satisfied that the failure to pay is due to conditions beyond the control of the Member.

Procedure

Article 20

The General Assembly shall meet in regular annual sessions and in such special sessions as occasion may require. Special sessions shall be convoked by the Secretary-General at the request of the Security Council or of a majority of the Members of the United Nations.

Article 21

The General Assembly shall adopt its own rules of procedure. It shall elect its President for each session.

Article 22

The General Assembly may establish such subsidiary organs as it deems necessary for the performance of its functions.

CHAPTER V – THE SECURITY COUNCIL

Article 23

1. The Security Council shall consist of fifteen Members of the United Nations. The Republic of China, France, the Union of Soviet Socialist Republics, the United Kingdom of Great Britain and Northern Ireland, and the United States of America shall be permanent members of the Security Council. The General Assembly shall elect ten other Members of the United Nations to be non-permanent members of the Security Council, due regard being specially paid, in the first instance to the contribution of Members of the United Nations to the maintenance of international peace and security and to the other purposes of the Organization, and also to equitable geographical distribution.
2. The non-permanent members of the Security Council shall be elected for a term of two years. In the first election of the non-permanent members after the increase of the membership of the Security Council from eleven to fifteen, two of the four additional members shall be chosen for a term of one year. A retiring member shall not be eligible for immediate re-election.
3. Each member of the Security Council shall have one representative.

Functions and Powers

Article 24

1. In order to ensure prompt and effective action by the United Nations, its Members confer on the Security Council primary responsibility for the maintenance of international peace and security, and agree that in carrying out its duties under this responsibility the Security Council acts on their behalf.
2. In discharging these duties the Security Council shall act in accordance with the Purposes and Principles of the United Nations. The specific powers granted to the Security Council for the discharge of these duties are laid down in Chapters VI, VII, VIII, and XII.
3. The Security Council shall submit annual and, when necessary, special reports to the General Assembly for its consideration.

Article 25

The Members of the United Nations agree to accept and carry out the decisions of the Security Council in accordance with the present Charter.

Article 26

In order to promote the establishment and maintenance of international peace and security with the least diversion for armaments of the world's human and economic resources, the Security Council shall be responsible for formulating, with the assistance of the Military Staff Committee referred to in Article 47, plans to be submitted to the Members of the United Nations for the establishment of a system for the regulation of armaments.

Voting

Article 27

1. Each member of the Security Council shall have one vote.
2. Decisions of the Security Council on procedural matters shall be made by an affirmative vote of nine members.

3. Decisions of the Security Council on all other matters shall be made by an affirmative vote of nine members including the concurring votes of the permanent members; provided that, in decisions under Chapter VI, and under paragraph 3 of Article 52, a party to a dispute shall abstain from voting.

Procedure

Article 28

1. The Security Council shall be so organized as to be able to function continuously. Each member of the Security Council shall for this purpose be represented at all times at the seat of the Organization.
2. The Security Council shall hold periodic meetings at which each of its members may, if it so desires, be represented by a member of the government or by some other specially designated representative.
3. The Security Council may hold meetings at such places other than the seat of the Organization as in its judgment will best facilitate its work.

Article 29

The Security Council may establish such subsidiary organs as it deems necessary for the performance of its functions.

Article 30

The Security Council shall adopt its own rules of procedure, including the method of selecting its President.

Article 31

Any Member of the United Nations which is not a member of the Security Council may participate, without vote, in the discussion of any question brought before the Security Council whenever the latter considers that the interests of that Member are specially affected.

Article 32

Any Member of the United Nations which is not a member of the Security Council or any state which is not a Member of the United Nations, if it is a party to a dispute under consideration by the Security Council, shall be invited to participate, without vote, in the discussion relating to the dispute. The Security Council shall lay down such conditions as it deems just for the participation of a state which is not a Member of the United Nations.

CHAPTER VI – PACIFIC SETTLEMENT OF DISPUTES

Article 33

1. The parties to any dispute, the continuance of which is likely to endanger the maintenance of international peace and security, shall, first of all, seek a solution by negotiation, enquiry, mediation, conciliation, arbitration, judicial settlement, resort to regional agencies or arrangements, or other peaceful means of their own choice.
2. The Security Council shall, when it deems necessary, call upon the parties to settle their dispute by such means.

Article 34
The Security Council may investigate any dispute, or any situation which might lead to international friction or give rise to a dispute, in order to determine whether the continuance of the dispute or situation is likely to endanger the maintenance of international peace and security.

Article 35
1. Any Member of the United Nations may bring any dispute, or any situation of the nature referred to in Article 34, to the attention of the Security Council or of the General Assembly.
2. A state which is not a Member of the United Nations may bring to the attention of the Security Council or of the General Assembly any dispute to which it is a party if it accepts in advance, for the purposes of the dispute, the obligations of pacific settlement provided in the present Charter.
3. The proceedings of the General Assembly in respect of matters brought to its attention under this Article will be subject to the provisions of Articles 11 and 12.

Article 36
1. The Security Council may, at any stage of a dispute of the nature referred to in Article 33 or of a situation of like nature, recommend appropriate procedures or methods of adjustment.
2. The Security Council should take into consideration any procedures for the settlement of the dispute which have already been adopted by the parties.
3. In making recommendations under this Article the Security Council should also take into consideration that legal disputes should as a general rule be referred by the parties to the International Court of Justice in accordance with the provisions of the Statute of the Court.

Article 37
1. Should the parties to a dispute of the nature referred to in Article 33 fail to settle it by the means indicated in that Article, they shall refer it to the Security Council.
2. If the Security Council deems that the continuance of the dispute is in fact likely to endanger the maintenance of international peace and security, it shall decide whether to take action under Article 36 or to recommend such terms of settlement as it may consider appropriate.

Article 38
Without prejudice to the provisions of Articles 33 to 37, the Security Council may, if all the parties to any dispute so request, make recommendations to the parties with a view to a pacific settlement of the dispute.

CHAPTER VII – ACTION WITH RESPECT TO THREATS TO THE PEACE, BREACHES OF THE PEACE, AND ACTS OF AGGRESSION

Article 39
The Security Council shall determine the existence of any threat to the peace, breach of the peace, or act of aggression and shall make recommendations, or decide what measures shall be taken in accordance with Articles 41 and 42, to maintain or restore international peace and security.

Article 40
In order to prevent an aggravation of the situation, the Security Council may, before making the recommendations or deciding upon the measures provided for in Article 39, call upon the parties concerned

to comply with such provisional measures as it deems necessary or desirable. Such provisional measures shall be without prejudice to the rights, claims, or position of the parties concerned. The Security Council shall duly take account of failure to comply with such provisional measures.

Article 41

The Security Council may decide what measures not involving the use of armed force are to be employed to give effect to its decisions, and it may call upon the Members of the United Nations to apply such measures. These may include complete or partial interruption of economic relations and of rail, sea, air, postal, telegraphic, radio, and other means of communication, and the severance of diplomatic relations.

Article 42

Should the Security Council consider that measures provided for in Article 41 would be inadequate or have proved to be inadequate, it may take such action by air, sea, or land forces as may be necessary to maintain or restore international peace and security. Such action may include demonstrations, blockade, and other operations by air, sea, or land forces of Members of the United Nations.

Article 43

1. All Members of the United Nations, in order to contribute to the maintenance of international peace and security, undertake to make available to the Security Council, on its call and in accordance with a special agreement or agreements, armed forces, assistance, and facilities, including rights of passage, necessary for the purpose of maintaining international peace and security.
2. Such agreement or agreements shall govern the numbers and types of forces, their degree of readiness and general location, and the nature of the facilities and assistance to be provided.
3. The agreement or agreements shall be negotiated as soon as possible on the initiative of the Security Council. They shall be concluded between the Security Council and Members or between the Security Council and groups of Members and shall be subject to ratification by the signatory states in accordance with their respective constitutional processes.

Article 44

When the Security Council has decided to use force it shall, before calling upon a Member not represented on it to provide armed forces in fulfilment of the obligations assumed under Article 43, invite that Member, if the Member so desires, to participate in the decisions of the Security Council concerning the employment of contingents of that Member's armed forces.

Article 45

In order to enable the United Nations to take urgent military measures Members shall hold immediately available national air-force contingents for combined international enforcement action. The strength and degree of readiness of these contingents and plans for their combined action shall be determined, within the limits laid down in the special agreement or agreements referred to in Article 43, by the Security Council with the assistance of the Military Staff Committee.

Article 46

Plans for the application of armed force shall be made by the Security Council with the assistance of the Military Staff Committee.

Article 47

1. There shall be established a Military Staff Committee to advise and assist the Security Council on all questions relating to the Security Council's military requirements for the maintenance of international peace and security, the employment and command of forces placed at its disposal, the regulation of armaments, and possible disarmament.
2. The Military Staff Committee shall consist of the Chiefs of Staff of the permanent members of the Security Council or their representatives. Any Member of the United Nations not permanently represented on the Committee shall be invited by the Committee to be associated with it when the efficient discharge of the Committee's responsibilities requires the participation of that Member in its work.
3. The Military Staff Committee shall be responsible under the Security Council for the strategic direction of any armed forces placed at the disposal of the Security Council. Questions relating to the command of such forces shall be worked out subsequently.
4. The Military Staff Committee, with the authorization of the Security Council and after consultation with appropriate regional agencies, may establish regional subcommittees.

Article 48

1. The action required to carry out the decisions of the Security Council for the maintenance of international peace and security shall be taken by all the Members of the United Nations or by some of them, as the Security Council may determine.
2. Such decisions shall be carried out by the Members of the United Nations directly and through their action in the appropriate international agencies of which they are members.

Article 49

The Members of the United Nations shall join in affording mutual assistance in carrying out the measures decided upon by the Security Council.

Article 50

If preventive or enforcement measures against any state are taken by the Security Council, any other state, whether a Member of the United Nations or not, which finds itself confronted with special economic problems arising from the carrying out of those measures shall have the right to consult the Security Council with regard to a solution of those problems.

Article 51

Nothing in the present Charter shall impair the inherent right of individual or collective self-defense if an armed attack occurs against a Member of the United Nations, until the Security Council has taken measures necessary to maintain international peace and security. Measures taken by Members in the exercise of this right of self-defence shall be immediately reported to the Security Council and shall not in any way affect the authority and responsibility of the Security Council under the present Charter to take at any time such action as it deems necessary in order to maintain or restore international peace and security.

CHAPTER VIII – REGIONAL ARRANGEMENTS

Article 52

1. Nothing in the present Charter precludes the existence of regional arrangements or agencies for dealing with such matters relating to the maintenance of international peace and security as are appro-

priate for regional action, provided that such arrangements or agencies and their activities are consistent with the Purposes and Principles of the United Nations.

2. The Members of the United Nations entering into such arrangements or constituting such agencies shall make every effort to achieve pacific settlement of local disputes through such regional arrangements or by such regional agencies before referring them to the Security Council.

3. The Security Council shall encourage the development of pacific settlement of local disputes through such regional arrangements or by such regional agencies either on the initiative of the states concerned or by reference from the Security Council.

4. This Article in no way impairs the application of Articles 34 and 35.

Article 53

1. The Security Council shall, where appropriate, utilize such regional arrangements or agencies for enforcement action under its authority. But no enforcement action shall be taken under regional arrangements or by regional agencies without the authorization of the Security Council, with the exception of measures against any enemy state, as defined in paragraph 2 of this Article, provided for pursuant to Article 107 or in regional arrangements directed against renewal of aggressive policy on the part of any such state, until such time as the Organization may, on request of the Governments concerned, be charged with the responsibility for preventing further aggression by such a state.

2. The term enemy state as used in paragraph 1 of this Article applies to any state which during the Second World War has been an enemy of any signatory of the present Charter.

Article 54

The Security Council shall at all times be kept fully informed of activities undertaken or in contemplation under regional arrangements or by regional agencies for the maintenance of international peace and security.

CHAPTER IX – INTERNATIONAL ECONOMIC AND SOCIAL CO-OPERATION

Article 55

With a view to the creation of conditions of stability and well-being which are necessary for peaceful and friendly relations among nations based on respect for the principle of equal rights and self-determination of peoples, the United Nations shall promote:

a. higher standards of living, full employment, and conditions of economic and social progress and development;

b. solutions of international economic, social, health, and related problems; and international cultural and educational co-operation; and

c. universal respect for, and observance of, human rights and fundamental freedoms for all without distinction as to race, sex, language, or religion.

Article 56

All Members pledge themselves to take joint and separate action in co-operation with the Organization for the achievement of the purposes set forth in Article 55.

Article 57

1. The various specialized agencies, established by intergovernmental agreement and having wide international responsibilities, as defined in their basic instruments, in economic, social, cultural, edu-

cational, health, and related fields, shall be brought into relationship with the United Nations in accordance with the provisions of Article 63.
2. Such agencies thus brought into relationship with the United Nations are hereinafter referred to as specialized agencies.

Article 58
The Organization shall make recommendations for the coordination of the policies and activities of the specialized agencies.

Article 59
The Organization shall, where appropriate, initiate negotiations among the states concerned for the creation of any new specialized agencies required for the accomplishment of the purposes set forth in Article 55.

Article 60
Responsibility for the discharge of the functions of the Organization set forth in this Chapter shall be vested in the General Assembly and, under the authority of the General Assembly, in the Economic and Social Council, which shall have for this purpose the powers set forth in Chapter X.

CHAPTER X – THE ECONOMIC AND SOCIAL COUNCIL

Composition

Article 61
1. The Economic and Social Council shall consist of fifty-four Members of the United Nations elected by the General Assembly.
2. Subject to the provisions of paragraph 3, eighteen members of the Economic and Social Council shall be elected each year for a term of three years. A retiring member shall be eligible for immediate re-election.
3. At the first election after the increase in the membership of the Economic and Social Council from twenty-seven to fifty-four members, in addition to the members elected in place of the nine members whose term of office expires at the end of that year, twenty-seven additional members shall be elected. Of these twenty-seven additional members, the term of office of nine members so elected shall expire at the end of one year, and of nine other members at the end of two years, in accordance with arrangements made by the General Assembly.
4. Each member of the Economic and Social Council shall have one representative.

Functions and Powers

Article 62
1. The Economic and Social Council may make or initiate studies and reports with respect to international economic, social, cultural, educational, health, and related matters and may make recommendations with respect to any such matters to the General Assembly, to the Members of the United Nations, and to the specialized agencies concerned.
2. It may make recommendations for the purpose of promoting respect for, and observance of, human rights and fundamental freedoms for all.

3. It may prepare draft conventions for submission to the General Assembly, with respect to matters falling within its competence.
4. It may call, in accordance with the rules prescribed by the United Nations, international conferences on matters falling within its competence.

Article 63
1. The Economic and Social Council may enter into agreements with any of the agencies referred to in Article 57, defining the terms on which the agency concerned shall be brought into relationship with the United Nations. Such agreements shall be subject to approval by the General Assembly.
2. It may coordinate the activities of the specialized agencies through consultation with and recommendations to such agencies and through recommendations to the General Assembly and to the Members of the United Nations.

Article 64
1. The Economic and Social Council may take appropriate steps to obtain regular reports from the specialized agencies. It may make arrangements with the Members of the United Nations and with the specialized agencies to obtain reports on the steps taken to give effect to its own recommendations and to recommendations on matters falling within its competence made by the General Assembly.
2. It may communicate its observations on these reports to the General Assembly.

Article 65
The Economic and Social Council may furnish information to the Security Council and shall assist the Security Council upon its request.

Article 66
1. The Economic and Social Council shall perform such functions as fall within its competence in connection with the carrying out of the recommendations of the General Assembly.
2. It may, with the approval of the General Assembly, perform services at the request of Members of the United Nations and at the request of specialized agencies.
3. It shall perform such other functions as are specified elsewhere in the present Charter or as may be assigned to it by the General Assembly.

Article 67
1. Each member of the Economic and Social Council shall have one vote.
2. Decisions of the Economic and Social Council shall be made by a majority of the members present and voting.

Procedure

Article 68
The Economic and Social Council shall set up commissions in economic and social fields and for the promotion of human rights, and such other commissions as may be required for the performance of its functions.

Article 69

The Economic and Social Council shall invite any Member of the United Nations to participate, without vote, in its deliberations on any matter of particular concern to that Member.

Article 70

The Economic and Social Council may make arrangements for representatives of the specialized agencies to participate, without vote, in its deliberations and in those of the commissions established by it, and for its representatives to participate in the deliberations of the specialized agencies.

Article 71

The Economic and Social Council may make suitable arrangements for consultation with nongovernmental organizations which are concerned with matters within its competence. Such arrangements may be made with international organizations and, where appropriate, with national organizations after consultation with the Member of the United Nations concerned.

Article 72

1. The Economic and Social Council shall adopt its own rules of procedure, including the method of selecting its President.
2. The Economic and Social Council shall meet as required in accordance with its rules, which shall include provision for the convening of meetings on the request of a majority of its members.

CHAPTER XI – DECLARATION REGARDING NON-SELF-GOVERNING TERRITORIES

Article 73

Members of the United Nations which have or assume responsibilities for the administration of territories whose peoples have not yet attained a full measure of self-government recognize the principle that the interests of the inhabitants of these territories are paramount, and accept as a sacred trust the obligation to promote to the utmost, within the system of international peace and security established by the present Charter, the well-being of the inhabitants of these territories, and, to this end:

a. to ensure, with due respect for the culture of the peoples concerned, their political, economic, social, and educational advancement, their just treatment, and their protection against abuses;
b. to develop self-government, to take due account of the political aspirations of the peoples, and to assist them in the progressive development of their free political institutions, according to the particular circumstances of each territory and its peoples and their varying stages of advancement;
c. to further international peace and security;
d. to promote constructive measures of development, to encourage research, and to co-operate with one another and, when and where appropriate, with specialized international bodies with a view to the practical achievement of the social, economic, and scientific purposes set forth in this Article; and
e. to transmit regularly to the Secretary-General for information purposes, subject to such limitation as security and constitutional considerations may require, statistical and other information of a technical nature relating to economic, social, and educational conditions in the territories for which they are respectively responsible other than those territories to which Chapter XII and XIII apply.

Article 74

Members of the United Nations also agree that their policy in respect of the territories to which this Chapter applies, no less than in respect of their metropolitan areas, must be based on the general principle of good-neighbourliness, due account being taken of the interests and well-being of the rest of the world, in social, economic, and commercial matters.

CHAPTER XII – INTERNATIONAL TRUSTEESHIP SYSTEM

Article 75

The United Nations shall establish under its authority an international trusteeship system for the administration and supervision of such territories as may be placed thereunder by subsequent individual agreements. These territories are hereinafter referred to as trust territories.

Article 76

The basic objectives of the trusteeship system, in accordance with the Purposes of the United Nations laid down in Article 1 of the present Charter, shall be:

a. to further international peace and security;
b. to promote the political, economic, social, and educational advancement of the inhabitants of the trust territories, and their progressive development towards self-government or independence as may be appropriate to the particular circumstances of each territory and its peoples and the freely expressed wishes of the peoples concerned, and as may be provided by the terms of each trusteeship agreement;
c. to encourage respect for human rights and for fundamental freedoms for all without distinction as to race, sex, language, or religion, and to encourage recognition of the interdependence of the peoples of the world; and
d. to ensure equal treatment in social, economic, and commercial matters for all Members of the United Nations and their nationals and also equal treatment for the latter in the administration of justice without prejudice to the attainment of the foregoing objectives and subject to the provisions of Article 80.

Article 77

1. The trusteeship system shall apply to such territories in the following categories as may be placed thereunder by means of trusteeship agreements:

a. territories now held under mandate;
b. territories which may be detached from enemy states as a result of the Second World War; and
c. territories voluntarily placed under the system by states responsible for their administration.

2. It will be a matter for subsequent agreement as to which territories in the foregoing categories will be brought under the trusteeship system and upon what terms.

Article 78

The trusteeship system shall not apply to territories which have become Members of the United Nations, relationship among which shall be based on respect for the principle of sovereign equality.

Article 79
The terms of trusteeship for each territory to be placed under the trusteeship system, including any alteration or amendment, shall be agreed upon by the states directly concerned, including the mandatory power in the case of territories held under mandate by a Member of the United Nations, and shall be approved as provided for in Articles 83 and 85.

Article 80
1. Except as may be agreed upon in individual trusteeship agreements, made under Articles 77, 79, and 81, placing each territory under the trusteeship system, and until such agreements have been concluded, nothing in this Chapter shall be construed in or of itself to alter in any manner the rights whatsoever of any states or any peoples or the terms of existing international instruments to which Members of the United Nations may respectively be parties.
2. Paragraph 1 of this Article shall not be interpreted as giving grounds for delay or postponement of the negotiation and conclusion of agreements for placing mandated and other territories under the trusteeship system as provided for in Article 77.

Article 81
The trusteeship agreement shall in each case include the terms under which the trust territory will be administered and designate the authority which will exercise the administration of the trust territory. Such authority, hereinafter called the administering authority, may be one or more states or the Organization itself.

Article 82
There may be designated, in any trusteeship agreement, a strategic area or areas which may include part or all of the trust territory to which the agreement applies, without prejudice to any special agreement or agreements made under Article 43.

Article 83
1. All functions of the United Nations relating to strategic areas, including the approval of the terms of the trusteeship agreements and of their alteration or amendment, shall be exercised by the Security Council.
2. The basic objectives set forth in Article 76 shall be applicable to the people of each strategic area.
3. The Security Council shall, subject to the provisions of the trusteeship agreements and without prejudice to security considerations, avail itself of the assistance of the Trusteeship Council to perform those functions of the United Nations under the trusteeship system relating to political. economic, social, and educational matters in the strategic areas.

Article 84
It shall be the duty of the administering authority to ensure that the trust territory shall play its part in the maintenance of international peace and security. To this end the administering authority may make use of volunteer forces, facilities, and assistance from the trust territory in carrying out the obligations towards the Security Council undertaken in this regard by the administering authority, as well as for local defence and the maintenance of law and order within the trust territory.

Article 85

1. The functions of the United Nations with regard to trusteeship agreements for all areas not designated as strategic, including the approval of the terms of the trusteeship agreements and of their alteration or amendment, shall be exercised by the General Assembly.
2. The Trusteeship Council, operating under the authority of the General Assembly, shall assist the General Assembly in carrying out these functions.

CHAPTER XIII – THE TRUSTEESHIP COUNCIL

Composition

Article 86

1. The Trusteeship Council shall consist of the following Members of the United Nations:

a. those Members administering trust territories;
b. such of those Members mentioned by name in Article 23 as are not administering trust territories; and
c. as many other Members elected for three-year terms by the General Assembly as may be necessary to ensure that the total number of members of the Trusteeship Council is equally divided between those Members of the United Nations which administer trust territories and those which do not.

2. Each member of the Trusteeship Council shall designate one specially qualified person to represent it therein.

Functions and Powers

Article 87

The General Assembly and, under its authority, the Trusteeship Council, in carrying out theirfunctions, may:

a. consider reports submitted by the administering authority;
b. accept petitions and examine them in consultation with the administering authority;
c. provide for periodic visits to the respective trust territories at times agreed upon with the administering authority; and
d. take these and other actions in conformity with the terms of the trusteeship agreements.

Article 88

The Trusteeship Council shall formulate a questionnaire on the political, economic, social, and educational advancement of the inhabitants of each trust territory, and the administering authority for each trust territory within the competence of the General Assembly shall make an annual report to the General Assembly upon the basis of such questionnaire.

Voting

Article 89

1. Each member of the Trusteeship Council shall have one vote.
2. Decisions of the Trusteeship Council shall be made by a majority of the members present and voting.

Procedure

Article 90
1. The Trusteeship Council shall adopt its own rules of procedure, including the method of selecting its President.
2. The Trusteeship Council shall meet as required in accordance with its rules, which shall include provision for the convening of meetings on the request of a majority of its members.

Article 91
The Trusteeship Council shall, when appropriate, avail itself of the assistance of the Economic and Social Council and of the specialized agencies in regard to matters with which they are respectively concerned.

CHAPTER XIV – THE INTERNATIONAL COURT OF JUSTICE

Article 92
The International Court of Justice shall be the principal judicial organ of the United Nations. It shall function in accordance with the annexed Statute which is based upon the Statute of the Permanent Court of International Justice and forms an integral part of the present Charter.

Article 93
1. All Members of the United Nations are ipso facto parties to the Statute of the International Court of Justice.
2. A state which is not a Member of the United Nations may become a party to the Statute of the International Court of Justice on conditions to be determined in each case by the General Assembly upon the recommendation of the Security Council.

Article 94
1. Each Member of the United Nations undertakes to comply with the decision of the International Court of Justice in any case to which it is a party.
2. If any party to a case fails to perform the obligations incumbent upon it under a judgment rendered by the Court, the other party may have recourse to the Security Council, which may, if it deems necessary, make recommendations or decide upon measures to be taken to give effect to the judgment.

Article 95
Nothing in the present Charter shall prevent Members of the United Nations from entrusting the solution of their differences to other tribunals by virtue of agreements already in existence or which may be concluded in the future.

Article 96
1. The General Assembly or the Security Council may request the International Court of Justice to give an advisory opinion on any legal question.
2. Other organs of the United Nations and specialized agencies, which may at any time be so authorized by the General Assembly, may also request advisory opinions of the Court on legal questions arising within the scope of their activities.

CHAPTER XV – THE SECRETARIAT

Article 97
The Secretariat shall comprise a Secretary-General and such staff as the Organization may require. The Secretary-General shall be appointed by the General Assembly upon the recommendation of the Security Council. He shall be the chief administrative officer of the Organization.

Article 98
The Secretary-General shall act in that capacity in all meetings of the General Assembly, of the Security Council, of the Economic and Social Council, and of the Trusteeship Council, and shall perform such other functions as are entrusted to him by these organs. The Secretary-General shall make an annual report to the General Assembly on the work of the Organization.

Article 99
The Secretary-General may bring to the attention of the Security Council any matter which in his opinion may threaten the maintenance of international peace and security.

Article 100
1. In the performance of their duties the Secretary-General and the staff shall not seek or receive instructions from any government or from any other authority external to the Organization. They shall refrain from any action which might reflect on their position as international officials responsible only to the Organization.
2. Each Member of the United Nations undertakes to respect the exclusively international character of the responsibilities of the Secretary-General and the staff and not to seek to influence them in the discharge of their responsibilities.

Article 101
1. The staff shall be appointed by the Secretary-General under regulations established by the General Assembly.
2. Appropriate staffs shall be permanently assigned to the Economic and Social Council, the Trusteeship Council, and, as required, to other organs of the United Nations. These staffs shall form a part of the Secretariat.
3. The paramount consideration in the employment of the staff and in the determination of the conditions of service shall be the necessity of securing the highest standards of efficiency, competence, and integrity. Due regard shall be paid to the importance of recruiting the staff on as wide a geographical basis as possible.

CHAPTER XVI – MISCELLANEOUS PROVISIONS

Article 102
1. Every treaty and every international agreement entered into by any Member of the United Nations after the present Charter comes into force shall as soon as possible be registered with the Secretariat and published by it.
2. No party to any such treaty or international agreement which has not been registered in accordance with the provisions of paragraph I of this Article may invoke that treaty or agreement before any organ of the United Nations.

Article 103

In the event of a conflict between the obligations of the Members of the United Nations under the present Charter and their obligations under any other international agreement, their obligations under the present Charter shall prevail.

Article 104

The Organization shall enjoy in the territory of each of its Members such legal capacity as may be necessary for the exercise of its functions and the fulfilment of its purposes.

Article 105

1. The Organization shall enjoy in the territory of each of its Members such privileges and immunities as are necessary for the fulfilment of its purposes.
2. Representatives of the Members of the United Nations and officials of the Organization shall similarly enjoy such privileges and immunities as are necessary for the independent exercise of their functions in connection with the Organization.
3. The General Assembly may make recommendations with a view to determining the details of the application of paragraphs 1 and 2 of this Article or may propose conventions to the Members of the United Nations for this purpose.

CHAPTER XVII – TRANSITIONAL SECURITY ARRANGEMENTS

Article 106

Pending the coming into force of such special agreements referred to in Article 43 as in the opinion of the Security Council enable it to begin the exercise of its responsibilities under Article 42, the parties to the Four-Nation Declaration, signed at Moscow October 30, 1943, and France, shall, in accordance with the provisions of paragraph 5 of that Declaration, consult with one another and as occasion requires with other Members of the United Nations with a view to such joint action on behalf of the Organization as may be necessary for the purpose of maintaining international peace and security.

Article 107

Nothing in the present Charter shall invalidate or preclude action, in relation to any state which during the Second World War has been an enemy of any signatory to the present Charter, taken or authorized as a result of that war by the Governments having responsibility for such action.

CHAPTER XVIII – AMENDMENTS

Article 108

Amendments to the present Charter shall come into force for all Members of the United Nations when they have been adopted by a vote of two thirds of the members of the General Assembly and ratified in accordance with their respective constitutional processes by two thirds of the Members of the United Nations, including all the permanent members of the Security Council.

Article 109

1. A General Conference of the Members of the United Nations for the purpose of reviewing the present Charter may be held at a date and place to be fixed by a two-thirds vote of the members of the General Assembly and by a vote of any seven members of the Security Council. Each Member of the United Nations shall have one vote in the conference.
2. Any alteration of the present Charter recommended by a two-thirds vote of the conference shall take effect when ratified in accordance with their respective constitutional processes by two thirds of the Members of the United Nations including all the permanent members of the Security Council.
3. If such a conference has not been held before the tenth annual session of the General Assembly following the coming into force of the present Charter, the proposal to call such a conference shall be placed on the agenda of that session of the General Assembly, and the conference shall be held if so decided by a majority vote of the members of the General Assembly and by a vote of any seven members of the Security Council.

CHAPTER XIX – RATIFICATION AND SIGNATURE

Article 110

1. The present Charter shall be ratified by the signatory states in accordance with their respective constitutional processes.
2. The ratifications shall be deposited with the Government of the United States of America, which shall notify all the signatory states of each deposit as well as the Secretary-General of the Organization when he has been appointed.
3. The present Charter shall come into force upon the deposit of ratifications by the Republic of China, France, the Union of Soviet Socialist Republics, the United Kingdom of Great Britain and Northern Ireland, and the United States of America, and by a majority of the other signatory states. A protocol of the ratifications deposited shall thereupon be drawn up by the Government of the United States of America which shall communicate copies thereof to all the signatory states.
4. The states signatory to the present Charter which ratify it after it has come into force will become original Members of the United Nations on the date of the deposit of their respective ratifications.

Article 111

The present Charter, of which the Chinese, French, Russian, English, and Spanish texts are equally authentic, shall remain deposited in the archives of the Government of the United States of America. Duly certified copies thereof shall be transmitted by that Government to the Governments of the other signatory states.

IN FAITH WHEREOF the representatives of the Governments of the United Nations have signed the present Charter.

DONE at the city of San Francisco the twenty-sixth day of June, one thousand nine hundred and forty-five.

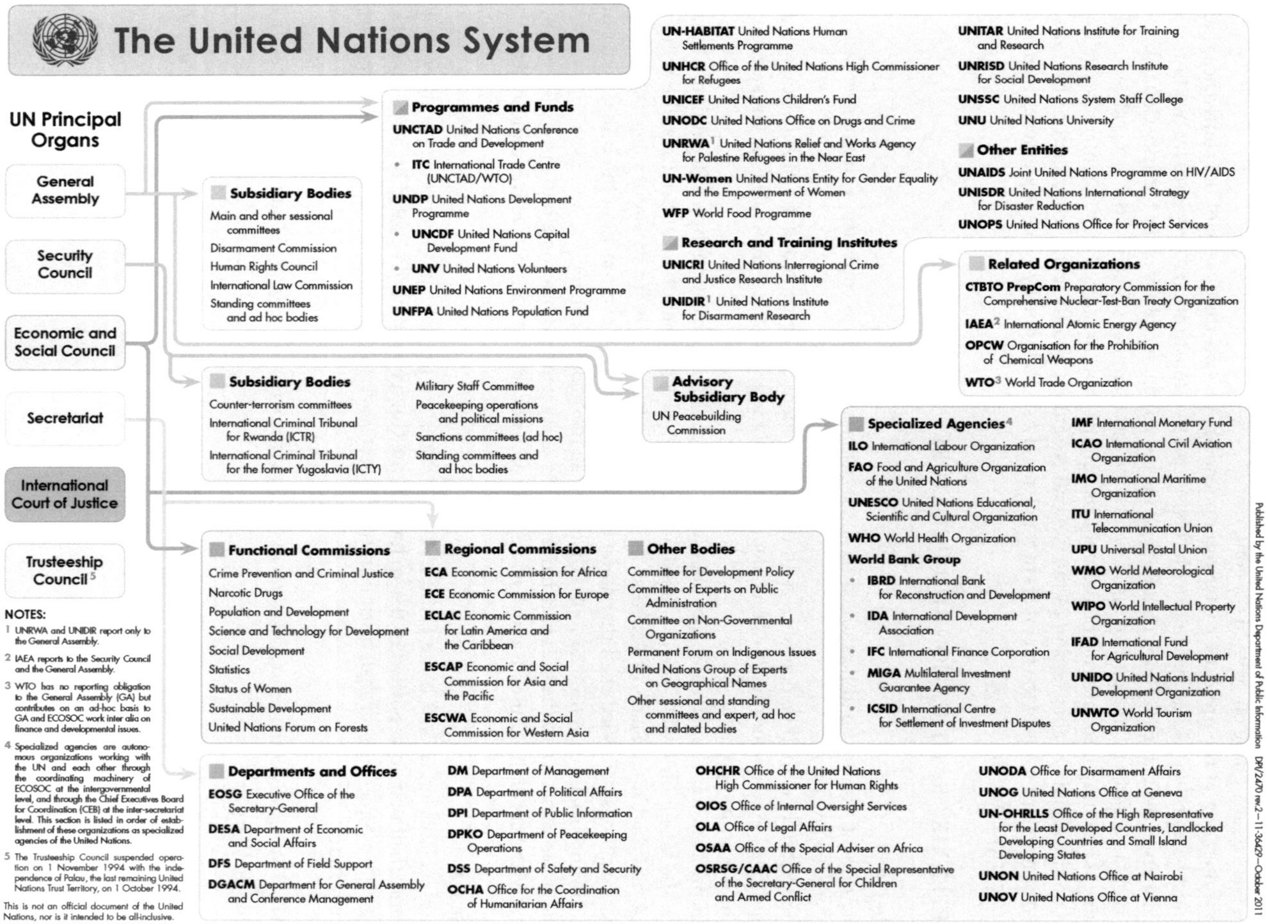

Figure 1

Source: Published by the United Nations Department of Public Information DPI/2470 rev.2—11-36429—October 2011.
The full document can be accessed at: https://unstats.un.org/unsd/statcom/doc12/WelcomeKit.pdf

Statute of the International Court of Justice, 1945

[*Note:* The Statute of the International Court of Justice forms an integral part of the UN Charter and is annexed to it.

Members of the United Nations are *ipso facto* parties to the Statute. However, in accordance with Article 93(2) of the UN Charter, States not members of the UN can also become parties to the Statute. That was the case, for example with Japan, Lichtenstein, San Marino and Switzerland.]

Article 1
The International Court of Justice established by the Charter of the United Nations as the principal judicial organ of the United Nations shall be constituted and shall function in accordance with the provisions of the present Statute.

CHAPTER I - ORGANIZATION OF THE COURT

Article 2
The Court shall be composed of a body of independent judges, elected regardless of their nationality from among persons of high moral character, who possess the qualifications required in their respective countries for appointment to the highest judicial offices, or are jurisconsults of recognized competence in international law.

Article 3
1. The Court shall consist of fifteen members, no two of whom may be nationals of the same state.
2. A person who for the purposes of membership in the Court could be regarded as a national of more than one state shall be deemed to be a national of the one in which he ordinarily exercises civil and political rights.

Article 4
1. The members of the Court shall be elected by the General Assembly and by the Security Council from a list of persons nominated by the national groups in the Permanent Court of Arbitration, in accordance with the following provisions.
2. In the case of Members of the United Nations not represented in the Permanent Court of Arbitration, candidates shall be nominated by national groups appointed for this purpose by their governments under the same conditions as those prescribed for members of the Permanent Court of Arbitration by Article 44 of the Convention of The Hague of 1907 for the pacific settlement of international disputes.
3. The conditions under which a state which is a party to the present Statute but is not a Member of the United Nations may participate in electing the members of the Court shall, in the absence of a special agreement, be laid down by the General Assembly upon recommendation of the Security Council.

Article 5

1. At least three months before the date of the election, the Secretary-General of the United Nations shall address a written request to the members of the Permanent Court of Arbitration belonging to the states which are parties to the present Statute, and to the members of the national groups appointed under Article 4, paragraph 2, inviting them to undertake, within a given time, by national groups, the nomination of persons in a position to accept the duties of a member of the Court.
2. No group may nominate more than four persons, not more than two of whom shall be of their own nationality. In no case may the number of candidates nominated by a group be more than double the number of seats to be filled.

Article 6

Before making these nominations, each national group is recommended to consult its highest court of justice, its legal faculties and schools of law, and its national academies and national sections of international academies devoted to the study of law.

Article 7

1. The Secretary-General shall prepare a list in alphabetical order of all the persons thus nominated. Save as provided in Article 12, paragraph 2, these shall be the only persons eligible.
2. The Secretary-General shall submit this list to the General Assembly and to the Security Council.

Article 8

The General Assembly and the Security Council shall proceed independently of one another to elect the members of the Court.

Article 9

At every election, the electors shall bear in mind not only that the persons to be elected should individually possess the qualifications required, but also that in the body as a whole the representation of the main forms of civilization and of the principal legal systems of the world should be assured.

Article 10

1. Those candidates who obtain an absolute majority of votes in the General Assembly and in the Security Council shall be considered as elected.
2. Any vote of the Security Council, whether for the election of judges or for the appointment of members of the conference envisaged in Article 12, shall be taken without any distinction between permanent and non-permanent members of the Security Council.
3. In the event of more than one national of the same state obtaining an absolute majority of the votes both of the General Assembly and of the Security Council, the eldest of these only shall be considered as elected.

Article 11

If, after the first meeting held for the purpose of the election, one or more seats remain to be filled, a second and, if necessary, a third meeting shall take place.

Article 12

1. If, after the third meeting, one or more seats still remain unfilled, a joint conference consisting of six members, three appointed by the General Assembly and three by the Security Council, may be

formed at any time at the request of either the General Assembly or the Security Council, for the purpose of choosing by the vote of an absolute majority one name for each seat still vacant, to submit to the General Assembly and the Security Council for their respective acceptance.
2. If the joint conference is unanimously agreed upon any person who fulfils the required conditions, he may be included in its list, even though he was not included in the list of nominations referred to in Article 7.
3. If the joint conference is satisfied that it will not be successful in procuring an election, those members of the Court who have already been elected shall, within a period to be fixed by the Security Council, proceed to fill the vacant seats by selection from among those candidates who have obtained votes either in the General Assembly or in the Security Council.
4. In the event of an equality of votes among the judges, the eldest judge shall have a casting vote.

Article 13
1. The members of the Court shall be elected for nine years and may be re-elected; provided, however, that of the judges elected at the first election, the terms of five judges shall expire at the end of three years and the terms of five more judges shall expire at the end of six years.
2. The judges whose terms are to expire at the end of the above-mentioned initial periods of three and six years shall be chosen by lot to be drawn by the Secretary-General immediately after the first election has been completed.
3. The members of the Court shall continue to discharge their duties until their places have been filled. Though replaced, they shall finish any cases which they may have begun.
4. In the case of the resignation of a member of the Court, the resignation shall be addressed to the President of the Court for transmission to the Secretary-General. This last notification makes the place vacant.

Article 14
Vacancies shall be filled by the same method as that laid down for the first election subject to the following provision: the Secretary-General shall, within one month of the occurrence of the vacancy, proceed to issue the invitations provided for in Article 5, and the date of the election shall be fixed by the Security Council.

Article 15
A member of the Court elected to replace a member whose term of office has not expired shall hold office for the remainder of his predecessor's term.

Article 16
1. No member of the Court may exercise any political or administrative function, or engage in any other occupation of a professional nature.
2. Any doubt on this point shall be settled by the decision of the Court.

Article 17
1. No member of the Court may act as agent, counsel, or advocate in any case.
2. No member may participate in the decision of any case in which he has previously taken part as agent, counsel, or advocate for one of the parties, or as a member of a national or international court, or of a commission of enquiry, or in any other capacity.
3. Any doubt on this point shall be settled by the decision of the Court.

Article 18

1. No member of the Court can be dismissed unless, in the unanimous opinion of the other members, he has ceased to fulfil the required conditions.
2. Formal notification thereof shall be made to the Secretary-General by the Registrar.
3. This notification makes the place vacant.

Article 19

The members of the Court, when engaged on the business of the Court, shall enjoy diplomatic privileges and immunities.

Article 20

Every member of the Court shall, before taking up his duties, make a solemn declaration in open court that he will exercise his powers impartially and conscientiously.

Article 21

1. The Court shall elect its President and Vice-President for three years; they may be re-elected.
2. The Court shall appoint its Registrar and may provide for the appointment of such other officers as may be necessary.

Article 22

1. The seat of the Court shall be established at The Hague. This, however, shall not prevent the Court from sitting and exercising its functions elsewhere whenever the Court considers it desirable.
2. The President and the Registrar shall reside at the seat of the Court.

Article 23

1. The Court shall remain permanently in session, except during the judicial vacations, the dates and duration of which shall be fixed by the Court.
2. Members of the Court are entitled to periodic leave, the dates and duration of which shall be fixed by the Court, having in mind the distance between The Hague and the home of each judge.
3. Members of the Court shall be bound, unless they are on leave or prevented from attending by illness or other serious reasons duly explained to the President, to hold themselves permanently at the disposal of the Court.

Article 24

1. If, for some special reason, a member of the Court considers that he should not take part in the decision of a particular case, he shall so inform the President.
2. If the President considers that for some special reason one of the members of the Court should not sit in a particular case, he shall give him notice accordingly.
3. If in any such case the member Court and the President disagree, the matter shall be settled by the decision of the Court.

Article 25

1. The full Court shall sit except when it is expressly provided otherwise in the present Statute.
2. Subject to the condition that the number of judges available to constitute the Court is not thereby reduced below eleven, the Rules of the Court may provide for allowing one or more judges, according to circumstances and in rotation, to be dispensed from sitting.
3. A quorum of nine judges shall suffice to constitute the Court.

Article 26

1. The Court may from time to time form one or more chambers, composed of three or more judges as the Court may determine, for dealing with particular categories of cases; for example, labour cases and cases relating to transit and communications.
2. The Court may at any time form a chamber for dealing with a particular case. The number of judges to constitute such a chamber shall be determined by the Court with the approval of the parties.
3. Cases shall be heard and determined by the chambers provided for in this article if the parties so request.

Article 27

A judgment given by any of the chambers provided for in Articles 26 and 29 shall be considered as rendered by the Court.

Article 28

The chambers provided for in Articles 26 and 29 may, with the consent of the parties, sit and exercise their functions elsewhere than at The Hague.

Article 29

With a view to the speedy dispatch of business, the Court shall form annually a chamber composed of five judges which, at the request of the parties, may hear and determine cases by summary procedure. In addition, two judges shall be selected for the purpose of replacing judges who find it impossible to sit.

Article 30

1. The Court shall frame rules for carrying out its functions. In particular, it shall lay down rules of procedure.
2. The Rules of the Court may provide for assessors to sit with the Court or with any of its chambers, without the right to vote.

Article 31

1. Judges of the nationality of each of the parties shall retain their right to sit in the case before the Court.
2. If the Court includes upon the Bench a judge of the nationality of one of the parties, any other party may choose a person to sit as judge. Such person shall be chosen preferably from among those persons who have been nominated as candidates as provided in Articles 4 and 5.
3. If the Court includes upon the Bench no judge of the nationality of the parties, each of these parties may proceed to choose a judge as provided in paragraph 2 of this Article.
4. The provisions of this Article shall apply to the case of Articles 26 and 29. In such cases, the President shall request one or, if necessary, two of the members of the Court forming the chamber to give place to the members of the Court of the nationality of the parties concerned, and, failing such, or if they are unable to be present, to the judges specially chosen by the parties.
5. Should there be several parties in the same interest, they shall, for the purpose of the preceding provisions, be reckoned as one party only. Any doubt upon this point shall be settled by the decision of the Court.
6. Judges chosen as laid down in paragraphs 2, 3, and 4 of this Article shall fulfil the conditions required by Articles 2, 17 (paragraph 2), 20, and 24 of the present Statute. They shall take part in the decision on terms of complete equality with their colleagues.

Article 32

1. Each member of the Court shall receive an annual salary.
2. The President shall receive a special annual allowance.
3. The Vice-President shall receive a special allowance for every day on which he acts as President.
4. The judges chosen under Article 31, other than members of the Court, shall receive compensation for each day on which they exercise their functions.
5. These salaries, allowances, and compensation shall be fixed by the General Assembly. They may not be decreased during the term of office.
6. The salary of the Registrar shall be fixed by the General Assembly on the proposal of the Court.
7. Regulations made by the General Assembly shall fix the conditions under which retirement pensions may be given to members of the Court and to the Registrar, and the conditions under which members of the Court and the Registrar shall have their travelling expenses refunded.
8. The above salaries, allowances, and compensation shall be free of all taxation.

Article 33

The expenses of the Court shall be borne by the United Nations in such a manner as shall be decided by the General Assembly.

CHAPTER II - COMPETENCE OF THE COURT

Article 34

1. Only states may be parties in cases before the Court.
2. The Court, subject to and in conformity with its Rules, may request of public international organizations information relevant to cases before it, and shall receive such information presented by such organizations on their own initiative.
3. Whenever the construction of the constituent instrument of a public international organization or of an international convention adopted thereunder is in question in a case before the Court, the Registrar shall so notify the public international organization concerned and shall communicate to it copies of all the written proceedings.

Article 35

1. The Court shall be open to the states parties to the present Statute.
2. The conditions under which the Court shall be open to other states shall, subject to the special provisions contained in treaties in force, be laid down by the Security Council, but in no case shall such conditions place the parties in a position of inequality before the Court.
3. When a state which is not a Member of the United Nations is a party to a case, the Court shall fix the amount which that party is to contribute towards the expenses of the Court. This provision shall not apply if such state is bearing a share of the expenses of the Court.

Article 36

1. The jurisdiction of the Court comprises all cases which the parties refer to it and all matters specially provided for in the Charter of the United Nations or in treaties and conventions in force.
2. The states parties to the present Statute may at any time declare that they recognize as compulsory ipso facto and without special agreement, in relation to any other state accepting the same obligation, the jurisdiction of the Court in all legal disputes concerning:

a. the interpretation of a treaty;
b. any question of international law;

c. the existence of any fact which, if established, would constitute a breach of an international obligation;
d. the nature or extent of the reparation to be made for the breach of an international obligation.

3. The declarations referred to above may be made unconditionally or on condition of reciprocity on the part of several or certain states, or for a certain time.

4. Such declarations shall be deposited with the Secretary-General of the United Nations, who shall transmit copies thereof to the parties to the Statute and to the Registrar of the Court.

5. Declarations made under Article 36 of the Statute of the Permanent Court of International Justice and which are still in force shall be deemed, as between the parties to the present Statute, to be acceptances of the compulsory jurisdiction of the International Court of Justice for the period which they still have to run and in accordance with their terms.

6. In the event of a dispute as to whether the Court has jurisdiction, the matter shall be settled by the decision of the Court.

Article 37

Whenever a treaty or convention in force provides for reference of a matter to a tribunal to have been instituted by the League of Nations, or to the Permanent Court of International Justice, the matter shall, as between the parties to the present Statute, be referred to the International Court of Justice.

Article 38

1. The Court, whose function is to decide in accordance with international law such disputes as are submitted to it, shall apply:

a. international conventions, whether general or particular, establishing rules expressly recognized by the contesting states;
b. international custom, as evidence of a general practice accepted as law;
c. the general principles of law recognized by civilized nations;
d. subject to the provisions of Article 59, judicial decisions and the teachings of the most highly qualified publicists of the various nations, as subsidiary means for the determination of rules of law.

2. This provision shall not prejudice the power of the Court to decide a case ex aequo et bono, if the parties agree thereto.

CHAPTER III - PROCEDURE

Article 39

1. The official languages of the Court shall be French and English. If the parties agree that the case shall be conducted in French, the judgment shall be delivered in French. If the parties agree that the case shall be conducted in English, the judgment shall be delivered in English.

2. In the absence of an agreement as to which language shall be employed, each party may, in the pleadings, use the language which it prefers; the decision of the Court shall be given in French and English. In this case the Court shall at the same time determine which of the two texts shall be considered as authoritative.

3. The Court shall, at the request of any party, authorize a language other than French or English to be used by that party.

Article 40

1. Cases are brought before the Court, as the case may be, either by the notification of the special agreement or by a written application addressed to the Registrar. In either case the subject of the dispute and the parties shall be indicated.
2. The Registrar shall forthwith communicate the application to all concerned.
3. He shall also notify the Members of the United Nations through the Secretary-General, and also any other states entitled to appear before the Court.

Article 41

1. The Court shall have the power to indicate, if it considers that circumstances so require, any provisional measures which ought to be taken to preserve the respective rights of either party.
2. Pending the final decision, notice of the measures suggested shall forthwith be given to the parties and to the Security Council.

Article 42

1. The parties shall be represented by agents.
2. They may have the assistance of counsel or advocates before the Court.
3. The agents, counsel, and advocates of parties before the Court shall enjoy the privileges and immunities necessary to the independent exercise of their duties.

Article 43

1. The procedure shall consist of two parts: written and oral.
2. The written proceedings shall consist of the communication to the Court and to the parties of memorials, counter-memorials and, if necessary, replies; also all papers and documents in support.
3. These communications shall be made through the Registrar, in the order and within the time fixed by the Court.
4. A certified copy of every document produced by one party shall be communicated to the other party.
5. The oral proceedings shall consist of the hearing by the Court of witnesses, experts, agents, counsel, and advocates.

Article 44

1. For the service of all notices upon persons other than the agents, counsel, and advocates, the Court shall apply direct to the government of the state upon whose territory the notice has to be served.
2. The same provision shall apply whenever steps are to be taken to procure evidence on the spot.

Article 45

The hearing shall be under the control of the President or, if he is unable to preside, of the Vice-President; if neither is able to preside, the senior judge present shall preside.

Article 46

The hearing in Court shall be public, unless the Court shall decide otherwise, or unless the parties demand that the public be not admitted.

Article 47

1. Minutes shall be made at each hearing and signed by the Registrar and the President.
2. These minutes alone shall be authentic.

Article 48

The Court shall make orders for the conduct of the case, shall decide the form and time in which each party must conclude its arguments, and make all arrangements connected with the taking of evidence.

Article 49

The Court may, even before the hearing begins, call upon the agents to produce any document or to supply any explanations. Formal note shall be taken of any refusal.

Article 50

The Court may, at any time, entrust any individual, body, bureau, commission, or other organization that it may select, with the task of carrying out an enquiry or giving an expert opinion.

Article 51

During the hearing any relevant questions are to be put to the witnesses and experts under the conditions laid down by the Court in the rules of procedure referred to in Article 30.

Article 52

After the Court has received the proofs and evidence within the time specified for the purpose, it may refuse to accept any further oral or written evidence that one party may desire to present unless the other side consents.

Article 53

1. Whenever one of the parties does not appear before the Court, or fails to defend its case, the other party may call upon the Court to decide in favour of its claim.
2. The Court must, before doing so, satisfy itself, not only that it has jurisdiction in accordance with Articles 36 and 37, but also that the claim is well founded in fact and law.

Article 54

1. When, subject to the control of the Court, the agents, counsel, and advocates have completed their presentation of the case, the President shall declare the hearing closed.
2. The Court shall withdraw to consider the judgment.
3. The deliberations of the Court shall take place in private and remain secret.

Article 55

1. All questions shall be decided by a majority of the judges present.
2. In the event of an equality of votes, the President or the judge who acts in his place shall have a casting vote.

Article 56

1. The judgment shall state the reasons on which it is based.
2. It shall contain the names of the judges who have taken part in the decision.

Article 57
If the judgment does not represent in whole or in part the unanimous opinion of the judges, any judge shall be entitled to deliver a separate opinion.

Article 58
The judgment shall be signed by the President and by the Registrar. It shall be read in open court, due notice having been given to the agents.

Article 59
The decision of the Court has no binding force except between the parties and in respect of that particular case.

Article 60
The judgment is final and without appeal. In the event of dispute as to the meaning or scope of the judgment, the Court shall construe it upon the request of any party.

Article 61
1. An application for revision of a judgment may be made only when it is based upon the discovery of some fact of such a nature as to be a decisive factor, which fact was, when the judgment was given, unknown to the Court and also to the party claiming revision, always provided that such ignorance was not due to negligence.
2. The proceedings for revision shall be opened by a judgment of the Court expressly recording the existence of the new fact, recognizing that it has such a character as to lay the case open to revision, and declaring the application admissible on this ground.
3. The Court may require previous compliance with the terms of the judgment before it admits proceedings in revision.
4. The application for revision must be made at latest within six months of the discovery of the new fact.
5. No application for revision may be made after the lapse of ten years from the date of the judgment.

Article 62
1. Should a state consider that it has an interest of a legal nature which may be affected by the decision in the case, it may submit a request to the Court to be permitted to intervene.
2. It shall be for the Court to decide upon this request.

Article 63
1. Whenever the construction of a convention to which states other than those concerned in the case are parties is in question, the Registrar shall notify all such states forthwith.
2. Every state so notified has the right to intervene in the proceedings; but if it uses this right, the construction given by the judgment will be equally binding upon it.

Article 64
Unless otherwise decided by the Court, each party shall bear its own costs.

CHAPTER IV - ADVISORY OPINIONS

Article 65

1. The Court may give an advisory opinion on any legal question at the request of whatever body may be authorized by or in accordance with the Charter of the United Nations to make such a request.
2. Questions upon which the advisory opinion of the Court is asked shall be laid before the Court by means of a written request containing an exact statement of the question upon which an opinion is required, and accompanied by all documents likely to throw light upon the question.

Article 66

1. The Registrar shall forthwith give notice of the request for an advisory opinion to all states entitled to appear before the Court.
2. The Registrar shall also, by means of a special and direct communication, notify any state entitled to appear before the Court or international organization considered by the Court, or, should it not be sitting, by the President, as likely to be able to furnish information on the question, that the Court will be prepared to receive, within a time limit to be fixed by the President, written statements, or to hear, at a public sitting to be held for the purpose, oral statements relating to the question.
3. Should any such state entitled to appear before the Court have failed to receive the special communication referred to in paragraph 2 of this Article, such state may express a desire to submit a written statement or to be heard; and the Court will decide.
4. States and organizations having presented written or oral statements or both shall be permitted to comment on the statements made by other states or organizations in the form, to the extent, and within the time limits which the Court, or, should it not be sitting, the President, shall decide in each particular case. Accordingly, the Registrar shall in due time communicate any such written statements to states and organizations having submitted similar statements.

Article 67

The Court shall deliver its advisory opinions in open court, notice having been given to the Secretary-General and to the representatives of Members of the United Nations, of other states and of international organizations immediately concerned.

Article 68

In the exercise of its advisory functions the Court shall further be guided by the provisions of the present Statute which apply in contentious cases to the extent to which it recognizes them to be applicable.

CHAPTER V - AMENDMENT

Article 69

Amendments to the present Statute shall be effected by the same procedure as is provided by the Charter of the United Nations for amendments to that Charter, subject however to any provisions which the General Assembly upon recommendation of the Security Council may adopt concerning the participation of states which are parties to the present Statute but are not Members of the United Nations.

Article 70

The Court shall have power to propose such amendments to the present Statute as it may deem necessary, through written communications to the Secretary-General, for consideration in conformity with the provisions of Article 69.

Convention on the Privileges and Immunities of the United Nations, New York 13 February 1946

[*Note:* the Convention was adopted by the UN General Assembly, on February 13, 1946 and entered into force on September 17, 1946, in accordance with Section 32. Timor-Leste is the last country which acceded to the Convention in January 2015.

Status since February 2018: 162 States Parties.]

Whereas Article 104 of the Charter of the United Nations provides that the Organization shall enjoy in the territory of each of its Members such legal capacity as may be necessary for the exercise of its functions and the fulfilment of its purposes and

Whereas Article 105 of the Charter of the United Nations provides that the Organization shall enjoy in the territory of each of its Members such privileges and immunities as are necessary for the fulfilment of its purposes and that representatives of the Members of the United Nations and officials of the Organization shall similarly enjoy such privileges and immunities as are necessary for the independent exercise of their functions in connection with the Organization;
Consequently the General Assembly by a Resolution adopted on the 13 February 1946, approved the following Convention and proposed it for accession by each Member of the United Nations.

Article I – Juridictional personality

Section 1

The United Nations shall possess juridical personality. It shall have the capacity:
(a) to contract;
(b) to acquire and dispose of immovable and movable property;
(c) to institute legal proceedings.

Article II – Property, funds and assets

Section 2

The United Nations, its property and assets wherever located and by whomsoever held, shall enjoy immunity from every form of legal process except insofar as in any particular case it has expressly waived its immunity. It is, however, understood that no waiver of immunity shall extend to any measure of execution.

Section 3

The premises of the United Nations shall be inviolable. The property and assets of the United Nations, wherever located and by whomsoever held, shall be immune from search, requisition, confiscation, expropriation and any other form of interference, whether by executive, administrative, judicial or legislative action.

Section 4

The archives of the United Nations, and in general all documents belonging to it or held by it, shall be inviolable wherever located.

Section 5

Without being restricted by financial controls, regulations or moratoria of any kind,
(a) the United Nations may hold funds, gold or currency of any kind and operate accounts in any currency;
(b) the United Nations shall be free to transfer its funds, gold or currency from one country to another or within any country and to convert any currency held by it into any other currency.

Section 6

In exercising its rights under section 5 above, the United Nations shall pay due regard to any representations made by the Government of any Member insofar as it is considered that effect can be given to such representations without detriment to the interests of the United Nations.

Section 7

The United Nations, its assets, income and other property shall be:
(a) exempt from all direct taxes; it is understood, however, that the United Nations will not claim exemption from taxes which are, in fact, no more than charges for public utility services;
(b) exempt from customs duties and prohibitions and restrictions on imports and exports in respect of articles imported or exported by the United Nations for its official use. It is understood, however, that articles imported under such exemption will not be sold in the country into which they were imported except under conditions agreed with the Government of that country;
(c) exempt from customs duties and prohibitions and restrictions on imports and exports in respect of its publications.

Section 8

While the United Nations will not, as a general rule, claim exemption from excise duties and from taxes on the sale of movable and immovable property which form part of the price to be paid, nevertheless when the United Nations is making important purchases for official use of property on which such duties and taxes have been charged or are chargeable, Members will, whenever possible, make appropriate administrative arrangements for the remission or return of the amount of duty or tax.

Article III – Facilities in respect of communications

Section 9

The United Nations shall enjoy in the territory of each Member for its official communications treatment not less favourable than that accorded by the Government of that Member to any other Government including its diplomatic mission in the matter of priorities, rates and taxes on mails, cables, telegrams, radiograms, telephotos, telephone and other communications; and press rates for information to the press and radio. No censorship shall be applied to the official correspondence and other official communications of the United Nations.

Section 10

The United Nations shall have the right to use codes and to despatch and receive its correspondence by courier or in bags, which shall have the same immunities and privileges as diplomatic couriers and bags.

Article IV – The representatives of members

Section 11

Representatives of Members to the principal and subsidiary organs of the United Nations and to conferences convened by the United Nations, shall, while exercising their functions and during their journey to and from the place of meeting, enjoy the following privileges and immunities:

(a) immunity from personal arrest of detention and from seizure of their personal baggage, and, in respect of words spoken or written and all acts done by them in their capacity as representatives, immunity from legal process of every kind;
(b) inviolability for all papers and documents;
(c) the right to use codes and to receive papers or correspondence by courier or in sealed bags;
(d) exemption in respect of themselves and their spouses from immigration restrictions, alien registration or national service obligations in the state they are visiting or through which they are passing in the exercise of their functions;
(e) the same facilities in respect of currency or exchange restrictions as are accorded to representatives of foreign governments on temporary official missions;
(f) the same immunities and facilities in respect of their personal baggage as are accorded to diplomatic envoys, and also
(g) such other privileges, immunities and facilities not inconsistent with the foregoing as diplomatic envoys enjoy, except that they shall have no right to claim exemption from customs duties on goods imported (otherwise than as part of their personal baggage) or from excise duties or sales taxes.

Section 12

In order to secure, for the representatives of Members to the principal and subsidiary organs of the United Nations and to conferences convened by the United Nations, complete freedom of speech and independence in the discharge of their duties, the immunity from legal process in respect of words spoken or written and all acts done by them in discharging their duties shall continue to be accorded, notwithstanding that the persons concerned are no longer the representatives of Members.

Section 13

Where the incidence of any form of taxation depends upon residence, periods during which the representatives of Members to the principal and subsidiary organs of the United Nations and to conferences convened by the United Nations are present in a state for the discharge of their duties shall not be considered as periods of residence.

Section 14

Privileges and immunities are accorded to the representatives of Members not for the personal benefit of the individuals themselves, but in order to safeguard the independent exercise of their functions in connection with the United Nations. Consequently a Member not only has the right but is under a duty to waive the immunity of its representative in any case where in the opinion of the Member the immunity would impede the course of justice, and it can be waived without prejudice to the purpose for which the immunity is accorded.

Section 15

The provisions of sections 11, 12 and 13 are not applicable between a representative and the authorities of the State of which he is a national or of which he is or has been the representative.

Section 16

In this article the expression "representatives" shall be deemed to include all delegates, deputy delegates, advisers, technical experts and secretaries of delegations.

Article V – Officials

Section 17

The Secretary-General will specify the categories of officials to which the provisions of this article and article VII shall apply. He shall submit these categories to the General Assembly. Thereafter these categories shall be communicated to the Governments of all Members. The names of the officials included in these categories shall from time to time be made known to the Governments of Members.

Section 18

Officials of the United Nations shall:

(a) be immune from legal process in respect of words spoken or written and all acts performed by them in their official capacity;

(b) be exempt from taxation on the salaries and emoluments paid to them by the United Nations;

(c) be immune from national service obligations;

(d) be immune, together with their spouses and relatives dependent on them, from immigration restrictions and alien registration;

(e) be accorded the same privileges in respect of exchange facilities as are accorded to the officials of comparable ranks forming part of diplomatic missions to the Government concerned;

(f) be given, together with their spouses and relatives dependent on them, the same repatriation facilities in time of international crisis as diplomatic envoys;
(g) have the right to import free of duty their furniture and effects at the time of first taking up their post in the country in question.

Section 19

In addition to the immunities and privileges specified in section 18, the Secretary-General and all Assistant Secretaries-General shall be accorded in respect of themselves, their spouses and minor children, the privileges and immunities exemptions and facilities accorded to diplomatic envoys, in accordance with international law.

Section 20

Privileges and immunities are granted to officials in the interests of the United Nations and not for the personal benefit of the individuals themselves. The Secretary-General shall have the right and the duty to waive the immunity of any official in any case where, in his opinion, the immunity would impede the course of justice and can be waived without prejudice to the interests of the United Nations. In the case of the Secretary-General, the Security Council shall have the right to waive immunity.

Section 21

The United Nations shall cooperate at all times with the appropriate authorities of Members to facilitate the proper administration of justice, secure the observance of police regulations and prevent the occurrence of any abuse in connection with the privileges, immunities and facilities mentioned in this article.

Article VI – Experts on missions for the united nations

Section 22

Experts (other than officials coming within the scope of article V) performing missions for the United Nations shall be accorded such privileges and immunities as are necessary for the independent exercise of their functions during the period of their missions, including the time spent on journeys in connection with their missions. In particular they shall be accorded:
(a) immunity from personal arrest or detention and from seizure of their personal baggage;
(b) in respect of words spoken or written and acts done by them in the course of the performance of their mission, immunity from legal process of every kind. This immunity from legal process shall continue to be accorded notwithstanding that the persons concerned are no longer employed on missions for the United Nations;
(c) inviolability for all papers and documents;
(d) for the purpose of their communications with the United Nations, the right to use codes and to receive papers or correspondence by courier or in sealed bags;
(e) the same facilities in respect of currency or exchange restrictions as are accorded to representatives of foreign governments on temporary official missions;
(f) the same immunities and facilities in respect of their personal baggage as are accorded to diplomatic envoys.

Section 23

Privileges and immunities are granted to experts in the interests of the United Nations and not for the personal benefit of the individuals themselves. The Secretary-General shall have the right and the duty to waive the immunity of any expert in any case where, in his opinion, the immunity would impede the course of justice and it can be waived without prejudice to the interests of the United Nations.

Article VII – United nations laissez-passer

Section 24

The United Nations may issue United Nations laissez-passer to its officials. These laissez-passers shall be recognized and accepted as valid travel documents by the authorities of Members, taking into account the provision of section 25.

Section 25

Applications for visas (where required) from the holders of United Nations laissez-passer, when accompanied by a certificate that they are travelling on the business of the United Nations, shall be dealt with as speedily as possible. In addition, such persons shall be granted facilities for speedy travel.

Section 26

Similar facilities to those specified in section 25 shall be accorded to experts and other persons who, though not be holders of United Nations laissez-passer, have a certificate that they are travelling on the business of the United Nations.

Section 27

The Secretary-General, Assistant Secretaries-General and Directors travelling on United Nations laissez-passer on the business of the United Nations shall be granted the same facilities as are accorded to diplomatic envoys.

Section 28

The provisions of this article may be applied to the comparable officials of specialized agencies if the agreements for relationship made under Article 63 of the Charter so provide.

Article VIII – Settlement of disputes

Section 29

The United Nations shall make provisions for appropriate modes of settlement of:
(a) disputes arising out of contracts or other disputes of a private law character to which the United Nations is a party;
(b) disputes involving any official of the United Nations who by reason of his official position enjoys immunity, if immunity has not been waived by the Secretary-General.

Section 30

All differences arising out of the interpretation or application of the present convention shall be referred to the International Court of Justice, unless in any case it is agreed by the parties to have recourse to another mode of settlement. If a difference arises between the United Nations on the one hand and a Member on the other hand, a request shall be made for an advisory opinion on any legal question involved in accordance with Article 96 of the Charter and Article 65 of the Statute of the Court. The opinion given by the Court shall be accepted as decisive by the parties.

Final article

Section 31

This convention is submitted to every Member of the United Nations for accession.

Section 32

Accession shall be effected by deposit of an instrument with the Secretary-General of the United Nations and the Convention shall come into force as regards each Member on the date of deposit of each instrument of accession.

Section 33

The Secretary-General shall inform all Members of the United Nations of the deposit of each accession.

Section 34

It is understood that, when an instrument of accession is deposited on behalf of any Member, the Member will be in a position under its own law to give effect to the terms of this Convention.

Section 35

This Convention shall continue in force as between the United Nations and every Member which has deposited an instrument of accession for so long as that member remains a Member of the United Nations, or until a revised general convention has been approved by the General Assembly and that Member has become a party to this revised convention.

Section 36

The Secretary-General may conclude with any Member or Members supplementary agreements adjusting the provisions of this Convention so far as that Member of those Members are concerned. These supplementary agreements shall in each case be subject to the approval of the General Assembly.

Agreement Between the United Nations and the United States Regarding the Headquarters of the United Nations, 1947

[*Note:* the Agreement between the United Nations and the United States of America was signed at Lake Success, New York on June 26, 1947, and approved by the General Assembly on October 31, 1947]

The United Nations and the United States of America:

Desiring to conclude an agreement for the purpose of carrying out the resolution adopted by the General Assembly on 14 December 1946 to establish the seat of the United Nations in the City of New York and to regulate questions arising as a result thereof;
Have appointed as their representatives for this purpose: The United Nations:
Trygve Lie, Secretary-General, and The United States of America:
George C. MARSHALL, Secretary of State,
Who have agreed as follows:

Article I – Definitions

Section 1

In this agreement:
(a) The expression "headquarters district" means:
  (1) the area defined as such in Annex 1;
  (2) any other lands or buildings which from time to time may be included therein by supplemental agreement with the appropriate American authorities;
(b) the expression "appropriate American authorities" means such federal, state, or local authorities in the United States as may be appropriate in the context and in accordance with the laws and customs of the United States, including the laws and customs of the State and local government involved;
(c) the expression "General Convention" means the Convention on the Privileges and Immunities of the United Nations approved by the General Assembly of the United Nations on 13 February 1946, as acceded to by the United States;
(d) the expression "United Nations" means the international organization established by the Charter of the United Nations, hereinafter referred to as the "Charter";
(e) the expression "Secretary-General" means the Secretary-General of the United Nations.

Article II – The headquarters district

Section 2

The seat of the United Nations shall be the headquarters district.

Section 3

The appropriate American authorities shall take whatever action may be necessary to assure that the United Nations shall not be dispossessed of its property in the headquarters district, except as provided in Section 22 in the event that the United Nations ceases to use the same, provided that the United Nations shall reimburse the appropriate American authorities for any costs incurred, after consultation with the United Nations, in liquidating by eminent domain proceedings or otherwise any adverse claims.

Section 4

(a) The United Nations may establish and operate in the headquarters district:
  (1) its own short-wave sending and receiving radio broadcasting facilities, including emergency link equipment, which may be 932922-51-13 used on the same frequencies (within the tolerances prescribed for the broadcasting service by applicable United States regulations) for radio-telegraph, radio-teletype, radio-telephone, radio-telephoto, and similar services;
  (2) one point-to-point circuit between the headquarters district and the office of the United Nations in Geneva (using single sideband equipment) to be used exclusively for the exchange of broadcasting programmes and inter-office communications;
  (3) low power, micro wave, low or medium frequencies, facilities for communication within headquarters buildings only, or such other buildings as may temporarily be used by the United Nations;
  (4) facilities for point-to-point communications to the same extent and subject to the same conditions as committed under applicable rules and regulations for amateur operation in the United States except that such rules and regulations shall not be applied in a manner inconsistent with the inviolability of the headquarters district provided by Section 9 (a);
  (5) such other radio facilities as may be specified by supplemental agreement between the United Nations and the appropriate American authorities.

(b) The United Nations shall make arrangements for the operation of the services referred to in this section with the International Telecommunication Union, the appropriate agencies of the Government of the United States and the appropriate agencies of other affected Governments with regard to all frequencies and similar matters.

(c) The facilities provided for in this section may, to the extent necessary for efficient operation, be established and operated outside the headquarters district. The appropriate American authorities will, on request of the United Nations, make arrangements, on such terms and in such manner as may be agreed upon by supplemental agreement, for the acquisition or use by the United Nations of appropriate premises for such purposes and the inclusion of such premises in the headquarters district.

Section 5

In the event that the United Nations should find it necessary and desirable to establish and operate an aerodrome, the conditions for the location, use and operation of such an aerodrome and the conditions under which there shall be entry into and exit therefrom shall be the subject of a supplemental agreement.

Section 6

In the event that the United Nations should propose to organize its own postal service, the conditions under which such service shall be set up shall be the subject of a supplemental agreement.

Article III – Law and authority in the headquarters district

Section 7

(a) The headquarters district shall be under the control and authority of the United Nations as provided in this agreement.
(b) Except as otherwise provided in this agreement or in the General Convention, the federal, state and local law of the United States shall apply within the headquarters district.
(c) Except as otherwise provided in this agreement or in the General Convention, the federal, state and local courts of the United States shall have jurisdiction over acts done and transactions taking place in the headquarters district as provided in applicable federal, state and local laws.
(d) The federal, state and local courts of the United States, when dealing with cases arising out of or relating to acts done or transactions taking place in the headquarters district, shall take into account the regulations enacted by the United Nations under Section 8.

Section 8

The United Nations shall have the power to make regulations, operative within the headquarters district, for the purpose of establishing therein conditions in all respects necessary for the full execution of its functions. No federal, state or local law or regulation of the United States which is inconsistent with a regulation of the United Nations authorized by this section shall, to the extent of such inconsistency, be applicable within the headquarters district. Any dispute, between the United Nations and the United States, as to whether a regulation of the United Nations is authorized by this section or as to whether a federal, state or local law or regulation is inconsistent with any regulation of the United Nations authorized by this section, shall be promptly settled as provided in Section 21. Pending such settlement, the regulation of the United Nations shall apply, and the federal, state or local law or regulation shall be inapplicable in the headquarters district to the extent that the United Nations claims it to be inconsistent with the regulation of the United Nations. This section shall not prevent the reasonable application of fire protection regulations of the appropriate American authorities.

Section 9

(a) The headquarters district shall be inviolable. Federal, state or local officers or officials of the United States, whether administrative, judicial, military or police, shall not enter the headquarters district to perform any official duties therein except with the consent of and under conditions agreed to by the Secretary-General. The service of legal process, including the seizure of private property, may take place within the headquarters district only with the consent of and under conditions approved by the Secretary-General.
(b) Without prejudice to the provisions of the General Convention or Article IV of this agreement, the United Nations shall prevent the headquarters district from becoming a refuge either for persons who are avoiding arrest under the federal, state, or local law of the United States or are required by the Government of the United States for extradition to another country, or for persons who are endeavouring to avoid service of legal process.

Section 10

The United Nations may expel or exclude persons from the headquarters district for violation of its regulations adopted under Section 8 or for other cause. Persons who violate such regulations shall be subject to other penalties or to detention under arrest only in accordance with the provisions of such laws or regulations as may be adopted by the appropriate American authorities.

Article IV – Communications and transit

Section 11

The federal, state or local authorities of the United States shall not impose any impediments to transit to or from the headquarters district of (1) representatives of Members or officials of the United Nations, or of specialized agencies as defined in Article 57, paragraph 2, of the Charter, or the families of such representatives or officials; (2) experts performing missions for the United Nations or for such specialized agencies; (3) representatives of the press, or of radio, film or other information agencies, who have been accredited by the United Nations (or by such a specialized agency) in its discretion after consultation with the United States; (4) representatives of nongovernmental organizations recognized by the United Nations for the purpose of consultation under Article 71 of the Charter; or (5) other persons invited to the headquarters district by the United Nations or by such specialized agency on official business. The appropriate American authorities shall afford any necessary protection to such persons while in transit to or from the headquarters district. This section does not apply to general interruptions of transportation which are to be dealt with as provided in Section 17, and does not impair the effectiveness of generally applicable laws and regulations as to the operation of means of transportation.

Section 12

The provisions of Section 11 shall be. applicable irrespective of the relations existing between the Governments of the persons referred to in that section and the Government of the United States.

Section 13

(a) Laws and regulations in force in the United States regarding the entry of aliens shall not be applied in such manner as to interfere with the privileges referred to in Section 11. When visas are required for persons referred to in that Section, they shall be granted without charge and as promptly as possible.

(b) Laws and regulations in force in the United States regarding the residence of aliens shall not be applied in such manner as to interfere with the privileges referred to in Section 11 and, specifically, shall not be applied in such manner as to require any such person to leave the United States on account of any activities performed by him in his official capacity. In case of abuse of such privileges of residence by any such person in activities in the United States outside his official capacity, it is understood that the privileges referred to in Section 11 shall not be construed to grant him exemption from the laws and regulations of the United States regarding the continued residence of aliens, provided that:

    (1) No proceedings shall be instituted under such laws or regulations to require any such person to leave the United States except with the prior approval of the Secretary of State of the United States. Such approval shall be given only after consultation with the appropriate Member in the case of a representative of a Member (or a member of his family) or with the Secretary-General or the principal executive officer of the appropriate specialized agency in the case of any other person referred to in Section 11;

    (2) A representative of the Member concerned, the Secretary-General or the principal Executive Officer of the appropriate specialized agency, as the case may be, shall have the right to appear in any such proceedings on behalf of the person against whom they are instituted;

    (3) Persons who are entitled to diplomatic privileges and immunities under Section 15 or under the General Convention shall not be required to leave the United States otherwise than in accordance with the customary procedure applicable to diplomatic envoys accredited to the United States.

(c) This section does not prevent the requirement of reasonable evidence to establish that persons claiming the rights granted by Section 11 come within the classes described- in that section, or the reasonable application of quarantine and health regulations.

(d) Except as provided above in this section and in the General Convention, the United States retains full control and authority over the entry of persons or property into the territory of the United States and the conditions under which persons may remain or reside there.

(e) The Secretary-General shall, at the request of the appropriate American authorities, enter into discussions with such authorities, with a view to making arrangements for registering the arrival and departure of persons who have been granted visas valid only for transit to and from the headquarters district and sojourn therein and in its immediate vicinity.

(f) The United Nations shall, subject to the foregoing provisions of this section, have the exclusive right to authorize or prohibit entry of persons and property into the headquarters district and to prescribe the conditions under which persons may remain or reside there.

Section 14

The Secretary-General and the appropriate American authorities shall, at the request of either of them, consult as to methods of facilitating entrance into the United States, and the use of available means of transportation, by persons coming from abroad who wish to visit the headquarters district and do not enjoy the rights referred to in this Article.

Article V – Resident representatives to the United Nations

Section 15

(1) Every person designated by a Member as the principal resident representative to the United Nations of such Member or as a resident representative with the rank of ambassador or minister plenipotentiary,
(2) Such resident members of their staffs as may be agreed upon between the Secretary-General, the Government of the United States and the Government of the Member concerned,
(3) Every person designated by a Member of a specialized agency, as defined in Article 57, paragraph 2, of the Charter, as its principal resident representative, with the rank of ambassador or minister plenipotentiary at the headquarters of such agency in the United States, and
(4) Such other principal resident representatives of members of a specialized agency and such resident members of the staffs of representatives of a specialized agency as may be agreed upon between the principal executive officer of the specialized agency, the Government of the United States and the Government of the Member concerned, shall whether residing inside or outside the headquarters district, be entitled in the territory of the United States to the same privileges and immunities, subject to corresponding conditions and obligations, as it accords to diplomatic envoys accredited to it. In the case of Members whose governments are not recognized by the United States, such privileges and immunities need be extended to such representatives, or persons on the staffs of such representatives, only within the headquarters district, at their residences and offices outside the district, in transit between the district and such residences and offices, and in transit on official business to or from foreign countries.

Article VI – Police protection of the headquarters district

Section 16

(a) The appropriate American authorities shall exercise due diligence to ensure that the tranquillity of the headquarters district is not disturbed by the unauthorized entry of groups of persons from outside or by disturbances in its immediate vicinity and shall cause to be provided on the boundaries of the headquarters district such police protection as is required for these purposes.
(b) If so requested by the Secretary-General, the appropriate American authorities shall provide a sufficient number of police for the preservation of law and order in the headquarters district, and for the removal therefrom of persons as requested under the authority of the United Nations. The United Nations shall, if requested, enter into arrangements with the appropriate American authorities to reimburse them for the reasonable cost of such services.

Article VII – Public services and protection of the headquarters district

Section 17

(a) The appropriate American authorities will exercise to the extent requested by the Secretary-General the powers which they possess with respect to the supplying of public services to ensure that the headquarters district shall be supplied on equitable terms with the necessary public services, including electricity, water, gas, post, telephone, telegraph, transportation, drainage, collection of refuse, fire protection, snow removal, etcetera. In case of any interruption or threatened interruption of any such services, the appropriate American authorities will consider the needs of the United Nations as being of equal importance with the similar needs of essential agencies of the Government of the United States, and will take steps accordingly, to ensure that the work of the United Nations is not prejudiced.

(b) Special provisions with reference to maintenance of utilities and underground construction are contained in Annex 2.

Section 18

The appropriate American authorities shall take all reasonable steps to ensure that the amenities of the headquarters district are not prejudiced and the purposes for which the district is required are not obstructed by any use made of the land in the vicinity of the district. The United Nations shall on its part take all reasonable steps to ensure that the amenities of the land in the vicinity of the headquarters district are not prejudiced by any use made of le land in the headquarters district by the United Nations.

Section 19

It is agreed that no form of racial or religious discrimination shall be permitted within the headquarters district.

Article VIII – Matters relating to the operation of this agreement

Section 20

The Secretary-General and the appropriate American authorities shall settle by agreement the channels through which they will communicate regarding the application of the provisions of this agreement and other questions affecting the headquarters district, and may enter into such supplemental agreements as may be necessary to fulfil the purposes of this agreement. In making supplemental agreements with the Secretary-General, the United States shall consult with the appropriate state and local authorities. If the Secretary-General so requests, the Secretary of State of the United States shall appoint a special representative for the purpose of liaison with the Secretary-General.

Section 21

(a) Any dispute between the United Nations and the United States concerning the interpretation or application of this agreement or of any supplemental agreement, which is not settled by negotiation or other agreed mode of settlement, shall be referred for final decision to a tribunal of three arbitrators, one to be named by the Secretary-General, one to be named by the Secretary of State of the United States, and the third to be chosen by the two, or, if they should fail to agree upon a third, then by the President of the International Court of Justice.

(b) The Secretary-General or the United States may ask the General Assembly to request of the International Court of Justice an advisory opinion on any legal question arising in the course of such proceedings. Pending the receipt of the opinion of the Court, an interim decision of the arbitral tribunal shall be observed by both parties. Thereafter, the arbitral tribunal shall render a final decision, having regard to the opinion of the Court.

Article IX – Miscellaneous provisions

Section 22

(a) The United Nations shall not dispose of all or any part of the land owned by it in the headquarters district without the consent of the United States. If the United States is unwilling to consent to a disposition which the United Nations wishes to make of all or any part of such land, the United States shall buy the same from the United Nations at a price to be determined as provided in paragraph (d) of this section.
(b) If the seat of the United Nations is removed from the headquarters district, all right, title and interest of the United Nations in and to real property in the headquarters district or any part of it shall, on request of either the United Nations or the United States be assigned and conveyed to the United States. In the absence of such a request, the same shall be assigned and conveyed to the sub-division of a state in which it is located or, if such sub-division shall not desire it, then to the state in which it is located. If none of the foregoing desire the same, it may be disposed of as provided in paragraph (a) of this Section.
(c) If the United Nations disposes of all or any part of the headquarters district, the provisions of other sections of this agreement which apply to the headquarters district shall immediately cease to apply to the land and buildings so disposed of.
(d) The price to be paid for any conveyance under this section shall, in default of agreement, be the then fair value of the land, buildings and installations, to be determined under the procedure provided in Section 21.

Section 23

The seat of the United Nations shall not be removed from the headquarters district unless the United Nations should so decide.

Section 24

This agreement shall cease to be in force if the seat of the United Nations is removed from the territory of the United States, except for such provisions as may be applicable in connection with the orderly termination of the operations of the United Nations at its seat in the United States and the disposition of its property therein.

Section 25

Wherever this agreement imposes obligations on the appropriate American authorities, the Government of the United States shall have the ultimate responsibility for the fulfilment of such obligations by the appropriate American authorities.

Section 26

The provisions of this agreement shall be complementary to the provisions of the General Convention. In so far as any provision of this agreement and any provisions of the General Convention relate to the same subject matter, the two provisions shall, wherever possible, be treated as complementary, so that both provisions shall be applicable and neither shall narrow the effect of the other; but in any case of absolute conflict, the provisions of this agreement shall prevail.

Section 27

This agreement shall be construed in the light of its primary purpose to enable the United Nations at its headquarters in the United States, fully and efficiently to discharge its responsibilities and fulfil its purposes.

Section 28

This agreement shall be brought into effect by an exchange of notes between the Secretary-General, duly authorized pursuant to a resolution of the General Assembly of the United Nations, and the appropriate executive officer of the United States, duly authorized pursuant to appropriate action of the Congress. In witness whereof the respective representatives have signed this Agreement and have affixed their seals hereto.
Done in duplicate, in the English and French languages, both authentic, at Lake Success, this twenty-sixth day of June, 1947.

[...]

Draft Model Status-of-Forces Agreement Between The United Nations and Host Countries[1], 1990

[*Note:* the Draft Model Status-of-Forces Agreement between the United Nations and host countries was prepared by and included in the Annex of the Report of the UN Secretary General of 9 October 1990 (UN. Doc. A/25/594).

It was intended to serve: (a) as a basis for the drafting of individual agreements between the United Nations and countries on whose territory peace-keeping operations are deployed and (b) as a basis for an agreement with a host country in operations where no United Nations military personnel are deployed.

The Model is drafted on the basis of the established practice and earlier status-of-forces agreements.]

I. DEFINITIONS

1. For the purpose of the present Agreement the following definitions shall apply:[2]

II. APPLICATION OF THE PRESENT AGREEMENT

2. Unless specifically provided otherwise, the provisions of the present Agreement and any obligation undertaken by [Government][3] or any privilege, immunity, facility or concession granted to the United Nations peace-keeping operation or any member thereof apply in [the area of operations/territory] only.

III. APPLICATION OF THE CONVENTION

3. The Convention on the Privileges and Immunities of the United Nations of 13 February 1946 shall apply to the United Nations peace-keeping operation subject to the provisions specified in the present Agreement.[4] or

---

1 This title corresponds to the terminology used in paragraph 11 of General Assembly resolution 44/49 dated 8 December 1989. While it has been used for working purposed, the precise character of the agreement of course will vary according to the type of the United Nations peace-keeping operation concerned.

2 This section will contain definitions of the main terms used in the agreement such as: "Participating State" means a State contributing personnel to the military and/or civilian components of the United Nations peace-keeping operation. "Convention" means the Convention on the Privileges and Immunities of the United Nations adopted by the General Assembly of the United Nations on 13 February 1946.

3 The term Government as used in the present Agreement will be defined to mean the Government of the host country or Administration having de facto authority over the territory and/or area of operation in question.

4 As a general rule, the basic privileges and immunities of a United Nations peace-keeping operation consist of provisions that flow from the Convention on the Privileges and Immunities of the United Nations adopted by the General Assembly on 13 February 1946. However, while the Convention is in force with respect to 124 Member States, there are a number of States that are not a party to it and there may also be United Nations operations involving relations with entities other than States. Thus, in such cases, the Status Agreement itself must provide specifically for the application of the Convention.

4. The United Nations peace-keeping operation, its property, funds and assets, and its members, including the Special Representative/Commander, shall enjoy the privileges and immunities specified in the present Agreement as well as those provided for in the Convention, to which [host country] is a Party.[5]

5. Article II of the Convention, which applies to the United Nations peace-keeping operation, shall also apply to the property, funds and assets of participating States used in connection with the United Nations peace-keeping operation.

IV. STATUS OF THE PEACE-KEEPING OPERATION

6. The United Nations peace-keeping operation and its members shall refrain from any action or activity incompatible with the impartial and international nature of their duties or inconsistent with the spirit of the present arrangements. The United Nations peace-keeping operation and its members shall respect all local laws and regulations. The Special Representative/Commander shall take all appropriate measures to ensure the observance of those obligations.

7. The Government undertakes to respect the exclusively international nature of the United Nations peace-keeping operation.

United Nations flag and vehicle markings

8. The Government recognizes the right of the United Nations peace-keeping operation to display within [host country territory] the United Nations flag on its headquarters, camps or other premises, vehicles, vessels and otherwise as decided by the Special Representative/Commander. Other flags or pennants may be displayed only in exceptional cases. In these cases, the United Nations peace-keeping operation shall give sympathetic consideration to observations or requests of the Government of [host country].

9. Vehicles, vessels and aircraft of the United Nations peace-keeping operation shall carry a distinctive United Nations identification, which shall be notified to the Government.

Communications

10. The United Nations peace-keeping operation shall enjoy the facilities in respect to communications provided in article III of the Convention and shall, in co-ordination with the Government, use such facilities as may be required for the performance of its task. Issues with respect to communications which may arise and which are not specifically provided for in the present Agreement shall be dealt with pursuant to the relevant provisions of the Convention.

11. Subject to the provisions of paragraph 10:

(a) The United Nations peace-keeping operation shall have authority to install and operate radio sending and receiving stations as well as satellite systems to connect appropriate points within the territory of [host country/territory] with each other and with United Nations offices in other countries, and to exchange traffic with the United Nations global telecommunications network. The telecommunication services shall be operated in accordance with the International Telecommunication Convention and Regulations and the frequencies on which any such station may be operated shall

---

5 Provision to be used where the host country is a party to the said Convention.

be decided upon in co-operation with the Government and shall be communicated by the United Nations to the International Frequency Registration Board.

(b) The United Nations peace-keeping operation shall enjoy, within the territory of [host country/territory], the right to unrestricted communication by radio (including satellite, mobile and handheld radio), telephone, telegraph, facsimile or any other means, and of establishing the necessary facilities for maintaining such communications within and between premises of the United Nations peace-keeping operation, including the laying of cables and land lines and the establishment of fixed and mobile radio sending, receiving and repeater stations. The frequencies on which the radio will operate shall be decided upon in co-operation with the Government. It is understood that connections with the local system of telegraphs, telex and telephones may be made only after consultation and in accordance with arrangements with the Government. it being further understood that the use of the local system of telegraphs, telex and telephones will be charged at the most favourable rate.

(c) The United Nations peace-keeping operation may make arrangements through its own facilities for the processing and transport of private mail addressed to or emanating from members of the United Nations peace-keeping operation. The Government shall be informed of the nature of such arrangements and shall not interfere with or apply censorship to the mail of the United Nations peace-keeping operation or its members. In the event that postal arrangements applying to private mail of members of the United Nations peace-keeping operation are extended to transfer of currency or the transport of packages and parcels, the conditions under which such operations are conducted shall be agreed with the Government.

Travel and transport

12. The United Nations peace-keeping operation and its members shall enjoy, together with its vehicles, vessels, aircraft and equipment, freedom of movement throughout the [host country/territory]. That freedom shall, with respect to large movements of personnel, stores or vehicles through airports or on railways or roads used for general traffic within the [host country/territory], be co-ordinated with the Government. The Government undertakes to supply the United Nations peace-keeping operation, where necessary, with maps and other information, including locations of mine fields and other dangers and impediments, which may be useful in facilitating its movements.
13. Vehicles, including all military vehicles, vessels and aircraft of the United Nations peace-keeping operation shall not be subject to registration or licensing by the Government provided that all such vehicles shall carry the third party insurance required by relevant legislation.
14. The United Nations peace-keeping operation may use roads, bridges, canals and other waters, port facilities and airfields without the payment of dues, tolls or charges, including wharfage charges. However, the United Nations peace-keeping operation will not claim exemption from charges which are in fact charges for services rendered.

Privileges and immunities of the United Nations peace-keeping operation

15. The United Nations peace-keeping operation, as a subsidiary organ of the United Nations, enjoys the status, privileges and immunities of the United Nations [as provided for in the present Agreement][6]

6 In case of other party is not party to the Convention.

[in accordance with the Convention).[7] The provision of article II of the Convention which applies to the United Nations peace-keeping operation shall also apply to the property, funds and assets of participating States used in [host country/territory] in connection with the national Contingents serving in the United Nations peace-keeping operation, as provided for in paragraph 5 of the present Agreement. The Government recognizes the right of the United Nations peace-keeping operation in particular:

(a) To import, free of duty or other restrictions, equipment, provisions, supplies and other good: which are for the exclusive and official use of the United Nations peace-keeping operation or for resale in the commissaries provided for hereinafter;
(b) To establish, maintain and operate commissaries at its headquarters, camps and posts for the benefit of the members of the United Nations peace-keeping operation, but not of locally recruited personnel. Such commissaries may provide goods of a consumable nature and other articles to be specified in advance. The Special Representative/Commander shall take all necessary measures to prevent abuse of such commissaries and the sale or resale of such goods to persons other than members of the United Nations peace-keeping operation, and he shall give sympathetic consideration to observations or requests of the Government concerning the operation of the commissaries;
(c) To clear ex customs and excise warehouse, free of duty or other restrictions, equipment, provisions, supplies and other goods which are for the exclusive and official use of the United Nations peace-keeping operation or for resale in the commissaries provided for above;
(d) To re-export or otherwise dispose of such equipment, as far as it is still usable, all unconsumed provisions, supplies and other goods so imported or cleared ex customs and excise warehouse which are not transferred, or otherwise disposed of, on terms and conditions to be agreed upon, to the competent local authorities of the [host country/territory] or to an entity nominated by them.

To the end that such importation, clearances, transfer or exportation may be effected with the least possible delay, a mutually satisfactory procedure, including documentation, shall be agreed between the United Nations peace-keeping operation and the Government at the earliest possible date.

V. FACILITIES FOR THE UNITED NATIONS PEACE-KEEPING OPERATION

Premises required for conducting the operational and administrative activities of the United Nations peace-keeping operation and for accommodating members of the peace-keeping operation

16. The Government of [host country] shall provide without cost to the United Nations peace-keeping operation and in agreement with the Special Representative/Commander such areas for headquarters, camps or other premises as may be necessary for the conduct of the operational and administrative activities of the United Nations peace-keeping operation and for the accommodation of the members of the United Nations peace-keeping operation. Without prejudice to the tact that all such premises remain [host country] territory, they shall be inviolable and subject to the exclusive control and authority of the United Nations. Where United Nations troops are co-located with military personnel of the host country, a permanent, direct and immediate access by the United Nations peace-keeping operation to those premises shall be guaranteed.

17. The Government undertakes to assist the United Nations peace-keeping operation as far as possible in obtaining and making available, where applicable, water, electricity and other facilities free of charge, or, where this is not possible, at the most favourable rate, and in the case of interruption or threatened interruption of service, to give as far as is within its powers the same priority to the needs of

7 In case the other party is a party to the Convention.

the United Nations peace-keeping operation as to essential government services. Where such utilities or facilities are not provided free of charge, payment shall be made by the United Nations peace-keeping operation on terms to be agreed with the comp tent authority. The United Nations peace-keeping operation shall be responsible for the maintenance and upkeep of facilities so provided,
18. The United Nations peace-keeping operation shall have the right, where necessary, to generate, within its premises, electricity for its use and to transmit and distribute such electricity.
19. The United Nations alone may consent to the entry of any government officials or of any other person net member of the United Nations peace-keeping operation to such premises.

Provisions, supplies and services, and sanitary arrangements

20. The Government undertakes to assist the United Nations peace-keeping operation as far as possible in obtaining equipment, provisions, supplies and other goods and services from local sources required for its subsistence and operations. In making purchases on the local market, the United Nations peace-keeping operation shall, on the basis of observations made and information provided by the Government in that respect, avoid any adverse effect on the local economy. The Government shall exempt the United Nations peace-keeping operation from general sales taxes in respect of all official local purchases.
21. The United Nations peace-keeping operation and the Government shall co-operate with respect to sanitary services and shall extend to each other the fullest co-operation in matters concerning health, particularly with respect to the control of communicable diseases, in accordance with international conventions.

Recruitment of local personnel

22. The United Nations peace-keeping operation may recruit locally such personnel as it requires. Upon the request of the Special Representative/Commander, the Government undertakes to facilitate the recruitment of qualified local staff by the United Nations peace-keeping operation and to accelerate the process of such recruitment.

Currency

23. The Government undertakes to make available to the United Nations peace-keeping operation, against reimbursement in mutually acceptable currency, [local]currency required for the use of the United Nations peace-keeping operation, including the pay of its members, at the rate of exchange most favourable to the United Nations peace-keeping operation.

VI. STATUS OF THE MEMBERS OF THE UNITED NATIONS PEACE-KEEPING OPERATION

Privileges and immunities

24. The Special Representative, the Commander of the military component of the United Nations peacekeeping operation, the head of the United Nations civilian police, and such high-ranking members of the Special Representative/Commander's staff as may be agreed upon with the Government shall have the status specified in sections 19 and 27 of the Convention, provided that the privileges and immunities therein referred to shall be those accorded to diplomatic envoys by [national or international] law.

25. Members of the United Nations Secretarial assigned to the civilian component to serve with the United Nations peace-keeping operation remain officials of the United Nations entitled to the privileges and immunities of articles V and VII of the Convention.
26. Military observers, United Nations civilian police and civilian personnel other than United Nations officials whose names are for the purpose notified to the Government by the Special Representative/Commander shall be considered as experts on mission within the meaning of article VI of the Convention.
27. Military personnel of national contingents assigned to the military component of the United Nations peace-keeping operation shall have the privileges and immunities specifically provided for in the present Agreement.
28. Unless otherwise specified in the present Agreement, locally recruited members of the United Nations peace-keeping operation shall enjoy the immunities concerning official acts and exemption from taxation and national service obligations provided for in sections 18 (a), (b)and (c) of the Convention.
29. Members of the United Nations peace-keeping operation shall be exempt from taxation on the pay and emoluments received from the United Nations or from a participating State and any income received from outside [host country/territory]. They shall also be exempt from all other direct taxes, except municipal rates for services enjoyed, and from all registration fees and charges.
30. Members of the United Nations peace-keeping operation shall have the right to import free of duty their personal effects in connection with their arrival in [host country/territory]. They shall be subject to the laws and regulations of [host country/territory] governing customs and foreign exchange with respect to personal property not required by them by reason of their presence in [host country/territory] with the United Nations peace-keeping operation. Special facilities will be granted by the Government for the speedy processing of entry and exit formalities for all members of the United Nations peace-keeping operation, including the military component, upon prior written notification. On departure from [host country/territory], members of the United Nations peace-keeping operation may, notwithstanding the above-mentioned exchange regulations, take with them such funds as the Special Representative/Commander certifies ware received in pay and emoluments from the United Nations or from a participating State and are a reasonable residue thereof. Special arrangements shall be made for the implementation of the present provisions in the interest of the Government and the members of the United Nations peace-keeping operation.
31. The Special Representative/Commander shall co-operate with the Government and shall render all assistance within its power in ensuring the observance of the customs and fiscal laws and regulations of [host country territory] by the members of the United Nations peace-keeping operation, in accordance with the present Agreement.

Entry, residence and departure

32. The Special Representative/Commander and members of the United Nations peace-keeping operation shall, whenever so required by the Special Representative/Commander, have the right to enter into, reside in and depart from [host country/territory].
33. The Government of [host country/territory) undertakes to facilitate the entry into and departure from [host country/territory) of the Special Representative/Commander and members of the United Nations peace-keeping operation and shall be kept informed of such movement. For that purpose, the Special Representative/Commander and members of the United Nations peace-keeping operation shall be exempt from passport and visa regulations and immigration inspection and restrictions on entering

into or departing from [host country/territory]. They shall also be exempt from any regulations governing the residence of aliens in [host count y/territory], including registration, but shall not be considered as acquiring any right to permanent rasidanee or domicile in [host country/territory].
34. For the purpose of such· entry or departure, members of the United Nations peace-keeping operation shall only be required to have: (a) an individual or collective movement order issued by or under the authority of the Special Representative/Commander or any appropriate authority of a participating State; and (b) a personal identity card issued in accordance with paragraph 35 of the present Agreement, except in the case of first entry, when the personal identity card issued by the appropriate authorities of a participating State shall be accepted in lieu of the said identity card.

Identification

35. The Special Representative/Commander shall issue to each member of the United Nations peace-keeping operation before or as soon as possible after such member's first entry into [host country/territory], as well as to all locally recruited personnel, a numbered identity card, which shall show full name, date of birth, title or rank, service (if appropriate) and photograph. Except as provided for in paragraph 34 of the present Agreement, such identity card shall be the only document required of a member of the United Nations peace-keeping operation.
36. Members of the United Nations peace-keeping operation as well as locally recruited personnel shall be required to present, but not to surrender, their [United Nations peace-keeping operation] identity cards upon demand of an appropriate official of the Government.

Uniform and arms

37. Military members and the United Nations civilian police of the United Nations peace-keeping operation shall wear, while performing official duties, the national military or police uniform of their respective States with standard United Nations accoutrements. United Nations Security Officers and Field Service Officers may wear the United Nations uniform. The wearing of civilian dress by the above-mentioned members of the United Nations peace-keeping operation may be authorized by the Special Representative/Commander at other times. Military members and civilian police of the United Nations peace-keeping operation and United Nations Security Officers designated by the Special Representative/Commander may possess and carry arms while on duty in accordance with their orders.

Permits and licences

38. The Government agrees to accept as valid, without tax or fee, a permit or licence issued by the Special Representative/Commander for the operation by any member of the United Nations peacekeeping operation, including locally recruited personnel, of any [United Nations peace-keeping operation] transport or communication equipment and for the practice of any profession or occupation in connection with the functioning of the United Nations peace-keeping operation, provided that no licence to drive a vehicle or pilot an aircraft shall be issued to any person who is not already in possession of an appropriate and valid licence.
39. Without prejudice to the provisions of paragraph 37, the Government further agrees to accept as valid, without tax or fee, a permit or licence issued by the Special Representative/Commander to a member of the United Nations peace-keeping operation for the carrying or use of firearms or ammunition in connection with the functioning of the United Nations peace-keeping operation.

Military police, arrest and transfer of custody, and mutual assistance

40. The Special Representative shall take all appropriate measures to ensure the maintenance of discipline and good order among members of the United Nations peace-keeping operation, as well as locally recruited personnel. To this end personnel designated by the Special Representative/Commander shall police the premises of the United Nations peace-keeping operation and such areas where its members are deployed. Elsewhere such personnel shall be employed only subject to arrangements with the Government and in liaison with it in so far as such employment is necessary to maintain discipline and order among members of the United Nations peace-keeping operation.

41. The military police of the United Nations peace-keeping operation shall have the power of arrest over the military members of the United Nations peace-keeping operation. Military personnel placed under arrest outside their own contingent areas shall be transferred to their contingent Commander for appropriate disciplinary action. The personnel mentioned in paragraph 40 above may take into custody any other person on the premises of the United Nations peace-keeping operation. Such other person shall be delivered immediately to the nearest appropriate official of the Government for the purpose of dealing with any offence or disturbance on such premises.

42. Subject to the provisions of paragraphs 24 and 26, officials of the Government may take into custody any member of the United Nations peace-keeping operation

(a) When so required by the Special Representative/Commander; or

(b) When such a member of the United Nations peace-keeping operation is apprehended in the commission or attempted Commission of a criminal offence. Such person shall be delivered immediately, together with any weapons or other item seized, to the nearest appropriate representative of the United Nations peace-keeping operation, whereafter the provisions of paragraph 47 shall apply mutatis mutandis.

43. When a person is taken into custody under paragraph 41 or paragraph 42 (b), the United Nations peace-keeping operation or the Government, as the case may be, may make a preliminary interrogation but may not delay the transfer of custody. Following such transfer, the person concerned shall be made available upon request to the arresting authority for further interrogation.

44. The United Nations peace-keeping operation and the Government shall assist each other in carrying out all necessary investigations into offences in respect of which either or both have an interest, in the production of witnesses and in the collection and production of evidence, including the seizure of and, if appropriate, the banding over of items connected wi.th an offence. The banding over of any such items may be made subject to the return within the terms specified by the authority delivering them. Each shall notify the other of the disposition of any case in the outcome of which the other may have an interest or in which there has been a transfer of custody under the provisions of paragraphs 41-43.

45. The Government shall ensure the prosecution of persons subject to its criminal jurisdiction who are accused of acts in relation to the United Nations peace-keeping operation or its members which, if committed in relation to the forces of the Government, would have rendered such acts liable to prosecution.

Jurisdiction

46. All members of the United Nations peace-keeping operation including locally recruited personnel shall be immune from legal process in respect of words spoken or written and all acts performed by them in their official capacity. Such immunity shall continue even after they cease to be members of or employed by the United Nations peace-keeping operation and after the expiration of the other provisions of the present Agreement.

47. Should the Government consider that any member of the United Nations peace-keeping operation has committed a criminal offence, it shall promptly inform the Special Representative/Commander and present to him any evidence available to it. Subject to the provisions of paragraph 24:

(a) If the accused person is a member of the civilian component or a civilian member of the military component, the Special Representative/Commander shall conduct any necessary supplementary inquiry and then agree with the Government whether or not crimik.al proceedings should be instituted. Failing such agreement, the question shall be resolved as provided in paragraph 53 of the present Agreement.

(b) Military members of the military component of the United Nations peace-keeping operation shall be subject to the exclusive jurisdiction of their respective participating States in respect of any criminal offences which may be committed by them in [host country/territory].

48. The Secretary-General of the United Nations will obtain assurances from Governments of participating States that they will be prepared to exercise jurisdiction with respect to crimes or offences which may be committed by members of their national contingents serving with the peace-keeping operation.[8]

49. If any civil proceeding is instituted against a member of the United Nations peace-keeping operation before any court of [host country/territory], the Special Representative/Commander shall be notified immediately, and he shall certify to the court whether or not the proceeding is related to the official duties of such member:

(a) If the Special Representative/Commander certifies that the proceeding is related to official duties, such proceeding shall be discontinued and the provisions of paragraph 51 of the present Agreement shall apply.

(b) If the Special Representative certifies that the proceeding is not related to official duties, the proceeding may continue. If the Special Representative/Commander certifies that a member of the United Nations peace-keeping operation is unable because of official duties or authorized absence to protect his interests in the proceeding, the court shall at the defendant's request suspend the proceeding until the elimination of the disability, but for not more than ninety days. Property of a member of the United Nations peace-keeping operation that is certified by the Special Representative/Commander to be needed by the defendant for the fulfilment of his official duties shall be free from seizure for the satisfaction of a judgement, decision or order. The personal liberty of a member of the United Nations peace-keeping operation shall not be restricted in a civil proceeding, whether to enforce a judgement, decision or order, to compel an oath or for any other reason.

Deceased members

50. The Special Representative/Commander shall have the right to take charge of and dispose of the body of a member of the United Nations peace-keeping operation who dies in [host country/territory], as well as that member's personal property located within [host country/territory], in accordance with United Nations procedures.

---

8 This provision has been inserted in the model agreement in order that all issues pertaining to this section be covered. Upon conclusion of a specific agreement, the provision in question could instead be inserted in a memorandum of understanding where further clarifications on the terms of an agreement are usually provided.

VII. SETTLEMENT OF DISPUTES

51. Except as provided in paragraph 53, any dispute or claim of a private law character to which the United Nations peace-keeping operation or any member thereof is a party and over which the courts of [host country/territory] do not have jurisdiction because of any provision of the present Agreement, shall be settled by a standing claims commission to be established for that purpose. One member of the commission shall be appointed by the Secretary-General of the United Nations, one member by the Government and a chairman jointly by the Secretary-General and the Government. If no agreement as to the chairman is reached within thirty days of the appointment of the first member of the commission, the President of the International Court of Justice may, at the request of either the Secretary-General of the United Nations or the Government, appoint the chairman. Any vacancy on the commission shall be filled by the same method prescribed for the original appointment, provided that the thirty-day period there prescribed shall start as soon as there is a vacancy in the chairmanship. The commission shall determine its own procedures, provided that any two members shall constitute a quorum for all purposes (except for a period of thirty days after the creation of a vacancy) and all decisions shall require the approval of any two members. The awards of the commission shall be final and binding, unless the Secretary-General of the United Nations and the Government permit an appeal to a tribunal established in accordance with paragraph 53. The awards of the commission shall be notified to the parties and, if against a member of the United Nations peace-keeping operation, the Special Representative/Commander or the Secretary-General of the United Nations shall use his best endeavours to ensure compliance.

52. Disputes concerning the terms of employment and conditions of service of locally recruited personnel shall be settled by the administrative procedures to be established by the Special Representative/Commander.

53. Any other dispute between the United Nations peace-keeping operation and the Government, and any appeal that both of them agree to allow from the award of the claims commission established pursuant to paragraph 51 shall, unless otherwise agreed by the parties, be submitted to a tribunal of three arbitrators. The provisions relating to the establishment and procedures of the claims commission shall apply, mutatis mutandis, to the establishment and procedures of the tribunal. The decisions of the tribunal shall be final and binding on both parties.

54. All differences between the United Nations and the Government of [host country/territory] arising out of the interpretation or application of the present arrangements which involve a question of principle concerning the Convention shall be dealt with in accordance with the procedure of section 30 of the Convention.[9]

VIII. SUPPLEMENTAL ARRANGEMENTS

55. The Special Representative/Commander and the Government may conclude supplemental arrangements to the present Agreement.

---

9 In case the other party to the present Agreement is a party to the Convention.

IX. LIAISON

56. The Special Representative/Commander and the Government shall take appropriate measures to ensure close and reciprocal liaison at every appropriate level.

X. MISCELLANEOUS PROVISIONS

57. Wherever the resent Agreement refers to the privileges, immunities and rights of the United Nations peace-keeping operation and to the facilities the [host country/territory] undertakes to provide to the United Nations peace-keeping operation, the Government shall have the ultimate responsibility for the implementation and fulfilment of such privileges, immunities, rights and facilities by the appropriate local [host country/territory] authorities.
58. The present Agreement is concluded for the sole purpose of assisting in the implementation of Security Council/General Assembly resolution [number and date of resolution] and has no bearing upon the respective positions of the parties concerning the status of [territory].[10]
59. The present Agreement shall enter into force on ....
60. The present Agreement shall remain in force until the departure of the final element of the United Nations peace-keeping operation from [host country/territory] except that:
(a) The provisions of paragraphs 46 and 53 [and 54][11] shall remain in force.
(b) The provisions of paragraph 51 shall remain in force until all claims have been settled that arose prior to the termination of the present Agreement and were submitted prior to or within three months of such termination.

10 The insertion of this provision in an agreement is subject to its relevancy.
11 See footnote i.

Statutes of the United Nations Dispute Tribunal and the United Nations Appeals Tribunal, 2008

[*Note:* the Statutes of the United Nations Dispute Tribunal and the United Nations Appeals Tribunal were adopted by the General Assembly resolution 63/253 of 24 December 2008]

Annex I: Statute of the United Nations Dispute Tribunal

Article 1
A tribunal is established by the present statute as the first instance of the two-tier formal system of administration of justice, to be known as the United Nations Dispute Tribunal.

Article 2
1. The Dispute Tribunal shall be competent to hear and pass judgement on an application filed by an individual, as provided for in article 3, paragraph 1, of the present statute, against the Secretary-General as the Chief Administrative Officer of the United Nations:
(a) To appeal an administrative decision that is alleged to be in non-compliance with the terms of appointment or the contract of employment. The terms "contract" and "terms of appointment" include all pertinent regulations and rules and all relevant administrative issuances in force at the time of alleged non-compliance;
(b) To appeal an administrative decision imposing a disciplinary measure;
(c) To enforce the implementation of an agreement reached through mediation pursuant to article 8, paragraph 2, of the present statute.
2. The Dispute Tribunal shall be competent to hear and pass judgement on an application filed by an individual requesting the Dispute Tribunal to suspend, during the pendency of the management evaluation, the implementation of a contested administrative decision that is the subject of an ongoing management evaluation, where the decision appears prima facie to be unlawful, in cases of particular urgency, and where its implementation would cause irreparable damage. The decision of the Dispute Tribunal on such an application shall not be subject to appeal.
3. The Dispute Tribunal shall be competent to permit or deny leave to an application to file a friend-ofthe-court brief by a staff association.
4. The Dispute Tribunal shall be competent to permit an individual who is entitled to appeal the same administrative decision under paragraph 1 (a) of the present article to intervene in a matter brought by another staff member under the same paragraph.
5. The Dispute Tribunal shall be competent to hear and pass judgement on an application filed against a specialized agency brought into relationship with the United Nations in accordance with the provisions of Articles 57 and 63 of the Charter of the United Nations or other international organization or entity established by a treaty and participating in the common system of conditions of service, where a special agreement has been concluded between the agency, organization or entity concerned and the Secretary-General of the United Nations to accept the terms of the jurisdiction of the Dispute Tribunal,

consonant with the present statute. Such special agreement shall provide that the agency, organization or entity concerned shall be bound by the judgements of the Dispute Tribunal and be responsible for the payment of any compensation awarded by the Dispute Tribunal in respect of its own staff members and shall include, inter alia, provisions concerning its participation in the administrative arrangements for the functioning of the Dispute Tribunal and concerning its sharing of the expenses of the Dispute Tribunal. Such special agreement shall also contain other provisions required for the Dispute Tribunal to carry out its functions vis-à-vis the agency, organization or entity.

6. In the event of a dispute as to whether the Dispute Tribunal has competence under the present statute, the Dispute Tribunal shall decide on the matter.

7. As a transitional measure, the Dispute Tribunal shall be competent to hear and pass judgement on:

(a) A case transferred to it from a joint appeals board or a joint disciplinary committee established by the United Nations, or from another similar body established by a separately administered fund or programme;

(b) A case transferred to it from the United Nations Administrative Tribunal, as decided by the General Assembly.

Article 3

1. An application under article 2, paragraph 1, of the present statute may be filed by:

(a) Any staff member of the United Nations, including the United Nations Secretariat or separately administered United Nations funds and programmes;

(b) Any former staff member of the United Nations, including the United Nations Secretariat or separately administered United Nations funds and programmes;

(c) Any person making claims in the name of an incapacitated or deceased staff member of the United Nations, including the United Nations Secretariat or separately administered United Nations funds and programmes.

2. A request for a suspension of action under article 2, paragraph 2, of the present statute may be filed by an individual, as provided for in paragraph 1 of the present article.

Article 4

1. The Dispute Tribunal shall be composed of three full-time judges and two half-time judges.

2. The judges shall be appointed by the General Assembly on the recommendation of the Internal Justice Council in accordance with Assembly resolution 62/228. No two judges shall be of the same nationality. Due regard shall be given to geographical distribution and gender balance.

3. To be eligible for appointment as a judge, a person shall:

(a) Be of high moral character; and

(b) Possess at least 10 years of judicial experience in the field of administrative law, or the equivalent within one or more national jurisdictions.

4. A judge of the Dispute Tribunal shall be appointed for one non-renewable term of seven years. As a transitional measure, two of the judges (one full-time judge and one half-time judge) initially appointed, to be determined by drawing of lots, shall serve three years and may be reappointed to the same Dispute Tribunal for a further non-renewable term of seven years. A current or former judge of the United Nations Appeals Tribunal shall not be eligible to serve in the Dispute Tribunal.

5. A judge of the Dispute Tribunal appointed to replace a judge whose term of office has not expired shall hold office for the remainder of his or her predecessor's term, and may be reappointed for one nonrenewable term of seven years, provided that the unexpired term is less than three years.

6. A judge of the Dispute Tribunal shall not be eligible for any appointment within the United Nations, except another judicial post, for a period of five years following his or her term of office.

7. The Dispute Tribunal shall elect a President.
8. A judge of the Dispute Tribunal shall serve in his or her personal capacity and enjoy full independence.
9. A judge of the Dispute Tribunal who has, or appears to have, a conflict of interest shall recuse himself or herself from the case. Where a party requests such recusal, the decision shall be taken by the President of the Dispute Tribunal.
10. A judge of the Dispute Tribunal may only be removed by the General Assembly in case of misconduct or incapacity.
11. A judge of the Dispute Tribunal may resign, by notifying the General Assembly through the Secretary-General of the United Nations. The resignation shall take effect from the date of notification, unless the notice of resignation specifies a later date.

Article 5

The three full-time judges of the Dispute Tribunal shall exercise their functions in New York, Geneva and Nairobi, respectively. However, the Dispute Tribunal may decide to hold sessions at other duty stations, as required by its caseload.

Article 6

1. The Secretary-General of the United Nations shall make the administrative arrangements necessary for the functioning of the Dispute Tribunal, including provisions for the travel and related costs of staff whose physical presence before the Dispute Tribunal is deemed necessary by the Dispute Tribunal and for judges to travel as necessary to hold sessions at other duty stations.
2. The Registries of the Dispute Tribunal shall be established in New York, Geneva and Nairobi, each consisting of a Registrar and such other staff as necessary.
3. The expenses of the Dispute Tribunal shall be borne by the United Nations.
4. Compensation ordered by the Dispute Tribunal shall be paid by the United Nations Secretariat or separately administered United Nations funds and programmes, as applicable and appropriate, or by the specialized agency, organization or entity that has accepted the jurisdiction of the Dispute Tribunal.

Article 7

1. Subject to the provisions of the present statute, the Dispute Tribunal shall establish its own rules of procedure, which shall be subject to approval by the General Assembly.
2. The rules of procedure of the Dispute Tribunal shall include provisions concerning:

(a) Organization of work;
(b) Presentation of submissions and the procedure to be followed in respect thereto;
(c) Procedures for maintaining the confidentiality and inadmissibility of verbal or written statements made during the mediation process;
(d) Intervention by persons not party to the case whose rights may be affected by the judgement;
(e) Oral hearings;
(f) Publication of judgements;
(g) Functions of the Registries;
(h) Procedure for summary dismissal;
(i) Evidentiary procedure;
(j) Suspension of implementation of contested administrative decisions;
(k) Procedure for the recusal of judges;
(l) Other matters relating to the functioning of the Dispute Tribunal.

Article 8

1. An application shall be receivable if:

(a) The Dispute Tribunal is competent to hear and pass judgement on the application, pursuant to article 2 of the present statute;

(b) An applicant is eligible to file an application, pursuant to article 3 of the present statute;

(c) An applicant has previously submitted the contested administrative decision for management evaluation, where required; and

(d) The application is filed within the following deadlines:

(i) In cases where a management evaluation of the contested decision is required:

a. Within 90 calendar days of the applicant's receipt of the response by management to his or her submission; or

b. Within 90 calendar days of the expiry of the relevant response period for the management evaluation if no response to the request was provided. The response period shall be 30 calendar days after the submission of the decision to management evaluation for disputes arising at Headquarters and 45 calendar days for other offices;

(ii) In cases where a management evaluation of the contested decision is not required, within 90 calendar days of the applicant's receipt of the administrative decision;

(iii) The deadlines provided for in subparagraphs (d) (i) and (ii) of the present paragraph shall be extended to one year if the application is filed by any person making claims in the name of an incapacitated or deceased staff member of the United Nations, including the United Nations Secretariat or separately administered United Nations funds and programmes;

(iv) Where the parties have sought mediation of their dispute within the deadlines for the filing of an application under subparagraph (d) of the present paragraph, but did not reach an agreement, the application is filed within 90 calendar days after the mediation has broken down in accordance with the procedures laid down in the terms of reference of the Mediation Division.

2. An application shall not be receivable if the dispute arising from the contested administrative decision had been resolved by an agreement reached through mediation. However, an applicant may file an application to enforce the implementation of an agreement reached through mediation, which shall be receivable if the agreement has not been implemented and the application is filed within 90 calendar days after the last day for the implementation as specified in the mediation agreement or, when the mediation agreement is silent on the matter, after the thirtieth day from the date of the signing of the agreement.

3. The Dispute Tribunal may decide in writing, upon written request by the applicant, to suspend or waive the deadlines for a limited period of time and only in exceptional cases. The Dispute Tribunal shall not suspend or waive the deadlines for management evaluation.

4. Notwithstanding paragraph 3 of the present article, an application shall not be receivable if it is filed more than three years after the applicant's receipt of the contested administrative decision.

5. The filing of an application shall not have the effect of suspending the implementation of the contested administrative decision.

6. An application and other submissions shall be filed in any of the official languages of the United Nations.

Article 9

1. The Dispute Tribunal may order production of documents or such other evidence as it deems necessary.

2. The Dispute Tribunal shall decide whether the personal appearance of the applicant or any other person is required at oral proceedings and the appropriate means for satisfying the requirement of personal appearance.
3. The oral proceedings of the Dispute Tribunal shall be held in public unless the Dispute Tribunal decides, at its own initiative or at the request of either party, that exceptional circumstances require the proceedings to be closed.

Article 10
1. The Dispute Tribunal may suspend proceedings in a case at the request of the parties for a time to be specified by it in writing.
2. At any time during the proceedings, the Dispute Tribunal may order an interim measure, which is without appeal, to provide temporary relief to either party, where the contested administrative decision appears prima facie to be unlawful, in cases of particular urgency, and where its implementation would cause irreparable damage. This temporary relief may include an order to suspend the implementation of the contested administrative decision, except in cases of appointment, promotion or termination.
3. At any time during the deliberations, the Dispute Tribunal may propose to refer the case to mediation. With the consent of the parties, it shall suspend the proceedings for a time to be specified by it. If a mediation agreement is not reached within this period of time, the Dispute Tribunal shall continue with its proceedings unless the parties request otherwise.
4. Prior to a determination of the merits of a case, should the Dispute Tribunal find that a relevant procedure prescribed in the Staff Regulations and Rules or applicable administrative issuances has not been observed, the Dispute Tribunal may, with the concurrence of the Secretary-General of the United Nations, remand the case for institution or correction of the required procedure, which, in any case, should not exceed three months. In such cases, the Dispute Tribunal may order the payment of compensation for procedural delay to the applicant for such loss as may have been caused by such procedural delay, which is not to exceed the equivalent of three months' net base salary.
5. As part of its judgement, the Dispute Tribunal may order one or both of the following:
(a) Rescission of the contested administrative decision or specific performance, provided that, where the contested administrative decision concerns appointment, promotion or termination, the Dispute Tribunal shall also set an amount of compensation that the respondent may elect to pay as an alternative to the rescission of the contested administrative decision or specific performance ordered, subject to subparagraph (b) of the present paragraph;
(b) Compensation, which shall normally not exceed the equivalent of two years' net base salary of the applicant. The Dispute Tribunal may, however, in exceptional cases order the payment of a higher compensation and shall provide the reasons for that decision.
6. Where the Dispute Tribunal determines that a party has manifestly abused the proceedings before it, it may award costs against that party.
7. The Dispute Tribunal shall not award exemplary or punitive damages.
8. The Dispute Tribunal may refer appropriate cases to the Secretary-General of the United Nations or the executive heads of separately administered United Nations funds and programmes for possible action to enforce accountability.
9. Cases before the Dispute Tribunal shall normally be considered by a single judge. However, the President of the United Nations Appeals Tribunal may, within seven calendar days of a written request by the President of the Dispute Tribunal, authorize the referral of a case to a panel of three judges of the Dispute Tribunal, when necessary, by reason of the particular complexity or importance of the case. Cases referred to a panel of three judges shall be decided by a majority vote.

Article 11

1. The judgements of the Dispute Tribunal shall be issued in writing and shall state the reasons, facts and law on which they are based.
2. The deliberations of the Dispute Tribunal shall be confidential.
3. The judgements of the Dispute Tribunal shall be binding upon the parties, but are subject to appeal in accordance with the statute of the United Nations Appeals Tribunal. In the absence of such appeal, they shall be executable following the expiry of the time provided for appeal in the statute of the Appeals Tribunal.
4. The judgements of the Dispute Tribunal shall be drawn up in any of the official languages of the United Nations, in two originals, which shall be deposited in the archives of the United Nations.
5. A copy of the judgement shall be communicated to each party in the case. The applicant shall receive a copy in the language in which the application was submitted unless he or she requests a copy in another official language of the United Nations.
6. The judgements of the Dispute Tribunal shall be published, while protecting personal data, and made generally available by the Registry of the Tribunal.

Article 12

1. Either party may apply to the Dispute Tribunal for a revision of an executable judgement on the basis of the discovery of a decisive fact which was, at the time the judgement was rendered, unknown to the Dispute Tribunal and to the party applying for revision, always provided that such ignorance was not due to negligence. The application must be made within 30 calendar days of the discovery of the fact and within one year of the date of the judgement.
2. Clerical or arithmetical mistakes, or errors arising therein from any accidental slip or omission, may at any time be corrected by the Dispute Tribunal, either on its own motion or on the application of any of the parties.
3. Either party may apply to the Dispute Tribunal for an interpretation of the meaning or the scope of the final judgement, provided that it is not under consideration by the Appeals Tribunal.
4. Once a judgement is executable under article 11, paragraph 3, of the present statute, either party may apply to the Dispute Tribunal for an order for execution of the judgement if the judgement requires execution within a certain period of time and such execution has not been carried out.

Article 13

The present statute may be amended by decision of the General Assembly.

Annex II - Statute of the United Nations Appeals Tribunal

Article 1

A tribunal is established by the present statute as the second instance of the two-tier formal system of administration of justice, to be known as the United Nations Appeals Tribunal.

Article 2

1. The Appeals Tribunal shall be competent to hear and pass judgement on an appeal filed against a judgement rendered by the United Nations Dispute Tribunal in which it is asserted that the Dispute Tribunal has:

(a) Exceeded its jurisdiction or competence;
(b) Failed to exercise jurisdiction vested in it;

(c) Erred on a question of law;
(d) Committed an error in procedure, such as to affect the decision of the case; or
(e) Erred on a question of fact, resulting in a manifestly unreasonable decision.

2. An appeal may be filed by either party (i.e., the applicant, a person making claims in the name of an incapacitated or deceased applicant, or the respondent) to a judgement of the Dispute Tribunal.

3. The Appeals Tribunal may affirm, reverse, modify or remand the judgement of the Dispute Tribunal. It may also issue all orders necessary or appropriate in aid of its jurisdiction and consonant with the present statute.

4. In cases of appeal under paragraph 1 (e) of the present article, the Appeals Tribunal shall be competent:
(a) To affirm, reverse or modify findings of fact of the Dispute Tribunal on the basis of substantial evidence in the written record; or
(b) To remand the case to the Dispute Tribunal for additional findings of fact, subject to paragraph 5 of the present article, if it determines that further findings of fact are necessary.

5. In exceptional circumstances, and where the Appeals Tribunal determines that the facts are likely to be establish ed with documentary evidence, including written testimony, it may receive such additional evidence if that is in the interest of justice and the efficient and expeditious resolution of the proceedings. Where this is not the case, or where the Appeals Tribunal determines that a decision cannot be taken without oral testimony or other forms of non-written evidence, it shall remand the case to the Dispute Tribunal. The evidence under this paragraph shall not include evidence that was known to either party and should have been presented at the level of the Dispute Tribunal.

6. Where the Appeals Tribunal remands a case to the Dispute Tribunal, it may order that the case be considered by a different judge of the Dispute Tribunal.

7. For the purposes of the present article, "written record" means anything that has been entered in the formal record of the Dispute Tribunal, including submissions, evidence, testimony, motions, objections, rulings and the judgement, and any evidence received in accordance with paragraph 5 of the present article.

8. In the event of a dispute as to whether the Appeals Tribunal has competence under the present statute, the Appeals Tribunal shall decide on the matter.

9. The Appeals Tribunal shall be competent to hear and pass judgement on an appeal of a decision of the Standing Committee acting on behalf of the Unite d Nations Joint Staff Pension Board, alleging nonobservance of the regulations of the United Nations Joint Staff Pension Fund, submitted by:
(a) Any staff member of a member organization of the Pension Fund which has accepted the jurisdiction of the Appeals Tribunal in Pension Fund cases who is eligible under article 21 of the regulations of the Fund as a participant in the Fund, even if his or her employment has ceased, and any person who has acceded to such staff member's rights upon his or her death;
(b) Any other person who can show that he or she is entitled to rights under the regulations of the Pension Fund by virtue of the participation in the Fund of a staff member of such member organization. In such cases, remands, if any, shall be to the Standing Committee acting on behalf of the United Nations Joint Staff Pension Board.

10. The Appeals Tribunal shall be competent to hear and pass judgement on an application filed against a specialized agency brought into relationship with the United Nations in accordance with the provisions of Articles 57 and 63 of the Charter of the United Nations or other international organization or entity established by a treaty and participating in the common system of conditions of service, where a special agreement has been concluded between the agency, organization or entity concerned and the Secretary-General of the United Nations to accept the terms of the jurisdiction of the Appeals Tribunal,

consonant with the present statute. Such special agreement shall provide that the agency, organization or entity concerned shall be bound by the judgements of the Appeals Tribunal and be responsible for the payment of any compensation awarded by the Appeals Tribunal in respect of its own staff members and shall include, inter alia, provisions concerning its participation in the administrative arrangements for the functioning of the Appeals Tribunal and concerning its sharing of the expenses of the Appeals Tribunal. Such special agreement shall also contain other provisions required for the Appeals Tribunal to carry out its functions vis-a-vis the agency, organization or entity. Such special agreement may only be concluded if the agency, organization or entity utilizes a neutral first instance process that includes a written record and a written decision providing reasons, fact and law. In such cases remands, if any, shall be to the first instance process of the agency, organization or entity.

Article 3

1. The Appeals Tribunal shall be composed of seven judges.
2. The judges shall be appointed by the General Assembly on the recommendation of the Internal Justice Council in accordance with General Assembly resolution 62/228. No two judges shall be of the same nationality. Due regard shall be given to geographical distribution and gender balance.
3. To be eligible for appointment as a judge, a person shall:
(a) Be of high moral character; and
(b) Possess at least 15 years of judicial experience in the field of administrative law, or the equivalent within one or more national jurisdictions.
4. A judge of the Appeals Tribunal shall be appointed for one non-renewable term of seven years. As a transitional measure, three of the judges initially appointed, to be determined by drawing of lots, shall serve three years and may be reappointed to the same Appeals Tribunal for a further non-renewable term of seven years. A current or former judge of the Dispute Tribunal shall not be eligible to serve in the Appeals Tribunal.
5. A judge of the Appeals Tribunal appointed to replace a judge whose term of office has not expired shall hold office for the remainder of his or her predecessor's term and may be reappointed for one non-renewable term of seven years, provided that the unexpired term is less than three years.
6. A judge of the Appeals Tribunal shall not be eligible for any appointment within the United Nations, except another judicial post, for a period of five years following his or her term of office.
7. The Appeals Tribunal shall elect a President and two Vice-Presidents.
8. A judge of the Appeals Tribunal shall serve in his or her personal capacity and enjoy full independence.
9. A judge of the Appeals Tribunal who has, or appears to have, a conflict of interest shall recuse himself or herself from the case. Where a party requests such recusal, the decision shall be taken by the President of the Appeals Tribunal.
10. A judge of the Appeals Tribunal may only be removed by the General Assembly in case of misconduct or incapacity.
11. A judge of the Appeals Tribunal may resign, by notifying the General Assembly through the Secretary-General of the United Nations. The resignation shall take effect from the date of notification, unless the notice of resignation specifies a later date.

Article 4

1. The Appeals Tribunal shall exercise its functions in New York. However, it may decide to hold sessions in Geneva or Nairobi, as required by its caseload.

2. The Appeals Tribunal shall hold ordinary sessions at dates to be fixed by its rules of procedure, subject to the determination of its President that there is a sufficient number of cases to justify holding the session.
3. Extraordinary sessions may be convoked by the President, as required by the caseload.

Article 5
1. The Secretary-General of the United Nations shall make the administrative arrangements necessary for the functioning of the Appeals Tribunal, including provisions for the travel and related costs of staff whose physical presence before the Appeals Tribunal is deemed necessary by the Appeals Tribunal and for judges to travel as necessary to hold sessions in Geneva and Nairobi.
2. The Registry of the Appeals Tribunal shall be established in New York. It shall consist of a Registrar and such other staff as necessary.
3. The expenses of the Appeals Tribunal shall be borne by the United Nations.
4. Compensation ordered by the Appeals Tribunal shall be paid by the United Nations Secretariat or separately administered United Nations funds and programmes, as applicable and appropriate, or by the specialized agency, organization or entity that has accepted the jurisdiction of the Appeals Tribunal.

Article 6
1. Subject to the provisions of the present statute, the Appeals Tribunal shall establish its own rules of procedure, which shall be subject to approval by the General Assembly.
2. The rules of procedure of the Appeals Tribunal shall include provisions concerning:
(a) Election of the President and Vice-Presidents;
(b) Composition of the Appeals Tribunal for its sessions;
(c) Organization of work;
(d) Presentation of submissions and the procedure to be followed in respect thereto;
(e) Procedures for maintaining the confidentiality and inadmissibility of verbal or written statements made during the mediation process;
(f) Intervention by persons not party to the case whose rights may have been affected by the judgement of the Dispute Tribunal and whose rights might therefore also be affected by the judgement of the Appeals Tribunal;
(g) The filing of friend-of-court briefs, upon motion and with the permission of the Appeals Tribunal;
(h) Oral proceedings;
(i) Publication of judgements;
(j) Functions of the Registry;
(k) Procedure for the recusal of judges;
(l) Other matters relating to the functioning of the Appeals Tribunal.

Article 7
1. An appeal shall be receivable if:
(a) The Appeals Tribunal is competent to hear and pass judgement on the appeal, pursuant to article 2, paragraph 1, of the present statute;
(b) The appellant is eligible to file the appeal, pursuant to article 2, paragraph 2, of the present statute; and
(c) The appeal is filed within 45 calendar days of the receipt of the judgement of the Dispute Tribunal or, where the Appeals Tribunal has decided to waive or suspend that deadline in accordance with paragraph 3 of the present article, within the period specified by the Appeals Tribunal.

2. For purposes of applications alleging non-observance of the regulations of the United Nations Joint Staff Pension Fund arising out of a decision of the United Nations Joint Staff Pension Board, an application shall be receivable if filed within 90 calendar days of receipt of the Board's decision.
3. The Appeals Tribunal may decide in writing, upon written request by the applicant, to suspend or waive the deadlines for a limited period of time and only in exceptional cases. The Appeals Tribunal shall not suspend or waive the deadlines for management evaluation.
4. Notwithstanding paragraph 3 of the present article, an application shall not be receivable if it is filed more than one year after the judgement of the Dispute Tribunal.
5. The filing of appeals shall have the effect of suspending the execution of the judgement contested.
6. An appeal and other submissions shall be filed in any of the official languages of the United Nations.

Article 8

1. The Appeals Tribunal may order production of documents or such other evidence as it deems necessary, subject to article 2 of the present statute.
2. The Appeals Tribunal shall decide whether the personal appearance of the appellant or any other person is required at oral proceedings and the appropriate means to achieve that purpose.
3. The judges assigned to a case will determine whether to hold oral proceedings.
4. The oral proceedings of the Appeals Tribunal shall be held in public unless the Appeals Tribunal decides, at its own initiative or at the request of either party, that exceptional circumstances require the proceedings to be closed.

Article 9

1. The Appeals Tribunal may order one or both of the following:
(a) Rescission of the contested administrative decision or specific performance, provided that, where the contested administrative decision concerns appointment, promotion or termination, the Appeals Tribunal shall also set an amount of compensation that the respondent may elect to pay as an alternative to the rescission of the contested administrative decision or specific performance ordered, subject to subparagraph (b) of the present paragraph;
(b) Compensation, which shall normally not exceed the equivalent of two years' net base salary of the applicant. The Appeals Tribunal may, however, in exceptional cases order the payment of a higher compensation and shall provide the reasons for that decision.
2. Where the Appeals Tribunal determines that a party has manifestly abused the appeals process, it may award costs against that party.
3. The Appeals Tribunal shall not award exemplary or punitive damages.
4. At any time during the proceedings, the Appeals Tribunal may order an interim measure to provide temporary relief to either party to prevent irreparable harm and to maintain consistency with the judgement of the Dispute Tribunal.
5. The Appeals Tribunal may refer appropriate cases to the Secretary-General of the United Nations or executive heads of separately administered United Nations funds and programmes for possible action to enforce accountability.

Article 10

1. Cases before the Appeals Tribunal shall normally be reviewed by a panel of three judges and shall be decided by a majority vote.
2. Where the President or any two judges sitting on a particular case consider that the case raises a significant question of law, at any time before judgement is rendered, the case may be referred for consideration by the whole Appeals Tribunal. A quorum in such cases shall be five judges.

3. The judgements of the Appeals Tribunal shall be issued in writing and shall state the reasons, facts and law on which they are based.
4. The deliberations of the Appeals Tribunal shall be confidential.
5. The judgements of the Appeals Tribunal shall be binding upon the parties.
6. The judgements of the Appeals Tribunal shall be final and without appeal, subject to the provisions of article 11 of the present statute.
7. The judgements of the Appeals Tribunal shall be drawn up in any of the official languages of the United Nations, in two originals, which shall be deposited in the archives of the United Nations.
8. A copy of the judgement shall be communicated to each party in the case. The applicant shall receive a copy in the language in which the appeal was submitted unless he or she requests a copy in another official language of the United Nations.
9. The judgements of the Appeals Tribunal shall be published, while protecting personal data, and made generally available by the Registry of the Tribunal.

Article 11
1. Subject to article 2 of the present statute, either party may apply to the Appeals Tribunal for a revision of a judgement on the basis of the discovery of a decisive fact which was, at the time the judgement was rendered, unknown to the Appeals Tribunal and to the party applying for revision, always provided that such ignorance was not due to negligence. The application must be made within 30 calendar days of the discovery of the fact and within one year of the date of the judgement.
2. Clerical or arithmetical mistakes, or errors arising therein from any accidental slip or omission, may at any time be corrected by the Appeals Tribunal, either on its own motion or on the application of any of the parties.
3. Either party may apply to the Appeals Tribunal for an interpretation of the meaning or scope of the judgement.
4. Where the judgement requires execution within a certain period of time and such execution has not been carried out, either party may apply to the Appeals Tribunal for an order for execution of the judgement.

Article 12
The present statute may be amended by decision of the General Assembly.

II. North Atlantic Treaty Organization (NATO)

The North Atlantic Treaty (NATO), 1949

[*Note:* the North Atlantic Treaty was adopted in Washington, D.C., on April 4, 1949 and entered into force on August 24, 1949.

Status since February 2018: 28 Members]

The Parties to this Treaty reaffirm their faith in the purposes and principles of the Charter of the United Nations and their desire to live in peace with all peoples and all governments.

They are determined to safeguard the freedom, common heritage and civilisation of their peoples, founded on the principles of democracy, individual liberty and the rule of law. They seek to promote stability and well-being in the North Atlantic area.

They are resolved to unite their efforts for collective defence and for the preservation of peace and security. They therefore agree to this North Atlantic Treaty :

Article 1
The Parties undertake, as set forth in the Charter of the United Nations, to settle any international dispute in which they may be involved by peaceful means in such a manner that international peace and security and justice are not endangered, and to refrain in their international relations from the threat or use of force in any manner inconsistent with the purposes of the United Nations.

Article 2
The Parties will contribute toward the further development of peaceful and friendly international relations by strengthening their free institutions, by bringing about a better understanding of the principles upon which these institutions are founded, and by promoting conditions of stability and wellbeing. They will seek to eliminate conflict in their international economic policies and will encourage economic collaboration between any or all of them.

Article 3
In order more effectively to achieve the objectives of this Treaty, the Parties, separately and jointly, by means of continuous and effective self-help and mutual aid, will maintain and develop their individual and collective capacity to resist armed attack.

Article 4
The Parties will consult together whenever, in the opinion of any of them, the territorial integrity, political independence or security of any of the Parties is threatened.

Article 5
The Parties agree that an armed attack against one or more of them in Europe or North America shall be considered an attack against them all and consequently they agree that, if such an armed attack occurs, each of them, in exercise of the right of individual or collective self-defence recognised by Article 51 of the Charter of the United Nations, will assist the Party or Parties so attacked by taking forthwith, individually and in concert with the other Parties, such action as it deems necessary, including the use of armed force, to restore and maintain the security of the North Atlantic area. Any such armed attack and all measures taken as a result thereof shall immediately be reported to the Security Council. Such measures shall be terminated when the Security Council has taken the measures necessary to restore and maintain international peace and security.

Article 6
For the purpose of Article 5, an armed attack on one or more of the Parties is deemed to include an armed attack

- on the territory of any of the Parties in Europe or North America, on the Algerian Departments of France
- on the territory of or on the Islands under the jurisdiction of any of the Parties in the North Atlantic area north of the Tropic of Cancer; on the forces, vessels, or aircraft of any of the Parties, when in or over these territories or any other area in Europe in which occupation forces of any of the Parties were stationed on the date when the Treaty entered into force or the Mediterranean Sea or the North Atlantic area north of the Tropic of Cancer.

Article 7
This Treaty does not affect, and shall not be interpreted as affecting in any way the rights and obligations under the Charter of the Parties which are members of the United Nations, or the primary responsibility of the Security Council for the maintenance of international peace and security.

Article 8
Each Party declares that none of the international engagements now in force between it and any other of the Parties or any third State is in conflict with the provisions of this Treaty, and undertakes not to enter into any international engagement in conflict with this Treaty.

Article 9
The Parties hereby establish a Council, on which each of them shall be represented, to consider matters concerning the implementation of this Treaty. The Council shall be so organised as to be able to meet promptly at any time. The Council shall set up such subsidiary bodies as may be necessary; in particular it shall establish immediately a defence committee which shall recommend measures for the implementation of Articles 3 and 5.

Article 10
The Parties may, by unanimous agreement, invite any other European State in a position to further the principles of this Treaty and to contribute to the security of the North Atlantic area to accede to this Treaty. Any State so invited may become a Party to the Treaty by depositing its instrument of accession with the Government of the United States of America. The Government of the United States of America will inform each of the Parties of the deposit of each such instrument of accession.

Article 11
This Treaty shall be ratified and its provisions carried out by the Parties in accordance with their respective constitutional processes. The instruments of ratification shall be deposited as soon as possible with

the Government of the United States of America, which will notify all the other signatories of each deposit. The Treaty shall enter into force between the States which have ratified it as soon as the ratifications of the majority of the signatories, including the ratifications of Belgium, Canada, France, Luxembourg, the Netherlands, the United Kingdom and the United States, have been deposited and shall come into effect with respect to other States on the date of the deposit of their ratifications.

Article 12
After the Treaty has been in force for ten years, or at any time thereafter, the Parties shall, if any of them so requests, consult together for the purpose of reviewing the Treaty, having regard for the factors then affecting peace and security in the North Atlantic area, including the development of universal as well as regional arrangements under the Charter of the United Nations for the maintenance of international peace and security.

Article 13
After the Treaty has been in force for twenty years, any Party may cease to be a Party one year after its notice of denunciation has been given to the Government of the United States of America, which will inform the Governments of the other Parties of the deposit of each notice of denunciation.

Article 14
This Treaty, of which the English and French texts are equally authentic, shall be deposited in the archives of the Government of the United States of America. Duly certified copies will be transmitted by that Government to the Governments of other signatories.

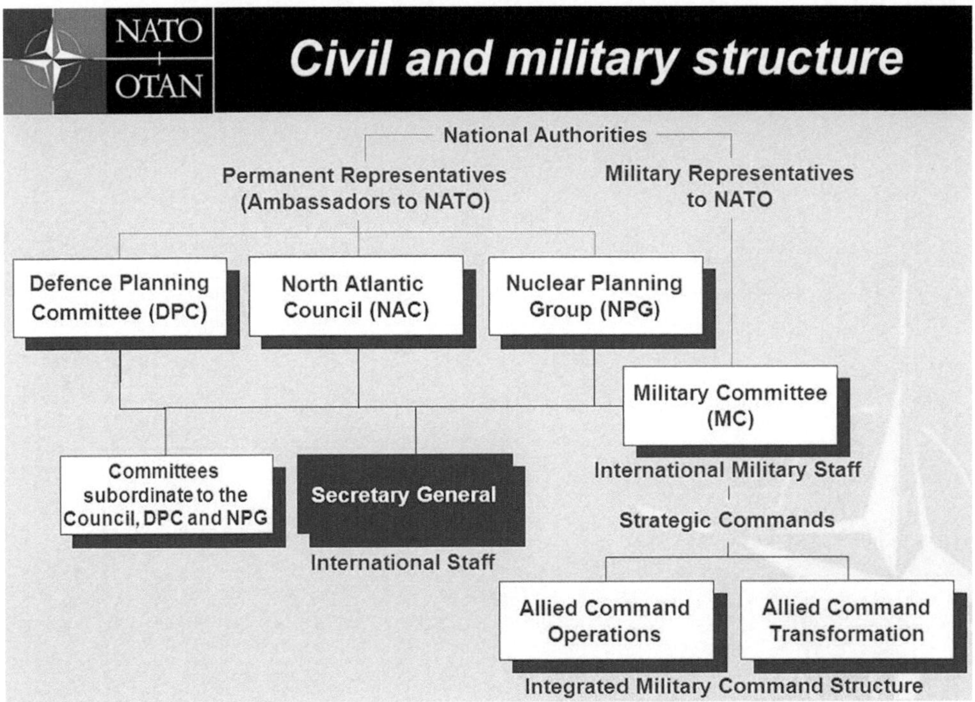

Figure 2: NATO Civil and Military structure
Source: Excerpt from North Atlantic Treaty Organisation - ppt download, http://slideplayer.com/slide/5334376/

III. Organization for Security and Cooperation in Europe (OSCE)

Final Act of the Conference on Security and Co-Operation in Europe, 1975

[*Note:* the Conference on Security and Cooperation (CSCE) commenced its activities by the adoption of the Final Act in Helsinki, on August 1, 1975. In 1994 the Conference was renamed into the Organization for Security and Cooperation in Europe (OSCE). Currently it presents the world's largest security organization in which participate 57 States from North America, Europe and Asia].

Motivated by the political will, in the interest of peoples, to improve and intensify their relations and to contribute in Europe to peace, security, justice and co-operation as well as to rapprochement among themselves and with the other States of the world,
Determined, in consequence, to give full effect to the results of the Conference and to assure, among their States and throughout Europe, the benefits deriving from those results and thus to broaden, deepen and make continuing and lasting the process of détente,
The High Representatives of the participating States have solemnly adopted the following:

Questions relating to Security in Europe

The States participating in the Conference on Security and Co-operation in Europe,
Reaffirming their objective of promoting better relations among themselves and ensuring conditions in which their people can live in true and lasting peace free from any threat to or attempt against their security;
Convinced of the need to exert efforts to make détente both a continuing and an increasingly viable and comprehensive process, universal in scope, and that the implementation of the results of the Conference on Security and Co-operation in Europe will be a major contribution to this process;
Considering that solidarity among peoples, as well as the common purpose of the participating States in achieving the aims as set forth by the Conference on Security and Co-operation in Europe, should lead to the development of better and closer relations among them in all fields and thus to overcoming the confrontation stemming from the character of their past relations, and to better mutual understanding;
Mindful of their common history and recognizing that the existence of elements common to their traditions and values can assist them in developing their relations, and desiring to search, fully taking into account the individuality and diversity of their positions and views, for possibilities of joining their efforts with a view to overcoming distrust and increasing confidence, solving the problems that separate them and cooperating in the interest of mankind;
Recognizing the indivisibility of security in Europe as well as their common interest in the development of co-operation throughout Europe and among themselves and expressing their intention to pursue efforts accordingly;

Recognizing the close link between peace and security in Europe and in the world as a whole and conscious of the need for each of them to make its contribution to the strengthening of world peace and security and to the promotion of fundamental rights, economic and social progress and well-being for all peoples;
Have adopted the following:

(a) Declaration on Principles Guiding Relations between Participating States

The participating States,
Reaffirming their commitment to peace, security and justice and the continuing development of friendly relations and co-operation;
Recognizing that this commitment, which reflects the interest and aspirations of peoples, constitutes for each participating State a present and future responsibility, heightened by experience of the past;
Reaffirming, in conformity with their membership in the United Nations and in accordance with the purposes and principles of the United Nations, their full and active support for the United Nations and for the enhancement of its role and effectiveness in strengthening international peace, security and justice, and in promoting the solution of international problems, as well as the development of friendly relations and co-operation among States;
Expressing their common adherence to the principles which are set forth below and are in conformity with the Charter of the United Nations, as well as their common will to act, in the application of these principles, in conformity with the purposes and principles of the Charter of the United Nations;
Declare their determination to respect and put into practice, each of them in its relations with all other participating States, irrespective of their political, economic or social systems as well as of their size, geographical location or level of economic development, the following principles, which all are of primary significance, guiding their mutual relations:

I. Sovereign equality, respect for the rights inherent in sovereignty

The participating States will respect each other's sovereign equality and individuality as well as all the rights inherent in and encompassed by its sovereignty, including in particular the right of every State to juridical equality, to territorial integrity and to freedom and political independence. They will also respect each other's right freely to choose and develop its political, social, economic and cultural systems as well as its right to determine its laws and regulations.
Within the framework of international law, all the participating States have equal rights and duties. They will respect each other's right to define and conduct as it wishes its relations with other States in accordance with international law and in the spirit of the present Declaration. They consider that their frontiers can be changed, in accordance with international law, by peaceful means and by agreement. They also have the right to belong or not to belong to international organizations, to be or not to be a party to bilateral or multilateral treaties including the right to be or not to be a party to treaties of alliance; they also have the right to neutrality.

II. Refraining from the threat or use of force

The participating States will refrain in their mutual relations, as well as in their international relations in general, from the threat or use of force against the territorial integrity or political independence of any State, or in any other manner inconsistent with the purposes of the United Nations and with the

present Declaration. No consideration may be invoked to serve to warrant resort to the threat or use of force in contravention of this principle.
Accordingly, the participating States will refrain from any acts constituting a threat of force or direct or indirect use of force against another participating State. Likewise they will refrain from any manifestation of force for the purpose of inducing another participating State to renounce the full exercise of its sovereign rights. Likewise they will also refrain in their mutual relations from any act of reprisal by force.
No such threat or use of force will be employed as a means of settling disputes, or questions likely to give rise to disputes, between them.

III. Inviolability of frontiers

The participating States regard as inviolable all one another's frontiers as well as the frontiers of all States in Europe and therefore they will refrain now and in the future from assaulting these frontiers.
Accordingly, they will also refrain from any demand for, or act of, seizure and usurpation of part or all of the territory of any participating State.

IV. Territorial integrity of States

The participating States will respect the territorial integrity of each of the participating States.
Accordingly, they will refrain from any action inconsistent with the purposes and principles of the Charter of the United Nations against the territorial integrity, political independence or the unity of any participating State, and in particular from any such action constituting a threat or use of force.
The participating States will likewise refrain from making each other's territory the object of military occupation or other direct or indirect measures of force in contravention of international law, or the object of acquisition by means of such measures or the threat of them. No such occupation or acquisition will be recognized as legal.

V. Peaceful settlement of disputes

The participating States will settle disputes among them by peaceful means in such a manner as not to endanger international peace and security, and justice.
They will endeavour in good faith and a spirit of co-operation to reach a rapid and equitable solution on the basis of international law.
For this purpose they will use such means as negotiation, enquiry, mediation, conciliation, arbitration, judicial settlement or other peaceful means of their own choice including any settlement procedure agreed to in advance of disputes to which they are parties.
In the event of failure to reach a solution by any of the above peaceful means, the parties to a dispute will continue to seek a mutually agreed way to settle the dispute peacefully.
Participating States, parties to a dispute among them, as well as other participating States, will refrain from any action which might aggravate the situation to such a degree as to endanger the maintenance of international peace and security and thereby make a peaceful settlement of the dispute more difficult.

VI. Non-intervention in internal affairs

The participating States will refrain from any intervention, direct or indirect, individual or collective, in the internal or external affairs falling within the domestic jurisdiction of another participating State, regardless of their mutual relations.
They will accordingly refrain from any form of armed intervention or threat of such intervention against another participating State.
They will likewise in all circumstances refrain from any other act of military, or of political, economic or other coercion designed to subordinate to their own interest the exercise by another participating State of the rights inherent in its sovereignty and thus to secure advantages of any kind.
Accordingly, they will, inter alia, refrain from direct or indirect assistance to terrorist activities, or to subversive or other activities directed towards the violent overthrow of the regime of another participating State.

VII. Respect for human rights and fundamental freedoms, including the freedom of thought, conscience, religion or belief

The participating States will respect human rights and fundamental freedoms, including the freedom of thought, conscience, religion or belief, for all without distinction as to race, sex, language or religion.
They will promote and encourage the effective exercise of civil, political, economic, social, cultural and other rights and freedoms all of which derive from the inherent dignity of the human person and are essential for his free and full development.
Within this framework the participating States will recognize and respect the freedom of the individual to profess and practice, alone or in community with others, religion or belief acting in accordance with the dictates of his own conscience.
The participating States on whose territory national minorities exist will respect the right of persons belonging to such minorities to equality before the law, will afford them the full opportunity for the actual enjoyment of human rights and fundamental freedoms and will, in this manner, protect their legitimate interests in this sphere.
The participating States recognize the universal significance of human rights and fundamental freedoms, respect for which is an essential factor for the peace, justice and well-being necessary to ensure the development of friendly relations and co-operation among themselves as among all States.
They will constantly respect these rights and freedoms in their mutual relations and will endeavour jointly and separately, including in co-operation with the United Nations, to promote universal and effective respect for them.
They confirm the right of the individual to know and act upon his rights and duties in this field.
In the field of human rights and fundamental freedoms, the participating States will act in conformity with the purposes and principles of the Charter of the United Nations and with the Universal Declaration of Human Rights. They will also fulfil their obligations as set forth in the international declarations and agreements in this field, including inter alia the International Covenants on Human Rights, by which they may be bound.

VIII. Equal rights and self-determination of peoples

The participating States will respect the equal rights of peoples and their right to self-determination, acting at all times in conformity with the purposes and principles of the Charter of the United Nations and with the relevant norms of international law, including those relating to territorial integrity of States.

By virtue of the principle of equal rights and self-determination of peoples, all peoples always have the right, in full freedom, to determine, when and as they wish, their internal and external political status, without external interference, and to pursue as they wish their political, economic, social and cultural development.

The participating States reaffirm the universal significance of respect for and effective exercise of equal rights and self-determination of peoples for the development of friendly relations among themselves as among all States; they also recall the importance of the elimination of any form of violation of this principle.

IX. Co-operation among States

The participating States will develop their co-operation with one another and with all States in all fields in accordance with the purposes and principles of the Charter of the United Nations. In developing their co-operation the participating States will place special emphasis on the fields as set forth within the framework of the Conference on Security and Co-operation in Europe, with each of them making its contribution in conditions of full equality.

They will endeavour, in developing their co-operation as equals, to promote mutual understanding and confidence, friendly and good-neighbourly relations among themselves, international peace, security and justice. They will equally endeavour, in developing their co-operation, to improve the well-being of peoples and contribute to the fulfilment of their aspirations through, inter alia, the benefits resulting from increased mutual knowledge and from progress and achievement in the economic, scientific, technological, social, cultural and humanitarian fields. They will take steps to promote conditions favourable to making these benefits available to all; they will take into account the interest of all in the narrowing of differences in the levels of economic development, and in particular the interest of developing countries throughout the world.

They confirm that governments, institutions, organizations and persons have a relevant and positive role to play in contributing toward the achievement of these aims of their co-operation.

They will strive, in increasing their co-operation as set forth above, to develop closer relations among themselves on an improved and more enduring basis for the benefit of peoples.

X. Fulfilment in good faith of obligations under international law

The participating States will fulfil in good faith their obligations under international law, both those obligations arising from the generally recognized principles and rules of international law and those obligations arising from treaties or other agreements, in conformity with international law, to which they are parties.

In exercising their sovereign rights, including the right to determine their laws and regulations, they will conform with their legal obligations under international law; they will furthermore pay due regard to and implement the provisions in the Final Act of the Conference on Security and Co-operation in Europe.

The participating States confirm that in the event of a conflict between the obligations of the members of the United Nations under the Charter of the United Nations and their obligations under any treaty or other international agreement, their obligations under the Charter will prevail, in accordance with Article 103 of the Charter of the United Nations.

All the principles set forth above are of primary significance and, accordingly, they will be equally and unreservedly applied, each of them being interpreted taking into account the others.
The participating States express their determination fully to respect and apply these principles, as set forth in the present Declaration, in all aspects, to their mutual relations and co-operation in order to ensure to each participating State the benefits resulting from the respect and application of these principles by all.
The participating States, paying due regard to the principles above and, in particular, to the first sentence of the tenth principle, "Fulfilment in good faith of obligations under international law", note that the present Declaration does not affect their rights and obligations, nor the corresponding treaties and other agreements and arrangements.
The participating States express the conviction that respect for these principles will encourage the development of normal and friendly relations and the progress of co-operation among them in all fields.
They also express the conviction that respect for these principles will encourage the development of political contacts among them which in time would contribute to better mutual understanding of their positions and views.
The participating States declare their intention to conduct their relations with all other States in the spirit of the principles contained in the present Declaration.
[...]

Co-operation in the Field of Economics, of Science and Technology and of the Environment

[...]

Questions relating to Security and Co-operation in the Mediterranean

[...]

Co-operation in Humanitarian and Other Fields

[...]

Follow-up to the Conference

The participating States,
Having considered and evaluated the progress made at the Conference on Security and Co-operation in Europe,
Considering further that, within the broader context of the world, the Conference is an important part of the process of improving security and developing co-operation in Europe and that its results will contribute significantly to this process,
Intending to implement the provisions of the Final Act of the Conference in order to give full effect to its results and thus to further the process of improving security and developing co-operation in Europe,
Convinced that, in order to achieve the aims sought by the Conference, they should make further unilateral, bilateral and multilateral efforts and continue, in the appropriate forms set forth below, the multilateral process initiated by the Conference,
1. Declare their resolve, in the period following the Conference, to pay due regard to and implement the provisions of the Final Act of the Conference:

(a) unilaterally, in all cases which lend themselves to such action;
(b) bilaterally, by negotiations with other participating States;
(c) multilaterally, by meetings of experts of the participating States, and also within the framework of existing international organizations, such as the United Nations Economic Commission for Europe and UNESCO, with regard to educational, scientific and cultural co-operation;
2. Declare furthermore their resolve to continue the multilateral process initiated by the Conference:
(a) by proceeding to a thorough exchange of views both on the implementation of the provisions of the Final Act and of the tasks defined by the Conference, as well as, in the context of the questions dealt with by the latter, on the deepening of their mutual relations, the improvement of security and the development of co-operation in Europe, and the development of the process of détente in the future;
(b) by organizing to these ends meetings among their representatives, beginning with a meeting at the level of representatives appointed by the Ministers of Foreign Affairs. This meeting will define the appropriate modalities for the holding of other meetings which could include further similar meetings and the possibility of a new Conference;
3. The first of the meetings indicated above will be held at Belgrade in 1977. A preparatory meeting to organize this meeting will be held at Belgrade on 15 June 1977. The preparatory meeting will decide on the date, duration, agenda and other modalities of the meeting of representatives appointed by the Ministers of Foreign Affairs;
4. The rules of procedure, the working methods and the scale of distribution for the expenses of the Conference will, mutatis mutandis, be applied to the meetings envisaged in paragraphs 1 (c), 2 and 3 above. All the above-mentioned meetings will be held in the participating States in rotation. The services of a technical secretariat will be provided by the host country.

The original of this Final Act, drawn up in English, French, German, Italian, Russian and Spanish, will be transmitted to the Government of the Republic of Finland, which will retain it in its archives. Each of the participating States will receive from the Government of the Republic of Finland a true copy of this Final Act.
The text of this Final Act will be published in each participating State, which will disseminate it and make it known as widely as possible.
The Government of the Republic of Finland is requested to transmit to the Secretary-General of the United Nations the text of this Final Act, which is not eligible for registration under Article 102 of the Charter of the United Nations, with a view to its circulation to all the members of the Organization as an official document of the United Nations.
The Government of the Republic of Finland is also requested to transmit the text of this Final Act to the Director-General of UNESCO and to the Executive Secretary of the United Nations Economic Commission for Europe.
Wherefore, the undersigned High Representatives of the participating States, mindful of the high political significance which they attach to the results of the Conference, and declaring their determination to act in accordance with the provisions contained in the above texts, have subscribed their signatures below:
at Helsinki, on 1st August 1975.

OSCE structure

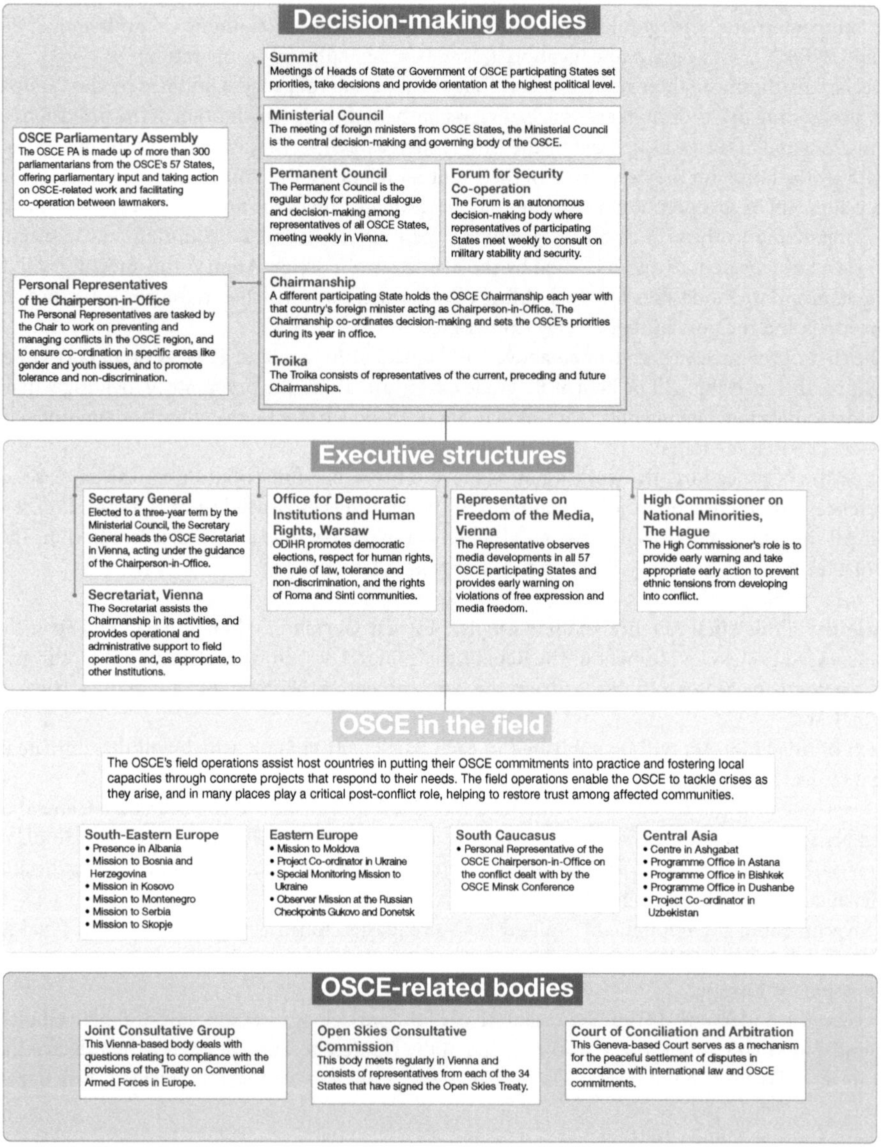

Figure 3
Source: Excerpt from What is the OSCE?
Factsheet can be accessed at https://www.osce.org/whatistheosce/factsheet?download=true

IV. World Trade Organization (WTO)

Agreement Establishing The World Trade Organization, 1994

[*Note:* The World Trade Organization was created by the Uruguay Round Negotiations held from 1986-1994. The Agreement Establishing the World Trade Organization was signed in Marrakesh, on April 15, 1994. It updated the General Agreement on Tariffs and Trade (GATT) of 1948 and incorporated in the WTO Agreement, the Organization officially commenced on January 1, 1995 under the Marrakesh Agreement. Currently it is the only international organization dealing with the global rules of trade between nations.

Status since February 2018: 164 Members.]

The *Parties* to this Agreement,

Recognizing that their relations in the field of trade and economic endeavour should be conducted with a view to raising standards of living, ensuring full employment and a large and steadily growing volume of real income and effective demand, and expanding the production of and trade in goods and services, while allowing for the optimal use of the world's resources in accordance with the objective of sustainable development, seeking both to protect and preserve the environment and to enhance the means for doing so in a manner consistent with their respective needs and concerns at different levels of economic development,
Recognizing further that there is need for positive efforts designed to ensure that developing countries, and especially the least developed among them, secure a share in the growth in international trade commensurate with the needs of their economic development,
Being desirous of contributing to these objectives by entering into reciprocal and mutually advantageous arrangements directed to the substantial reduction of tariffs and other barriers to trade and to the elimination of discriminatory treatment in international trade relations,
Resolved, therefore, to develop an integrated, more viable and durable multilateral trading system encompassing the General Agreement on Tariffs and Trade, the results of past trade liberalization efforts, and all of the results of the Uruguay Round of Multilateral Trade Negotiations,
Determined to preserve the basic principles and to further the objectives underlying this multilateral trading system,
Agree as follows:

Article I – Establishment of the Organization
The World Trade Organization (hereinafter referred to as "the WTO") is hereby established.

Article II – Scope of the WTO
1. The WTO shall provide the common institutional framework for the conduct of trade relations among its Members in matters related to the agreements and associated legal instruments included in the Annexes to this Agreement.

2. The agreements and associated legal instruments included in Annexes 1, 2 and 3 (hereinafter referred to as "Multilateral Trade Agreements") are integral parts of this Agreement, binding on all Members.
3. The agreements and associated legal instruments included in Annex 4 (hereinafter referred to as "Plurilateral Trade Agreements") are also part of this Agreement for those Members that have Page 10 accepted them, and are binding on those Members. The Plurilateral Trade Agreements do not create either obligations or rights for Members that have not accepted them.
4. The General Agreement on Tariffs and Trade 1994 as specified in Annex 1A (hereinafter referred to as "GATT 1994") is legally distinct from the General Agreement on Tariffs and Trade, dated 30 October 1947, annexed to the Final Act Adopted at the Conclusion of the Second Session of the Preparatory Committee of the United Nations Conference on Trade and Employment, as subsequently rectified, amended or modified (hereinafter referred to as "GATT 1947").

Article III – Functions of the WTO

1. The WTO shall facilitate the implementation, administration and operation, and further the objectives, of this Agreement and of the Multilateral Trade Agreements, and shall also provide the framework for the implementation, administration and operation of the Plurilateral Trade Agreements.
2. The WTO shall provide the forum for negotiations among its Members concerning their multilateral trade relations in matters dealt with under the agreements in the Annexes to this Agreement. The WTO may also provide a forum for further negotiations among its Members concerning their multilateral trade relations, and a framework for the implementation of the results of such negotiations, as may be decided by the Ministerial Conference.
3. The WTO shall administer the Understanding on Rules and Procedures Governing the Settlement of Disputes (hereinafter referred to as the "Dispute Settlement Understanding" or "DSU") in Annex 2 to this Agreement.
4. The WTO shall administer the Trade Policy Review Mechanism (hereinafter referred to as the "TPRM") provided for in Annex 3 to this Agreement.
5. With a view to achieving greater coherence in global economic policy-making, the WTO shall cooperate, as appropriate, with the International Monetary Fund and with the International Bank for Reconstruction and Development and its affiliated agencies.

Article IV – Structure of the WTO

1. There shall be a Ministerial Conference composed of representatives of all the Members, which shall meet at least once every two years. The Ministerial Conference shall carry out the functions of the WTO and take actions necessary to this effect. The Ministerial Conference shall have the authority to take decisions on all matters under any of the Multilateral Trade Agreements, if so requested by a Member, in accordance with the specific requirements for decision-making in this Agreement and in the relevant Multilateral Trade Agreement.
2. There shall be a General Council composed of representatives of all the Members, which shall meet as appropriate. In the intervals between meetings of the Ministerial Conference, its functions shall be conducted by the General Council. The General Council shall also carry out the functions assigned to it by this Agreement. The General Council shall establish its rules of procedure and approve the rules of procedure for the Committees provided for in paragraph 7.
3. The General Council shall convene as appropriate to discharge the responsibilities of the Dispute Settlement Body provided for in the Dispute Settlement Understanding. The Dispute Settlement Body may have its own chairman and shall establish such rules of procedure as it deems necessary for the fulfilment of those responsibilities.

4. The General Council shall convene as appropriate to discharge the responsibilities of the Trade Policy Review Body provided for in the TPRM. The Trade Policy Review Body may have its own chairman and shall establish such rules of procedure as it deems necessary for the fulfilment of those responsibilities.
5. There shall be a Council for Trade in Goods, a Council for Trade in Services and a Council for Trade-Related Aspects of Intellectual Property Rights (hereinafter referred to as the "Council for TRIPS"), which shall operate under the general guidance of the General Council. The Council for Trade in Goods shall oversee the functioning of the Multilateral Trade Agreements in Annex 1A. The Council for Trade in Services shall oversee the functioning of the General Agreement on Trade in Services (hereinafter referred to as "GATS"). The Council for TRIPS shall oversee the functioning of the Agreement on Trade-Related Aspects of Intellectual Property Rights (hereinafter referred to as the "Agreement on TRIPS"). These Councils shall carry out the functions assigned to them by their respective agreements and by the General Council. They shall establish their respective rules of procedure subject to the approval of the General Council. Membership in these Councils shall be open to representatives of all Members. These Councils shall meet as necessary to carry out their functions.
6. The Council for Trade in Goods, the Council for Trade in Services and the Council for TRIPS shall establish subsidiary bodies as required. These subsidiary bodies shall establish their respective rules of procedure subject to the approval of their respective Councils.
7. The Ministerial Conference shall establish a Committee on Trade and Development, a Committee on Balance-of-Payments Restrictions and a Committee on Budget, Finance and Administration, which shall carry out the functions assigned to them by this Agreement and by the Multilateral Trade Agreements, and any additional functions assigned to them by the General Council, and may establish such additional Committees with such functions as it may deem appropriate. As part of its functions, the Committee on Trade and Development shall periodically review the special provisions in the Multilateral Trade Agreements in favour of the least-developed country Members and report to the General Council for appropriate action. Membership in these Committees shall be open to representatives of all Members.
8. The bodies provided for under the Plurilateral Trade Agreements shall carry out the functions assigned to them under those Agreements and shall operate within the institutional framework of the WTO. These bodies shall keep the General Council informed of their activities on a regular basis.

Article V – Relations with Other Organizations

1. The General Council shall make appropriate arrangements for effective cooperation with other intergovernmental organizations that have responsibilities related to those of the WTO.
2. The General Council may make appropriate arrangements for consultation and cooperation with non-governmental organizations concerned with matters related to those of the WTO.

Article VI – The Secretariat

1. There shall be a Secretariat of the WTO (hereinafter referred to as "the Secretariat") headed by a Director-General.
2. The Ministerial Conference shall appoint the Director-General and adopt regulations setting out the powers, duties, conditions of service and term of office of the Director-General.
3. The Director-General shall appoint the members of the staff of the Secretariat and determine their duties and conditions of service in accordance with regulations adopted by the Ministerial Conference.
4. The responsibilities of the Director-General and of the staff of the Secretariat shall be exclusively international in character. In the discharge of their duties, the Director-General and the staff of the

Secretariat shall not seek or accept instructions from any government or any other authority external to the WTO. They shall refrain from any action which might adversely reflect on their position as international officials. The Members of the WTO shall respect the international character of the responsibilities of the Director-General and of the staff of the Secretariat and shall not seek to influence them in the discharge of their duties.

Article VII – Budget and Contributions

1. The Director-General shall present to the Committee on Budget, Finance and Administration the annual budget estimate and financial statement of the WTO. The Committee on Budget, Finance and Administration shall review the annual budget estimate and the financial statement presented by the Director-General and make recommendations thereon to the General Council. The annual budge estimate shall be subject to approval by the General Council.
2. The Committee on Budget, Finance and Administration shall propose to the General Council financial regulations which shall include provisions setting out:
(a) the scale of contributions apportioning the expenses of the WTO among its Members; and
(b) the measures to be taken in respect of Members in arrears.
The financial regulations shall be based, as far as practicable, on the regulations and practices of GATT 1947.
3. The General Council shall adopt the financial regulations and the annual budget estimate by a two-thirds majority comprising more than half of the Members of the WTO.
4. Each Member shall promptly contribute to the WTO its share in the expenses of the WTO in accordance with the financial regulations adopted by the General Council.

Article VIII – Status of the WTO

1. The WTO shall have legal personality, and shall be accorded by each of its Members such legal capacity as may be necessary for the exercise of its functions.
2. The WTO shall be accorded by each of its Members such privileges and immunities as are necessary for the exercise of its functions.
3. The officials of the WTO and the representatives of the Members shall similarly be accorded by each of its Members such privileges and immunities as are necessary for the independent exercise of their functions in connection with the WTO.
4. The privileges and immunities to be accorded by a Member to the WTO, its officials, and the representatives of its Members shall be similar to the privileges and immunities stipulated in the Convention on the Privileges and Immunities of the Specialized Agencies, approved by the General Assembly of the United Nations on 21 November 1947.
5. The WTO may conclude a headquarters agreement.

Article IX – Decision-Making

1. The WTO shall continue the practice of decision-making by consensus followed under GATT 1947.[1] Except as otherwise provided, where a decision cannot be arrived at by consensus, the matter at issue shall be decided by voting. At meetings of the Ministerial Conference and the General Council, each Member of the WTO shall have one vote. Where the European Communities exercise their right to

1 The body concerned shall be deemed to have decided by consensus on a matter submitted for its consideration, if no Member, present at the meeting when the decision is taken, formally objects to the proposed decision.

vote, they shall have a number of votes equal to the number of their member States[2] which are Members of the WTO. Decisions of the Ministerial Conference and the General Council shall be taken by a majority of the votes cast, unless otherwise provided in this Agreement or in the relevant Multilateral Trade Agreement.[3]

2. The Ministerial Conference and the General Council shall have the exclusive authority to adopt interpretations of this Agreement and of the Multilateral Trade Agreements. In the case of an interpretation of a Multilateral Trade Agreement in Annex 1, they shall exercise their authority on the basis of a recommendation by the Council overseeing the functioning of that Agreement. The decision to adopt an interpretation shall be taken by a three-fourths majority of the Members. This paragraph shall not be used in a manner that would undermine the amendment provisions in Article X.

3. In exceptional circumstances, the Ministerial Conference may decide to waive an obligation imposed on a Member by this Agreement or any of the Multilateral Trade Agreements, provided that any such decision shall be taken by three fourths[4] of the Members unless otherwise provided for in this paragraph.

(a) A request for a waiver concerning this Agreement shall be submitted to the Ministerial Conference for consideration pursuant to the practice of decision-making by consensus. The Ministerial Conference shall establish a time-period, which shall not exceed 90 days, to consider the request. If consensus is not reached during the time-period, any decision to grant a waiver shall be taken by three fourths4 of the Members.

(b) A request for a waiver concerning the Multilateral Trade Agreements in Annexes 1A or 1B or 1C and their annexes shall be submitted initially to the Council for Trade in Goods, the Council for Trade in Services or the Council for TRIPS, respectively, for consideration during a time-period which shall not exceed 90 days. At the end of the time-period, the relevant Council shall submit a report to the Ministerial Conference.

4. A decision by the Ministerial Conference granting a waiver shall state the exceptional circumstances justifying the decision, the terms and conditions governing the application of the waiver, and the date on which the waiver shall terminate. Any waiver granted for a period of more than one year shall be reviewed by the Ministerial Conference not later than one year after it is granted, and thereafter annually until the waiver terminates. In each review, the Ministerial Conference shall examine whether the exceptional circumstances justifying the waiver still exist and whether the terms and conditions attached to the waiver have been met. The Ministerial Conference, on the basis of the annual review, may extend, modify or terminate the waiver.

5. Decisions under a Plurilateral Trade Agreement, including any decisions on interpretations and waivers, shall be governed by the provisions of that Agreement.

Article X – Amendments

1. Any Member of the WTO may initiate a proposal to amend the provisions of this Agreement or the Multilateral Trade Agreements in Annex 1 by submitting such proposal to the Ministerial Confer-

---

2 The number of votes of the European Communities and their member States shall in no case exceed the number of the member States of the European Communities.

3 Decisions by the General Council when convened as the Dispute Settlement Body shall be taken only in accordance with the provisions of paragraph 4 of Article 2 of the Dispute Settlement Understanding.

4 A decision to grant a waiver in respect of any obligation subject to a transition period or a period for staged implementation that the requesting Member has not performed by the end of the relevant period shall be taken only by consensus.

ence. The Councils listed in paragraph 5 of Article IV may also submit to the Ministerial Conference proposals to amend the provisions of the corresponding Multilateral Trade Agreements in Annex 1 the functioning of which they oversee. Unless the Ministerial Conference decides on a longer period, for a period of 90 days after the proposal has been tabled formally at the Ministerial Conference any decision by the Ministerial Conference to submit the proposed amendment to the Members for acceptance shall be taken by consensus. Unless the provisions of paragraphs 2, 5 or 6 apply, that decision shall specify whether the provisions of paragraphs 3 or 4 shall apply. If consensus is reached, the Ministerial Conference shall forthwith submit the proposed amendment to the Members for acceptance. If consensus is not reached at a meeting of the Ministerial Conference within the established period, the Ministerial Conference shall decide by a two-thirds majority of the Members whether to submit the proposed amendment to the Members for acceptance. Except as provided in paragraphs 2, 5 and 6, the provisions of paragraph 3 shall apply to the proposed amendment, unless the Ministerial Conference decides by a three-fourths majority of the Members that the provisions of paragraph 4 shall apply.

2. Amendments to the provisions of this Article and to the provisions of the following Articles shall take effect only upon acceptance by all Members:
Article IX of this Agreement;
Articles I and II of GATT 1994;
Article II:1 of GATS;
Article 4 of the Agreement on TRIPS.

3. Amendments to provisions of this Agreement, or of the Multilateral Trade Agreements in Annexes 1A and 1C, other than those listed in paragraphs 2 and 6, of a nature that would alter the rights and obligations of the Members, shall take effect for the Members that have accepted them upon acceptance by two thirds of the Members and thereafter for each other Member upon acceptance by it. The Ministerial Conference may decide by a three-fourths majority of the Members that any amendment made effective under this paragraph is of such a nature that any Member which has not accepted it within a period specified by the Ministerial Conference in each case shall be free to withdraw from the WTO or to remain a Member with the consent of the Ministerial Conference.

4. Amendments to provisions of this Agreement or of the Multilateral Trade Agreements in Annexes 1A and 1C, other than those listed in paragraphs 2 and 6, of a nature that would not alter the rights and obligations of the Members, shall take effect for all Members upon acceptance by two thirds of the Members.

5. Except as provided in paragraph 2 above, amendments to Parts I, II and III of GATS and the respective annexes shall take effect for the Members that have accepted them upon acceptance by two thirds of the Members and thereafter for each Member upon acceptance by it. The Ministerial Conference may decide by a three-fourths majority of the Members that any amendment made effective under the preceding provision is of such a nature that any Member which has not accepted it within a period specified by the Ministerial Conference in each case shall be free to withdraw from the WTO or to remain a Member with the consent of the Ministerial Conference. Amendments to Parts IV, V and VI of GATS and the respective annexes shall take effect for all Members upon acceptance by two thirds of the Members.

6. Notwithstanding the other provisions of this Article, amendments to the Agreement on TRIPS meeting the requirements of paragraph 2 of Article 71 thereof may be adopted by the Ministerial Conference without further formal acceptance process.

7. Any Member accepting an amendment to this Agreement or to a Multilateral Trade Agreement in Annex 1 shall deposit an instrument of acceptance with the Director-General of the WTO within the period of acceptance specified by the Ministerial Conference.

8. Any Member of the WTO may initiate a proposal to amend the provisions of the Multilateral Trade Agreements in Annexes 2 and 3 by submitting such proposal to the Ministerial Conference. The decision to approve amendments to the Multilateral Trade Agreement in Annex 2 shall be made by consensus and these amendments shall take effect for all Members upon approval by the Ministerial Conference. Decisions to approve amendments to the Multilateral Trade Agreement in Annex 3 shall take effect for all Members upon approval by the Ministerial Conference.
9. The Ministerial Conference, upon the request of the Members parties to a trade agreement, may decide exclusively by consensus to add that agreement to Annex 4. The Ministerial Conference, upon the request of the Members parties to a Plurilateral Trade Agreement, may decide to delete that Agreement from Annex 4.
10. Amendments to a Plurilateral Trade Agreement shall be governed by the provisions of that Agreement.

Article XI – Original Membership

1. The contracting parties to GATT 1947 as of the date of entry into force of this Agreement, and the European Communities, which accept this Agreement and the Multilateral Trade Agreements and for which Schedules of Concessions and Commitments are annexed to GATT 1994 and for which Schedules of Specific Commitments are annexed to GATS shall become original Members of the WTO.
2. The least-developed countries recognized as such by the United Nations will only be required to undertake commitments and concessions to the extent consistent with their individual development, financial and trade needs or their administrative and institutional capabilities.

Article XII – Accession

1. Any State or separate customs territory possessing full autonomy in the conduct of its external commercial relations and of the other matters provided for in this Agreement and the Multilateral Trade Agreements may accede to this Agreement, on terms to be agreed between it and the WTO. Such accession shall apply to this Agreement and the Multilateral Trade Agreements annexed thereto.
2. Decisions on accession shall be taken by the Ministerial Conference. The Ministerial Conference shall approve the agreement on the terms of accession by a two-thirds majority of the Members of the WTO.
3. Accession to a Plurilateral Trade Agreement shall be governed by the provisions of that Agreement.

Article XIII – Non-Application of Multilateral Trade Agreements between Particular Members

1. This Agreement and the Multilateral Trade Agreements in Annexes 1 and 2 shall not apply as between any Member and any other Member if either of the Members, at the time either becomes a Member, does not consent to such application.
2. Paragraph 1 may be invoked between original Members of the WTO which were contracting parties to GATT 1947 only where Article XXXV of that Agreement had been invoked earlier and was effective as between those contracting parties at the time of entry into force for them of this Agreement.
3. Paragraph 1 shall apply between a Member and another Member which has acceded under Article XII only if the Member not consenting to the application has so notified the Ministerial Conference before the approval of the agreement on the terms of accession by the Ministerial Conference.
4. The Ministerial Conference may review the operation of this Article in particular cases at the request of any Member and make appropriate recommendations.
5. Non-application of a Plurilateral Trade Agreement between parties to that Agreement shall be governed by the provisions of that Agreement.

Article XIV – Acceptance, Entry into Force and Deposit

1. This Agreement shall be open for acceptance, by signature or otherwise, by contracting parties to GATT 1947, and the European Communities, which are eligible to become original Members of the WTO in accordance with Article XI of this Agreement. Such acceptance shall apply to this Agreement and the Multilateral Trade Agreements annexed hereto. This Agreement and the Multilateral Trade Agreements annexed hereto shall enter into force on the date determined by Ministers in accordance with paragraph 3 of the Final Act Embodying the Results of the Uruguay Round of Multilateral Trade Negotiations and shall remain open for acceptance for a period of two years following that date unless the Ministers decide otherwise. An acceptance following the entry into force of this Agreement shall enter into force on the 30th day following the date of such acceptance.
2. A Member which accepts this Agreement after its entry into force shall implement those concessions and obligations in the Multilateral Trade Agreements that are to be implemented over a period of time starting with the entry into force of this Agreement as if it had accepted this Agreement on the date of its entry into force.
3. Until the entry into force of this Agreement, the text of this Agreement and the Multilateral Trade Agreements shall be deposited with the Director-General to the CONTRACTING PARTIES to GATT 1947. The Director-General shall promptly furnish a certified true copy of this Agreement and the Multilateral Trade Agreements, and a notification of each acceptance thereof, to each government and the European Communities having accepted this Agreement. This Agreement and the Multilateral Trade Agreements, and any amendments thereto, shall, upon the entry into force of this Agreement, be deposited with the Director-General of the WTO.
4. The acceptance and entry into force of a Plurilateral Trade Agreement shall be governed by the provisions of that Agreement. Such Agreements shall be deposited with the Director-General to the CONTRACTING PARTIES to GATT 1947. Upon the entry into force of this Agreement, such Agreements shall be deposited with the Director-General of the WTO.

Article XV – Withdrawal

1. Any Member may withdraw from this Agreement. Such withdrawal shall apply both to this Agreement and the Multilateral Trade Agreements and shall take effect upon the expiration of six months from the date on which written notice of withdrawal is received by the Director-General of the WTO.
2. Withdrawal from a Plurilateral Trade Agreement shall be governed by the provisions of that Agreement.

Article XVI – Miscellaneous Provisions

1. Except as otherwise provided under this Agreement or the Multilateral Trade Agreements, the WTO shall be guided by the decisions, procedures and customary practices followed by the CONTRACTING PARTIES to GATT 1947 and the bodies established in the framework of GATT 1947.
2. To the extent practicable, the Secretariat of GATT 1947 shall become the Secretariat of the WTO, and the Director-General to the CONTRACTING PARTIES to GATT 1947, until such time as the Ministerial Conference has appointed a Director-General in accordance with paragraph 2 of Article VI of this Agreement, shall serve as Director-General of the WTO.
3. In the event of a conflict between a provision of this Agreement and a provision of any of the Multilateral Trade Agreements, the provision of this Agreement shall prevail to the extent of the conflict.
4. Each Member shall ensure the conformity of its laws, regulations and administrative procedures with its obligations as provided in the annexed Agreements.
5. No reservations may be made in respect of any provision of this Agreement. Reservations in respect of any of the provisions of the Multilateral Trade Agreements may only be made to the extent provided

for in those Agreements. Reservations in respect of a provision of a Plurilateral Trade Agreement shall be governed by the provisions of that Agreement.

6. This Agreement shall be registered in accordance with the provisions of Article 102 of the Charter of the United Nations.

DONE at Marrakesh this fifteenth day of April one thousand nine hundred and ninety-four, in a single copy, in the English, French and Spanish languages, each text being authentic.

Explanatory Notes:

The terms "country" or "countries" as used in this Agreement and the Multilateral Trade Agreements are to be understood to include any separate customs territory Member of the WTO.

In the case of a separate customs territory Member of the WTO, where an expression in this Agreement and the Multilateral Trade Agreements is qualified by the term "national", such expression shall be read as pertaining to that customs territory, unless otherwise specified.

LIST OF ANNEXES

ANNEX 1

ANNEX 1A: Multilateral Agreements on Trade in Goods

General Agreement on Tariffs and Trade 1994

Agreement on Agriculture

Agreement on the Application of Sanitary and Phytosanitary Measures

Agreement on Textiles and Clothing

Agreement on Technical Barriers to Trade

Agreement on Trade-Related Investment Measures

Agreement on Implementation of Article VI of the General Agreement on Tariffs and Trade 1994

Agreement on Implementation of Article VII of the General Agreement on Tariffs and Trade 1994

Agreement on Preshipment Inspection

Agreement on Rules of Origin

Agreement on Import Licensing Procedures

Agreement on Subsidies and Countervailing Measures

Agreement on Safeguards

ANNEX 1B: General Agreement on Trade in Services and Annexes

ANNEX 1C: Agreement on Trade-Related Aspects of Intellectual Property Rights

ANNEX 2

Understanding on Rules and Procedures Governing the Settlement of Disputes

ANNEX 3

Trade Policy Review Mechanism

ANNEX 4

Plurilateral Trade Agreements

Agreement on Trade in Civil Aircraft

Agreement on Government Procurement

International Dairy Agreement

International Bovine Meat Agreement

Understanding on rules and procedures governing the settlement of disputes

Annex 2 of the WTO Agreement

Article 1

Coverage and Application

1. The rules and procedures of this Understanding shall apply to disputes brought pursuant to the consultation and dispute settlement provisions of the agreements listed in Appendix 1 to this Understanding (referred to in this Understanding as the "covered agreements"). The rules and procedures of this Understanding shall also apply to consultations and the settlement of disputes between Members concerning their rights and obligations under the provisions of the Agreement Establishing the World Trade Organization (referred to in this Understanding as the "WTO Agreement") and of this Understanding taken in isolation or in combination with any other covered agreement.
2. The rules and procedures of this Understanding shall apply subject to such special or additional rules and procedures on dispute settlement contained in the covered agreements as are identified in Appendix 2 to this Understanding. To the extent that there is a difference between the rules and procedures of this Understanding and the special or additional rules and procedures set forth in Appendix 2, the special or additional rules and procedures in Appendix 2 shall prevail. In disputes involving rules and procedures under more than one covered agreement, if there is a conflict between special or additional rules and procedures of such agreements under review, and where the parties to the dispute cannot agree on rules and procedures within 20 days of the establishment of the panel, the Chairman of the Dispute Settlement Body provided for in paragraph 1 of Article 2 (referred to in this Understanding as the "DSB"), in consultation with the parties to the dispute, shall determine the rules and procedures to be followed within 10 days after a request by either Member. The Chairman shall be guided by the principle that special or additional rules and procedures should be used where possible, and the rules and procedures set out in this Understanding should be used to the extent necessary to avoid conflict.

Article 2

Administration

1. The Dispute Settlement Body is hereby established to administer these rules and procedures and, except as otherwise provided in a covered agreement, the consultation and dispute settlement provisions of the covered agreements. Accordingly, the DSB shall have the authority to establish panels, adopt panel and Appellate Body reports, maintain surveillance of implementation of rulings and recommendations, and authorize suspension of concessions and other obligations under the covered agreements. With respect to disputes arising under a covered agreement which is a Plurilateral Trade Agreement, the term "Member" as used herein shall refer only to those Members that are parties to the relevant Plurilateral Trade Agreement. Where the DSB administers the dispute settlement provisions of a Plurilateral Trade Agreement, only those Members that are parties to that Agreement may participate in decisions or actions taken by the DSB with respect to that dispute.
2. The DSB shall inform the relevant WTO Councils and Committees of any developments in disputes related to provisions of the respective covered agreements.

3. The DSB shall meet as often as necessary to carry out its functions within the time-frames provided in this Understanding.
4. Where the rules and procedures of this Understanding provide for the DSB to take a decision, it shall do so by consensus[1].

Article 3

General Provisions
1. Members affirm their adherence to the principles for the management of disputes heretofore applied under Articles XXII and XXIII of GATT 1947, and the rules and procedures as further elaborated and modified herein.
2. The dispute settlement system of the WTO is a central element in providing security and predictability to the multilateral trading system. The Members recognize that it serves to preserve the rights and obligations of Members under the covered agreements, and to clarify the existing provisions of those agreements in accordance with customary rules of interpretation of public international law. Recommendations and rulings of the DSB cannot add to or diminish the rights and obligations provided in the covered agreements.
3. The prompt settlement of situations in which a Member considers that any benefits accruing to it directly or indirectly under the covered agreements are being impaired by measures taken by another Member is essential to the effective functioning of the WTO and the maintenance of a proper balance between the rights and obligations of Members.
4. Recommendations or rulings made by the DSB shall be aimed at achieving a satisfactory settlement of the matter in accordance with the rights and obligations under this Understanding and under the covered agreements.
5. All solutions to matters formally raised under the consultation and dispute settlement provisions of the covered agreements, including arbitration awards, shall be consistent with those agreements and shall not nullify or impair benefits accruing to any Member under those agreements, nor impede the attainment of any objective of those agreements.
6. Mutually agreed solutions to matters formally raised under the consultation and dispute settlement provisions of the covered agreements shall be notified to the DSB and the relevant Councils and Committees, where any Member may raise any point relating thereto.
7. Before bringing a case, a Member shall exercise its judgement as to whether action under these procedures would be fruitful. The aim of the dispute settlement mechanism is to secure a positive solution to a dispute. A solution mutually acceptable to the parties to a dispute and consistent with the covered agreements is clearly to be preferred. In the absence of a mutually agreed solution, the first objective of the dispute settlement mechanism is usually to secure the withdrawal of the measures concerned if these are found to be inconsistent with the provisions of any of the covered agreements. The provision of compensation should be resorted to only if the immediate withdrawal of the measure is impracticable and as a temporary measure pending the withdrawal of the measure which is inconsistent with a covered agreement. The last resort which this Understanding provides to the Member invoking the dispute settlement procedures is the possibility of suspending the application of concessions or other

---

1 The DSB shall be deemed to have decided by consensus on a matter submitted for its consideration, if no Member, present at the meeting of the DSB when the decision is taken, formally objects to the proposed decision.

obligations under the covered agreements on a discriminatory basis vis-à-vis the other Member, subject to authorization by the DSB of such measures.
8. In cases where there is an infringement of the obligations assumed under a covered agreement, the action is considered *prima facie* to constitute a case of nullification or impairment. This means that there is normally a presumption that a breach of the rules has an adverse impact on other Members parties to that covered agreement, and in such cases, it shall be up to the Member against whom the complaint has been brought to rebut the charge.
9. The provisions of this Understanding are without prejudice to the rights of Members to seek authoritative interpretation of provisions of a covered agreement through decision-making under the WTO Agreement or a covered agreement which is a Plurilateral Trade Agreement.
10. It is understood that requests for conciliation and the use of the dispute settlement procedures should not be intended or considered as contentious acts and that, if a dispute arises, all Members will engage in these procedures in good faith in an effort to resolve the dispute. It is also understood that complaints and counter-complaints in regard to distinct matters should not be linked.
11. This Understanding shall be applied only with respect to new requests for consultations under the consultation provisions of the covered agreements made on or after the date of entry into force of the WTO Agreement. With respect to disputes for which the request for consultations was made under GATT 1947 or under any other predecessor agreement to the covered agreements before the date of entry into force of the WTO Agreement, the relevant dispute settlement rules and procedures in effect immediately prior to the date of entry into force of the WTO Agreement shall continue to apply[2].
12. Notwithstanding paragraph 11, if a complaint based on any of the covered agreements is brought by a developing country Member against a developed country Member, the complaining party shall have the right to invoke, as an alternative to the provisions contained in Articles 4, 5, 6 and 12 of this Understanding, the corresponding provisions of the Decision of 5 April 1966 (BISD 14S/18), except that where the Panel considers that the time-frame provided for in paragraph 7 of that Decision is insufficient to provide its report and with the agreement of the complaining party, that time-frame may be extended. To the extent that there is a difference between the rules and procedures of Articles 4, 5, 6 and 12 and the corresponding rules and procedures of the Decision, the latter shall prevail.

Article 4

Consultations

1. Members affirm their resolve to strengthen and improve the effectiveness of the consultation procedures employed by Members.
2. Each Member undertakes to accord sympathetic consideration to and afford adequate opportunity for consultation regarding any representations made by another Member concerning measures affecting the operation of any covered agreement taken within the territory of the former[3].
3. If a request for consultations is made pursuant to a covered agreement, the Member to which the request is made shall, unless otherwise mutually agreed, reply to the request within 10 days after the date of its receipt and shall enter into consultations in good faith within a period of no more than 30

2 This paragraph shall also be applied to disputes on which panel reports have not been adopted or fully implemented.

3 Where the provisions of any other covered agreement concerning measures taken by regional or local governments or authorities within the territory of a Member contain provisions different from the provisions of this paragraph, the provisions of such other covered agreement shall prevail.

days after the date of receipt of the request, with a view to reaching a mutually satisfactory solution. If the Member does not respond within 10 days after the date of receipt of the request, or does not enter into consultations within a period of no more than 30 days, or a period otherwise mutually agreed, after the date of receipt of the request, then the Member that requested the holding of consultations may proceed directly to request the establishment of a panel.

4. All such requests for consultations shall be notified to the DSB and the relevant Councils and Committees by the Member which requests consultations. Any request for consultations shall be submitted in writing and shall give the reasons for the request, including identification of the measures at issue and an indication of the legal basis for the complaint.

5. In the course of consultations in accordance with the provisions of a covered agreement, before resorting to further action under this Understanding, Members should attempt to obtain satisfactory adjustment of the matter.

6. Consultations shall be confidential, and without prejudice to the rights of any Member in any further proceedings.

7. If the consultations fail to settle a dispute within 60 days after the date of receipt of the request for consultations, the complaining party may request the establishment of a panel. The complaining party may request a panel during the 60-day period if the consulting parties jointly consider that consultations have failed to settle the dispute.

8. In cases of urgency, including those which concern perishable goods, Members shall enter into consultations within a period of no more than 10 days after the date of receipt of the request. If the consultations have failed to settle the dispute within a period of 20 days after the date of receipt of the request, the complaining party may request the establishment of a panel.

9. In cases of urgency, including those which concern perishable goods, the parties to the dispute, panels and the Appellate Body shall make every effort to accelerate the proceedings to the greatest extent possible.

10. During consultations Members should give special attention to the particular problems and interests of developing country Members.

11. Whenever a Member other than the consulting Members considers that it has a substantial trade interest in consultations being held pursuant to paragraph 1 of Article XXII of GATT 1994, paragraph 1 of Article XXII of GATS, or the corresponding provisions in other covered agreements[4], such Member may notify the consulting Members and the DSB, within 10 days after the date of the circulation of the request for consultations under said Article, of its desire to be joined in the consultations. Such Member shall be joined in the consultations, provided that the Member to which the request for consultations was addressed agrees that the claim of substantial interest is well-founded. In that event they shall so inform the DSB. If the request to be joined in the consultations is not accepted, the applicant Member

4 The corresponding consultation provisions in the covered agreements are listed hereunder: Agreement on Agriculture, Article 19; Agreement on the Application of Sanitary and Phytosanitary Measures, paragraph 1 of Article 11; Agreement on Textiles and Clothing, paragraph 4 of Article 8; Agreement on Technical Barriers to Trade, paragraph 1 of Article 14; Agreement on Trade-Related Investment Measures, Article 8; Agreement on Implementation of Article VI of GATT 1994, paragraph 2 of Article 17; Agreement on Implementation of Article VII of GATT 1994, paragraph 2 of Article 19; Agreement on Preshipment Inspection, Article 7; Agreement on Rules of Origin, Article 7; Agreement on Import Licensing Procedures, Article 6; Agreement on Subsidies and Countervailing Measures, Article 30; Agreement on Safeguards, Article 14; Agreement on Trade-Related Aspects of Intellectual Property Rights, Article 64.1; and any corresponding consultation provisions in Plurilateral Trade Agreements as determined by the competent bodies of each Agreement and as notified to the DSB.

shall be free to request consultations under paragraph 1 of Article XXII or paragraph 1 of Article XXIII of GATT 1994, paragraph 1 of Article XXII or paragraph 1 of Article XXIII of GATS, or the corresponding provisions in other covered agreements.

Article 5

Good Offices, Conciliation and Mediation

1. Good offices, conciliation and mediation are procedures that are undertaken voluntarily if the parties to the dispute so agree.
2. Proceedings involving good offices, conciliation and mediation, and in particular positions taken by the parties to the dispute during these proceedings, shall be confidential, and without prejudice to the rights of either party in any further proceedings under these procedures.
3. Good offices, conciliation or mediation may be requested at any time by any party to a dispute. They may begin at any time and be terminated at any time. Once procedures for good offices, conciliation or mediation are terminated, a complaining party may then proceed with a request for the establishment of a panel.
4. When good offices, conciliation or mediation are entered into within 60 days after the date of receipt of a request for consultations, the complaining party must allow a period of 60 days after the date of receipt of the request for consultations before requesting the establishment of a panel. The complaining party may request the establishment of a panel during the 60-day period if the parties to the dispute jointly consider that the good offices, conciliation or mediation process has failed to settle the dispute.
5. If the parties to a dispute agree, procedures for good offices, conciliation or mediation may continue while the panel process proceeds.
6. The Director-General may, acting in an *ex officio* capacity, offer good offices, conciliation or mediation with the view to assisting Members to settle a dispute.

Article 6

Establishment of Panels

1. If the complaining party so requests, a panel shall be established at the latest at the DSB meeting following that at which the request first appears as an item on the DSB's agenda, unless at that meeting the DSB decides by consensus not to establish a panel[5].
2. The request for the establishment of a panel shall be made in writing. It shall indicate whether consultations were held, identify the specific measures at issue and provide a brief summary of the legal basis of the complaint sufficient to present the problem clearly. In case the applicant requests the establishment of a panel with other than standard terms of reference, the written request shall include the proposed text of special terms of reference.

Article 7

Terms of Reference of Panels

1. Panels shall have the following terms of reference unless the parties to the dispute agree otherwise within 20 days from the establishment of the panel:

---

5 If the complaining party so requests, a meeting of the DSB shall be convened for this purpose within 15 days of the request, provided that at least 10 days' advance notice of the meeting is given.

"To examine, in the light of the relevant provisions in (name of the covered agreement(s) cited by the parties to the dispute), the matter referred to the DSB by (name of party) in document ... and to make such findings as will assist the DSB in making the recommendations or in giving the rulings provided for in that/those agreement(s)."

2. Panels shall address the relevant provisions in any covered agreement or agreements cited by the parties to the dispute.

3. In establishing a panel, the DSB may authorize its Chairman to draw up the terms of reference of the panel in consultation with the parties to the dispute, subject to the provisions of paragraph 1. The terms of reference thus drawn up shall be circulated to all Members. If other than standard terms of reference are agreed upon, any Member may raise any point relating thereto in the DSB.

Article 8

Composition of Panels

1. Panels shall be composed of well-qualified governmental and/or non-governmental individuals, including persons who have served on or presented a case to a panel, served as a representative of a Member or of a contracting party to GATT 1947 or as a representative to the Council or Committee of any covered agreement or its predecessor agreement, or in the Secretariat, taught or published on international trade law or policy, or served as a senior trade policy official of a Member.

2. Panel members should be selected with a view to ensuring the independence of the members, a sufficiently diverse background and a wide spectrum of experience.

3. Citizens of Members whose governments[6] are parties to the dispute or third parties as defined in paragraph 2 of Article 10 shall not serve on a panel concerned with that dispute, unless the parties to the dispute agree otherwise.

4. To assist in the selection of panelists, the Secretariat shall maintain an indicative list of governmental and non-governmental individuals possessing the qualifications outlined in paragraph 1, from which panelists may be drawn as appropriate. That list shall include the roster of non-governmental panelists established on 30 November 1984 (BISD 31S/9), and other rosters and indicative lists established under any of the covered agreements, and shall retain the names of persons on those rosters and indicative lists at the time of entry into force of the WTO Agreement. Members may periodically suggest names of governmental and non-governmental individuals for inclusion on the indicative list, providing relevant information on their knowledge of international trade and of the sectors or subject matter of the covered agreements, and those names shall be added to the list upon approval by the DSB. For each of the individuals on the list, the list shall indicate specific areas of experience or expertise of the individuals in the sectors or subject matter of the covered agreements.

5. Panels shall be composed of three panelists unless the parties to the dispute agree, within 10 days from the establishment of the panel, to a panel composed of five panelists. Members shall be informed promptly of the composition of the panel.

6. The Secretariat shall propose nominations for the panel to the parties to the dispute. The parties to the dispute shall not oppose nominations except for compelling reasons.

7. If there is no agreement on the panelists within 20 days after the date of the establishment of a panel, at the request of either party, the Director-General, in consultation with the Chairman of the DSB and the Chairman of the relevant Council or Committee, shall determine the composition of the panel by

---

6 In the case where customs unions or common markets are parties to a dispute, this provision applies to citizens of all member countries of the customs unions or common markets.

appointing the panelists whom the Director-General considers most appropriate in accordance with any relevant special or additional rules or procedures of the covered agreement or covered agreements which are at issue in the dispute, after consulting with the parties to the dispute. The Chairman of the DSB shall inform the Members of the composition of the panel thus formed no later than 10 days after the date the Chairman receives such a request.
8. Members shall undertake, as a general rule, to permit their officials to serve as panelists.
9. Panelists shall serve in their individual capacities and not as government representatives, nor as representatives of any organization. Members shall therefore not give them instructions nor seek to influence them as individuals with regard to matters before a panel.
10. When a dispute is between a developing country Member and a developed country Member the panel shall, if the developing country Member so requests, include at least one panelist from a developing country Member.
11. Panelists' expenses, including travel and subsistence allowance, shall be met from the WTO budget in accordance with criteria to be adopted by the General Council, based on recommendations of the Committee on Budget, Finance and Administration.

Article 9

Procedures for Multiple Complainants
1. Where more than one Member requests the establishment of a panel related to the same matter, a single panel may be established to examine these complaints taking into account the rights of all Members concerned. A single panel should be established to examine such complaints whenever feasible.
2. The single panel shall organize its examination and present its findings to the DSB in such a manner that the rights which the parties to the dispute would have enjoyed had separate panels examined the complaints are in no way impaired. If one of the parties to the dispute so requests, the panel shall submit separate reports on the dispute concerned. The written submissions by each of the complainants shall be made available to the other complainants, and each complainant shall have the right to be present when any one of the other complainants presents its views to the panel.
3. If more than one panel is established to examine the complaints related to the same matter, to the greatest extent possible the same persons shall serve as panelists on each of the separate panels and the timetable for the panel process in such disputes shall be harmonized.

Article 10

Third Parties
1. The interests of the parties to a dispute and those of other Members under a covered agreement at issue in the dispute shall be fully taken into account during the panel process.
2. Any Member having a substantial interest in a matter before a panel and having notified its interest to the DSB (referred to in this Understanding as a "third party") shall have an opportunity to be heard by the panel and to make written submissions to the panel. These submissions shall also be given to the parties to the dispute and shall be reflected in the panel report.
3. Third parties shall receive the submissions of the parties to the dispute to the first meeting of the panel.
4. If a third party considers that a measure already the subject of a panel proceeding nullifies or impairs benefits accruing to it under any covered agreement, that Member may have recourse to normal dispute settlement procedures under this Understanding. Such a dispute shall be referred to the original panel wherever possible.

Article 11

Function of Panels

The function of panels is to assist the DSB in discharging its responsibilities under this Understanding and the covered agreements. Accordingly, a panel should make an objective assessment of the matter before it, including an objective assessment of the facts of the case and the applicability of and conformity with the relevant covered agreements, and make such other findings as will assist the DSB in making the recommendations or in giving the rulings provided for in the covered agreements. Panels should consult regularly with the parties to the dispute and give them adequate opportunity to develop a mutually satisfactory solution.

Article 12

Panel Procedures

1. Panels shall follow the Working Procedures in Appendix 3 unless the panel decides otherwise after consulting the parties to the dispute.
2. Panel procedures should provide sufficient flexibility so as to ensure high-quality panel reports, while not unduly delaying the panel process.
3. After consulting the parties to the dispute, the panelists shall, as soon as practicable and whenever possible within one week after the composition and terms of reference of the panel have been agreed upon, fix the timetable for the panel process, taking into account the provisions of paragraph 9 of Article 4, if relevant.
4. In determining the timetable for the panel process, the panel shall provide sufficient time for the parties to the dispute to prepare their submissions.
5. Panels should set precise deadlines for written submissions by the parties and the parties should respect those deadlines.
6. Each party to the dispute shall deposit its written submissions with the Secretariat for immediate transmission to the panel and to the other party or parties to the dispute. The complaining party shall submit its first submission in advance of the responding party's first submission unless the panel decides, in fixing the timetable referred to in paragraph 3 and after consultations with the parties to the dispute, that the parties should submit their first submissions simultaneously. When there are sequential arrangements for the deposit of first submissions, the panel shall establish a firm time-period for receipt of the responding party's submission. Any subsequent written submissions shall be submitted simultaneously.
7. Where the parties to the dispute have failed to develop a mutually satisfactory solution, the panel shall submit its findings in the form of a written report to the DSB. In such cases, the report of a panel shall set out the findings of fact, the applicability of relevant provisions and the basic rationale behind any findings and recommendations that it makes. Where a settlement of the matter among the parties to the dispute has been found, the report of the panel shall be confined to a brief description of the case and to reporting that a solution has been reached.
8. In order to make the procedures more efficient, the period in which the panel shall conduct its examination, from the date that the composition and terms of reference of the panel have been agreed upon until the date the final report is issued to the parties to the dispute, shall, as a general rule, not exceed six months. In cases of urgency, including those relating to perishable goods, the panel shall aim to issue its report to the parties to the dispute within three months.
9. When the panel considers that it cannot issue its report within six months, or within three months in cases of urgency, it shall inform the DSB in writing of the reasons for the delay together with an

estimate of the period within which it will issue its report. In no case should the period from the establishment of the panel to the circulation of the report to the Members exceed nine months.
10. In the context of consultations involving a measure taken by a developing country Member, the parties may agree to extend the periods established in paragraphs 7 and 8 of Article 4. If, after the relevant period has elapsed, the consulting parties cannot agree that the consultations have concluded, the Chairman of the DSB shall decide, after consultation with the parties, whether to extend the relevant period and, if so, for how long. In addition, in examining a complaint against a developing country Member, the panel shall accord sufficient time for the developing country Member to prepare and present its argumentation. The provisions of paragraph 1 of Article 20 and paragraph 4 of Article 21 are not affected by any action pursuant to this paragraph.
11. Where one or more of the parties is a developing country Member, the panel's report shall explicitly indicate the form in which account has been taken of relevant provisions on differential and more favourable treatment for developing country Members that form part of the covered agreements which have been raised by the developing country Member in the course of the dispute settlement procedures.
12. The panel may suspend its work at any time at the request of the complaining party for a period not to exceed 12 months. In the event of such a suspension, the time-frames set out in paragraphs 8 and 9 of this Article, paragraph 1 of Article 20, and paragraph 4 of Article 21 shall be extended by the amount of time that the work was suspended. If the work of the panel has been suspended for more than 12 months, the authority for establishment of the panel shall lapse.

Article 13

Right to Seek Information
1. Each panel shall have the right to seek information and technical advice from any individual or body which it deems appropriate. However, before a panel seeks such information or advice from any individual or body within the jurisdiction of a Member it shall inform the authorities of that Member. A Member should respond promptly and fully to any request by a panel for such information as the panel considers necessary and appropriate. Confidential information which is provided shall not be revealed without formal authorization from the individual, body, or authorities of the Member providing the information.
2. Panels may seek information from any relevant source and may consult experts to obtain their opinion on certain aspects of the matter. With respect to a factual issue concerning a scientific or other technical matter raised by a party to a dispute, a panel may request an advisory report in writing from an expert review group. Rules for the establishment of such a group and its procedures are set forth in Appendix 4.

Article 14

Confidentiality
1. Panel deliberations shall be confidential.
2. The reports of panels shall be drafted without the presence of the parties to the dispute in the light of the information provided and the statements made.
3. Opinions expressed in the panel report by individual panelists shall be anonymous.

Article 15

Interim Review Stage

1. Following the consideration of rebuttal submissions and oral arguments, the panel shall issue the descriptive (factual and argument) sections of its draft report to the parties to the dispute. Within a period of time set by the panel, the parties shall submit their comments in writing.
2. Following the expiration of the set period of time for receipt of comments from the parties to the dispute, the panel shall issue an interim report to the parties, including both the descriptive sections and the panel's findings and conclusions. Within a period of time set by the panel, a party may submit a written request for the panel to review precise aspects of the interim report prior to circulation of the final report to the Members. At the request of a party, the panel shall hold a further meeting with the parties on the issues identified in the written comments. If no comments are received from any party within the comment period, the interim report shall be considered the final panel report and circulated promptly to the Members.
3. The findings of the final panel report shall include a discussion of the arguments made at the interim review stage. The interim review stage shall be conducted within the time-period set out in paragraph 8 of Article 12.

Article 16

Adoption of Panel Reports

1. In order to provide sufficient time for the Members to consider panel reports, the reports shall not be considered for adoption by the DSB until 20 days after the date they have been circulated to the Members.
2. Members having objections to a panel report shall give written reasons to explain their objections for circulation at least 10 days prior to the DSB meeting at which the panel report will be considered.
3. The parties to a dispute shall have the right to participate fully in the consideration of the panel report by the DSB, and their views shall be fully recorded.
4. Within 60 days after the date of circulation of a panel report to the Members, the report shall be adopted at a DSB meeting[77] unless a party to the dispute formally notifies the DSB of its decision to appeal or the DSB decides by consensus not to adopt the report. If a party has notified its decision to appeal, the report by the panel shall not be considered for adoption by the DSB until after completion of the appeal. This adoption procedure is without prejudice to the right of Members to express their views on a panel report.

Article 17

Appellate Review Standing Appellate Body

1. A standing Appellate Body shall be established by the DSB. The Appellate Body shall hear appeals from panel cases. It shall be composed of seven persons, three of whom shall serve on any one case. Persons serving on the Appellate Body shall serve in rotation. Such rotation shall be determined in the working procedures of the Appellate Body.

---

7 If a meeting of the DSB is not scheduled within this period at a time that enables the requirements of paragraphs 1 and 4 of Article 16 to be met, a meeting of the DSB shall be held for this purpose.

2. The DSB shall appoint persons to serve on the Appellate Body for a four-year term, and each person may be reappointed once. However, the terms of three of the seven persons appointed immediately after the entry into force of the WTO Agreement shall expire at the end of two years, to be determined by lot. Vacancies shall be filled as they arise. A person appointed to replace a person whose term of office has not expired shall hold office for the remainder of the predecessor's term.
3. The Appellate Body shall comprise persons of recognized authority, with demonstrated expertise in law, international trade and the subject matter of the covered agreements generally. They shall be unaffiliated with any government. The Appellate Body membership shall be broadly representative of membership in the WTO. All persons serving on the Appellate Body shall be available at all times and on short notice, and shall stay abreast of dispute settlement activities and other relevant activities of the WTO. They shall not participate in the consideration of any disputes that would create a direct or indirect conflict of interest.
4. Only parties to the dispute, not third parties, may appeal a panel report. Third parties which have notified the DSB of a substantial interest in the matter pursuant to paragraph 2 of Article 10 may make written submissions to, and be given an opportunity to be heard by, the Appellate Body.
5. As a general rule, the proceedings shall not exceed 60 days from the date a party to the dispute formally notifies its decision to appeal to the date the Appellate Body circulates its report. In fixing its timetable the Appellate Body shall take into account the provisions of paragraph 9 of Article 4, if relevant. When the Appellate Body considers that it cannot provide its report within 60 days, it shall inform the DSB in writing of the reasons for the delay together with an estimate of the period within which it will submit its report. In no case shall the proceedings exceed 90 days.
6. An appeal shall be limited to issues of law covered in the panel report and legal interpretations developed by the panel.
7. The Appellate Body shall be provided with appropriate administrative and legal support as it requires.
8. The expenses of persons serving on the Appellate Body, including travel and subsistence allowance, shall be met from the WTO budget in accordance with criteria to be adopted by the General Council, based on recommendations of the Committee on Budget, Finance and Administration.

Procedures for Appellate Review

9. Working procedures shall be drawn up by the Appellate Body in consultation with the Chairman of the DSB and the Director-General, and communicated to the Members for their information.
10. The proceedings of the Appellate Body shall be confidential. The reports of the Appellate Body hall be drafted without the presence of the parties to the dispute and in the light of the information provided and the statements made.
11. Opinions expressed in the Appellate Body report by individuals serving on the Appellate Body shall be anonymous.
12. The Appellate Body shall address each of the issues raised in accordance with paragraph 6 during the appellate proceeding.
13. The Appellate Body may uphold, modify or reverse the legal findings and conclusions of the panel.

Adoption of Appellate Body Reports

14. An Appellate Body report shall be adopted by the DSB and unconditionally accepted by the parties to the dispute unless the DSB decides by consensus not to adopt the Appellate Body report within

30 days following its circulation to the Members[8]. This adoption procedure is without prejudice to the right of Members to express their views on an Appellate Body report.

Article 18

Communications with the Panel or Appellate Body

1. There shall be no *ex parte* communications with the panel or Appellate Body concerning matters under consideration by the panel or Appellate Body.
2. Written submissions to the panel or the Appellate Body shall be treated as confidential, but shall be made available to the parties to the dispute. Nothing in this Understanding shall preclude a party to a dispute from disclosing statements of its own positions to the public. Members shall treat as confidential information submitted by another Member to the panel or the Appellate Body which that Member has designated as confidential. A party to a dispute shall also, upon request of a Member, provide a non-confidential summary of the information contained in its written submissions that could be disclosed to the public.

Article 19

Panel and Appellate Body Recommendations

1. Where a panel or the Appellate Body concludes that a measure is inconsistent with a covered agreement, it shall recommend that the Member concerned[9] bring the measure into conformity with that agreement[10]. In addition to its recommendations, the panel or Appellate Body may suggest ways in which the Member concerned could implement the recommendations.
2. In accordance with paragraph 2 of Article 3, in their findings and recommendations, the panel and Appellate Body cannot add to or diminish the rights and obligations provided in the covered agreements.

Article 20

Time-frame for DSB Decisions

Unless otherwise agreed to by the parties to the dispute, the period from the date of establishment of the panel by the DSB until the date the DSB considers the panel or appellate report for adoption shall as a general rule not exceed nine months where the panel report is not appealed or 12 months where the report is appealed. Where either the panel or the Appellate Body has acted, pursuant to paragraph 9 of Article 12 or paragraph 5 of Article 17, to extend the time for providing its report, the additional time taken shall be added to the above periods.

---

8 If a meeting of the DSB is not scheduled during this period, such a meeting of the DSB shall be held for this purpose.

9 The "Member concerned" is the party to the dispute to which the panel or Appellate Body recommendations are directed. "http://www.wto.org/english/tratop_e/dispu_e/dsu_e.htm".

10 With respect to recommendations in cases not involving a violation of GATT 1994 or any other covered agreement, see Article 26.

Article 21

Surveillance of Implementation of Recommendations and Rulings

1. Prompt compliance with recommendations or rulings of the DSB is essential in order to ensure effective resolution of disputes to the benefit of all Members.
2. Particular attention should be paid to matters affecting the interests of developing country Members with respect to measures which have been subject to dispute settlement.
3. At a DSB meeting held within 30 days[11] after the date of adoption of the panel or Appellate Body report, the Member concerned shall inform the DSB of its intentions in respect of implementation of the recommendations and rulings of the DSB. If it is impracticable to comply immediately with the recommendations and rulings, the Member concerned shall have a reasonable period of time in which to do so. The reasonable period of time shall be:
(a) the period of time proposed by the Member concerned, provided that such period is approved by the DSB; or, in the absence of such approval,
(b) a period of time mutually agreed by the parties to the dispute within 45 days after the date of adoption of the recommendations and rulings; or, in the absence of such agreement,
(c) a period of time determined through binding arbitration within 90 days after the date of adoption of the recommendations and rulings[12]. In such arbitration, a guideline for the arbitrator[13] should be that the reasonable period of time to implement panel or Appellate Body recommendations should not exceed 15 months from the date of adoption of a panel or Appellate Body report. However, that time may be shorter or longer, depending upon the particular circumstances.
4. Except where the panel or the Appellate Body has extended, pursuant to paragraph 9 of Article 12 or paragraph 5 of Article 17, the time of providing its report, the period from the date of establishment of the panel by the DSB until the date of determination of the reasonable period of time shall not exceed 15 months unless the parties to the dispute agree otherwise. Where either the panel or the Appellate Body has acted to extend the time of providing its report, the additional time taken shall be added to the 15-month period; provided that unless the parties to the dispute agree that there are exceptional circumstances, the total time shall not exceed 18 months.
5. Where there is disagreement as to the existence or consistency with a covered agreement of measures taken to comply with the recommendations and rulings such dispute shall be decided through recourse to these dispute settlement procedures, including wherever possible resort to the original panel. The panel shall circulate its report within 90 days after the date of referral of the matter to it. When the panel considers that it cannot provide its report within this time frame, it shall inform the DSB in writing of the reasons for the delay together with an estimate of the period within which it will submit its report.
6. The DSB shall keep under surveillance the implementation of adopted recommendations or rulings. The issue of implementation of the recommendations or rulings may be raised at the DSB by any Member at any time following their adoption. Unless the DSB decides otherwise, the issue of implementation of the recommendations or rulings shall be placed on the agenda of the DSB meeting after six months following the date of establishment of the reasonable period of time pursuant to paragraph 3

---

11 If a meeting of the DSB is not scheduled during this period, such a meeting of the DSB shall be held for this purpose.

12 If the parties cannot agree on an arbitrator within ten days after referring the matter to arbitration, the arbitrator shall be appointed by the Director-General within ten days, after consulting the parties.

13 The expression "arbitrator" shall be interpreted as referring either to an individual or a group.

and shall remain on the DSB's agenda until the issue is resolved. At least 10 days prior to each such DSB meeting, the Member concerned shall provide the DSB with a status report in writing of its progress in the implementation of the recommendations or rulings.

7. If the matter is one which has been raised by a developing country Member, the DSB shall consider what further action it might take which would be appropriate to the circumstances.

8. If the case is one brought by a developing country Member, in considering what appropriate action might be taken, the DSB shall take into account not only the trade coverage of measures complained of, but also their impact on the economy of developing country Members concerned.

Article 22

Compensation and the Suspension of Concessions

1. Compensation and the suspension of concessions or other obligations are temporary measures available in the event that the recommendations and rulings are not implemented within a reasonable period of time. However, neither compensation nor the suspension of concessions or other obligations is preferred to full implementation of a recommendation to bring a measure into conformity with the covered agreements. Compensation is voluntary and, if granted, shall be consistent with the covered agreements.

2. If the Member concerned fails to bring the measure found to be inconsistent with a covered agreement into compliance therewith or otherwise comply with the recommendations and rulings within the reasonable period of time determined pursuant to paragraph 3 of Article 21, such Member shall, if so requested, and no later than the expiry of the reasonable period of time, enter into negotiations with any party having invoked the dispute settlement procedures, with a view to developing mutually acceptable compensation. If no satisfactory compensation has been agreed within 20 days after the date of expiry of the reasonable period of time, any party having invoked the dispute settlement procedures may request authorization from the DSB to suspend the application to the Member concerned of concessions or other obligations under the covered agreements.

3. In considering what concessions or other obligations to suspend, the complaining party shall apply the following principles and procedures:

(a) the general principle is that the complaining party should first seek to suspend concessions or other obligations with respect to the same sector(s) as that in which the panel or Appellate Body has found a violation or other nullification or impairment;

(b) if that party considers that it is not practicable or effective to suspend concessions or other obligations with respect to the same sector(s), it may seek to suspend concessions or other obligations in other sectors under the same agreement;

(c) if that party considers that it is not practicable or effective to suspend concessions or other obligations with respect to other sectors under the same agreement, and that the circumstances are serious enough, it may seek to suspend concessions or other obligations under another covered agreement;

(d) in applying the above principles, that party shall take into account:

  (i) the trade in the sector or under the agreement under which the panel or Appellate Body has found a violation or other nullification or impairment, and the importance of such trade to that party;

  (ii) the broader economic elements related to the nullification or impairment and the broader economic consequences of the suspension of concessions or other obligations;

(e) if that party decides to request authorization to suspend concessions or other obligations pursuant to subparagraphs (b) or (c), it shall state the reasons therefor in its request. At the same time as the request is forwarded to the DSB, it also shall be forwarded to the relevant Councils and also, in the case of a request pursuant to subparagraph (b), the relevant sectoral bodies;

(f) for purposes of this paragraph, "sector" means:

 (i) with respect to goods, all goods;

 (ii) with respect to services, a principal sector as identified in the current "Services Sectoral Classification List" which identifies such sectors[14];

 (iii) with respect to trade-related intellectual property rights, each of the categories of intellectual property rights covered in Section 1, or Section 2, or Section 3, or Section 4, or Section 5, or Section 6, or Section 7 of Part II, or the obligations under Part III, or Part IV of the Agreement on TRIPS;

(g) for purposes of this paragraph, "agreement" means:

 (i) with respect to goods, the agreements listed in Annex 1A of the WTO Agreement, taken as a whole as well as the Plurilateral Trade Agreements in so far as the relevant parties to the dispute are parties to these agreements;

 (ii) with respect to services, the GATS;

 (iii) with respect to intellectual property rights, the Agreement on TRIPS.

4. The level of the suspension of concessions or other obligations authorized by the DSB shall be equivalent to the level of the nullification or impairment.

5. The DSB shall not authorize suspension of concessions or other obligations if a covered agreement prohibits such suspension.

6. When the situation described in paragraph 2 occurs, the DSB, upon request, shall grant authorization to suspend concessions or other obligations within 30 days of the expiry of the reasonable period of time unless the DSB decides by consensus to reject the request. However, if the Member concerned objects to the level of suspension proposed, or claims that the principles and procedures set forth in paragraph 3 have not been followed where a complaining party has requested authorization to suspend concessions or other obligations pursuant to paragraph 3(b) or (c), the matter shall be referred to arbitration. Such arbitration shall be carried out by the original panel, if members are available, or by an arbitrator[15] appointed by the Director-General and shall be completed within 60 days after the date of expiry of the reasonable period of time. Concessions or other obligations shall not be suspended during the course of the arbitration.

7. The arbitrator[16] acting pursuant to paragraph 6 shall not examine the nature of the concessions or other obligations to be suspended but shall determine whether the level of such suspension is equivalent to the level of nullification or impairment. The arbitrator may also determine if the proposed suspension 166 Documents on the Law of International Organizations of concessions or other obligations is allowed under the covered agreement. However, if the matter referred to arbitration includes a claim that the principles and procedures set forth in paragraph 3 have not been followed, the arbitrator shall examine that claim. In the event the arbitrator determines that those principles and procedures have not been followed, the complaining party shall apply them consistent with paragraph 3. The parties shall accept the arbitrator's decision as final and the parties concerned shall not seek a second arbi-

14 The list in document MTN.GNS/W/120 identifies eleven sectors.

15 The expression "arbitrator" shall be interpreted as referring either to an individual or a group.

16 The expression "arbitrator" shall be interpreted as referring either to an individual or a group or to the members of the original panel when serving in the capacity of arbitrator.

tration. The DSB shall be informed promptly of the decision of the arbitrator and shall upon request, grant authorization to suspend concessions or other obligations where the request is consistent with the decision of the arbitrator, unless the DSB decides by consensus to reject the request.
8. The suspension of concessions or other obligations shall be temporary and shall only be applied until such time as the measure found to be inconsistent with a covered agreement has been removed, or the Member that must implement recommendations or rulings provides a solution to the nullification or impairment of benefits, or a mutually satisfactory solution is reached. In accordance with paragraph 6 of Article 21, the DSB shall continue to keep under surveillance the implementation of adopted recommendations or rulings, including those cases where compensation has been provided or concessions or other obligations have been suspended but the recommendations to bring a measure into conformity with the covered agreements have not been implemented.
9. The dispute settlement provisions of the covered agreements may be invoked in respect of measures affecting their observance taken by regional or local governments or authorities within the territory of a Member. When the DSB has ruled that a provision of a covered agreement has not been observed, the responsible Member shall take such reasonable measures as may be available to it to ensure its observance. The provisions of the covered agreements and this Understanding relating to compensation and suspension of concessions or other obligations apply in cases where it has not been possible to secure such observance[17].

Article 23

Strengthening of the Multilateral System
1. When Members seek the redress of a violation of obligations or other nullification or impairment of benefits under the covered agreements or an impediment to the attainment of any objective of the covered agreements, they shall have recourse to, and abide by, the rules and procedures of this Understanding.
2. In such cases, Members shall:
(a) not make a determination to the effect that a violation has occurred, that benefits have been nullified or impaired or that the attainment of any objective of the covered agreements has been impeded, except through recourse to dispute settlement in accordance with the rules and procedures of this Understanding, and shall make any such determination consistent with the findings contained in the panel or Appellate Body report adopted by the DSB or an arbitration award rendered under this Understanding;
(b) follow the procedures set forth in Article 21 to determine the reasonable period of time for the Member concerned to implement the recommendations and rulings; and (c) follow the procedures set forth in Article 22 to determine the level of suspension of concessions or other obligations and obtain DSB authorization in accordance with those procedures before suspending concessions or other obligations under the covered agreements in response to the failure of the Member concerned to implement the recommendations and rulings within that reasonable period of time.

---

17 Where the provisions of any covered agreement concerning measures taken by regional or local governments or authorities within the territory of a Member contain provisions different from the provisions of this paragraph, the provisions of such covered agreement shall prevail.

Article 24

Special Procedures Involving Least-Developed Country Members

1. At all stages of the determination of the causes of a dispute and of dispute settlement procedures involving a least-developed country Member, particular consideration shall be given to the special situation of least-developed country Members. In this regard, Members shall exercise due restraint in raising matters under these procedures involving a least-developed country Member. If nullification or impairment is found to result from a measure taken by a least-developed country Member, complaining parties shall exercise due restraint in asking for compensation or seeking authorization to suspend the application of concessions or other obligations pursuant to these procedures.
2. In dispute settlement cases involving a least-developed country Member, where a satisfactory solution has not been found in the course of consultations the Director-General or the Chairman of the DSB shall, upon request by a least-developed country Member offer their good offices, conciliation and mediation with a view to assisting the parties to settle the dispute, before a request for a panel is made. The Director-General or the Chairman of the DSB, in providing the above assistance, may consult any source which either deems appropriate.

Article 25

Arbitration

1. Expeditious arbitration within the WTO as an alternative means of dispute settlement can facilitate the solution of certain disputes that concern issues that are clearly defined by both parties.
2. Except as otherwise provided in this Understanding, resort to arbitration shall be subject to mutual agreement of the parties which shall agree on the procedures to be followed. Agreements to resort to arbitration shall be notified to all Members sufficiently in advance of the actual commencement of the arbitration process.
3. Other Members may become party to an arbitration proceeding only upon the agreement of the parties which have agreed to have recourse to arbitration. The parties to the proceeding shall agree to abide by the arbitration award. Arbitration awards shall be notified to the DSB and the Council or Committee of any relevant agreement where any Member may raise any point relating thereto.
4. Articles 21 and 22 of this Understanding shall apply *mutatis mutandis* to arbitration awards.

Article 26

1. Non-Violation Complaints of the Type Described in Paragraph 1(b) of Article XXIII of GATT 1994

Where the provisions of paragraph 1(b) of Article XXIII of GATT 1994 are applicable to a covered agreement, a panel or the Appellate Body may only make rulings and recommendations where a party to the dispute considers that any benefit accruing to it directly or indirectly under the relevant covered agreement is being nullified or impaired or the attainment of any objective of that Agreement is being impeded as a result of the application by a Member of any measure, whether or not it conflicts with the provisions of that Agreement. Where and to the extent that such party considers and a panel or the Appellate Body determines that a case concerns a measure that does not conflict with the provisions of a covered agreement to which the provisions of paragraph 1(b) of Article XXIII of GATT 1994 are applicable, the procedures in this Understanding shall apply, subject to the following:

(a) the complaining party shall present a detailed justification in support of any complaint relating to a measure which does not conflict with the relevant covered agreement;
(b) where a measure has been found to nullify or impair benefits under, or impede the attainment of objectives, of the relevant covered agreement without violation thereof, there is no obligation to withdraw the measure. However, in such cases, the panel or the Appellate Body shall recommend that the Member concerned make a mutually satisfactory adjustment;
(c) notwithstanding the provisions of Article 21, the arbitration provided for in paragraph 3 of Article 21, upon request of either party, may include a determination of the level of benefits which have been nullified or impaired, and may also suggest ways and means of reaching a mutually satisfactory adjustment; such suggestions shall not be binding upon the parties to the dispute;
(d) notwithstanding the provisions of paragraph 1 of Article 22, compensation may be part of a mutually satisfactory adjustment as final settlement of the dispute.

2. Complaints of the Type Described in Paragraph 1(c) of Article XXIII of GATT 1994

Where the provisions of paragraph 1(c) of Article XXIII of GATT 1994 are applicable to a covered agreement, a panel may only make rulings and recommendations where a party considers that any benefit accruing to it directly or indirectly under the relevant covered agreement is being nullified or impaired or the attainment of any objective of that Agreement is being impeded as a result of the existence of any situation other than those to which the provisions of paragraphs 1(a) and 1(b) of Article XXIII of GATT 1994 are applicable. Where and to the extent that such party considers and a panel determines that the matter is covered by this paragraph, the procedures of this Understanding shall apply only up to and including the point in the proceedings where the panel report has been circulated to the Members. The dispute settlement rules and procedures contained in the Decision of 12 April 1989 (BISD 36S/61-67) shall apply to consideration for adoption, and surveillance and implementation of recommendations and rulings. The following shall also apply:
(a) the complaining party shall present a detailed justification in support of any argument made with respect to issues covered under this paragraph;
(b) in cases involving matters covered by this paragraph, if a panel finds that cases also involve dispute settlement matters other than those covered by this paragraph, the panel shall circulate a report to the DSB addressing any such matters and a separate report on matters falling under this paragraph.

Article 27

Responsibilities of the Secretariat
1. The Secretariat shall have the responsibility of assisting panels, especially on the legal, historical and procedural aspects of the matters dealt with, and of providing secretarial and technical support.
2. While the Secretariat assists Members in respect of dispute settlement at their request, there may also be a need to provide additional legal advice and assistance in respect of dispute settlement to developing country Members. To this end, the Secretariat shall make available a qualified legal expert from the WTO technical cooperation services to any developing country Member which so requests. This expert shall assist the developing country Member in a manner ensuring the continued impartiality of the Secretariat.
3. The Secretariat shall conduct special training courses for interested Members concerning these dispute settlement procedures and practices so as to enable Members' experts to be better informed in this regard.

WTO structure

All WTO members may participate in all councils, etc., except Appellate Body, Dispute Settlement panels, and plurilateral committees.

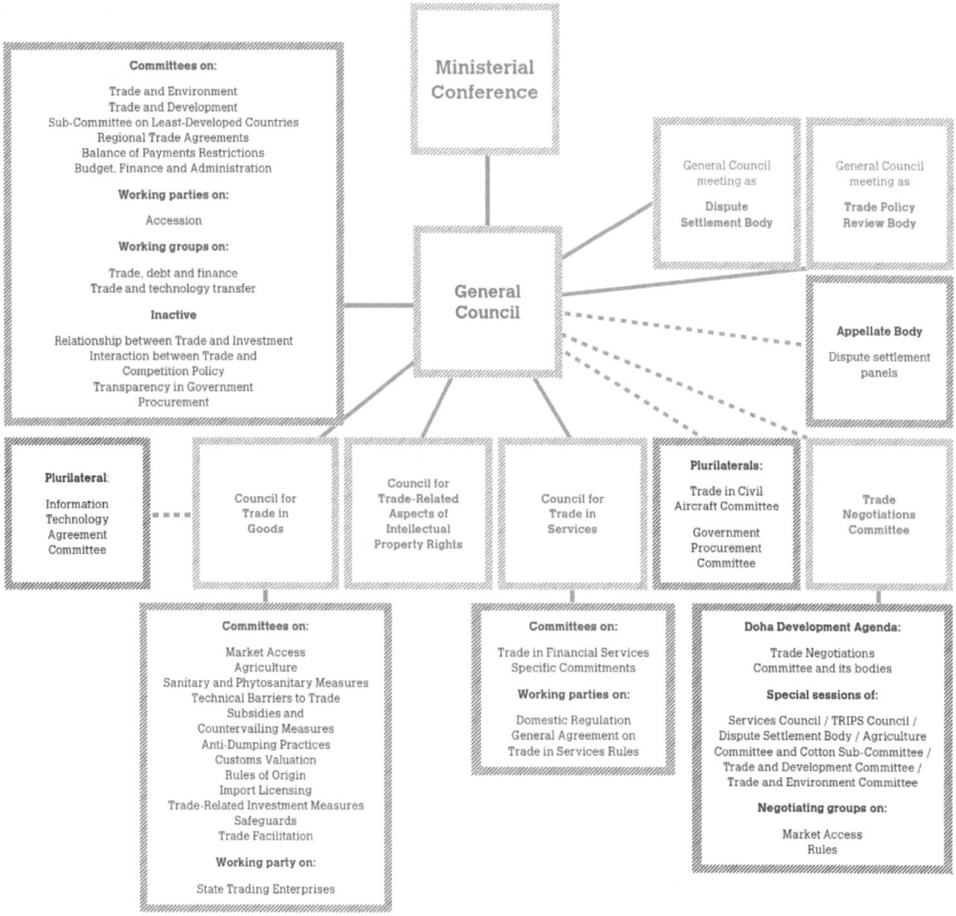

Figure 4
Source: WTO organization chart, can be accessed at:
https://www.wto.org/english/thewto_e/whatis_e/tif_e/org2_e.htm

V. Other Documents

Convention on the Representation of States in their Relations with International Organizations of a Universal Character, Vienna, 1975

[*Note:* the Convention was adopted by the UN Conference on the Representation of States in their Relations with International Organizations held in Vienna, Austria, from 4 February to 14 March 1975. It was opened for signature at Vienna on 14 March 1975 at the Federal Ministry for Foreign Affairs of the Republic of Austria. After 30 September 1975, it remained open for signature at the UN Headquarters in New York until 30 March 1976, the closing date for signature.

Status since May 2018: 20 signatories and 34 Parties. The Convention has not yet entered into force. In accordance with Article 89 it shall enter into force on the thirtieth day following the date of deposit of the 35th instrument of ratification or accession.]

The States Parties to the present Convention,

Recognizing the increasingly important role of multilateral diplomacy in relations between States and the responsibilities of the United Nations, its specialized agencies and other international organizations of a universal character within the international community,
Having in mind the purposes and principles of the Charter of the United Nations concerning the sovereign equality of States, the maintenance of international peace and security and the promotion of friendly relations and cooperation among States,
Recalling the work of codification and progressive development of international law applicable to bilateral relations between States which was achieved by the Vienna Convention on Diplomatic Relations of 1961, the Vienna Convention on Consular Relations of 1963, and the Convention on Special Missions of 1969,
Believing that an international convention on the representation of States in their relations with international organizations of a universal character would contribute to the promotion of friendly relations and cooperation among States, irrespective of their political, economic and social systems,
Recalling the provisions of Article 105 of the Charter of the United Nations,
Recognizing that the purpose of privileges and immunities contained in the present Convention is not to benefit individuals but to ensure the efficient performance of their functions in connection with organizations and conferences,
Taking account of the Convention on the Privileges and Immunities of the United Nations of 1946, the Convention on the Privileges and Immunities of the Specialized Agencies of 1947 and other agreements in force between States and between States and international organizations,
Affirming that the rules of customary international law continue to govern questions not expressly regulated by the provisions of the present Convention,
Have agreed as follows:

PART I - INTRODUCTION

Article 1 Use of terms

1. For the purposes of the present Convention:

(1) "international organization" means an intergovernmental organization;

(2) "international organization of a universal character" means the United Nations, its specialized agencies, the International Atomic Energy Agency and any similar organization whose membership and responsibilities are on a worldwide scale;

(3) "Organization" means the international organization in question;

(4) "organ" means:
   (a) any principal or subsidiary organ of an international organization, or
   (b) any commission, committee or subgroup of any such organ, in which States are members;

(5) "conference" means a conference of States convened by or under the auspices of an international organization;

(6) "mission" means, as the case may be, the permanent mission or the permanent observer mission;

(7) "permanent mission" means a mission of permanent character, representing the State, sent by a State member of an international organization to the Organization;

(8) "permanent observer mission" means a mission of permanent character, representing the State, sent to an international organization by a State not a member of the Organization;

(9) "delegation" means, as the case may be, the delegation to an organ or the delegation to a conference;

(10) "delegation to an organ" means the delegation sent by a State to participate on its behalf in the proceedings of the organ;

(11) "delegation to a conference" means the delegation sent by a State to participate on its behalf in the conference;

(12) "observer delegation" means, as the case may be, the observer delegation to an organ or the observer delegation to a conference;

(13) "observer delegation to an organ" means the delegation sent by a State to participate on its behalf as an observer in the proceedings of the organ;

(14) "observer delegation to a conference" means the delegation sent by a State to participate on its behalf as an observer in the proceedings of the conference;

(15) "host State" means the State in whose territory:
   (a) the Organization has its seat or an office, or
   (b) a meeting of an organ or a conference is held;

(16) "sending State" means the State which sends:
   (a) a mission to the Organization at its seat or to an office of the Organization, or
   (b) a delegation to an organ or a delegation to a conference, or
   (c) an observer delegation to an organ or an observer delegation to a conference;

(17) "head of mission" means, as the case may be, the permanent representative or the permanent observer;

(18) "permanent representative" means the person charged by the sending State with the duty of acting as the head of the permanent mission;

(19) "permanent observer" means the person charged by the sending State with the duty of acting as the head of the permanent observer mission;

(20) "members of the mission" means the head of mission and the members of the staff;

(21) "head of delegation" means the delegate charged by the sending State with the duty of acting in that capacity;

(22) "delegate" means any person designated by a State to participate as its representative in the proceedings of an organ or in a conference;
(23) "members of the delegation" means the delegates and the members of the staff;
(24) "head of the observer delegation" means the observer delegate charged by the sending State with the duty of acting in that capacity;
(25) "observer delegate" means any person designated by a State to attend as an observer the proceedings of an organ or of a conference;
(26) "members of the observer delegation" means the observer delegates and the members of the staff;
(27) "members of the staff" means the members of the diplomatic staff, the administrative and technical staff and the service staff of the mission, the delegation or the observer delegation;
(28) "members of the diplomatic staff" means the members of the staff of the mission, the delegation or the observer delegation who enjoy diplomatic status for the purpose of the mission, the delegation or the observer delegation;
(29) "members of the administrative and technical staff" means the members of the staff employed in the administrative and technical service of the mission, the delegation or the observer delegation;
(30) "members of the service staff" means the members of the staff employed by the mission, the delegation or the observer delegation as household workers or for similar tasks;
(31) "private staff" means persons employed exclusively in the private service of the members of the mission or the delegation;
(32) "premises of the mission" means the buildings or parts of buildings and the land ancillary thereto, irrespective of ownership, used for the purpose of the mission, including the residence of the head of mission;
(33) "premises of the delegation" means the buildings or parts of buildings, irrespective of ownership, used solely as the offices of the delegation;
(34) "rules of the Organization" means, in particular, the constituent instruments, relevant decisions and resolutions, and established practice of the Organization.

2. The provisions of paragraph 1 of this article regarding the use of terms in the present Convention are without prejudice to the use of those terms or to the meanings which may be given to them in other international instruments or the internal law of any State.

Article 2 Scope of the present Convention

1. The present Convention applies to the representation of States in their relations with any international organization of a universal character, and to their representation at conferences convened by or under the auspices of such an organization, when the Convention has been accepted by the host State and the Organization has completed the procedure envisaged by article 90.
2. The fact that the present Convention does not apply to other international organizations is without prejudice to the application to the representation of States in their relations with such other organizations of any of the rules set forth in the Convention which would be applicable under international law independently of the Convention.
3. The fact that the present Convention does not apply to other conferences is without prejudice to the application to the representation of States at such other conferences of any of the rules set forth in the Convention which would be applicable under international law independently of the Convention.
4. Nothing in the present Convention shall preclude the conclusion of agreements between States or between States and international organizations making the Convention applicable in whole or in part to international organizations or conferences other than those referred to in paragraph 1 of this article.

Article 3 Relationship between the present Convention and the relevant rules of international organizations or conferences
The provisions of the present Convention are without prejudice to any relevant rules of the Organization or to any relevant rules of procedure of the Conference.

Article 4 Relationship between the present Convention and other international agreements
The provisions of the present Convention:
(a) are without prejudice to other international agreements in force between States or between States and international organizations of a universal character, and
(b) shall not preclude the conclusion of other international agreements regarding the representation of States in their relations with international organizations of a universal character or their representation at conferences convened by or under the auspices of such organizations.

PART II – MISSIONS TO INTERNATIONAL ORGANIZATIONS

Article 5 Establishment of missions
1. Member States may, if the rules of the Organization so permit, establish permanent missions for the performance of the functions mentioned in article 6.
2. Non-member States may, if the rules of the Organization so permit, establish permanent observer missions for the performance of the functions mentioned in article 7.
3. The Organization shall notify the host State of the institution of a mission prior to its establishment.

Article 6 Functions of the permanent mission
The functions of the permanent mission consist, inter alia, in:
(a) ensuring the representation of the sending State to the Organization;
(b) maintaining liaison between the sending State and the Organization;
(c) negotiating with and within the Organization;
(d) ascertaining activities in the Organization and reporting thereon to the Government of the sending State;
(e) ensuring the participation of the sending State in the activities of the Organization;
(f) protecting the interests of the sending State in relation to the Organization;
(g) promoting the realization of the purposes and principles of the Organization by cooperating with and within the Organization.

Article 7 Functions of the permanent observer mission
The functions of the permanent observer mission consist, inter alia, in:
(a) ensuring the representation of the sending State and safeguarding its interests in relation to the Organization and maintaining liaison with it;
(b) ascertaining activities in the Organization and reporting thereon to the Government of the sending State;
(c) promoting cooperation with the Organization and negotiating with it.

Article 8 Multiple accreditation or appointment
1. The sending State may accredit the same person as head of mission to two or more international organizations or appoint a head of mission as a member of the diplomatic staff of another of its missions.

2. The sending State may accredit a member of the diplomatic staff of the mission as head of mission to other international organizations or appoint a member of the staff of the mission as a member of the staff of another of its missions.
3. Two or more States may accredit the same person as head of mission to the same international organization.

Article 9 Appointment of the members of the mission
Subject to the provisions of articles 14 and 73, the sending State may freely appoint the members of the mission.

Article 10 Credentials of the head of mission
The credentials of the head of mission shall be issued by the Head of State, by the Head of Government, by the Minister for Foreign Affairs or, if the rules of the Organization so permit, by another competent authority of the sending State and shall be transmitted to the Organization.

Article 11 Accreditation to organs of the Organization
1. A member State may specify in the credentials issued to its permanent representative that he is authorized to act as a delegate to one or more organs of the Organization.
2. Unless a member State provides otherwise, its permanent representative may act as a delegate to organs of the Organization for which there are no special requirements as regards representation.
3. A non-member State may specify in the credentials issued to its permanent observer that he is authorized to act as an observer delegate to one or more organs of the Organization when this is permitted by the rules of the Organization or the organ concerned.

Article 12 Full powers for the conclusion of a treaty with the Organization
1. The head of mission, by virtue of his functions and without having to produce full powers, is considered as representing his State for the purpose of adopting the text of a treaty between that State and the Organization.
2. The head of mission is not considered by virtue of his functions as representing his State for the purpose of signing a treaty, or signing a treaty *ad referendum*, between that State and the Organization unless it appears from the practice of the Organization, or from other circumstances, that the intention of the parties was to dispense with full powers.

Article 13 Composition of the mission
In addition to the head of mission, the mission may include diplomatic staff, administrative and technical staff and service staff.

Article 14 Size of the mission
The size of the mission shall not exceed what is reasonable and normal, having regard to the functions of the Organization, the needs of the particular mission and the circumstances and conditions in the host State.

Article 15 Notifications
1. The sending State shall notify the Organization of:

(a) the appointment, position, title and order of precedence of the members of the mission, their arrival, their final departure or the termination of their functions with the mission, and any other changes affecting their status that may occur in the course of their service with the mission;
(b) the arrival and final departure of any person belonging to the family of a member of the mission and forming part of his household and, where appropriate, the fact that a person becomes or ceases to be such a member of the family;
(c) the arrival and final departure of persons employed on the private staff of members of the mission and the termination of their employment as such;
(d) the beginning and the termination of the employment of persons resident in the host State as members of the staff of the mission or as persons employed on the private staff;
(e) the location of the premises of the mission and of the private residences enjoying inviolability under articles 23 and 29, as well as any other information that may be necessary to identify such premises and residences.

2. Where possible, prior notification of arrival and final departure shall also be given.
3. The Organization shall transmit to the host State the notification referred to in paragraphs 1 and 2 of this article.
4. The sending State may also transmit to the host State the notification referred to in paragraphs 1 and 2 of this article.

Article 16 Acting head of mission
If the post of head of mission is vacant, or if the head of mission is unable to perform his functions, the sending State may appoint an acting head of mission whose name shall be notified to the Organization and by it to the host State.

Article 17 Precedence
Precedence among permanent representatives shall be determined by the alphabetical order of the names of the States used in the Organization.
Precedence among permanent observers shall be determined by the alphabetical order of the names of the States used in the Organization.

Article 18 Location of the mission
Missions should be established in the locality where the Organization has its seat. However, if the rules of the Organization so permit and with the prior consent of the host State, the sending State may establish a mission or an office of a mission in a locality other than that in which the Organization has its seat.

Article 19 Use of flag and emblem
1. The mission shall have the right to use the flag and emblem of the sending State on its premises. The head of mission shall have the same right as regards his residence and means of transport.
2. In the exercise of the right accorded by this article regard shall be had to the laws, regulations and usages of the host State.

Article 20 General facilities
1. The host State shall accord to the mission all necessary facilities for the performance of its functions.

2. The Organization shall assist the mission in obtaining those facilities and shall accord to the mission such facilities as lie within its own competence.

Article 21 Premises and accommodation
1. The host State and the Organization shall assist the sending State in obtaining on reasonable terms premises necessary for the mission in the territory of the host State. Where necessary, the host State shall facilitate in accordance with its laws the acquisition of such premises.
2. Where necessary, the host State and the Organization shall also assist the mission in obtaining on reasonable terms suitable accommodation for its members.

Article 22 Assistance by the Organization in respect of privileges and immunities
1. The Organization shall, where necessary, assist the sending State, its mission and the members of its mission in securing the enjoyment of the privileges and immunities provided for under the present Convention.
2. The Organization shall, where necessary, assist the host State in securing the discharge of the obligations of the sending State, its mission and the members of its mission in respect of the privileges and immunities provided for under the present Convention.

Article 23 Inviolability of premises
1. The premises of the mission shall be inviolable. The agents of the host State may not enter them, except with the consent of the head of mission.
(a) The host State is under a special duty to take all appropriate steps to protect the premises of the mission against any intrusion or damage and to prevent any disturbance of the peace of the mission or impairment of its dignity.
(b) In case of an attack on the premises of the mission, the host State shall take all appropriate steps to prosecute and punish persons who have committed the attack.
2. The premises of the mission, their furnishings and other property thereon and the means of transport of the mission shall be immune from search, requisition, attachment or execution.

Article 24 Exemption of the premises from taxation
1. The premises of the mission of which the sending State or any person acting on its behalf is the owner or the lessee shall be exempt from all national, regional or municipal dues and taxes other than such as represent payment for specific services rendered.
2. The exemption from taxation referred to in this article shall not apply to such dues and taxes payable under the law of the host State by persons contracting with the sending State or with any person acting on its behalf.

Article 25 Inviolability of archives and documents
The archives and documents of the mission shall be inviolable at all times and wherever they may be.

Article 26 Freedom of movement
Subject to its laws and regulations concerning zones entry into which is prohibited or regulated for reasons of national security, the host State shall ensure freedom of movement and travel in its territory to all members of the mission and members of their families forming part of their households.

Article 27 Freedom of communication

1. The host State shall permit and protect free communication on the part of the mission for all official purposes. In communicating with the Government of the sending State, its permanent diplomatic missions, consular posts, permanent missions, permanent observer missions, special missions, delegations and observer delegations, wherever situated, the mission may employ all appropriate means, including couriers and messages in code or cipher. However, the mission may install and use a wireless transmitter only with the consent of the host State.
2. The official correspondence of the mission shall be inviolable. Official correspondence means all correspondence relating to the mission and its functions.
3. The bag of the mission shall not be opened or detained.
4. The packages constituting the bag of the mission must bear visible external marks of their character and may contain only documents or articles intended for the official use of the mission.
5. The courier of the mission, who shall be provided with an official document indicating his status and the number of packages constituting the bag, shall be protected by the host State in the performance of his functions. He shall enjoy personal inviolability and shall not be liable to any form of arrest or detention.
6. The sending State or the mission may designate couriers ad hoc of the mission. In such cases the provisions of paragraph 5 of this article shall also apply, except that the immunities therein mentioned shall cease to apply when the courier ad hoc has delivered to the consignee the mission's bag in his charge.
7. The bag of the mission may be entrusted to the captain of a ship or of a commercial aircraft scheduled to land at an authorized port of entry. He shall be provided with an official document indicating the number of packages constituting the bag, but he shall not be considered to be a courier of the mission. By arrangement with the appropriate authorities of the host State, the mission may send one of its members to take possession of the bag directly and freely from the captain of the ship or of the aircraft.

Article 28 Personal inviolability

The persons of the head of mission and of the members of the diplomatic staff of the mission shall be inviolable. They shall not be liable to any form of arrest or detention. The host State shall treat them with due respect and shall take all appropriate steps to prevent any attack on their persons, freedom or dignity and to prosecute and punish persons who have committed such attacks.

Article 29 Inviolability of residence and property

1. The private residence of the head of mission and of the members of the diplomatic staff of the mission shall enjoy the same inviolability and protection as the premises of the mission.
2. The papers, correspondence and, except as provided in paragraph 2 of article 30, the property of the head of mission or of members of the diplomatic staff of the mission shall also enjoy inviolability.

Article 30 Immunity from jurisdiction

1. The head of mission and the members of the diplomatic staff of the mission shall enjoy immunity from the criminal jurisdiction of the host State. They shall also enjoy immunity from its civil and administrative jurisdiction, except in the case of:

(a) a real action relating to private immovable property situated in the territory of the host State, unless the person in question holds it on behalf of the sending State for the purposes of the mission;
(b) an action relating to succession in which the person in question is involved as executor, administrator, heir or legatee as a private person and not on behalf of the sending State;

(c) an action relating to any professional or commercial activity exercised by the person in question in the host State outside his official functions.

2. No measures of execution may be taken in respect of the head of mission or a member of the diplomatic staff of the mission except in cases coming under subparagraphs *(a)*, *(b)* and *(c)* of paragraph 1 of this article, and provided that the measures concerned can be taken without infringing the inviolability of his person or of his residence.

3. The head of mission and the members of the diplomatic staff of the mission are not obliged to give evidence as witnesses.

4. The immunity of the head of mission or of a member of the diplomatic staff of the mission from the jurisdiction of the host State does not exempt him from the jurisdiction of the sending State.

Article 31 Waiver of immunity

1. The immunity from jurisdiction of the head of mission and members of the diplomatic staff of the mission and of persons enjoying immunity under article 36 may be waived by the sending State.

2. Waiver must always be express.

3. The initiation of proceedings by any of the persons referred to in paragraph 1 of this article shall preclude him from invoking immunity from jurisdiction in respect of any counterclaim directly connected with the principal claim.

4. Waiver of immunity from jurisdiction in respect of civil or administrative proceedings shall not be held to imply waiver of immunity in respect of the execution of the judgement, for which a separate waiver shall be necessary.

5. If the sending State does not waive the immunity of any of the persons mentioned in paragraph 1 of this article in respect of a civil action, it shall use its best endeavours to bring about a just settlement of the case.

Article 32 Exemption from social security legislation

1. Subject to the provisions of paragraph 3 of this article, the head of mission and the members of the diplomatic staff of the mission shall with respect to services rendered for the sending State be exempt from social security provisions which may be in force in the host State.

2. The exemption provided for in paragraph I of this article shall also apply to persons who are in the sole private employ of the head of mission or of a member of the diplomatic staff of the mission, on condition:

(a) that such employed persons are not nationals of or permanently resident in the host State; and

(b) that they are covered by the social security provisions which may be in force in the sending State or a third State.

3. The head of mission and the members of the diplomatic staff of the mission who employ persons to whom the exemption provided for in paragraph 2 of this article does not apply shall observe the obligations which the social security provisions of the host State impose upon employers.

4. The exemption provided for in paragraphs 1 and 2 of this article shall not preclude voluntary participation in the social security system of the host State provided that such participation is permitted by that State.

5. The provisions of this article shall not affect bilateral or multilateral agreements concerning social security concluded previously and shall not prevent the conclusion of such agreements in the future.

Article 33 Exemption from dues and taxes

1. The head of mission and the members of the diplomatic staff of the mission shall be exempt from all dues and taxes, personal or real, national, regional or municipal, except:
(a) indirect taxes of a kind which are normally incorporated in the price of goods or services;
(b) dues and taxes on private immovable property situated in the territory of the host State, unless the person concerned holds it on behalf of the sending State for the purposes of the mission;
(c) estate, succession or inheritance duties levied by the host State, subject to the provisions of paragraph 4 of article 38;
(d) dues and taxes on private income having its source in the host State and capital taxes on investments made in commercial undertakings in the host State;
(e) charges levied for specific services rendered;
(f) registration, court or record fees, mortgage dues and stamp duty, with respect to immovable property, subject to the provisions of article 24.

Article 34 Exemption from personal services

The host State shall exempt the head of mission and the members of the diplomatic staff of the mission from all personal services, from all public service of any kind whatsoever, and from military obligations such as those connected with requisitioning, military contributions and billeting.

Article 35 Exemption from customs duties and inspection

1. The host State shall, in accordance with such laws and regulations as it may adopt, permit entry of and grant exemption from all customs duties, taxes and related charges other than charges for storage, cartage and similar services, on:
(a) articles for the official use of the mission;
(b) articles for the personal use of the head of mission or a member of the diplomatic staff of the mission, including articles intended for his establishment.

2. The personal baggage of the head of mission or a member of the diplomatic staff of the mission shall be exempt from inspection, unless there are serious grounds for presuming that it contains articles not covered by the exemptions mentioned in paragraph 1 of this article, or articles the import or export of which is prohibited by the law or controlled by the quarantine regulations of the host State. In such cases, inspection shall be conducted only in the presence of the person enjoying the exemption or of his authorized representative.

Article 36 Privileges and immunities of other persons

The members of the family of the head of mission forming part of his household and the members of the family of a member of the diplomatic staff of the mission forming part of his household shall, if they are not nationals of or permanently resident in the host State, enjoy the privileges and immunities specified in articles 28, 29, 30, 32, 33, 34 and in paragraphs 1(b) and 2 of article 35.

Members of the administrative and technical staff of the mission, together with members of their families forming part of their respective households who are not nationals of or permanently resident in the host State, shall enjoy the privileges and immunities specified in articles 28, 29, 30, 32, 33 and 34, except that the immunity from civil and administrative jurisdiction of the host State specified in paragraph 1 of article 30 shall not extend to acts performed outside the course of their duties. They shall also enjoy the privileges specified in paragraph 1 *(b)* of article 35 in respect of articles imported at the time of final installation.

Members of the service staff of the mission who are not nationals of or permanently resident in the host State shall enjoy immunity in respect of acts performed in the course of their duties, exemption from dues and taxes on the emoluments they receive by reason of their employment and the exemption specified in article 32.
Private staff of members of the mission shall, if they are not nationals of or permanently resident in the host State, be exempt from dues and taxes on the emoluments they receive by reason of their employment. In other respects, they may enjoy privileges and immunities only to the extent admitted by the host State. However, the host State must exercise its jurisdiction over those persons in such a manner as not to interfere unduly with the performance of the functions of the mission.

Article 37 Nationals and permanent residents of the host State
1. Except in so far as additional privileges and immunities may be granted by the host State, the head of mission or any member of the diplomatic staff of the mission who is a national of or permanently resident in that State shall enjoy only immunity from jurisdiction and inviolability in respect of official acts performed in the exercise of his functions.
2. Other members of the staff of the mission who are nationals of or permanently resident in the host State shall enjoy only immunity from jurisdiction in respect of official acts performed in the exercise of their functions. In all other respects, those members, and persons on the private staff who are nationals of or permanently resident in the host State, shall enjoy privileges and immunities only to the extent admitted by the host State. However, the host State must exercise its jurisdiction over those members and persons in such a manner as not to interfere unduly with the performance of the functions of the mission.

Article 38 Duration of privileges and immunities
1. Every person entitled to privileges and immunities shall enjoy them from the moment he enters the territory of the host State on proceeding to take up his post or, if already in its territory, from the moment when his appointment is notified to the host State by the Organization or by the sending State.
2. When the functions of a person enjoying privileges and immunities have come to an end, such privileges and immunities shall normally cease at the moment when he leaves the territory, or on the expiry of a reasonable period in which to do so. However, with respect to acts performed by such a person in the exercise of his functions as a member of the mission, immunity shall continue to subsist.
3. In the event of the death of a member of the mission, the members of his family shall continue to enjoy the privileges and immunities to which they are entitled until the expiry of a reasonable period in which to leave the territory.
4. In the event of the death of a member of the mission not a national of or permanently resident in the host State or of a member of his family forming part of his household, the host State shall permit the withdrawal of the movable property of the deceased, with the exception of any property acquired in the territory the export of which was prohibited at the time of his death. Estate, succession and inheritance duties shall not be levied on movable property which is in the host State solely because of the presence there of the deceased as a member of the mission or of the family of a member of the mission.

Article 39 Professional or commercial activity
1. The head of mission and members of the diplomatic staff of the mission shall not practise for personal profit any professional or commercial activity in the host State.
2. Except insofar as such privileges and immunities may be granted by the host State, members of the administrative and technical staff and persons forming part of the household of a member of the mis-

sion shall not, when they practise a professional or commercial activity for personal profit, enjoy any privilege or immunity in respect of acts performed in the course of or in connection with the practise of such activity.

Article 40 End of functions

The functions of the head of mission or of a member of the diplomatic staff of the mission shall come to an end, inter alia:

(a) on notification of their termination by the sending State to the Organization;
(b) if the mission is finally or temporarily recalled.

Article 41 Protection of premises, property and archives

1. When the mission is temporarily or finally recalled, the host State must respect and protect the premises, property and archives of the mission. The sending State must take all appropriate measures to terminate this special duty of the host State as soon as possible. It may entrust custody of the premises, property and archives of the mission to the Organization if it so agrees, or to a third State acceptable to the host State.
2. The host State, if requested by the sending State, shall grant the latter facilities for removing the property and archives of the mission from the territory of the host State.

PART III – DELEGATIONS TO ORGANS AND TO CONFERENCES

Article 42 Sending of delegations

1. A State may send a delegation to an organ or to a conference in accordance with the rules of the Organization.
2. Two or more States may send the same delegation to an organ or to a conference in accordance with the rules of the Organization.

Article 43 Appointment of the members of the delegation

Subject to the provisions of articles 46 and 73, the sending State may freely appoint the members of the delegation.

Article 44 Credentials of delegates

The credentials of the head of delegation and of other delegates shall be issued by the Head of State, by the Head of Government, by the Minister for Foreign Affairs or, if the rules of the Organization or the rules of procedure of the conference so permit, by another competent authority of the sending State. They shall be transmitted, as the case may be, to the Organization or to the conference.

Article 45 Composition of the delegation

In addition to the head of delegation, the delegation may include other delegates, diplomatic staff, administrative and technical staff and service staff.

Article 46 Size of the delegation

The size of the delegation shall not exceed what is reasonable and normal, having regard, as the case may be, to the functions of the organ or the object of the conference, as well as the needs of the particular delegation and the circumstances and conditions in the host State.

Article 47 Notifications

1. The sending State shall notify the Organization or, as the case may be, the conference of:

(a) the composition of the delegation, including the position, title and order of precedence of the members of the delegation, and any subsequent changes therein;

(b) the arrival and final departure of members of the delegation and the termination of their functions with the delegation;

(c) the arrival and final departure of any person accompanying a member of the delegation;

(d) the beginning and the termination of the employment of persons resident in the host State as members of the staff of the delegation or as persons employed on the private staff;

(e) the location of the premises of the delegation and of the private accommodation enjoying inviolability under article 59, as well as any other information that may be necessary to identify such premises and accommodation.

2. Where possible, prior notification of arrival and final departure shall also be given.

3. The Organization or, as the case may be, the conference shall transmit to the host State the notifications referred to in paragraphs 1 and 2 of this article.

4. The sending State may also transmit to the host State the notifications referred to in paragraphs 1 and 2 of this article.

Article 48 Acting head of delegation

1. If the head of delegation is absent or unable to perform his functions, an acting head of delegation shall be designated from among the other delegates by the head of delegation or, in case he is unable to do so, by a competent authority of the sending State. The name of the acting head of delegation shall be notified, as the case may be, to the Organization or to the conference.

2. If a delegation does not have another delegate available to serve as acting head of delegation, another person may be designated for that purpose. In such case credentials must be issued and transmitted in accordance with article 44.

Article 49 Precedence

Precedence among delegations shall be determined by the alphabetical order of the names of the States used in the Organization.

Article 50 Status of the Head of State and persons of high rank

1. The Head of State or any member of a collegial body performing the functions of Head of State under the constitution of the State concerned, when he leads the delegation, shall enjoy in the host State or in a third State, in addition to what is granted by the present Convention, the facilities, privileges and immunities accorded by international law to Heads of State.

2. The Head of Government, the Minister for Foreign Affairs or other person of high rank, when he leads or is a member of the delegation, shall enjoy in the host State or in a third State, in addition to what is granted by the present Convention, the facilities, privileges and immunities accorded by international law to such persons.

Article 51 General facilities

1. The host State shall accord to the delegation all necessary facilities for the performance of its tasks.

2. The Organization or, as the case may be, the conference shall assist the delegation in obtaining those facilities and shall accord to the delegation such facilities as lie within its own competence.

Article 52 Premises and accommodation

If so requested, the host State and, where necessary, the Organization or the conference shall assist the sending State in obtaining on reasonable terms premises necessary for the delegation and suitable accommodation for its members.

Article 53 Assistance in respect of privileges and immunities

1. The Organization or, as the case may be, the Organization and the conference shall, where necessary, assist the sending State, its delegation and the members of its delegation in securing the enjoyment of the privileges and immunities provided for under the present Convention.
2. The Organization or, as the case may be, the Organization and the conference shall, where necessary, assist the host State in securing the discharge of the obligations of the sending State, its delegation and the members of its delegation in respect of the privileges and immunities provided for under the present Convention.

Article 54 Exemption of the premises from taxation

1. The sending State or any member of the delegation acting on behalf of the delegation shall be exempt from all national, regional or municipal dues and taxes in respect of the premises of the delegation other than such as represent payment for specific services rendered.
2. The exemption from taxation referred to in this article shall not apply to such dues and taxes payable under the law of the host State by persons contracting with the sending State or with a member of the delegation.

Article 55 Inviolability of archives and documents

The archives and documents of the delegation shall be inviolable at all times and wherever they may be.

Article 56 Freedom of movement

Subject to its laws and regulations concerning zones entry into which is prohibited or regulated for reasons of national security, the host State shall ensure to all members of the delegation such freedom of movement and travel in its territory as is necessary for the performance of the tasks of the delegation.

Article 57 Freedom of communication

1. The host State shall permit and protect free communication on the part of the delegation for all official purposes. In communicating with the Government of the sending State, its permanent diplomatic missions, consular posts, permanent missions, permanent observer missions, special missions, other delegations, and observer delegations, wherever situated, the delegation may employ all appropriate means, including couriers and messages in code or cipher. However, the delegation may install and use a wireless transmitter only with the consent of the host State.
2. The official correspondence of the delegation shall be inviolable. Official correspondence means all correspondence relating to the delegation and its tasks.
3. Where practicable, the delegation shall use the means of communication, including the bag and the courier, of the permanent diplomatic mission, of a consular post, of the permanent mission or of the permanent observer mission of the sending State.
4. The bag of the delegation shall not be opened or detained.

5. The packages constituting the bag of the delegation must bear visible external marks of their character and may contain only documents or articles intended for the official use of the delegation.
6. The courier of the delegation, who shall be provided with an official document indicating his status and the number of packages constituting the bag, shall be protected by the host State in the performance of his functions. He shall enjoy personal inviolability and shall not be liable to any form of arrest or detention.
7. The sending State or the delegation may designate couriers ad hoc of the delegation. In such cases the provisions of paragraph 6 of this article shall also apply, except that the immunities therein mentioned shall cease to apply when the courier ad hoc has delivered to the consignee the delegation's bag in his charge.
8. The bag of the delegation may be entrusted to the captain of a ship or of a commercial aircraft scheduled to land at an authorized port of entry. He shall be provided with an official document indicating the number of packages constituting the bag, but he shall not be considered to be a courier of the delegation. By arrangement with the appropriate authorities of the host State, the delegation may send one of its members to take possession of the bag directly and freely from the captain of the ship or of the aircraft.

Article 58 Personal inviolability

The persons of the head of delegation and of other delegates and members of the diplomatic staff of the delegation shall be inviolable. They shall not be liable, inter alia, to any form of arrest or detention. The host State shall treat them with due respect and shall take all appropriate steps to prevent any attack on their persons, freedom or dignity and to prosecute and punish persons who have committed such attacks.

Article 59 Inviolability of private accommodation and property

1. The private accommodation of the head of delegation and of other delegates and members of the diplomatic staff of the delegation shall enjoy inviolability and protection.
2. The papers, correspondence and, except as provided in paragraph 2 of article 60, the property of the head of delegation and of other delegates or members of the diplomatic staff of the delegation shall also enjoy inviolability.

Article 60 Immunity from jurisdiction

1. The head of delegation and other delegates and members of the diplomatic staff of the delegation shall enjoy immunity from the criminal jurisdiction of the host State, and immunity from its civil and administrative jurisdiction in respect of all acts performed in the exercise of their official functions.
2. No measures of execution may be taken in respect of such persons unless they can be taken without infringing their rights under articles 58 and 59.
3. Such persons are not obliged to give evidence as witnesses.
4. Nothing in this article shall exempt such persons from the civil and administrative jurisdiction of the host State in relation to an action for damages arising from an accident caused by a vehicle, vessel or aircraft, used or owned by the persons in question, where those damages are not recoverable from insurance.
5. Any immunity of such persons from the jurisdiction of the host State does not exempt them from the jurisdiction of the sending State.

Article 61 Waiver of immunity

1. The immunity from jurisdiction of the head of delegation and of other delegates and members of the diplomatic staff of the delegation and of persons enjoying immunity under article 66 may be waived by the sending State.
2. Waiver must always be express.
3. The initiation of proceedings by any of the persons referred to in paragraph 1 of this article shall preclude him from invoking immunity from jurisdiction in respect of any counterclaim directly connected with the principal claim.
4. Waiver of immunity from jurisdiction in respect of civil or administrative proceedings shall not be held to imply waiver of immunity in respect of the execution of the judgement, for which a separate waiver shall be necessary.
5. If the sending State does not waive the immunity of any of the persons mentioned in paragraph 1 of this article in respect of a civil action, it shall use its best endeavours to bring about a just settlement of the case.

Article 62 Exemption from social security legislation

1. Subject to the provisions of paragraph 3 of this article, the head of delegation and other delegates and members of the diplomatic staff of the delegation shall with respect to services rendered for the sending State be exempt from social security provisions which may be in force in the host State.
2. The exemption provided for in paragraph 1 of this article shall also apply to persons who are in the sole private employ of the head of delegation or of any other delegate or member of the diplomatic staff of the delegation, on condition:
(a) that such employed persons are not nationals of or permanently resident in the host State; and
(b) that they are covered by the social security provisions which may be in force in the sending State or a third State.
3. The head of delegation and other delegates and members of the diplomatic staff of the delegation who employ persons to whom the exemption provided for in paragraph 2 of this article does not apply shall observe the obligations which the social security provisions of the host State impose upon employers.
4. The exemption provided for in paragraphs 1 and 2 of this article shall not preclude voluntary participation in the social security system of the host State provided that such participation is permitted by that State.
5. The provisions of this article shall not affect bilateral or multilateral agreements concerning social security concluded previously and shall not prevent the conclusion of such agreements in the future.

Article 63 Exemption from dues and taxes

The head of delegation and other delegates and members of the diplomatic staff of the delegation shall be exempt, to the extent practicable, from all dues and taxes, personal or real, national, regional or municipal, except:
(a) indirect taxes of a kind which are normally incorporated in the price of goods or services;
(b) dues and taxes on private immovable property situated in the territory of the host State, unless the person concerned holds it on behalf of the sending State for the purposes of the delegation;
(c) estate, succession or inheritance duties levied by the host State, subject to the provisions of paragraph 4 of article 68;
(d) dues and taxes on private income having its source in the host State and capital taxes on investments made in commercial undertakings in the host State;

(e) charges levied for specific services rendered;
(f) registration, court or record fees, mortgage dues and stamp duty, with respect to immovable property, subject to the provisions of article 54.

Article 64 Exemption from personal services
The host State shall exempt the head of delegation and other delegates and members of the diplomatic staff of the delegation from all personal services, from all public service of any kind whatsoever, and from military obligations such as those connected with requisitioning, military contributions and billeting.

Article 65 Exemption from customs duties and inspection
1. The host State shall, in accordance with such laws and regulations as it may adopt, permit entry of and grant exemption from all customs duties, taxes and related charges other than charges for storage, cartage and similar services, on:
(a) articles for the official use of the delegation;
(b) articles for the personal use of the head of delegation or any other delegate or member of the diplomatic staff of the delegation, imported in his personal baggage at the time of his first entry into the territory of the host State to attend the meeting of the organ or conference.
2. The personal baggage of the head of delegation or any other delegate or member of the diplomatic staff of the delegation shall be exempt from inspection, unless there are serious grounds for presuming that it contains articles not covered by the exemptions mentioned in paragraph 1 of this article, or articles the import or export of which is prohibited by the law or controlled by the quarantine regulations of the host State. In such cases, inspection shall be conducted only in the presence of the person enjoying the exemption or of his authorized representative.

Article 66 Privileges and immunities of other persons
1. The members of the family of the head of delegation who accompany him and the members of the family of any other delegate or member of the diplomatic staff of the delegation who accompany him shall, if they are not nationals of or permanently resident in the host State, enjoy the privileges and immunities specified in articles 58, 60 and 64 and in paragraphs 1 (b) and 2 of article 65 and exemption from aliens' registration obligations.
2. Members of the administrative and technical staff of the delegation shall, if they are not nationals of or permanently resident in the host State, enjoy the privileges and immunities specified in articles 58, 59, 60, 62, 63 and 64. They shall also enjoy the privileges specified in paragraph 1 (b) of article 65 in respect of articles imported in their personal baggage at the time of their first entry into the territory of the host State for the purpose of attending the meeting of the organ or conference. Members of the family of a member of the administrative and technical staff who accompany him shall, if they are not nationals of or permanently resident in the host State, enjoy the privileges and immunities specified in articles 58, 60 and 64 and in paragraph 1 *(b)* of article 65 to the extent accorded to such a member of the staff.
3. Members of the service staff of the delegation who are not nationals of or permanently resident in the host State shall enjoy the same immunity in respect of acts performed in the course of their duties as is accorded to members of the administrative and technical staff of the delegation, exemption from dues and taxes on the emoluments they receive by reason of their employment and the exemption specified in article 62.

4. Private staff of members of the delegation shall, if they are not nationals of or permanently resident in the host State, be exempt from dues and taxes on the emoluments they receive by reason of their employment. In other respects, they may enjoy privileges and immunities only to the extent admitted by the host State. However, the host State must exercise its jurisdiction over those persons in such a manner as not to interfere unduly with the performance of the tasks of the delegation.

Article 67 Nationals and permanent residents of the host State

1. Except insofar as additional privileges and immunities may be granted by the host State the head of delegation or any other delegate or member of the diplomatic staff of the delegation who is a national of or permanently resident in that State shall enjoy only immunity from jurisdiction and inviolability in respect of official acts performed in the exercise of his functions.
2. Other members of the staff of the delegation and persons on the private staff who are nationals of or permanently resident in the host State shall enjoy privileges and immunities only to the extent admitted by the host State. However, the host State must exercise its jurisdiction over those members and persons in such a manner as not to interfere unduly with the performance of the tasks of the delegation.

Article 68 Duration of privileges and immunities

1. Every person entitled to privileges and immunities shall enjoy them from the moment he enters the territory of the host State for the purpose of attending the meeting of an organ or conference or, if already in its territory, from the moment when his appointment is notified to the host State by the Organization, by the conference or by the sending State.
2. When the functions of a person enjoying privileges and immunities have come to an end, such privileges and immunities shall normally cease at the moment when he leaves the territory, or on the expiry of a reasonable period in which to do so. However, with respect to acts performed by such a person in the exercise of his functions as a member of the delegation, immunity shall continue to subsist.
3. In the event of the death of a member of the delegation, the members of his family shall continue to enjoy the privileges and immunities to which they are entitled until the expiry of a reasonable period in which to leave the territory.
4. In the event of the death of a member of the delegation not a national of or permanently resident in the host State or of a member of his family accompanying him, the host State shall permit the withdrawal of the movable property of the deceased, with the exception of any property acquired in the territory the export of which was prohibited at the time of his death. Estate, succession and inheritance duties shall not be levied on movable property which is in the host State solely because of the presence there of the deceased as a member of the delegation or of the family of a member of the delegation.

Article 69 End of functions

The functions of the head of delegation or of any other delegate or member of the diplomatic staff of the delegation shall come to an end, inter alia:

(a) on notification of their termination by the sending State to the Organization or the conference;
(b) upon the conclusion of the meeting of the organ or the conference.

Article 70 Protection of premises, property and archives

1. When the meeting of an organ or a conference comes to an end, the host State must respect and protect the premises of the delegation so long as they are used by it, as well as the property and archives of the delegation. The sending State must take all appropriate measures to terminate this special duty of the host State as soon as possible.

2. The host State, if requested by the sending State, shall grant the latter facilities for removing the property and the archives of the delegation from the territory of the host State.

PART IV - OBSERVER DELEGATIONS TO ORGANS AND TO CONFERENCES

Article 71 Sending of observer delegations
A State may send an observer delegation to an organ or to a conference in accordance with the rules of the Organization.

Article 72 General provision concerning observer delegations
All the provisions of articles 43 to 70 of the present Convention shall apply to observer delegations.

PART V - GENERAL PROVISI ONS

Article 73 Nationality of the members of the mission, the delegation or the observer delegation
1. The head of mission and members of the diplomatic staff of the mission, the head of delegation, other delegates and members of the diplomatic staff of the delegation, the head of the observer delegation, other observer delegates and members of the diplomatic staff of the observer delegation should in principle be of the nationality of the sending State.
2. The head of mission and members of the diplomatic staff of the mission may not be appointed from among persons having the nationality of the host State except with the consent of that State, which may be withdrawn at any time.
3. Where the head of delegation, any other delegate or any member of the diplomatic staff of the delegation or the head of the observer delegation, any other observer delegate or any member of the diplomatic staff of the observer delegation is appointed from among persons having the nationality of the host State, the consent of that State shall be assumed if it has been notified of such appointment of a national of the host State and has made no objection.

Article 74 Laws concerning acquisition of nationality
Members of the mission, the delegation or the observer delegation not being nationals of the host State, and members of their families forming part of their household or, as the case may be, accompanying them, shall not, solely by the operation of the law of the host State, acquire the nationality of that State.

Article 75 Privileges and immunities in case of multiple functions
When members of the permanent diplomatic mission or of a consular post in the host State are included in a mission, a delegation or an observer delegation, they shall retain their privileges and immunities as members of their permanent diplomatic mission or consular post in addition to the privileges and immunities accorded by the present Convention.

Article 76 Cooperation between sending States and host States
Whenever necessary and to the extent compatible with the independent exercise of the functions of the mission, the delegation or the observer delegation, the sending State shall cooperate as fully as possible with the host State in the conduct of any investigation or prosecution carried out pursuant to the provisions of articles 23, 28, 29 and 58.

Article 77 Respect for the laws and regulations of the host State

1. Without prejudice to their privileges and immunities, it is the duty of all persons enjoying such privileges and immunities to respect the laws and regulations of the host State. They also have a duty not to interfere in the internal affairs of that State.
2. In case of grave and manifest violation of the criminal law of the host State by a person enjoying immunity from jurisdiction, the sending State shall, unless it waives the immunity of the person concerned, recall him, terminate his functions with the mission, the delegation or the observer delegation or secure his departure, as appropriate. The sending State shall take the same action in case of grave and manifest interference in the internal affairs of the host State. The provisions of this paragraph shall not apply in the case of any act that the person concerned performed in carrying out the functions of the mission or the tasks of the delegation or of the observer delegation.
3. The premises of the mission and the premises of the delegation shall not be used in any manner incompatible with the exercise of the functions of the mission or the performance of the tasks of the delegation.
4. Nothing in this article shall be construed as prohibiting the host State from taking such measures as are necessary for its own protection. In that event the host State shall, without prejudice to articles 84 and 85, consult the sending State in an appropriate manner in order to ensure that such measures do not interfere with the normal functioning of the mission, the delegation or the observer delegation.
5. The measures provided for in paragraph 4 of this article shall be taken with the approval of the Minister for Foreign Affairs or of any other competent minister in conformity with the constitutional rules of the host State.

Article 78 Insurance against third-party risks

The members of the mission, of the delegation or of the observer delegation shall comply with all obligations under the laws and regulations of the host State relating to third-party liability insurance for any vehicle, vessel or aircraft used or owned by them.

Article 79 Entry into the territory of the host State

1. The host State shall permit entry into its territory of:
(a) members of the mission and members of their families forming part of their respective households, and
(b) members of the delegation and members of their families accompanying them, and
(c) members of the observer delegation and members of their families accompanying them.
2. Visas, when required, shall be granted as promptly as possible to any person referred to in paragraph 1 of this article.

Article 80 Facilities for departure

The host State shall, if requested, grant facilities to enable persons enjoying privileges and immunities, other than nationals of the host State, and members of the families of such persons irrespective of their nationality, to leave its territory.

Article 81 Transit through the territory of a third State

1. If a head of mission or a member of the diplomatic staff of the mission, a head of delegation, other delegate or member of the diplomatic staff of the delegation, a head of an observer delegation, other observer delegate or member of the diplomatic staff of the observer delegation passes through or is in the territory of a third State which has granted him a passport visa if such visa was necessary, while

proceeding to take up or to resume his functions, or when returning to his own country, the third State shall accord him inviolability and such other immunities as may be required to ensure his transit.

2. The provisions of paragraph 1 of this article shall also apply in the case of:

(a) members of the family of the head of mission or of a member of the diplomatic staff of the mission forming part of his household and enjoying privileges and immunities, whether travelling with him or travelling separately to join him or to return to their country;

(b) members of the family of the head of delegation, of any other delegate or member of the diplomatic staff of the delegation who are accompanying him and enjoying privileges and immunities, whether travelling with him or travelling separately to join him or to return to their country;

(c) members of the family of the head of the observer delegation, of any other observer delegate or member of the diplomatic staff of the observer delegation, who are accompanying him and enjoy privileges and immunities whether travelling with him or travelling separately to join him or to return to their country.

3. In circumstances similar to those specified in paragraphs 1 and 2 of this article, third States shall not hinder the passage of members of the administrative and technical or service staff, and of members of their families, through their territories.

4. Third States shall accord to official correspondence and other official communications in transit, including messages in code or cipher, the same freedom and protection as the host State is bound to accord under the present Convention. They shall accord to the couriers of the mission, of the delegation or of the observer delegation, who have been granted a passport visa if such visa was necessary, and to the bags of the mission, of the delegation or of the observer delegation in transit the same inviolability and protection as the host State is bound to accord under the present Convention.

5. The obligations of third States under paragraphs 1, 2, 3 and 4 of this article shall also apply to the persons mentioned respectively in those paragraphs and to the official communications and bags of the mission, of the delegation or of the observer delegation when they are present in the territory of the third State owing to force majeure.

Article 82 Non-recognition of States or governments or absence of diplomatic or consular relations

1. The rights and obligations of the host State and of the sending State under the present Convention shall be affected neither by the non-recognition by one of those States of the other State or of its government nor by the non-existence or the severance of diplomatic or consular relations between them.

2. The establishment or maintenance of a mission, the sending or attendance of a delegation or of an observer delegation or any act in application of the present Convention shall not by itself imply recognition by the sending State of the host State or its government or by the host State of the sending State or its government.

Article 83 Non-discrimination

In the application of the provisions of the present Convention no discrimination shall be made as between States.

Article 84 Consultations

If a dispute between two or more States Parties arises out of the application or interpretation of the present Convention, consultations between them shall be held upon the request of any of them. At the request of any of the parties to the dispute, the Organization or the conference shall be invited to join in the consultations.

Article 85 Conciliation

1. If the dispute is not disposed of as a result of the consultations referred to in article 84 within one month from the date of their inception, any State participating in the consultations may bring the dispute before a conciliation commission constituted in accordance with the provisions of this article by giving written notice to the Organization and to the other States participating in the consultations.
2. Each conciliation commission shall be composed of three members: two members who shall be appointed respectively by each of the parties to the dispute, and a Chairman appointed in accordance with paragraph 3 of this article. Each State Party to the present Convention shall designate in advance a person to serve as a member of such a commission. It shall notify the designation to the Organization, which shall maintain a register of persons so designated. If it does not make the designation in advance, it may do so during the conciliation procedure up to the moment at which the Commission begins to draft the report which it is to prepare in accordance with paragraph 7 of this article.
3. The Chairman of the Commission shall be chosen by the other two members. If the other two members are unable to agree within one month from the notice referred to in paragraph 1 of this article or if one of the parties to the dispute has not availed itself of its right to designate a member of the Commission, the Chairman shall be designated at the request of one of the parties to the dispute by the chief administrative officer of the Organization. The appointment shall be made within a period of one month from such request. The chief administrative officer of the Organization shall appoint as the Chairman a qualified jurist who is neither an official of the Organization nor a national of any State party to the dispute.
4. Any vacancy shall be filled in the manner prescribed for the initial appointment.
5. The Commission shall function as soon as the Chairman has been appointed even if its composition is incomplete.
6. The Commission shall establish its own rules of procedure and shall reach its decisions and recommendations by a majority vote. It may recommend to the Organization, if the Organization is so authorized in accordance with the Charter of the United Nations, to request an advisory opinion from the International Court of Justice regarding the application or interpretation of the present Convention.
7. If the Commission is unable to obtain an agreement among the parties to the dispute on a settlement of the dispute within two months from the appointment of its Chairman, it shall prepare as soon as possible a report of its proceedings and transmit it to the parties to the dispute. The report shall include the Commission's conclusions upon the facts and questions of law and the recommendations which it has submitted to the parties to the dispute in order to facilitate a settlement of the dispute. The two months time limit may be extended by decision of the Commission. The recommendations in the report of the Commission shall not be binding on the parties to the dispute unless all the parties to the dispute have accepted them. Nevertheless, any party to the dispute may declare unilaterally that it will abide by the recommendations in the report so far as it is concerned.
8. Nothing in the preceding paragraphs of this article shall preclude the establishment of any other appropriate procedure for the settlement of disputes arising out of the application or interpretation of the present Convention or the conclusion of any agreement between the parties to the dispute to submit the dispute to a procedure instituted in the Organization or to any other procedure.
9. This article is without prejudice to provisions concerning the settlement of disputes contained in international agreements in force between States or between States and international organizations.

PART VI - FINAL CLAUSES

Article 86 Signature
The present Convention shall be open for signature by all States until 30 September 1975 at the Federal Ministry for Foreign Affairs of the Republic of Austria and subsequently, until 30 March 1976, at United Nations Headquarters in New York.

Article 87 Ratification
The present Convention is subject to ratification. The instruments of ratification shall be deposited with the Secretary-General of the United Nations.

Article 88 Accession
The present Convention shall remain open for accession by any State. The instruments of accession shall be deposited with the Secretary-General of the United Nations.

Article 89 Entry into force
1. The present Convention shall enter into force on the thirtieth day following the date of deposit of the thirty-fifth instrument of ratification or accession.
2. For each State ratifying or acceding to the Convention after the deposit of the thirty-fifth instrument of ratification or accession, the Convention shall enter into force on the thirtieth day after the deposit by such State of its instrument of ratification or accession.

Article 90 Implementation by organizations
After the entry into force of the present Convention, the competent organ of an international organization of a universal character may adopt a decision to implement the relevant provisions of the Convention. The Organization shall communicate the decision to the host State and to the depositary of the Convention.

Article 91 Notifications by the depositary
1. As depositary of the present Convention, the Secretary-General of the United Nations shall inform all States:
(a) of signatures to the Convention and of the deposit of instruments of ratification or accession, in accordance with articles 86, 87 and 88;
(b) of the date on which the Convention will enter into force, in accordance with article 89;
(c) of any decision communicated in accordance with article 90.
2. The Secretary-General of the United Nations shall also inform all States, as necessary, of other acts, notifications or communications relating to the present Convention.

Article 92 Authentic texts
The original of the present Convention, of which the Chinese, English, French, Russian and Spanish texts are equally authentic, shall be deposited with the Secretary-General of the United Nations, who shall send certified copies thereof to all States.

In WITNESS WHEREOF the undersigned Plenipotentiaries, being duly authorized thereto by their respective Governments, have signed the present Convention.
DONE at Vienna this fourteenth day of March, one thousand nine hundred and seventy-five.

Convention on the Law of Treaties Between States and International Organizations or Between International Organizations, Vienna, 1986

[*Note:* the Convention was adopted in Vienna on March 21, 1986.

Status since May 2018: 39 signatories and 44 parties. Pursuant to Article 85 international organizations, which are party to the Convention, are not counted for the purposes of the entry into force of the Convention. The Convention is not yet entered into force]

The Parties to the present Convention,

Considering the fundamental role of treaties in the history of international relations,
Recognizing the consensual nature of treaties and their ever-increasing importance as a source of international law,
Noting that the principles of free consent and of good faith and the *pacta sunt servanda* rule are universally recognized,
Affirming the importance of enhancing the process of codification and progressive development of international law at a universal level,
Believing that the codification and progressive development of the rules relating to treaties between States and international organizations or between international organizations are means of enhancing legal order in international relations and of serving the purposes of the United Nations,
Having in mind the principles of international law embodied in the Charter of the United Nations, such as the principles of the equal rights and self-determination of peoples, of the sovereign equality and independence of all States, of non-interference in the domestic affairs of States, of the prohibition of the threat or use of force and of universal respect for, and observance of, human rights and fundamental freedoms for all,
Bearing in mind the provisions of the Vienna Convention on the Law of Treaties of 1969,
Recognizing the relationship between the law of treaties between States and the law of treaties between States and international organizations or between international organizations,
Considering the importance of treaties between States and international organizations or between international organizations as a useful means of developing international relations and ensuring conditions for peaceful cooperation among nations, whatever their constitutional and social systems,
Having in mind the specific features of treaties to which international organizations are parties as subjects of international law distinct from States,
Noting that international organizations possess the capacity to conclude treaties, which is necessary for the exercise of their functions and the fulfilment of their purposes,
Recognizing that the practice of international organizations in concluding treaties with States or between themselves should be in accordance with their constituent instruments,

Affirming that nothing in the present Convention should be interpreted as affecting those relations between an international organization and its members which are regulated by the rules of the organization,

Affirming also that disputes concerning treaties, like other international disputes, should be settled, in conformity with the Charter of the United Nations, by peaceful means and in conformity with the principles of justice and international law,

Affirming also that the rules of customary international law will continue to govern questions not regulated by the provisions of the present Convention,

Have agreed as follows:

PART I - INTRODUCTION

Article 1 - Scope of the present Convention

The present Convention applies to:

(*a*) treaties between one or more States and one or more international organizations, and

(*b*) treaties between international organizations.

Article 2 - Use of terms

1. For the purposes of the present Convention:

(*a*) "treaty" means an international agreement governed by international law and concluded in written form:

  (i) between one or more States and one or more international organizations; or

  (ii) between international organizations, whether that agreement is embodied in a single instrument or in two or more related instruments and whatever its particular designation;

(*b*) "ratification" means the international act so named whereby a State establishes on the international plane its consent to be bound by a treaty;

(*b* bis) "act of formal confirmation" means an international act corresponding to that of ratification by a State, whereby an international organization establishes on the international plane its consent to be bound by a treaty;

(*b* ter) "acceptance", "approval" and "accession" mean in each case the international act so named whereby a State or an international organization establishes on the international plane its consent to be bound by a treaty;

(*c*) "full powers" means a document emanating from the competent authority of a State or from the competent organ of an international organization designating a person or persons to represent the State or the organization for negotiating, adopting or authenticating the text of a treaty, for expressing the consent of the State or of the organization to be bound by a treaty, or for accomplishing any other act with respect to a treaty;

(*d*) "reservation" means a unilateral statement, however phrased or named, made by a State or by an international organization when signing, ratifying, formally confirming, accepting, approving or acceding to a treaty, whereby it purports to exclude or to modify the legal effect of certain provisions of the treaty in their application to that State or to that organization;

(*e*) "negotiating State" and "negotiating organization" mean respectively:

  (i) a State, or

  (ii) an international organization, which took part in the drawing up and adoption of the text of the treaty;

(*f*) "contracting State" and "contracting organization" mean respectively:
  (i) a State, or
  (ii) an international organization, which has consented to be bound by the treaty, whether or not the treaty has entered into force;
(*g*) "party" means a State or an international organization which has consented to be bound by the treaty and for which the treaty is in force;
(*h*) "third State" and "third organization" mean respectively:
  (i) a State, or
  (ii) an international organization, not a party to the treaty;
(*i*) "international organization" means an intergovernmental organization;
(*j*) "rules of the organization" means, in particular, the constituent instruments, decisions and resolutions adopted in accordance with them, and established practice of the organization.

2. The provisions of paragraph 1 regarding the use of terms in the present Convention are without prejudice to the use of those terms or to the meanings which may be given to them in the internal law of any State or in the rules of any international organization.

Article 3 - International agreements not within the scope of the present Convention

The fact that the present Convention does not apply:
(i) to international agreements to which one or more States, one or more international organizations and one or more subjects of international law other than States or organizations are parties;
(ii) to international agreements to which one or more international organizations and one or more subjects of international law other than States or organizations are parties;
(iii) to international agreements not in written form between one or more States and one or more international organizations, or between international organizations; or
(iv) to international agreements between subjects of international law other than States or international organizations;

shall not affect:
  (*a*) the legal force of such agreements;
  (*b*) the application to them of any of the rules set forth in the present Convention to which they would be subject under international law independently of the Convention;
  (*c*) the application of the Convention to the relations between States and international organizations or to the relations of organizations as between themselves, when those relations are governed by international agreements to which other subjects of international law are also parties.

Article 4 - Non-retroactivity of the present Convention

Without prejudice to the application of any rules set forth in the present Convention to which treaties between one or more States and one or more international organizations or between international organizations would be subject under international law independently of the Convention, the Convention applies only to such treaties concluded after the entry into force of the present Convention with regard to those States and those organizations.

Article 5 - Treaties constituting international organizations and treaties adopted within an international organization

The present Convention applies to any treaty between one or more States and one or more international organizations which is the constituent instrument of an international organization and to any treaty adopted within an international organization, without prejudice to any relevant rules of the organization.

PART II – CONCLUSION AND ENTRY INTO FORCE OF TREATIES

SECTION 1. CONCLUSION OF TREATIES

Article 6 - Capacity of international organizations to conclude treaties
The capacity of an international organization to conclude treaties is governed by the rules of that organization.

Article 7- Full powers
1. A person is considered as representing a State for the purpose of adopting or authenticating the text of a treaty or for the purpose of expressing the consent of the State to be bound by a treaty if:
(*a*) that person produces appropriate full powers; or
(*b*) it appears from practice or from other circumstances that it was the intention of the States and international organizations concerned to consider that person as representing the State for such purposes without having to produce full powers.
2. In virtue of their functions and without having to produce full powers, the following are considered as representing their State:
(*a*) Heads of State, Heads of Government and Ministers for Foreign Affairs, for the purpose of performing all acts relating to the conclusion of a treaty between one or more States and one or more international organizations;
(*b*) representatives accredited by States to an international conference, for the purpose of adopting the text of a treaty between States and international organizations;
(*c*) representatives accredited by States to an international organization or one of its organs, for the purpose of adopting the text of a treaty in that organization or organ;
(*d*) heads of permanent missions to an international organization, for the purpose of adopting the text of a treaty between the accrediting States and that organization.
3. A person is considered as representing an international organization for the purpose of adopting or authenticating the text of a treaty, or expressing the consent of that organization to be bound by a treaty, if:
(*a*) that person produces appropriate full powers; or
(*b*) it appears from the circumstances that it was the intention of the States and international organizations concerned to consider that person as representing the organization for such purposes, in accordance with the rules of the organization, without having to produce full powers.

Article 8 - Subsequent confirmation of an act performed without authorization
An act relating to the conclusion of a treaty performed by a person who cannot be considered under article 7 as authorized to represent a State or an international organization for that purpose is without legal effect unless afterwards confirmed by that State or that organization.

Article 9 - Adoption of the text
1. The adoption of the text of a treaty takes place by the consent of all the States and international organizations or, as the case may be, all the organizations participating in its drawing up except as provided in paragraph 2.
2. The adoption of the text of a treaty at an international conference takes place in accordance with the procedure agreed upon by the participants in that conference. If, however, no agreement is reached on any such procedure, the adoption of the text shall take place by the vote of two thirds of the participants present and voting unless by the same majority they shall decide to apply a different rule.

Article 10 - Authentication of the text

1. The text of a treaty between one or more States and one or more international organizations is established as authentic and definitive:

(*a*) by such procedure as may be provided for in the text or agreed upon by the States and organizations participating in its drawing up; or

(*b*) failing such procedure, by the signature, signature *ad referendum* or initialling by the representatives of those States and those organizations of the text of the treaty or of the Final Act of a conference incorporating the text.

2. The text of a treaty between international organizations is established as authentic and definitive:

(*a*) by such procedure as may be provided for in the text or agreed upon by the organizations participating in its drawing up; or

(*b*) failing such procedure, by the signature, signature *ad referendum* or initialling by the representatives of those States and those organizations of the text of the treaty or of the Final Act of a conference incorporating the text.

Article 11 - Means of expressing consent to be bound by a treaty

1 The consent of a State to be bound by a treaty may be expressed by signature, exchange of instruments constituting a treaty, ratification, acceptance, approval or accession, or by any other means if so agreed.

2 The consent of an international organization to be bound by a treaty may be expressed by signature, exchange of instruments constituting a treaty, act of formal confirmation, acceptance, approval or accession, or by any other means if so agreed.

Article 12 - Consent to be bound by a treaty expressed by signature

1. The consent of a State or of an international organization to be bound by a treaty is expressed by the signature of the representative of that State or of that organization when:

(*a*) the treaty provides that signature shall have that effect;

(*b*) it is otherwise established that the negotiating States and negotiating organizations or, as the case may be, the negotiating organizations were agreed that signature should have that effect; or

(*c*) the intention of the State or organization to give that effect to the signature appears from the full powers of its representative or was expressed during the negotiation.

2. For the purposes of paragraph 1:

(*a*) the initialling of a text constitutes a signature of the treaty when it is established that the negotiating States and negotiating organizations or, as the case may be, the negotiating organizations so agreed;

(*b*) the signature *ad referendum* of a treaty by the representative of a State or an international organization, if confirmed by his State or organization, constitutes a full signature of the treaty.

Article 13 - Consent to be bound by a treaty expressed by an exchange of instruments constituting a treaty

The consent of States or of international organizations to be bound by a treaty constituted by instruments exchanged between them is expressed by that exchange when:

(*a*) the instruments provide that their exchange shall have that effect; or

(*b*) it is otherwise established that those States and those organizations or, as the case may be, those organizations were agreed that the exchange of instruments should have that effect.

Article 14 - Consent to be bound by a treaty expressed by ratification, act of formal confirmation, acceptance or approval

1. The consent of a State to be bound by a treaty is expressed by ratification when:
(*a*) the treaty provides for such consent to be expressed by means of ratification;
(*b*) it is otherwise established that the negotiating States and negotiating organizations were agreed that ratification should be required;
(*c*) the representative of the State has signed the treaty subject to ratification; or
(*d*) the intention of the State to sign the treaty subject to ratification appears from the full powers of its representative or was expressed during the negotiation.

2. The consent of an international organization to be bound by a treaty is expressed by an act of formal confirmation when:
(*a*) the treaty provides for such consent to be expressed by means of an act of formal confirmation;
(*b*) it is otherwise established that the negotiating States and negotiating organizations or, as the case may be, the negotiating organizations were agreed that an act of formal confirmation should be required;
(*c*) the representative of the organization has signed the treaty subject to an act of formal confirmation; or
(*d*) the intention of the organization to sign the treaty subject to an act of formal confirmation appears from the full powers of its representative or was expressed during the negotiation.

3. The consent of a State or of an international organization to be bound by a treaty is expressed by acceptance or approval under conditions similar to those which apply to ratification or, as the case may be, to an act of formal confirmation.

Article 15 - Consent to be bound by a treaty expressed by accession

The consent of a State or of an international organization to be bound by a treaty is expressed by accession when:
(*a*) the treaty provides that such consent may be expressed by that State or that organization by means of accession;
(*b*) it is otherwise established that the negotiating States and negotiating organizations or, as the case may be, the negotiating organizations were agreed that such consent may be expressed by that State or that organization by means of accession; or
(*c*) all the parties have subsequently agreed that such consent may be expressed by that State or that organization by means of accession.

Article 16 - Exchange or deposit of instruments of ratification, formal confirmation, acceptance, approval or accession

1. Unless the treaty otherwise provides, instruments of ratification, instruments relating to an act of formal confirmation or instruments of acceptance, approval or accession establish the consent of a State or of an international organization to be bound by a treaty between one or more States and one or more international organizations upon:
(*a*) their exchange between the contracting States and contracting organizations;
(*b*) their deposit with the depositary; or
(*c*) their notification to the contracting States and to the contracting organizations or to the depositary, if so agreed.

2. Unless the treaty otherwise provides, instruments relating to an act of formal confirmation or instruments of acceptance, approval or accession establish the consent of an international organization to be bound by a treaty between international organizations upon:
(*a*) their exchange between the contracting organizations;
(*b*) their deposit with the depositary; or
(*c*) their notification to the contracting organizations or to the depositary, if so agreed.

Article 17 - Consent to be bound by part of a treaty and choice of differing provisions
1. Without prejudice to articles 19 to 23, the consent of a State or of an international organization to be bound by part of a treaty is effective only if the treaty so permits, or if the contracting States and contracting organizations or, as the case may be, the contracting organizations so agree.
2. The consent of a State or of an international organization to be bound by a treaty which permits a choice between differing provisions is effective only if it is made clear to which of the provisions the consent relates.

Article 18 - Obligation not to defeat the object and purpose of a treaty prior to its entry into force
A State or an international organization is obliged to refrain from acts which would defeat the object and purpose of a treaty when:
(*a*) that State or that organization has signed the treaty or has exchanged instruments constituting the treaty subject to ratification, act of formal confirmation, acceptance or approval, until that State or that organization shall have made its intention clear not to become a party to the treaty; or
(*b*) that State or that organization has expressed its consent to be bound by the treaty, pending the entry into force of the treaty and provided that such entry into force is not unduly delayed.

SECTION 2. RESERVATIONS

Article 19 - Formulation of reservations
A State or an international organization may, when signing, ratifying, formally confirming, accepting, approving or acceding to a treaty, formulate a reservation unless:
(*a*) the reservation is prohibited by the treaty;
(*b*) the treaty provides that only specified reservations, which do not include the reservation in question, may be made; or
(*c*) in cases not falling under subparagraphs (a) and (b), the reservation is incompatible with the object and purpose of the treaty.

Article 20 - Acceptance of and objection to reservations
1. A reservation expressly authorized by a treaty does not require any subsequent acceptance by the contracting States and contracting organizations or, as the case may be, by the contracting organizations unless the treaty so provides.
2. When it appears from the limited number of the negotiating States and negotiating organizations or, as the case may be, of the negotiating organizations and the object and purpose of a treaty that the application of the treaty in its entirety between all the parties is an essential condition of the consent of each one to be bound by the treaty, a reservation requires acceptance by all the parties.
3. When a treaty is a constituent instrument of an international organization and unless it otherwise provides, a reservation requires the acceptance of the competent organ of that organization.
4. In cases not falling under the preceding paragraphs and unless the treaty otherwise provides:

(*a*) acceptance of a reservation by a contracting State or by a contracting organization constitutes the reserving State or international organization a party to the treaty in relation to the accepting State or organization if or when the treaty is in force for the reserving State or organization and for the accepting State or organization;
(*b*) an objection by a contracting State or by a contracting organization to a reservation does not preclude the entry into force of the treaty as between the objecting State or international organization and the reserving State or organization unless a contrary intention is definitely expressed by the objecting State or organization;
(*c*) an act expressing the consent of a State or of an international organization to be bound by the treaty and containing a reservation is effective as soon as at least one contracting State or one contracting organization has accepted the reservation.

5. For the purposes of paragraphs 2 and 4, and unless the treaty otherwise provides, a reservation is considered to have been accepted by a State or an international organization if it shall have raised no objection to the reservation by the end of a period of twelve months after it was notified of the reservation or by the date on which it expressed its consent to be bound by the treaty, whichever is later.

Article 21 - Legal effects of reservations and of objections to reservations

1. A reservation established with regard to another party in accordance with articles 19, 20 and 23:
(*a*) modifies for the reserving State or international organization in its relations with that other party the provisions of the treaty to which the reservation relates to the extent of the reservation; and
(*b*) modifies those provisions to the same extent for that other party in its relations with the reserving State or international organization.

2. The reservation does not modify the provisions of the treaty for the other parties to the treaty inter se.

3. When a State or an international organization objecting to a reservation has not opposed the entry into force of the treaty between itself and the reserving State or organization, the provisions to which the reservation relates do not apply as between the reserving State or organization and the objecting State or organization to the extent of the reservation.

Article 22 - Withdrawal of reservations and of objections to reservations

1. Unless the treaty otherwise provides, a reservation may be withdrawn at any time and the consent of a State or of an international organization which has accepted the reservation is not required for its withdrawal.

2. Unless the treaty otherwise provides, an objection to a reservation may be withdrawn at any time.

3. Unless the treaty otherwise provides, or it is otherwise agreed:
(*a*) the withdrawal of a reservation becomes operative in relation to a contracting State or a contracting organization only when notice of it has been received by that State or that organization;
(*b*) the withdrawal of an objection to a reservation becomes operative only when notice of it has been received by the State or international organization which formulated the reservation.

Article 23 - Procedure regarding reservations

1. A reservation, an express acceptance of a reservation and an objection to a reservation must be formulated in writing and communicated to the contracting States and contracting organizations and other States and international organizations entitled to become parties to the treaty.

2. If formulated when signing the treaty subject to ratification, act of formal confirmation, acceptance or approval, a reservation must be formally confirmed by the reserving State or international organ-

ization when expressing its consent to be bound by the treaty. In such a case the reservation shall be considered as having been made on the date of its confirmation.
3. An express acceptance of, or an objection to, a reservation made previously to confirmation of the reservation does not itself require confirmation.
4. The withdrawal of a reservation or of an objection to a reservation must be formulated in writing.

SECTION 3. ENTRY INTO FORCE AND PROVISIONAL APPLICATION OF TREATIES

Article 24 - Entry into force
1. A treaty enters into force in such manner and upon such date as it may provide or as the negotiating States and negotiating organizations or, as the case may be, the negotiating organizations may agree.
2. Failing any such provision or agreement, a treaty enters into force as soon as consent to be bound by the treaty has been established for all the negotiating States and negotiating organizations or, as the case may be, all the negotiating organizations.
3. When the consent of a State or of an international organization to be bound by a treaty is established on a date after the treaty has come into force, the treaty enters into force for that State or that organization on that date, unless the treaty otherwise provides.
4. The provisions of a treaty regulating the authentication of its text, the establishment of consent to be bound by the treaty, the manner or date of its entry into force, reservations, the functions of the depositary and other matters arising necessarily before the entry into force of the treaty apply from the time of the adoption of its text.

Article 25 - Provisional application
1. A treaty or a part of a treaty is applied provisionally pending its entry into force if:
(*a*) the treaty itself so provides; or
(*b*) the negotiating States and negotiating organizations or, as the case may be, the negotiating organizations have in some other manner so agreed.
2. Unless the treaty otherwise provides or the negotiating States and negotiating organizations or, as the case may be, the negotiating organizations have otherwise agreed, the provisional application of a treaty or a part of a treaty with respect to a State or an international organization shall be terminated if that State or that organization notifies the States and organizations with regard to which the treaty is being applied provisionally of its intention not to become a party to the treaty.

PART III – OBSERVANCE, APPLICATION AND INTERPRETATION OF TREATIES

SECTION 1. OBSERVANCE OF TREATIES

Article 26 - *Pacta sunt servanda*
Every treaty in force is binding upon the parties to it and must be performed by them in good faith.

Article 27 - Internal law of States, rules of international organizations and observance of treaties
1. A State party to a treaty may not invoke the provisions of its internal law as justification for its failure to perform the treaty.
2. An international organization party to a treaty may not invoke the rules of the organization as justification for its failure to perform the treaty.
3. The rules contained in the preceding paragraphs are without prejudice to article 46.

SECTION 2. APPLICATION OF TREATIES

Article 28 - Non-retroactivity of treaties
Unless a different intention appears from the treaty or is otherwise established, its provisions do not bind a party in relation to any act or fact which took place or any situation which ceased to exist before the date of the entry into force of the treaty with respect to that party.

Article 29 - Territorial scope of treaties
Unless a different intention appears from the treaty or is otherwise established, a treaty between one or more States and one or more international organizations is binding upon each State party in respect of its entire territory.

Article 30 - Application of successive treaties relating to the same subject matter
1. The rights and obligations of States and international organizations parties to successive treaties relating to the same subject matter shall be determined in accordance with the following paragraphs.
2. When a treaty specifies that it is subject to, or that it is not to be considered as incompatible with, an earlier or later treaty, the provisions of that other treaty prevail.
3. When all the parties to the earlier treaty are parties also to the later treaty but the earlier treaty is not terminated or suspended in operation under article 59, the earlier treaty applies to the extent that its provisions are compatible with those of the later treaty.
4. When the parties to the later treaty do not include all the parties to the earlier one:
(*a*) as between two parties, each of which is a party to both treaties, the same rule applies as in paragraph 3;
(*b*) as between a party to both treaties and a party to only one of the treaties, the treaty to which both are parties governs their mutual rights and obligations.
5. Paragraph 4 is without prejudice to article 41, or to any question of the termination or suspension of the operation of a treaty under article 60 or to any question of responsibility which may arise for a State or for an international organization from the conclusion or application of a treaty the provisions of which are incompatible with its obligations towards a State or an organization under another treaty.
6. The preceding paragraphs are without prejudice to the fact that, in the event of a conflict between obligations under the Charter of the United Nations and obligations under a treaty, the obligations under the Charter shall prevail.

SECTION 3. INTERPRETATION OF TREATIES

Article 31 - General rule of interpretation
1. A treaty shall be interpreted in good faith in accordance with the ordinary meaning to be given to the terms of the treaty in their context and in the light of its object and purpose.
2. The context for the purpose of the interpretation of a treaty shall comprise, in addition to the text, including its preamble and annexes:
(*a*) any agreement relating to the treaty which was made between all the parties in connection with the conclusion of the treaty;
(*b*) any instrument which was made by one or more parties in connection with the conclusion of the treaty and accepted by the other parties as an instrument related to the treaty.

3. There shall be taken into account, together with the context:

(*a*) any subsequent agreement between the parties regarding the interpretation of the treaty or the application of its provisions;

(*b*) any subsequent practice in the application of the treaty which establishes the agreement of the parties regarding its interpretation;

(*c*) any relevant rules of international law applicable in the relations between the parties.

4. A special meaning shall be given to a term if it is established that the parties so intended.

Article 32 - Supplementary means of interpretation

Recourse may be had to supplementary means of interpretation, including the preparatory work of the treaty and the circumstances of its conclusion, in order to confirm the meaning resulting from the application of article 31, or to determine the meaning when the interpretation according to article 31:

(*a*) leaves the meaning ambiguous or obscure; or

(*b*) leads to a result which is manifestly absurd or unreasonable.

Article 33 - Interpretation of treaties authenticated in two or more languages

1. When a treaty has been authenticated in two or more languages, the text is equally authoritative in each language, unless the treaty provides or the parties agree that, in case of divergence, a particular text shall prevail.

2. A version of the treaty in a language other than one of those in which the text was authenticated shall be considered an authentic text only if the treaty so provides or the parties so agree.

3. The terms of a treaty are presumed to have the same meaning in each authentic text.

4. Except where a particular text prevails in accordance with paragraph 1, when a comparison of the authentic texts discloses a difference of meaning which the application of articles 31 and 32 does not remove, the meaning which best reconciles the texts, having regard to the object and purpose of the treaty, shall be adopted.

SECTION 4. TREATIES AND THIRD STATES OR THIRD ORGANIZATIONS

Article 34 - General rule regarding third States and third organizations

A treaty does not create either obligations or rights for a third State or a third organization without the consent of that State or that organization.

Article 35 - Treaties providing for obligations for third States or third organizations

An obligation arises for a third State or a third organization from a provision of a treaty if the parties to the treaty intend the provision to be the means of establishing the obligation and the third State or the third organization expressly accepts that obligation in writing. Acceptance by the third organization of such an obligation shall be governed by the rules of that organization.

Article 36 - Treaties providing for rights for third States or third organizations

1. A right arises for a third State from a provision of a treaty if the parties to the treaty intend the provision to accord that right either to the third State, or to a group of States to which it belongs, or to all States, and the third State assents thereto. Its assent shall be presumed so long as the contrary is not indicated, unless the treaty otherwise provides.

2. A right arises for a third organization from a provision of a treaty if the parties to the treaty intend the provision to accord that right either to the third organization, or to a group of international organizations to which it belongs, or to all organizations, and the third organization assents thereto. Its assent shall be governed by the rules of the organization.
3. A State or an international organization exercising a right in accordance with paragraph 1 or 2 shall comply with the conditions for its exercise provided for in the treaty or established in conformity with the treaty.

Article 37 - Revocation or modification of obligations or rights of third States or third organizations
1. When an obligation has arisen for a third State or a third organization in conformity with article 35, the obligation may be revoked or modified only with the consent of the parties to the treaty and of the third State or the third organization, unless it is established that they had otherwise agreed.
2. When a right has arisen for a third State or a third organization in conformity with article 36, the right may not be revoked or modified by the parties if it is established that the right was intended not to be revocable or subject to modification without the consent of the third State or the third organization.
3. The consent of an international organization party to the treaty or of a third organization, as provided for in the foregoing paragraphs, shall be governed by the rules of that organization.

Article 38 - Rules in a treaty becoming binding on third States or third organizations through international custom
Nothing in articles 34 to 37 precludes a rule set forth in a treaty from becoming binding upon a third State or a third organization as a customary rule of international law, recognized as such.

PART IV – AMENDMENT AND MODIFICATION OF TREATIES

Article 39 - General rule regarding the amendment of treaties
1. A treaty may be amended by agreement between the parties. The rules laid down in Part II apply to such an agreement except insofar as the treaty may otherwise provide.
2. The consent of an international organization to an agreement provided for in paragraph 1 shall be governed by the rules of that organization.

Article 40 - Amendment of multilateral treaties
1. Unless the treaty otherwise provides, the amendment of multilateral treaties shall be governed by the following paragraphs.
2. Any proposal to amend a multilateral treaty as between all the parties must be notified to all the contracting States and all the contracting organizations, each one of which shall have the right to take part in:
(*a*) the decision as to the action to be taken in regard to such proposal;
(*b*) the negotiation and conclusion of any agreement for the amendment of the treaty.
3. Every State or international organization entitled to become a party to the treaty shall also be entitled to become a party to the treaty as amended.
4. The amending agreement does not bind any State or international organization already a party to the treaty which does not become a party to the amending agreement; article 30, paragraph 4 (*b*), applies in relation to such State or organization.

5. Any State or international organization which becomes a party to the treaty after the entry into force of the amending agreement shall, failing an expression of a different intention by that State or that organization:
(*a*) be considered as a party to the treaty as amended; and
(*b*) be considered as a party to the unamended treaty in relation to any party to the treaty not bound by the amending agreement.

Article 41 - Agreements to modify multilateral treaties between certain of the parties only
1. Two or more of the parties to a multilateral treaty may conclude an agreement to modify the treaty as between themselves alone if:
(*a*) the possibility of such a modification is provided for by the treaty; or
(*b*) the modification in question is not prohibited by the treaty and:
  (i) does not affect the enjoyment by the other parties of their rights under the treaty or the performance of their obligations;
  (ii) does not relate to a provision, derogation from which is incompatible with the effective execution of the object and purpose of the treaty as a whole.
2. Unless in a case falling under paragraph 1 (*a*) the treaty otherwise provides, the parties in question shall notify the other parties of their intention to conclude the agreement and of the modification to the treaty for which it provides.

PART V – INVALIDITY, TERMINATION AND SUSPENSION OF THE OPERATION OF TREATIES

SECTION 1. GENERAL PROVISIONS

Article 42 - Validity and continuance in force of treaties
1. The validity of a treaty or of the consent of a State or an international organization to be bound by a treaty may be impeached only through the application of the present Convention.
2. The termination of a treaty, its denunciation or the withdrawal of a party, may take place only as a result of the application of the provisions of the treaty or of the present Convention. The same rule applies to suspension of the operation of a treaty.

Article 43 - Obligations imposed by international law independently of a treaty
The invalidity, termination or denunciation of a treaty, the withdrawal of a party from it, or the suspension of its operation, as a result of the application of the present Convention or of the provisions of the treaty, shall not in any way impair the duty of any State or of any international organization to fulfil any obligation embodied in the treaty to which that State or that organization would be subject under international law independently of the treaty.

Article 44 - Separability of treaty provisions
1. A right of a party, provided for in a treaty or arising under article 56, to denounce, withdraw from or suspend the operation of the treaty may be exercised only with respect to the whole treaty unless the treaty otherwise provides or the parties otherwise agree.
2. A ground for invalidating, terminating, withdrawing from or suspending the operation of a treaty recognized in the present Convention may be invoked only with respect to the whole treaty except as provided in the following paragraphs or in article 60.

3. If the ground relates solely to particular clauses, it may be invoked only with respect to those clauses where:
(*a*) the said clauses are separable from the remainder of the treaty with regard to their application;
(*b*) it appears from the treaty or is otherwise established that acceptance of those clauses was not an essential basis of the consent of the other party or parties to be bound by the treaty as a whole; and
(*c*) continued performance of the remainder of the treaty would not be unjust.
4. In cases falling under articles 49 and 50, the State or international organization entitled to invoke the fraud or corruption may do so with respect either to the whole treaty or, subject to paragraph 3, to the particular clauses alone.
5. In cases falling under articles 51, 52 and 53, no separation of the provisions of the treaty is permitted.

Article 45 - Loss of a right to invoke a ground for invalidating, terminating, withdrawing from or suspending the operation of a treaty
1. A State may no longer invoke a ground for invalidating, terminating, withdrawing from or suspending the operation of a treaty under articles 46 to 50 or articles 60 and 62 if, after becoming aware of the facts:
(*a*) it shall have expressly agreed that the treaty is valid or remains in force or continues in operation, as the case may be; or
(*b*) it must by reason of its conduct be considered as having acquiesced in the validity of the treaty or in its maintenance in force or in operation, as the case may be.
2. An international organization may no longer invoke a ground for invalidating, terminating, withdrawing from or suspending the operation of a treaty under articles 46 to 50 or articles 60 and 62 if, after becoming aware of the facts:
(*a*) it shall have expressly agreed that the treaty is valid or remains in force or continues in operation, as the case may be; or
(*b*) it must by reason of the conduct of the competent organ be considered as having renounced the right to invoke that ground.

SECTION 2 - INVALIDITY OF TREATIES

Article 46 - Provisions of internal law of a State and rules of an international organization regarding competence to conclude treaties
1. A State may not invoke the fact that its consent to be bound by a treaty has been expressed in violation of a provision of its internal law regarding competence to conclude treaties as invalidating its consent unless that violation was manifest and concerned a rule of its internal law of fundamental importance.
2. An international organization may not invoke the fact that its consent to be bound by a treaty has been expressed in violation of the rules of the organization regarding competence to conclude treaties as invalidating its consent unless that violation was manifest and concerned a rule of fundamental importance.
3. A violation is manifest if it would be objectively evident to any State or any international organization conducting itself in the matter in accordance with the normal practice of States and, where appropriate, of international organizations and in good faith.

Article 47 - Specific restrictions on authority to express the consent of a State or an international organization

If the authority of a representative to express the consent of a State or of an international organization to be bound by a particular treaty has been made subject to a specific restriction, his omission to observe that restriction may not be invoked as invalidating the consent expressed by him unless the restriction was notified to the negotiating States and negotiating organizations prior to his expressing such consent.

Article 48 - Error

1. A State or an international organization may invoke an error in a treaty as invalidating its consent to be bound by the treaty if the error relates to a fact or situation which was assumed by that State or that organization to exist at the time when the treaty was concluded and formed an essential basis of the consent of that State or that organization to be bound by the treaty.
2. Paragraph 1 shall not apply if the State or international organization in question contributed by its own conduct to the error or if the circumstances were such as to put that State or that organization on notice of a possible error.
3. An error relating only to the wording of the text of a treaty does not affect its validity; article 80 then applies.

Article 49 - Fraud

A State or an international organization induced to conclude a treaty by the fraudulent conduct of a negotiating State or a negotiating organization may invoke the fraud as invalidating its consent to be bound by the treaty.

Article 50 - Corruption of a representative of a State or of an international organization

A State or an international organization the expression of whose consent to be bound by a treaty has been procured through the corruption of its representative directly or indirectly by a negotiating State or a negotiating organization may invoke such corruption as invalidating its consent to be bound by the treaty.

Article 51 - Coercion of a representative of a State or of an international organization

The expression by a State or an international organization of consent to be bound by a treaty which has been procured by the coercion of the representative of that State or that organization through acts or threats directed against him shall be without any legal effect.

Article 52 - Coercion of a State or of an international organization by the threat or use of force

A treaty is void if its conclusion has been procured by the threat or use of force in violation of the principles of international law embodied in the Chatter of the United Nations.

Article 53 - Treaties conflicting with a peremptory norm of general international law (*jus cogens*)

A treaty is void if, at the time of its conclusion, it conflicts with a peremptory norm of general international law. For the purposes of the present Convention, a peremptory norm of general international law is a norm accepted and recognized by the international community of States as a whole as a norm from which no derogation is permitted and which can be modified only by a subsequent norm of general international law having the same character.

SECTION 3 - TERMINATION AND SUSPENSION OF THE OPERATION OF TREATIES

Article 54 - Termination of or withdrawal from a treaty under its provisions or by consent of the parties

The termination of a treaty or the withdrawal of a party may take place:
(*a*) in conformity with the provisions of the treaty; or
(*b*) at any time by consent of all the parties after consultation with the contracting States and contracting organizations.

Article 55 - Reduction of the parties to a multilateral treaty below the number necessary for its entry into force

Unless the treaty otherwise provides, a multilateral treaty does not terminate by reason only of the fact that the number of the parties falls below the number necessary for its entry into force.

Article 56 - Denunciation of or withdrawal from a treaty containing no provision regarding termination, denunciation or withdrawal

1. A treaty which contains no provision regarding its termination and which does not provide for denunciation or withdrawal is not subject to denunciation or withdrawal unless:
(*a*) it is established that the parties intended to admit the possibility of denunciation or withdrawal; or
(*b*) a right of denunciation or withdrawal may be implied by the nature of the treaty.
2. A party shall give not less than twelve months' notice of its intention to denounce or withdraw from a treaty under paragraph 1.

Article 57- Suspension of the operation of a treaty under its provisions or by consent of the parties

The operation of a treaty in regard to all the parties or to a particular party may be suspended:
(*a*) in conformity with the provisions of the treaty; or
(*b*) at any time by consent of all the parties after consultation with the contracting States and contracting organizations.

Article 58 - Suspension of the operation of a multilateral treaty by agreement between certain of the parties only

1. Two or more parties to a multilateral treaty may conclude an agreement to suspend the operation of provisions of the treaty, temporarily and as between themselves alone, if:
(*a*) the possibility of such a suspension is provided for by the treaty; or
(*b*) the suspension in question is not prohibited by the treaty and:
  (i) does not affect the enjoyment by the other parties of their rights under the treaty or the performance of their obligations;
  (ii) is not incompatible with the object and purpose of the treaty.
2. Unless in a case falling under paragraph 1 (*a*) the treaty otherwise provides, the parties in question shall notify the other parties of their intention to conclude the agreement and of those provisions of the treaty the operation of which they intend to suspend.

Article 59 - Termination or suspension of the operation of a treaty implied by conclusion of a later treaty

1. A treaty shall be considered as terminated if all the parties to it conclude a later treaty relating to the same subject matter and:

(*a*) it appears from the later treaty or is otherwise established that the parties intended that the matter should be governed by that treaty; or
(*b*) the provisions of the later treaty are so far incompatible with those of the earlier one that the two treaties are not capable of being applied at the same time.

2. The earlier treaty shall be considered as only suspended in operation if it appears from the later treaty or is otherwise established that such was the intention of the parties.

Article 60 - Termination or suspension of the operation of a treaty as a consequence of its breach

1. A material breach of a bilateral treaty by one of the parties entitles the other to invoke the breach as a ground for terminating the treaty or suspending its operation in whole or in part.
2. A material breach of a multilateral treaty by one of the parties entitles:
(*a*) the other parties by unanimous agreement to suspend the operation of the treaty in whole or in part or to terminate it either:
    (i) in the relations between themselves and the defaulting State or international organization; or
    (ii) as between all the parties;
(*b*) a party specially affected by the breach to invoke it as a ground for suspending the operation of the treaty in whole or in part in the relations between itself and the defaulting State or international organization;
(*c*) any party other than the defaulting State or international organization to invoke the breach as a ground for suspending the operation of the treaty in whole or in part with respect to itself if the treaty is of such a character that a material breach of its provisions by one party radically changes the position of every party with respect to the further performance of its obligations under the treaty.
3. A material breach of a treaty, for the purposes of this article, consists in:
(*a*) a repudiation of the treaty not sanctioned by the present Convention; or
(*b*) the violation of a provision essential to the accomplishment of the object or purpose of the treaty.
4. The foregoing paragraphs are without prejudice to any provision in the treaty applicable in the event of a breach.
5. Paragraphs 1 to 3 do not apply to provisions relating to the protection of the human person contained in treaties of a humanitarian character, in particular to provisions prohibiting any form of reprisals against persons protected by such treaties.

Article 61 - Supervening impossibility of performance

1. A party may invoke the impossibility of performing a treaty as a ground for terminating or withdrawing from it if the impossibility results from the permanent disappearance or destruction of an object indispensable for the execution of the treaty. If the impossibility is temporary, it may be invoked only as a ground for suspending the operation of the treaty.
2. Impossibility of performance may not be invoked by a party as a ground for terminating, withdrawing from or suspending the operation of a treaty if the impossibility is the result of a breach by that party either of an obligation under the treaty or of any other international obligation owed to any other party to the treaty.

Article 62 - Fundamental change of circumstances

1. A fundamental change of circumstances which has occurred with regard to those existing at the time of the conclusion of a treaty, and which was not foreseen by the parties, may not be invoked as a ground for terminating or withdrawing from the treaty unless:

(*a*) the existence of those circumstances constituted an essential basis of the consent of the parties to be bound by the treaty; and
(*b*) the effect of the change is radically to transform the extent of obligations still to be performed under the treaty.
2. A fundamental change of circumstances may not be invoked as a ground for terminating or withdrawing from a treaty between two or more States and one or more international organizations if the treaty establishes a boundary.
3. A fundamental change of circumstances may not be invoked as a ground for terminating or withdrawing from a treaty if the fundamental change is the result of a breach by the party invoking it either of an obligation under the treaty or of any other international obligation owed to any other party to the treaty.
4. If, under the foregoing paragraphs, a party may invoke a fundamental change of circumstances as a ground for terminating or withdrawing from a treaty it may also invoke the change as a ground for suspending the operation of the treaty.

Article 63 - Severance of diplomatic or consular relations
The severance of diplomatic or consular relations between States Parties to a treaty between two or more States and one or more international organizations does not affect the legal relations established between those States by the treaty except insofar as the existence of diplomatic or consular relations is indispensable for the application of the treaty.

Article 64 - Emergence of a new peremptory norm of general international law (*jus cogens*)
If a new peremptory norm of general international law emerges, any existing treaty which is in conflict with that norm becomes void and terminates.

SECTION 4. PROCEDURE

Article 65 - Procedure to be followed with respect to invalidity, termination, withdrawal from or suspension of the operation of a treaty
1. A party which, under the provisions of the present Convention, invokes either a defect in its consent to be bound by a treaty or a ground for impeaching the validity of a treaty, terminating it, withdrawing from it or suspending its operation, must notify the other parties of its claim. The notification shall indicate the measure proposed to be taken with respect to the treaty and the reasons therefore.
2. If, after the expiry of a period which, except in cases of special urgency, shall not be less than three months after the receipt of the notification, no party has raised any objection, the party making the notification may carry out in the manner provided in article 67 the measure which it has proposed.
3. If, however, objection has been raised by any other party, the parties shall seek a solution through the means indicated in Article 33 of the Charter of the United Nations.
4. The notification or objection made by an international organization shall be governed by the rules of that organization.
5. Nothing in the foregoing paragraphs shall affect the rights or obligations of the parties under any provisions in force binding the parties with regard to the settlement of disputes.
6. Without prejudice to article 45, the fact that a State or an international organization has not previously made the notification prescribed in paragraph 1 shall not prevent it from making such notification in answer to another party claiming performance of the treaty or alleging its violation.

Article 66 - Procedures for judicial settlement, arbitration and conciliation

1. If, under paragraph 3 of article 65, no solution has been reached within a period of twelve months following the date on which the objection was raised, the procedures specified in the following paragraphs shall be followed.

2. With respect to a dispute concerning the application or the interpretation of article 53 or 64:

(*a*) if a State is a party to the dispute with one or more States, it may, by a written application, submit the dispute to the International Court of Justice for a decision;

(*b*) if a State is a party to the dispute to which one or more international organizations are parties, the State may, through a Member State of the United Nations if necessary, request the General Assembly or the Security Council or, where appropriate, the competent organ of an international organization which is a party to the dispute and is authorized in accordance with Article 96 of the Charter of the United Nations, to request an advisory opinion of the International Court of Justice in accordance with Article 65 of the Statute of the Court;

(*c*) if the United Nations or an international organization that is authorized in accordance with Article 96 of the Charter of the United Nations is a party to the dispute, it may request an advisory opinion of the International Court of Justice in accordance with Article 65 of the Statute of the Court;

(*d*) if an international organization other than those referred to in subparagraph (*c*) is a party to the dispute, it may, through a Member State of the United Nations, follow the procedure specified in subparagraph (*b*);

(*e*) the advisory opinion given pursuant to subparagraph (*b*), (*c*) or (*d*) shall be accepted as decisive by all the parties to the dispute concerned;

(*f*) if the request under subparagraph (*b*), (*c*) or (*d*) for an advisory opinion of the Court is not granted, any one of the parties to the dispute may, by written notification to the other party or parties, submit it to arbitration in accordance with the provisions of the Annex to the present Convention.

3. The provisions of paragraph 2 apply unless all the parties to a dispute referred to in that paragraph by common consent agree to submit the dispute to an arbitration procedure, including the one specified in the Annex to the present Convention.

4. With respect to a dispute concerning the application or the interpretation of any of the articles in Part V, other than articles 53 and 64, of the present Convention, any one of the parties to the dispute may set in motion the conciliation procedure specified in the Annex to the Convention by submitting a request to that effect to the Secretary-General of the United Nations.

Article 67 - Instruments for declaring invalid, terminating, withdrawing from or suspending the operation of a treaty

1. The notification provided for under article 65, paragraph 1, must be made in writing.

2. Any act declaring invalid, terminating, withdrawing from or suspending the operation of a treaty pursuant to the provisions of the treaty or of paragraphs 2 or 3 of article 65 shall be carried out through an instrument communicated to the other parties. If the instrument emanating from a State is not signed by the Head of State, Head of Government or Minister for Foreign Affairs, the representative of the State communicating it may be called upon to produce full powers. If the instrument emanates from an international organization, the representative of the organization communicating it may be called upon to produce full powers.

Article 68 - Revocation of notifications and instruments provided for in articles 65 and 67

A notification or instrument provided for in articles 65 or 67 may be revoked at any time before it takes effect.

SECTION 5. CONSEQUENCES OF THE INVALIDITY, TERMINATION OR SUSPENSION OF THE OPERATION OF A TREATY

Article 69 - Consequences of the invalidity of a treaty

1. A treaty the invalidity of which is established under the present Convention is void. The provisions of a void treaty have no legal force.
2. If acts have nevertheless been performed in reliance on such a treaty:
(*a*) each party may require any other party to establish as far as possible in their mutual relations the position that would have existed if the acts had not been performed;
(*b*) acts performed in good faith before the invalidity was invoked are not rendered unlawful by reason only of the invalidity of the treaty.
3. In cases falling under articles 49, 50, 51 or 52, paragraph 2 does not apply with respect to the party to which the fraud, the act of corruption or the coercion is imputable.
4. In the case of the invalidity of the consent of a particular State or a particular international organization to be bound by a multilateral treaty, the foregoing rules apply in the relations between that State or that organization and the parties to the treaty.

Article 70 - Consequences of the termination of a treaty

1. Unless the treaty otherwise provides or the parties otherwise agree, the termination of a treaty under its provisions or in accordance with the present Convention:
(*a*) releases the parties from any obligation further to perform the treaty;
(*b*) does not affect any right, obligation or legal situation of the parties created through the execution of the treaty prior to its termination.
2. If a State or an international organization denounces or withdraws from a multilateral treaty, paragraph 1 applies in the relations between that State or that organization and each of the other parties to the treaty from the date when such denunciation or withdrawal takes effect.

Article 71 - Consequences of the invalidity of a treaty which conflicts with a peremptory norm of general international law

1. In the case of a treaty which is void under article 53 the parties shall:
(*a*) eliminate as far as possible the consequences of any act performed in reliance on any provision which conflicts with the peremptory norm of general international law; and
(*b*) bring their mutual relations into conformity with the peremptory norm of general international law.
2. In the case of a treaty which becomes void and terminates under article 64, the termination of the treaty:
(*a*) releases the parties from any obligation further to perform the treaty;
(*b*) does not affect any right, obligation or legal situation of the parties created through the execution of the treaty prior to its termination; provided that those rights, obligations or situations may thereafter be maintained only to the extent that their maintenance is not in itself in conflict with the new peremptory norm of general international law.

Article 72 - Consequences of the suspension of the operation of a treaty

1. Unless the treaty otherwise provides or the parties otherwise agree, the suspension of the operation of a treaty under its provisions or in accordance with the present Convention:

(*a*) releases the parties between which the operation of the treaty is suspended from the obligation to perform the treaty in their mutual relations during the period of the suspension;
(*b*) does not otherwise affect the legal relations between the parties established by the treaty.
2. During the period of the suspension the parties shall refrain from acts tending to obstruct the resumption of the operation of the treaty.

PART VI – MISCELLANEOUS PROVISIONS

Article 73 - Relationship to the Vienna Convention on the Law of Treaties
As between States Parties to the Vienna Convention on the Law of Treaties of 1969, the relations of those States under a treaty between two or more States and one or more international organizations shall be governed by that Convention.

Article 74 - Questions not prejudged by the present Convention
1. The provisions of the present Convention shall not prejudge any question that may arise in regard to a treaty between one or more States and one or more international organizations from a succession of States or from the international responsibility of a State or from the outbreak of hostilities between States.
2. The provisions of the present Convention shall not prejudge any question that may arise in regard to a treaty from the international responsibility of an international organization, from the termination of the existence of the organization or from the termination of participation by a State in the membership of the organization.
3. The provisions of the present Convention shall not prejudge any question that may arise in regard to the establishment of obligations and rights for States members of an international organization under a treaty to which that organization is a party.

Article 75 - Diplomatic and consular relations and the conclusion of treaties
The severance or absence of diplomatic or consular relations between two or more States does not prevent the conclusion of treaties between two or more of those States and one or more international organizations. The conclusion of such a treaty does not in itself affect the situation in regard to diplomatic or consular relations.

Article 76 - Case of an aggressor State
The provisions of the present Convention are without prejudice to any obligation in relation to a treaty between one or more States and one or more international organizations which may arise for an aggressor State in consequence of measures taken in conformity with the Charter of the United Nations with reference to that State's aggression.

PART VII – DEPOSITARIES, NOTIFICATIONS, CORRECTONS AND REGISTRATION

Article 77 - Depositaries of treaties
1. The designation of the depositary of a treaty may be made by the negotiating States and negotiating organizations or, as the case may be, the negotiating organizations, either in the treaty itself or in some other manner. The depositary may be one or more States, an international organization or the chief administrative officer of the organization.

2. The functions of the depositary of a treaty are international in character and the depositary is under an obligation to act impartially in their performance. In particular, the fact that a treaty has not entered into force between certain of the parties or that a difference has appeared between a State or an international organization and a depositary with regard to the performance of the latter's functions shall not affect that obligation.

Article 78 - Functions of depositaries

1. The functions of a depositary, unless otherwise provided in the treaty or agreed by the contracting States and contracting organizations or, as the case may be, by the contracting organizations, comprise in particular:

(*a*) keeping custody of the original text of the treaty and of any full powers delivered to the depositary;

(*b*) preparing certified copies of the original text and preparing any further text of the treaty in such additional languages as may be required by the treaty and transmitting them to the parties and to the States and international organizations entitled to become parties to the treaty;

(*c*) receiving any signatures to the treaty and receiving and keeping custody of any instruments, notifications and communications relating to it;

(*d*) examining whether the signature or any instrument, notification or communication relating to the treaty is in due and proper form and, if need be, bringing the matter to the attention of the State or international organization in question;

(*e*) informing the parties and the States and international organizations entitled to become parties to the treaty of acts, notifications and communications relating to the treaty;

(*f*) informing the States and international organizations entitled to become parties to the treaty when the number of signatures or of instruments of ratification, instruments relating to an act of formal confirmation, or of instruments of acceptance, approval or accession required for the entry into force of the treaty has been received or deposited;

(*g*) registering the treaty with the Secretariat of the United Nations;

(*h*) performing the functions specified in other provisions of the present Convention.

2. In the event of any difference appearing between a State or an international organization and the depositary as to the performance of the latter's functions, the depositary shall bring the question to the attention of:

(*a*) the signatory States and organizations and the contracting States and contracting organizations; or

(*b*) where appropriate, the competent organ of the international organization concerned.

Article 79 - Notifications and communications

Except as the treaty or the present Convention otherwise provide, any notification or communication to be made by any State or any international organization under the present Convention shall:

(*a*) if there is no depositary, be transmitted direct to the States and organizations for which it is intended, or if there is a depositary, to the latter;

(*b*) be considered as having been made by the State or organization in question only upon its receipt by the State or organization to which it was transmitted or, as the case may be, upon its receipt by the depositary;

(*c*) if transmitted to a depositary, be considered as received by the State or organization for which it was intended only when the latter State or organization has been informed by the depositary in accordance with article 78, paragraph 1(*e*).

Article 80 - Correction of errors in texts or in certified copies of treaties

1. Where, after the authentication of the text of a treaty, the signatory States and international organizations and the contracting States and contracting organizations are agreed that it contains an error, the error shall, unless those States and organizations decide upon some other means of correction, be corrected:

(*a*) by having the appropriate correction made in the text and causing the correction to be initialled by duly authorized representatives;

(*b*) by executing or exchanging an instrument or instruments setting out the correction which it has been agreed to make; or

(*c*) by executing a corrected text of the whole treaty by the same procedure as in the case of the original ext.

2. Where the treaty is one for which there is a depositary, the latter shall notify the signatory States and international organizations and the contracting States and contracting organizations of the error and of the proposal to correct it and shall specify an appropriate time limit within which objection to the proposed correction may be raised. If, on the expiry of the time limit:

(*a*) no objection has been raised, the depositary shall make and initial the correction in the text and shall execute a procés-verbal of the rectification of the text and communicate a copy of it to the parties and to the States and organizations entitled to become parties to the treaty;

(*b*) an objection has been raised, the depositary shall communicate the objection to the signatory States and organizations and to the contracting States and contracting organizations.

3. The rules in paragraphs 1 and 2 apply also where the text has been authenticated in two or more languages and it appears that there is a lack of concordance which the signatory States and international organizations and the contracting States and contracting organizations agree should be corrected.

4. The corrected text replaces the defective text ab initio, unless the signatory States and international organizations and the contracting States and contracting organizations otherwise decide.

5. The correction of the text of a treaty that has been registered shall be notified to the Secretariat of the United Nations.

6. Where an error is discovered in a certified copy of a treaty, the depositary shall execute a procés-verbal specifying the rectification and communicate a copy of it to the signatory States and international organizations and to the contracting States and contracting organizations.

Article 81 - Registration and publication of treaties

1. Treaties shall, after their entry into force, be transmitted to the Secretariat of the United Nations for registration or filing and recording, as the case may be, and for publication.

2. The designation of a depositary shall constitute authorization for it to perform the acts specified in the preceding paragraph.

PART VIII – FINAL PROVISIONS

Article 82 - Signature

The present Convention shall be open for signature until 31 December 1986 at the Federal Ministry for Foreign Affairs of the Republic of Austria, and subsequently, until 30 June 1987, at United Nations Headquarters, New York by:

(*a*) all States;

(*b*) Namibia, represented by the United Nations Council for Namibia;

(*c*) international organizations invited to participate in the United Nations Conference on the Law of Treaties between States and International Organizations or between International Organizations.

Article 83 - Ratification or act of formal confirmation

The present Convention is subject to ratification by States and by Namibia, represented by the United Nations Council for Namibia, and to acts of formal confirmation by international organizations.

The instruments of ratification and those relating to acts of formal confirmation shall be deposited with the Secretary-General of the United Nations.

Article 84 - Accession

1. The present Convention shall remain open for accession by any State, by Namibia, represented by the United Nations Council for Namibia, and by any international organization which has the capacity to conclude treaties.
2. An instrument of accession of an international organization shall contain a declaration that it has the capacity to conclude treaties.
3. The instruments of accession shall be deposited with the Secretary-General of the United Nations.

Article 85 - Entry into force

1. The present Convention shall enter into force on the thirtieth day following the date of deposit of the thirty-fifth instrument of ratification or accession by States or by Namibia, represented by the United Nations Council for Namibia.
2. For each State or for Namibia, represented by the United Nations Council for Namibia, ratifying or acceding to the Convention after the condition specified in paragraph 1 has been fulfilled, the Convention shall enter into force on the thirtieth day after deposit by such State or by Namibia of its instrument of ratification or accession.
3. For each international organization depositing an instrument relating to an act of formal confirmation or an instrument of accession, the Convention shall enter into force on the thirtieth day after such deposit, or at the date the Convention enters into force pursuant to paragraph 1, whichever is later.

Article 86 - Authentic texts

The original of the present Convention, of which the Arabic, Chinese, English, French, Russian and Spanish texts are equally authentic, shall be deposited with the Secretary-General of the United Nations.

IN WITNESS WHEREOF the undersigned Plenipotentiaries, being duly authorized by their respective Governments, and duly authorized representatives of the United Nations Council for Namibia and of international organizations have signed the present Convention.

DONE at Vienna, this twenty-first day of March one thousand nine hundred and eighty-six.

Draft Articles on the Responsibility of International Organizations, 2011

[*Note:* Draft Articles on the Responsibility of International Organizations were prepared by the International Law Commission and adopted on its 63rd session of the Commission, held in 2011. The UN General Assembly took note of the Draft Articles in its Resolution 66/100 of December 9, 2011.]

Responsibility of international organizations

Part One

Introduction

Article 1 Scope of the present draft articles
1. The present draft articles apply to the international responsibility of an international organization for an internationally wrongful act.
2. The present draft articles also apply to the international responsibility of a State for an internationally wrongful act in connection with the conduct of an international organization.

Article 2 Use of terms
For the purposes of the present draft articles,
(a) "international organization" means an organization established by a treaty or other instrument governed by international law and possessing its own international legal personality. International organizations may include as members, in addition to States, other entities;
(b) "rules of the organization" means, in particular, the constituent instruments, decisions, resolutions and other acts of the international organization adopted in accordance with those instruments, and established practice of the organization;
(c) "organ of an international organization" means any person or entity which has that status in accordance with the rules of the organization;
(d) "agent of an international organization" means an official or other person or entity, other than an organ, who is charged by the organization with carrying out, or helping to carry out, one of its functions, and thus through whom the organization acts.

Part Two

The internationally wrongful act of an international organization

Chapter I General principles

Article 3 Responsibility of an international organization for its internationally wrongful acts
Every internationally wrongful act of an international organization entails the international responsibility of that organization.

Article 4 Elements of an internationally wrongful act of an international organization
There is an internationally wrongful act of an international organization when conduct consisting of an action or omission:
(a) is attributable to that organization under international law; and
(b) constitutes a breach of an international obligation of that organization.

Article 5 Characterization of an act of an international organization as internationally wrongful
The characterization of an act of an international organization as internationally wrongful is governed by international law.

Chapter II Attribution of conduct to an international organization

Article 6 Conduct of organs or agents of an international organization
1. The conduct of an organ or agent of an international organization in the performance of functions of that organ or agent shall be considered an act of that organization under international law, whatever position the organ or agent holds in respect of the organization.
2. The rules of the organization apply in the determination of the functions of its organs and agents.

Article 7 Conduct of organs of a State or organs or agents of an international organization placed at the disposal of another international organization
The conduct of an organ of a State or an organ or agent of an international organization that is placed at the disposal of another international organization shall be considered under international law an act of the latter organization if the organization exercises effective control over that conduct.

Article 8 Excess of authority or contravention of instructions
The conduct of an organ or agent of an international organization shall be considered an act of that organization under international law if the organ or agent acts in an official capacity and within the overall functions of that organization, even if the conduct exceeds the authority of that organ or agent or contravenes instructions.

Article 9 Conduct acknowledged and adopted by an international organization as its own
Conduct which is not attributable to an international organization under articles 6 to 8 shall nevertheless be considered an act of that organization under international law if and to the extent that the organization acknowledges and adopts the conduct in question as its own.

Chapter III

Breach of an international obligation

Article 10 Existence of a breach of an international obligation
1. There is a breach of an international obligation by an international organization when an act of that international organization is not in conformity with what is required of it by that obligation, regardless of the origin or character of the obligation concerned.
2. Paragraph 1 includes the breach of any international obligation that may arise for an international organization towards its members under the rules of the organization.

Article 11 International obligation in force for an international organization
An act of an international organization does not constitute a breach of an international obligation unless the organization is bound by the obligation in question at the time the act occurs.

Article 12 Extension in time of the breach of an international obligation
1. The breach of an international obligation by an act of an international organization not having a continuing character occurs at the moment when the act is performed, even if its effects continue.
2. The breach of an international obligation by an act of an international organization having a continuing character extends over the entire period during which the act continues and remains not in conformity with that obligation.
3. The breach of an international obligation requiring an international organization to prevent a given event occurs when the event occurs and extends over the entire period during which the event continues and remains not in conformity with that obligation.

Article 13 Breach consisting of a composite act
1. The breach of an international obligation by an international organization through a series of actions and omissions defined in aggregate as wrongful occurs when the action or omission occurs which, taken with the other actions or omissions, is sufficient to constitute the wrongful act.
2. In such a case, the breach extends over the entire period starting with the first of the actions or omissions of the series and lasts for as long as these actions or omissions are repeated and remain not in conformity with the international obligation.

Chapter IV

Responsibility of an international organization in connection with the act of a State or another international organization

Article 14 Aid or assistance in the commission of an internationally wrongful act
An international organization which aids or assists a State or another international organization in the commission of an internationally wrongful act by the State or the latter organization is internationally responsible for doing so if:
(a) the former organization does so with knowledge of the circumstances of the internationally wrongful act; and
(b) the act would be internationally wrongful if committed by that organization.

Article 15 Direction and control exercised over the commission of an internationally wrongful act
An international organization which directs and controls a State or another international organization in the commission of an internationally wrongful act by the State or the latter organization is internationally responsible for that act if:
(a) the former organization does so with knowledge of the circumstances of the internationally wrongful act; and
(b) the act would be internationally wrongful if committed by that organization.

Article 16 Coercion of a State or another international organization
An international organization which coerces a State or another international organization to commit an act is internationally responsible for that act if:
(a) the act would, but for the coercion, be an internationally wrongful act of the coerced State or international organization; and
(b) the coercing international organization does so with knowledge of the circumstances of the act.

Article 17 Circumvention of international obligations through decisions and authorizations addressed to members
1. An international organization incurs international responsibility if it circumvents one of its international obligations by adopting a decision binding member States or international organizations to commit an act that would be internationally wrongful if committed by the former organization.
2. An international organization incurs international responsibility if it circumvents one of its international obligations by authorizing member States or international organizations to commit an act that would be internationally wrongful if committed by the former organization and the act in question is committed because of that authorization.
3. Paragraphs 1 and 2 apply whether or not the act in question is internationally wrongful for the member States or international organizations to which the decision or authorization is addressed.

Article 18 Responsibility of an international organization member of another international organization
Without prejudice to draft articles 14 to 17, the international responsibility of an international organization that is a member of another international organization also arises in relation to an act of the latter under the conditions set out in draft articles 61 and 62 for States that are members of an international organization.

Article 19 Effect of this Chapter
This Chapter is without prejudice to the international responsibility of the State or international organization which commits the act in question, or of any other State or international organization.

Chapter V

Circumstances precluding wrongfulness

Article 20 Consent
Valid consent by a State or an international organization to the commission of a given act by another international organization precludes the wrongfulness of that act in relation to that State or the former organization to the extent that the act remains within the limits of that consent.

Article 21 Self-defence
The wrongfulness of an act of an international organization is precluded if and to the extent that the act constitutes a lawful measure of self-defence under international law.

Article 22 Countermeasures
1. Subject to paragraphs 2 and 3, the wrongfulness of an act of an international organization not in conformity with an international obligation towards a State or another international organization is precluded if and to the extent that the act constitutes a countermeasure taken in accordance with the substantive and procedural conditions required by international law, including those set forth in Chapter II of Part Four for countermeasures taken against another international organization.
2. Subject to paragraph 3, an international organization may not take countermeasures against a responsible member State or international organization unless:
(a) the conditions referred to in paragraph 1 are met;
(b) the countermeasures are not inconsistent with the rules of the organization; and
(c) no appropriate means are available for otherwise inducing compliance with the obligations of the responsible State or international organization concerning cessation of the breach and reparation.
3. Countermeasures may not be taken by an international organization against a member State or international organization in response to a breach of an international obligation under the rules of the organization unless such countermeasures are provided for by those rules.

Article 23 Force majeure
1. The wrongfulness of an act of an international organization not in conformity with an international obligation of that organization is precluded if the act is due to force majeure, that is, the occurrence of an irresistible force or of an unforeseen event, beyond the control of the organization, making it materially impossible in the circumstances to perform the obligation.
2. Paragraph 1 does not apply if:
(a) the situation of force majeure is due, either alone or in combination with other factors, to the conduct of the organization invoking it; or
(b) the organization has assumed the risk of that situation occurring.

Article 24 Distress
1. The wrongfulness of an act of an international organization not in conformity with an international obligation of that organization is precluded if the author of the act in question has no other reasonable way, in a situation of distress, of saving the author's life or the lives of other persons entrusted to the author's care.
2. Paragraph 1 does not apply if:
(a) the situation of distress is due, either alone or in combination with other factors, to the conduct of the organization invoking it; or
(b) the act in question is likely to create a comparable or greater peril.

Article 25 Necessity
1. Necessity may not be invoked by an international organization as a ground for precluding the wrongfulness of an act not in conformity with an international obligation of that organization unless the act:
(a) is the only means for the organization to safeguard against a grave and imminent peril an essential interest of its member States or of the international community as a whole, when the organization has, in accordance with international law, the function to protect the interest in question; and

(b) does not seriously impair an essential interest of the State or States towards which the international obligation exists, or of the international community as a whole.

2. In any case, necessity may not be invoked by an international organization as a ground for precluding wrongfulness if:

(a) the international obligation in question excludes the possibility of invoking necessity; or

(b) the organization has contributed to the situation of necessity.

Article 26 Compliance with peremptory norms

Nothing in this Chapter precludes the wrongfulness of any act of an international organization which is not in conformity with an obligation arising under a peremptory norm of general international law.

Article 27 Consequences of invoking a circumstance precluding wrongfulness

The invocation of a circumstance precluding wrongfulness in accordance with this Chapter is without prejudice to:

(a) compliance with the obligation in question, if and to the extent that the circumstance precluding wrongfulness no longer exists;

(b) the question of compensation for any material loss caused by the act in question.

Part Three

Content of the international responsibility of an international organization

Chapter I

General principles

Article 28 Legal consequences of an internationally wrongful act

The international responsibility of an international organization which is entailed by an internationally wrongful act in accordance with the provisions of Part Two involves legal consequences as set out in this Part.

Article 29 Continued duty of performance

The legal consequences of an internationally wrongful act under this Part do not affect the continued duty of the responsible international organization to perform the obligation breached.

Article 30 Cessation and non-repetition

The international organization responsible for the internationally wrongful act is under an obligation:

(a) to cease that act, if it is continuing;

(b) to offer appropriate assurances and guarantees of non-repetition, if circumstances so require.

Article 31 Reparation

1. The responsible international organization is under an obligation to make full reparation for the injury caused by the internationally wrongful act.

2. Injury includes any damage, whether material or moral, caused by the internationally wrongful act of an international organization.

Article 32 Relevance of the rules of the organization

1. The responsible international organization may not rely on its rules as justification for failure to comply with its obligations under this Part.

2. Paragraph 1 is without prejudice to the applicability of the rules of an international organization to the relations between the organization and its member States and organizations.

Article 33 Scope of international obligations set out in this Part

1. The obligations of the responsible international organization set out in this Part may be owed to one or more States, to one or more other organizations, or to the international community as a whole, depending in particular on the character and content of the international obligation and on the circumstances of the breach.

2. This Part is without prejudice to any right, arising from the international responsibility of an international organization, which may accrue directly to any person or entity other than a State or an international organization.

Chapter II

Reparation for injury

Article 34 Forms of reparation

Full reparation for the injury caused by the internationally wrongful act shall take the form of restitution, compensation and satisfaction, either singly or in combination, in accordance with the provisions of this Chapter.

Article 35 Restitution

An international organization responsible for an internationally wrongful act is under an obligation to make restitution, that is, to re-establish the situation which existed before the wrongful act was committed, provided and to the extent that restitution:

(a) is not materially impossible;

(b) does not involve a burden out of all proportion to the benefit deriving from restitution instead of compensation.

Article 36 Compensation

1. The international organization responsible for an internationally wrongful act is under an obligation to compensate for the damage caused thereby, insofar as such damage is not made good by restitution.

2. The compensation shall cover any financially assessable damage including loss of profits insofar as it is established.

Article 37 Satisfaction

1. The international organization responsible for an internationally wrongful act is under an obligation to give satisfaction for the injury caused by that act insofar as it cannot be made good by restitution or compensation.

2. Satisfaction may consist in an acknowledgement of the breach, an expression of regret, a formal apology or another appropriate modality.

3. Satisfaction shall not be out of proportion to the injury and may not take a form humiliating to the responsible international organization.

Article 38 Interest

1. Interest on any principal sum due under this Chapter shall be payable when necessary in order to ensure full reparation. The interest rate and mode of calculation shall be set so as to achieve that result.
2. Interest runs from the date when the principal sum should have been paid until the date the obligation to pay is fulfilled.

Article 39 Contribution to the injury

In the determination of reparation, account shall be taken of the contribution to the injury by wilful or negligent action or omission of the injured State or international organization or of any person or entity in relation to whom reparation is sought.

Article 40 Ensuring the fulfilment of the obligation to make reparation

1. The responsible international organization shall take all appropriate measures in accordance with its rules to ensure that its members provide it with the means for effectively fulfilling its obligations under this Chapter.
2. The members of a responsible international organization shall take all the appropriate measures that may be required by the rules of the organization in order to enable the organization to fulfil its obligations under this Chapter.

Chapter III

Serious breaches of obligations under peremptory norms of general international law

Article 41 Application of this Chapter

1. This Chapter applies to the international responsibility which is entailed by a serious breach by an international organization of an obligation arising under a peremptory norm of general international law.
2. A breach of such an obligation is serious if it involves a gross or systematic failure by the responsible international organization to fulfil the obligation.

Article 42 Particular consequences of a serious breach of an obligation under this Chapter

1. States and international organizations shall cooperate to bring to an end through lawful means any serious breach within the meaning of article 41.
2. No State or international organization shall recognize as lawful a situation created by a serious breach within the meaning of article 41, nor render aid or assistance in maintaining that situation.
3. This article is without prejudice to the other consequences referred to in this Part and to such further consequences that a breach to which this Chapter applies may entail under international law.

Part Four

The implementation of the international responsibility of an international organization

Chapter I

Invocation of the responsibility of an international organization

Article 43 Invocation of responsibility by an injured State or international organization
A State or an international organization is entitled as an injured State or an injured international organization to invoke the responsibility of another international organization if the obligation breached is owed to:
(a) that State or the former international organization individually;
(b) a group of States or international organizations including that State or the former international organization, or the international community as a whole, and the breach of the obligation:
(i) specially affects that State or that international organization; or
(ii) is of such a character as radically to change the position of all the other States and international organizations to which the obligation is owed with respect to the further performance of the obligation.

Article 44 Notice of claim by an injured State or international organization
1. An injured State or international organization which invokes the responsibility of another international organization shall give notice of its claim to that organization.
2. The injured State or international organization may specify in particular:
(a) the conduct that the responsible international organization should take in order to cease the wrongful act, if it is continuing;
(b) what form reparation should take in accordance with the provisions of

Part Three

Article 45 Admissibility of claims
1. An injured State may not invoke the responsibility of an international organization if the claim is not brought in accordance with any applicable rule relating to the nationality of claims.
2. When the rule of exhaustion of local remedies applies to a claim, an injured State or international organization may not invoke the responsibility of another international organization if any available and effective remedy has not been exhausted.

Article 46 Loss of the right to invoke responsibility
The responsibility of an international organization may not be invoked if:
(a) the injured State or international organization has validly waived the claim;
(b) the injured State or international organization is to be considered as having, by reason of its conduct, validly acquiesced in the lapse of the claim.

Article 47 Plurality of injured States or international organizations

Where several States or international organizations are injured by the same internationally wrongful act of an international organization, each injured State or international organization may separately invoke the responsibility of the international organization for the internationally wrongful act.

Article 48 Responsibility of an international organization and one or more States or international organizations

1. Where an international organization and one or more States or other international organizations are responsible for the same internationally wrongful act, the responsibility of each State or organization may be invoked in relation to that act.
2. Subsidiary responsibility may be invoked insofar as the invocation of the primary responsibility has not led to reparation.
3. Paragraphs 1 and 2:
(a) do not permit any injured State or international organization to recover, by way of compensation, more than the damage it has suffered;
(b) are without prejudice to any right of recourse that the State or international organization providing reparation may have against the other responsible States or international organizations.

Article 49 Invocation of responsibility by a State or an international organization other than an injured State or international organization

1. A State or an international organization other than an injured State or international organization is entitled to invoke the responsibility of another international organization in accordance with paragraph 4 if the obligation breached is owed to a group of States or international organizations, including the State or organization that invokes responsibility, and is established for the protection of a collective interest of the group.
2. A State other than an injured State is entitled to invoke the responsibility of an international organization in accordance with paragraph 4 if the obligation breached is owed to the international community as a whole.
3. An international organization other than an injured international organization is entitled to invoke the responsibility of another international organization in accordance with paragraph 4 if the obligation breached is owed to the international community as a whole and safeguarding the interest of the international community as a whole underlying the obligation breached is within the functions of the international organization invoking responsibility.
4. A State or an international organization entitled to invoke responsibility under paragraphs 1 to 3 may claim from the responsible international organization:
(a) cessation of the internationally wrongful act, and assurances and guarantees of non-repetition in accordance with draft article 30; and
(b) performance of the obligation of reparation in accordance with Part Three, in the interest of the injured State or international organization or of the beneficiaries of the obligation breached.
5. The requirements for the invocation of responsibility by an injured State or international organization under draft articles 44, 45, paragraph 2, and 46 apply to an invocation of responsibility by a State or international organization entitled to do so under paragraphs 1 to 4.

Article 50 Scope of this Chapter

This Chapter is without prejudice to the entitlement that a person or entity other than a State or an international organization may have to invoke the international responsibility of an international organization.

Chapter II Countermeasures

Article 51 Object and limits of countermeasures

1. An injured State or an injured international organization may only take countermeasures against an international organization which is responsible for an internationally wrongful act in order to induce that organization to comply with its obligations under Part Three.
2. Countermeasures are limited to the non-performance for the time being of international obligations of the State or international organization taking the measures towards the responsible international organization.
3. Countermeasures shall, as far as possible, be taken in such a way as to permit the resumption of performance of the obligations in question.
4. Countermeasures shall, as far as possible, be taken in such a way as to limit their effects on the exercise by the responsible international organization of its functions.

Article 52 Conditions for taking countermeasures by members of an international organization

1. Subject to paragraph 2, an injured State or international organization which is a member of a responsible international organization may not take countermeasures against that organization unless:
(a) the conditions referred to in article 51 are met;
(b) the countermeasures are not inconsistent with the rules of the organization; and
(c) no appropriate means are available for otherwise inducing compliance with the obligations of the responsible international organization concerning cessation of the breach and reparation.
2. Countermeasures may not be taken by an injured State or international organization which is a member of a responsible international organization against that organization in response to a breach of an international obligation under the rules of the organization unless such countermeasures are provided for by those rules.

Article 53 Obligations not affected by countermeasures

1. Countermeasures shall not affect:
(a) the obligation to refrain from the threat or use of force as embodied in the Charter of the United Nations;
(b) obligations for the protection of human rights;
(c) obligations of a humanitarian character prohibiting reprisals;
(d) other obligations under peremptory norms of general international law.
2. An injured State or international organization taking countermeasures is not relieved from fulfilling its obligations:
(a) under any dispute settlement procedure applicable between it and the responsible international organization;
(b) to respect any inviolability of organs or agents of the responsible international organization and of the premises, archives and documents of that organization.

Article 54 Proportionality of countermeasures

Countermeasures must be commensurate with the injury suffered, taking into account the gravity of the internationally wrongful act and the rights in question.

Article 55 Conditions relating to resort to countermeasures

1. Before taking countermeasures, an injured State or international organization shall:

(a) call upon the responsible international organization, in accordance with draft article 44, to fulfil its obligations under Part Three;

(b) notify the responsible international organization of any decision to take countermeasures and offer to negotiate with that organization.

2. Notwithstanding paragraph 1 (b), the injured State or international organization may take such urgent countermeasures as are necessary to preserve its rights.

3. Countermeasures may not be taken, and if already taken must be suspended without undue delay if:

(a) the internationally wrongful act has ceased; and

(b) the dispute is pending before a court or tribunal which has the authority to make decisions binding on the parties.

4. Paragraph 3 does not apply if the responsible international organization fails to implement the dispute settlement procedures in good faith.

Article 56 Termination of countermeasures

Countermeasures shall be terminated as soon as the responsible international organization has complied with its obligations under Part Three in relation to the internationally wrongful act.

Article 57 Measures taken by States or international organizations other than an injured State or organization

This Chapter does not prejudice the right of any State or international organization, entitled under article 49, paragraphs 1 to 3, to invoke the responsibility of another international organization, to take lawful measures against that organization to ensure cessation of the breach and reparation in the interest of the injured State or organization or of the beneficiaries of the obligation breached.

Part Five

Responsibility of a State in connection with the conduct of an international organization

Article 58 Aid or assistance by a State in the commission of an internationally wrongful act by an international organization

1. A State which aids or assists an international organization in the commission of an internationally wrongful act by the latter is internationally responsible for doing so if:

(a) the State does so with knowledge of the circumstances of the internationally wrongful act; and

(b) the act would be internationally wrongful if committed by that State.

2. An act by a State member of an international organization done in accordance with the rules of the organization does not as such engage the international responsibility of that State under the terms of this article.

Article 59 Direction and control exercised by a State over the commission of an internationally wrongful act by an international organization

1. A State which directs and controls an international organization in the commission of an internationally wrongful act by the latter is internationally responsible for that act if:
(a) the State does so with knowledge of the circumstances of the internationally wrongful act; and
(b) the act would be internationally wrongful if committed by that State.
2. An act by a State member of an international organization done in accordance with the rules of the organization does not as such engage the international responsibility of that State under the terms of this draft article.

Article 60 Coercion of an international organization by a State

A State which coerces an international organization to commit an act is internationally responsible for that act if:
(a) the act would, but for the coercion, be an internationally wrongful act of the coerced international organization; and
(b) the coercing State does so with knowledge of the circumstances of the act.

Article 61 Circumvention of international obligations of a State member of an international organization

1. A State member of an international organization incurs international responsibility if, by taking advantage of the fact that the organization has competence in relation to the subject-matter of one of the State's international obligations, it circumvents that obligation by causing the organization to commit an act that, if committed by the State, would have constituted a breach of the obligation.
2. Paragraph 1 applies whether or not the act in question is internationally wrongful for the international organization.

Article 62 Responsibility of a State member of an international organization for an internationally wrongful act of that organization

1. A State member of an international organization is responsible for an internationally wrongful act of that organization if:
(a) it has accepted responsibility for that act towards the injured party; or
(b) it has led the injured party to rely on its responsibility.
2. Any international responsibility of a State under paragraph 1 is presumed to be subsidiary.

Article 63 Effect of this Part

This Part is without prejudice to the international responsibility of the international organization which commits the act in question, or of any State or other international organization.

Part Six

General Provisions

Article 64 *Lex specialis*

These draft articles do not apply where and to the extent that the conditions for the existence of an internationally wrongful act or the content or implementation of the international responsibility of an international organization, or of a State in connection with the conduct of an international organization, are governed by special rules of international law. Such special rules of international law may be contained in the rules of the organization applicable to the relations between an international organization and its members.

Article 65 Questions of international responsibility not regulated by these draft articles
The applicable rules of international law continue to govern questions concerning the responsibility of an international organization or a State for an internationally wrongful act to the extent that they are not regulated by these draft articles.

Article 66 Individual responsibility
These draft articles are without prejudice to any question of the individual responsibility under international law of any person acting on behalf of an international organization or a State.

Article 67 Charter of the United Nations
These draft articles are without prejudice to the Charter of the United Nations.

PART TWO – CASES

I. International Courts

International Court of Justice

Conditions of Admission of a State to Membership in the United Nations (Article 4 of the Charter), ICJ Advisory Opinion, 28 May 1948 (First Admissions Case)

[*Note:*

Opinion requested by: the UN General Assembly resolution 113 (II)B adopted on 17 November 1947

Question before the Court:
"Is a Member of the United Nations which is called upon, in virtue of Article 4 of the Charter, to pronounce itself by its vote, either in the Security Council or in the General Assembly, on the admission of a State to membership in the United Nations, juridically entitled to make its consent to the admission dependent on conditions not expressly provided by paragraph 1 of the said Article? In particular, can such a Member, while it recognizes the conditions set forth in that provision to be fulfilled by the State concerned, subject its affirmative vote to the additional condition that other States be admitted to membership in the United Nations together with that State?"]

The Opinion:

[...]

The question put is in effect confined to the following point only: are the conditions stated in paragraph I of Article 4 exhaustive in character in the sense that an affirmative reply would lead to the conclusion that a Member is not legally entitled to make admission dependent on conditions not expressly provided for in that Article, while a negative reply would, on the contrary, authorize a Member to make admission dependent also on other conditions.

[...]

Having been asked to determine the character, exhaustive or otherwise, of the conditions stated in Article 4, the Court must in the first place consider the text of that Article. The English and French texts of paragraph I of Article 4 have the same meaning, and it is impossible to find any conflict between them. The text of this paragraph, by the enumeration which it contains and the choice of its terms, clearly demonstrates the intention of its authors to establish a legal rule which, while it fixes the conditions of admission, determines also the reasons for which admission may be refused; for the text does not differentiate between these two cases and any attempt to restrict it to one of them would be purely arbitrary.

The terms “Membership in the United Nations is open to all other peace-loving States which . . .” and *“Peuvent devenir Membres des Nations unies tous autres États pacifiques”*, indicate that States which fulfil the conditions stated have the qualifications requisite for admission. The natural meaning of the words used leads to the conclusion that these conditions constitute an exhaustive enumeration and are not merely stated by way of guidance or example. The provision would lose its significance and weight, if other conditions, unconnected with those laid down, could be demanded. The conditions stated in paragraph I of Article 4 must therefore be regarded not merely as the necessary conditions, but also as the conditions which suffice.

Nor can it be argued that the conditions enumerated represent only an indispensable minimum, in the sense that political considerations could be superimposed upon them, and prevent the admission of an applicant which fulfils them. Such an interpretation would be inconsistent with the terms of paragraph 2 of Article 4, which provide for the admission of “*tout Etat* remplissant ces conditions”-“any such State”. It would lead to conferring upon Members an indefinite and practically unlimited power of discretion in the imposition of new conditions. Such a power would be inconsistent with the very character of paragraph I of Article 4 which, by reason of the close connexion which it establishes between membership and the observance of the principles and obligations of the Charter, clearly constitutes a legal regulation of the question of the admission of new States. To warrant an interpretation other than that which ensues from the natural meaning of the words, a decisive reason would be required which has not been established.

Moreover, the spirit as well as the terms of the paragraph preclude the idea that considerations extraneous to these principles and obligations can prevent the admission of a State which complies with them. If the authors of the Charter had meant to leave Members free to import into the application of this provision considerations extraneous to the conditions laid down therein, they would undoubtedly have adopted a different wording.

[...]

Article 4 does not forbid the taking into account of any factor which it is possible reasonably and in good faith to connect with the conditions laid down in that Article. The taking into account of such factors is implied in the very wide and very elastic nature of the prescribed conditions; no relevant political factor that is to Say, none connected with the conditions of admission – is excluded.

It has been sought to deduce either from the second paragraph of Article 4, or from the political character of the organ recommending or deciding upon admission, arguments in favour of an interpretation of paragraph 1 of Article 4, to the effect that the fulfilment of the conditions provided for in that Article is necessary before the admission of a State can be recommended or decided upon, but that it does not preclude the Members of the Organization from advancing considerations of political expediency, extraneous to the conditions of Article 4.

But paragraph 2 is concerned only with the procedure for admission, while the preceding paragraph lays down the substantive law. This procedural character is clearly indicated by the words “will be effected”, which, by linking admission to the decision, point clearly to the fact that the paragraph is solely concerned with the manner in which admission is effected, and not with the subject of the judgment of the Organization, nor with the nature of the appreciation involved in that judgment, these two questions being dealt with in the preceding paragraph. Moreover, this paragraph, in referring to the “recommendation” of the Security Council and the “decision” of the General Assembly, is designed only to determine the respective functions of these two organs which consist in pronouncing upon the question whether or not the applicant State shall be admitted to membership after having established whether or not the prescribed conditions are fulfilled.

The political character of an organ cannot release it from the observance of the treaty provisions established by the Charter when they constitute limitations on its powers or criteria for its judgment. To ascertain whether an organ has freedom of choice for its decisions, reference must be made to the terms of its constitution. In this case, the limits of this freedom are fixed by Article 4 and allow for a wide liberty of appreciation. There is therefore no conflict between the functions of the political organs, on the one hand, and the exhaustive character of the prescribed conditions, on the other.

It has been sought to base on the political responsibilities assumed by the Security Council, in virtue of Article 24 of the Charter, an argument justifying the necessity for according to the Security Council as well as to the General Assembly complete freedom of appreciation in connexion with the admission of new Members. But Article 24, owing to the very general nature of its terms, cannot, in the absence of any provision, affect the special rules for admission which emerge from Article 4.

The foregoing considerations establish the exhaustive character of the conditions prescribed in Article 4.

***

The second part of the question concerns a demand on the part of a Member making its consent to the admission of an applicant dependent on the admission of other applicants.

Judged on the basis of the rule which the Court adopts in its interpretation of Article 4, such a demand clearly constitutes a new condition, since it is entirely unconnected with those prescribed in Article 4. It is also in an entirely different category from those conditions, since it makes admission dependent, not on the conditions required of applicants, qualifications which are supposed to be fulfilled, but on an extraneous consideration concerning States other than the applicant State.

The provisions of Article 4 necessarily imply that every application for admission should be examined and voted on separately and on its own merits; otherwise it would be impossible to determine whether a particular applicant fulfils the necessary conditions. To subject an affirmative vote for the admission of an applicant State to the condition that other States be admitted with that State would prevent Members from exercising their judgment in each case with complete liberty, within the scope of the prescribed conditions. Such a demand is incompatible with the letter and spirit of Article 4 of the Charter.

[...]

Reparations for Injuries Suffered in the Service of the United Nations (Article 4 of the Charter), ICJ Advisory Opinion, 11 April 1949

[*Note:*

Opinion requested by: *the UN General Assembly resolution 258(III) adopted on 3 December 1948.*

Questions before the Court:
"I. In the event of an agent of the United Nations in the performance of his duties suffering injury in circumstances involving the responsibility of a State, has the United Nations, as an Organization, the capacity to bring an international claim against the responsible de jure or de facto government with a view to obtaining the reparation due in respect of the damage caused (a) to the United Nations, (b) to the victim or to persons entitled through him?
II. In the event of an affirmative reply on point I (b), how is action by the United Nations to be reconciled with such rights as may be possessed by the State of which the victim is a national?"]

The Opinion:

[...]

The questions asked of the Court relate to the "capacity to bring an international claim"; accordingly, we must begin by defining what is meant by that capacity, and consider the characteristics of the Organization, so as to determine whether, in general, these characteristics do, or do not, include for the Organization a right to present an international claim.

Competence to bring an international claim is, for those possessing it, the capacity to resort to the customary methods recognized by international law for the establishment, the presentation and the settlement of claims. Among these methods may be mentioned protest, request for an enquiry, negotiation, and request for submission to an arbitral tribunal or to the Court in so far as this may be authorized by the Statute.

This capacity certainly belongs to the State; a State can bring an international claim against another State. Such a claim takes the form of a claim between two political entities, equal in law, similar in form, and both the direct subjects of international law. It is dealt with by means of negotiation, and cannot, in the present state of the law as to international jurisdiction, be submitted to a tribunal, except with the consent of the States concerned.

When the Organization brings a claim against one of its Members, this claim will be presented in the same manner, and regulated by the same procedure. It may, when necessary, be supported by the political means at the disposal of the Organization. In these ways the Organization would find a method for securing the observance of its rights by the Member against which it has a claim.

But, in the international sphere, has the Organization such a nature as involves the capacity to bring an international claim? In order to answer this question, the Court must first enquire whether the Charter has given the Organization such a position that it possesses, in regard to its Members, rights which it is entitled to ask them to respect. In other words, does the Organization possess international personality? This is no doubt a doctrinal expression, which has sometimes given rise to controversy.

But it will be used here to mean that if the Organization is recognized as having that personality, it is an entity capable of availing itself of obligations incumbent upon its Members.

To answer this question, which is not settled by the actual terms of the Charter, we must consider what characteristics it was intended thereby to give to the Organization.

The subjects of law in any legal system are not necessarily identical in their nature or in the extent of their rights, and their nature depends upon the needs of the community. Throughout its history, the development of international law has been influenced by the requirements of international life, and the progressive increase in the collective activities of States has already given rise to instances of action upon the international plane by certain entities which are not States. This development culminated in the establishment in June 1945 of an international organization whose purposes and principles are specified in the Charter of the United Nations. But to achieve these ends the attribution of international personality is indispensable.

The Charter has not been content to make the Organization created by it merely a centre "for harmonizing the actions of nations in the attainment of these common ends" (Article 1, para. 4). It has equipped that centre with organs, and has given it special tasks. It has defined the position of the Members in relation to the Organization by requiring them to give it every assistance in any action undertaken by it (Article 2, para. 5), and to accept and carry out the decisions of the Security Council; by authorizing the General Assembly to make recommendations to the Members; by giving the Organization legal capacity and privileges and immunities in the territory of each of its Members; and by providing for the conclusion of agreements between the Organization and its Members. Practice – in particular the conclusion of conventions to which the Organization is a party – has confirmed this character of the Organization, which occupies a position in certain respects in detachment from its Members, and which is under a duty to remind them, if need be, of certain obligations. It must be added that the Organization is a political body, charged with political tasks of an important character, and covering a wide field namely, the maintenance of international peace and security, the development of friendly relations among nations, and the achievement of international co-operation in the solution of problems of an economic, social, cultural or humanitarian character (Article 1); and in dealing with its Members it employs political means. The "Convention on the Privileges and Immunities of the United Nations" of 1946 creates rights and duties between each of the signatories and the Organization (see, in particular, Section 35). It is difficult to see how such a convention could operate except upon the international plane and as between parties possessing international personality.

In the opinion of the Court, the Organization was intended to exercise and enjoy, and is in fact exercising and enjoying, functions and rights which can only be explained on the basis of the possession of a large measure of international personality and the capacity to operate upon an international plane. It is at present the supreme type of international organization, and it could not carry out the intentions of its founders if it was devoid of international personality. It must be acknowledged that its Members, by entrusting certain functions to it, with the attendant duties and responsibilities, have clothed it with the competence required to enable those functions to be effectively discharged.

Accordingly, the Court has come to the conclusion that the Organization is an international person. That is not the same thing as saying that it is a State, which it certainly is not, or that its legal personality and rights and duties are the same as those of a State. Still less is it the same thing as saying that it is "a super-State", whatever that expression may mean. It does not even imply that all its rights and duties must be upon the international plane, any more than all the rights and duties of a State must be upon that plane. What it does mean is that it is a subject of international law and capable of possessing international rights and duties, and that it has capacity to maintain its rights by bringing international claims.

[...]

Whereas a State possesses the totality of international rights and duties recognized by international law, the rights and duties of an entity such as the Organization must depend upon its purposes and functions as specified or implied in its constituent documents and developed in practice. The functions of the Organization are of such a character that they could not be effectively discharged if they involved the concurrent action, on the international plane, of fifty-eight or more Foreign Offices, and the Court concludes that the Members have endowed the Organization with capacity to bring international claims when necessitated by the discharge of its functions.
What is the position as regards the claims mentioned in the request for an opinion? Question I is divided into two points, which must be considered in turn.

***

Question I *(a)* is as follows:

> "In the event of an agent of the United Nations in the performance of his duties suffering injury in circumstances involving the responsibility of a State, has the United Nations, as an Organization, the capacity to bring an international claim against the responsible *de jure* or *de facto* government with a view to obtaining the reparation due in respect of the damage caused (a) to the United Nations. . . .?"

The question is concerned solely with the reparation of damage caused to the Organization when one of its agents suffers injury at the same time. It cannot be doubted that the Organization has the capacity to bring an international claim against one of its Members which has caused injury to it by a breach of its international obligations towards it. The damage specified in Question I *(a)* means exclusively damage caused to the interests of the Organization itself, to its administrative machine, to its property and assets, and to the interests of which it is the guardian. It is clear that the Organization has the capacity to bring a claim for this damage. As the claim is based on the breach of an international obligation on the part of the Member held responsible by the Organization, the Member cannot contend that this obligation is governed by municipal law, and the Organization is justified in giving its claim the character of an international claim.

When the Organization has sustained damage resulting from a breach by a Member of its international obligations, it is impossible to see how it can obtain reparation unless it possesses capacity to bring an international claim. It cannot be supposed that in such an event all the Members of the Organization, save the defendant State, must combine to bring a claim against the defendant for the damage suffered by the Organization.

[...]

***

Question I *(b)* is as follows:

> . . ."has the United Nations, as an Organization, the capacity to bring an international claim . . . in respect of the damage caused
> . . . *(b)* to the victim or to persons entitled through him?"

[...]

[...] within the competence of the national State and not, as a general rule, within that of the Organization.

The Charter does not expressly confer upon the Organization the capacity to include, in its claim for reparation, damage caused to the victim or to persons entitled through him. The Court must therefore begin by enquiring whether the provisions of the Charter concerning the functions of the Organization, and the part played by its agents in the performance of those functions, imply for the Organization power to afford its agents the limited protection that would consist in the bringing of a claim on their behalf for reparation for damage suffered in such circumstances. Under international law, the Organization must be deemed to have those powers which, though not expressly provided in the Charter, are conferred upon it by necessary implication as being essential to the performance of its duties. This principle of law was applied by the Permanent Court of International Justice to the International Labour Organization in its Advisory Opinion No. 13 of July 23rd 1926 (Series B., No. 13, p. 18), and must be applied to the United Nations.

Having regard to its purposes and functions already referred to, the Organization may find it necessary, and has in fact found it necessary, to entrust its agents with important missions to be performed in disturbed parts of the world. Many missions, from their very nature, involve the agents in unusual dangers to which ordinary persons are not exposed. For the same reason, the injuries suffered by its agents in these circumstances will sometimes have occurred in such a manner that their national State would not be justified in bringing a claim for reparation on the ground of diplomatic protection, or, at any rate, would not feel disposed to do so. Both to ensure the efficient and independent performance of these missions and to afford effective support to its agents, the Organization must provide them with adequate protection.

[...]

For this purpose, the Members of the Organization have entered into certain undertakings, some of which are in the Charter and others in complementary agreements. The content of these undertakings need not be described here; but the Court must stress the importance of the duty to render to the Organization "every assistance" which is accepted by the Members in Article 2, paragraph 5, of the Charter. It must be noted that the effective working of the Organization – the accomplishment of its task, and the independence and effectiveness of the work of its agents – require that these undertakings should be strictly observed. For that purpose, it is necessary that, when an infringement occurs, the Organization should be able to call upon the responsible State to remedy its default, and, in particular, to obtain from the State reparation for the damage that the default may have caused to its agent. In order that the agent may perform his duties satisfactorily, he must feel that this protection is assured to him by the Organization, and that he may count on it. To ensure the independence of the agent, and, consequently, the independent action of the Organization itself, it is essential that in performing his duties he need not have to rely on any other protection than that of the Organization (save of course for the more direct and immediate protection due from the State in whose territory he may be). In particular, he should not have to rely on the protection of his own State. If he had to rely on that State, his independence might well be compromised, contrary to the principle applied by Article 100 of the Charter. And lastly, it is essential that – whether the agent belongs to a powerful or to a weak State; to one more affected or less affected, by the complications of international life; to one in sympathy or 'not in sympathy with the mission of the agent – he should know that in the performance of his duties he is under the protection of the Organization. This assurance is even more necessary when the agent is stateless.

Upon examination of the character of the functions entrusted to the Organization and of the nature of the missions of its agents, it becomes clear that the capacity of the Organization to exercise a measure of functional protection of its agents arises by necessary intendment out of the Charter.

The obligations entered into by States to enable the agents of the Organization to perform their duties are undertaken not in the interest of the agents, but in that of the Organization. When it claims redress for a breach of these obligations, the Organization is invoking its own right, the right that the obligations due to it should be respected. On this ground, it asks for reparation of the injury suffered, for "it is a principle of international law that the breach of an engagement involves an obligation to make reparation in an adequate form"; as was stated by the Permanent Court in its Judgment No. 8 of July 20th, 1927 (Series A., No. 9, p. 21). In claiming reparation based on the injury suffered by its agent, the Organization does not represent the agent, but is asserting its own right, the right to secure respect for undertakings entered into towards the Organization.

Having regard to the foregoing considerations, and to the undeniable right of the Organization to demand that its Members shall fulfil the obligations entered into by them in the interest of the good working of the Organization, the Court is of the opinion that, in the case of a breach of these obligations, the Organization has the capacity to claim adequate reparation, and that in assessing this reparation it is authorized to include the damage suffered by the victim or by persons entitled through him.

***

The question remains whether the Organization has "the capacity to bring an international claim against the responsible *de jure* or *de facto* government with a view to obtaining the reparation due in respect of the damage caused *(a)* to the United Nations, *(b)* to the victim or to persons entitled through him" when the defendant State is not a member of the Organization.

In considering this aspect of Question I *(a)* and *(b)*, it is necessary to keep in mind the reasons which have led the Court to give an affirmative answer to it when the defendant State is a Member of the Organization. It has now been established that the Organization has capacity to bring claims on the international plane, and that it possesses a right of functional protection in respect of its agents. Here again the Court is authorized to assume that the damage suffered involves the responsibility of a State, and it is not called upon to express an opinion upon the various ways in which that responsibility might be engaged. Accordingly the question is whether the Organization has capacity to bring a claim against the defendant State to recover reparation in respect of that damage or whether, on the contrary, the defendant State, not being a member, is justified in raising the objection that the Organization lacks the capacity to bring an international claim. On this point, the Court's opinion is that fifty States, representing the vast majority of the members of the international community, had the power, in conformity with international law, to bring into being an entity possessing objective international personality, and not merely personality recognized by them alone, together with capacity to bring international claims.

Accordingly, the Court arrives at the conclusion that an affirmative answer should be given to Question I *(a)* and *(b)* whether or not the defendant State is a Member of the United Nations.

***

[...]

Competence of the General Assembly for the Admission of a State to the United Nations, ICJ Advisory Opinion, 3 March 1950 (Second Admissions Case)

[*Note:*

Opinion requested by: the UN General Assembly resolution 296(IV) J adopted on 22 November 1949

Question before the Court:
"Can the admission of a State to membership in the United Nations, pursuant to Article 4, paragraph 2, of the Charter, be effected by a decision of the General Assembly when the Security Council has made no recommendation for admission by reason of the candidate failing to obtain the requisite majority or of the negative vote of a permanent Member upon a resolution so to recommend?"]

The Opinion:

[...]

The Court is, therefore, called upon to determine solely whether the General Assembly can make a decision to admit a State when the Security Council has transmitted no recommendation to it.

Article 4, paragraph 2, is as follows:

> "The admission of any such State to membership in the United Nations will be effected by a decision of the General Assembly upon the recommendation of the Security Council."

The Court has no doubt as to the meaning of this text. It requires two things to effect admission: a "recommendation" of the Security Council and a "decision" of the General Assembly. It is in the nature of things that the recommendation should come before the decision. The word "recommendation", and the word "upon" preceding it, imply the idea that the recommendation is the foundation of the decision to admit, and that the latter rests upon the recommendation. Both these acts are indispensable to form the judgment of the Organization to which the previous paragraph of Article 4 refers. The text under consideration means that the General Assembly can only decide to admit upon the recommendation of the Security Council; it determines the respective roles of the two organs whose combined action is required before admission can be effected: in other words, the recommendation of the Security Council is the condition precedent to the decision of the Assembly by which the admission is effected.

[...]

The conclusions to which the Court is led by the text of Article 4, paragraph 2, are fully confirmed by the structure of the Charter, and particularly by the relations established by it between the General Assembly and the Security Council.

The General Assembly and the Security Council are both principal organs of the United Nations. The Charter does not place the Security Council in a subordinate position. Article 24 confers upon it "primary responsibility for the maintenance of peace and security", and the Charter grants it for this purpose certain powers of decision. Under Articles 4, 5, and 6, the Security Council co-operates with the General Assembly in matters of admission to membership, of suspension from the exercise of the rights and privileges of membership, and of expulsion from the Organization. It has power, without the concurrence of the General Assembly, to reinstate the Member which was the object of the suspension, in its rights and privileges.

The organs to which Article 4 entrusts the judgment of the Organization in matters of admission have consistently interpreted the text in the sense that the General Assembly can decide to admit only on the basis of a recommendation of the Security Council. In particular, the Rules of Procedure of the General Assembly provide for consideration of the merits of an application and of the decision to be made upon it only "if the Security Council recommends the applicant State for membership" (Article 125). The Rules merely state that if the Security Council has not recommended the admission, the General Assembly may send back the application to the Security Council for further consideration (Article 126). This last step has been taken several times: it was taken in Resolution 296 (IV), the very one that embodies this Request for an Opinion.

To hold that the General Assembly has power to admit a State to membership in the absence of a recommendation of the Security Council would be to deprive the Security Council of an important power which has been entrusted to it by the Charter. It would almost nullify the role of the Security Council in the exercise of one of the essential functions of the Organization. It would mean that the Security Council would have merely to study the case, present a report, give advice, and express an opinion. This is not what Article 4, paragraph 2, says.

The Court cannot accept the suggestion made in one of the written statements submitted to the Court, that the General Assembly, in order to try to meet the requirement of Article 4, paragraph 2, could treat the absence of a recommendation as equivalent to what is described in that statement as an "unfavourable recommendation", upon which the General Assembly could base a decision to admit a State to membership.

Reference has also been made to a document of the San Francisco Conference, in order to put the possible case of an unfavourable recommendation being voted by the Security Council: 'such a recommendation has never been made in practice. In the opinion of the Court, Article 4, paragraph 2, envisages a favourable recommendation of the Security Council and that only. An unfavourable recommendation would not correspond to the provisions of Article 4, paragraph 2.

While keeping within the limits of a Request which deals with the scope of the powers of the General Assembly, it is enough for the Court to say that nowhere has the General Assembly received the power to change, to the point of reversing, the meaning of a vote of the Security Council.

In consequence, it is impossible to admit that the General Assembly has the power to attribute to a vote of the Security Council the character of a recommendation when the Council itself considers that no such recommendation has been made.

[...]

Effect of Awards of Compensation made by the U. N. Administrative Tribunal, ICJ Advisory Opinion, 13 July 1954

[*Note:*

Opinion requested by: the UN General Assembly resolution 785(VIII) A of 9 December 1953

Questions before the Court:
"(1) Having regard to the Statute of the United Nations Administrative Tribunal and to any other relevant instruments and to the relevant records, has the General Assembly the right on any grounds to refuse to give effect to an award of compensation made by that Tribunal in favour of a staff member of the United Nations whose contract of service has been terminated without his assent ?
(2) If the answer given by the Court to question (1) is in the affirmative, what are the principal grounds upon which the General Assembly could lawfully exercise such a right ?"]

The Opinion:

[...]

The legal power of the General Assembly to establish a tribunal competent to render judgments binding on the United Nations has been challenged. Accordingly, it is necessary to consider whether the General Assembly has been given this power by the Charter.

There is no express provision for the establishment of judicial bodies or organs and no indication to the contrary. However, in its Opinion – *Reparation for Injuries suffered in the Service of the United Nations*, Advisory Opinion: I.C.J. Reports 1949, p. 182 – the Court said:

> "Under international law, the Organization must be deemed to have those powers which, though not expressly provided in the Charter, are conferred upon it by necessary implication as being essential to the performance of its duties."

The Court must therefore begin by enquiring whether the provisions of the Charter concerning the relations between the staff members and the Organization imply for the Organization the power to establish a judicial tribunal to adjudicate upon disputes arising out of the contracts of service.

Under the provisions of Chapter XV of the Charter, the Secretariat, which is one of the principal organs of the United Nations, comprises the Secretary-General and the staff. The Secretary-General is appointed by the General Assembly, upon the recommendation of the Security Council, and he is "the chief administrative officer of the Organization". The staff members are "appointed by the Secretary-General under regulations established by the General Assembly". In the words of Article 101 (3) of the Charter, "The paramount consideration in the employment of the staff and in the determination of the conditions of service shall be the necessity of securing the highest standards of efficiency, competence and integrity".

The contracts of service between the Organization and the staff members are contained in letters of appointment. Each appointment is made subject to terms and conditions provided in the Staff Regulations and Staff Rules, together with such amendments as may be made from time to time.

When the Secretariat was organized, a situation arose in which the relations between the staff members and the Organization were governed by a complex code of law. This code consisted of the Staff

Regulations established by the General Assembly, defining the fundamental rights and obligations of the staff, and the Staff Rules, made by the Secretary-General in order to implement the Staff Regulations. It was inevitable that there would be disputes between the Organization and staff members as to their rights and duties. The Charter contains no provision which authorizes any of the principal organs of the United Nations to adjudicate upon these disputes, and Article 105 secures for the United Nations jurisdictional immunities in national courts. It would, in the opinion of the Court, hardly be consistent with the expressed aim of the Charter to promote freedom and justice for individuals and with the constant preoccupation of the United Nations Organization to promote this aim that it should afford no judicial or arbitral remedy to its own staff for the settlement of any disputes which may arise between it and them.

In these circumstances, the Court finds that the power to establish a tribunal, to do justice as between the Organization and the staff members, was essential to ensure the efficient working of the Secretariat, and to give effect to the paramount consideration of securing the highest standards of efficiency, competence and integrity. Capacity to do this arises by necessary intendment out of the Charter.

The existence of this capacity leads to the further enquiry as to the agency by which it may be exercised. Here, there can be no room for doubt.

In Article 7 of the Charter, after naming the six principal organs, it is provided in paragraph (2):

> "Such subsidiary organs, as may be found necessary may be established in accordance with the present Charter."

Article 22 provides:

> "The General Assembly may establish such subsidiary organs as it deems necessary for the performance of its functions."

Further, in Article 101, paragraph 1, the General Assembly is given power to regulate staff relations:

> "The Staff shall be appointed by the Secretary-General under regulations established by the General Assembly."

Accordingly, the Court finds that the power to establish a tribunal to do justice between the Organization and the staff members may be exercised by the General Assembly.

*

But that does not dispose of the problem before the Court. Some of the Governments that take the position that there are grounds which would justify the General Assembly in refusing to give effect to awards, agree that the powers of the General Assembly, and particularly its power to establish regulations under Article 101, imply the power to set up an administrative tribunal. They agree that the General Assembly would be able to establish a tribunal competent to hear and decide staff grievances, to prescribe its jurisdiction, and to authorize it to give a final decision, in the sense that no appeal could be taken as of right. They nevertheless contend that the implied power does not enable the General Assembly to establish a tribunal with authority to make decisions binding on the General Assembly itself.

In the first place, it is contended that there was no need to go so far, and that an implied power can only be exercised to the extent that the particular measure under consideration can be regarded as absolutely essential. There can be no doubt that the General Assembly in the exercise of its power could have set up a tribunal without giving finality to its judgments. In fact, however, it decided, after long deliberation, to invest the Tribunal with power to render judgments which would be "final and without appeal", and which would be binding on the United Nations. The precise nature and scope of the measures by which the power of creating a tribunal was to be exercised, was a matter for determination by the General Assembly alone.

*

It has been contended that the General Assembly cannot, by establishing the Administrative Tribunal, divest itself of the power conferred by paragraph (i) of Article 17 of the Charter, which reads:

> "The General Assembly shall consider and approve the budget of the Organization."

This provision confers a power on the General Assembly, for the exercise of which Article 18 requires the vote of a two-thirds majority. Accordingly, the establishment of a tribunal competent to make an award of compensation to which the General Assembly was bound to give effect would, it has been argued, contravene the provisions relating to the budgetary power. The Court is unable to accept this contention.

The Court notes that Article 17 of the Charter appears in a section of Chapter IV relating to the General Assembly, which is entitled "Functions and Powers". This Article deals with a function of the General Assembly and provides for the consideration and approval by it of the budget of the Organization. Consideration of the budget is thus an act which must be performed and the same is true of its approval, for without such approval there can be no budget.

But the function of approving the budget does not mean that the General Assembly has an absolute power to approve or disapprove the expenditure proposed to it; for some part of that expenditure arises out of obligations already incurred by the Organization, and to this extent the General Assembly has no alternative but to honour these engagements. The question, therefore, to be decided by the Court is whether these obligations comprise the awards of compensation made by the Administrative Tribunal in favour of staff members. The reply to this question must be in the affirmative. The obligatory character of these awards has been established by the considerations set out above relating to the authority of *res judicata* and the binding effect of the judgments of this Tribunal upon the United Nations Organization.

The Court therefore considers that the assignment of the budgetary function to the General Assembly cannot be regarded as conferring upon it the right to refuse to give effect to the obligation arising out of an award of the Administrative Tribunal.

*

It has also been contended that the implied power of the General Assembly to establish a tribunal cannot be carried so far as to enable the tribunal to intervene in matters falling within the province of the Secretary-General. The Court cannot accept this contention.

The General Assembly could at all times limit or control the powers of the Secretary-General in staff matters, by virtue of the provisions of Article 101. Acting under powers conferred by the Charter, the General Assembly authorized the intervention of the Tribunal to the extent that such intervention might result from the exercise of jurisdiction conferred upon the Tribunal by its Statute. Accordingly, when the Tribunal decides that particular action by the Secretary-General involves a breach of the contract of service, it is in no sense intervening in a Charter power of the Secretary-General, because the Secretary-Generals legal powers in staff matters have already been limited in this respect by the General Assembly.

*

A similar problem is involved in the contention that the General Assembly cannot authorize and the Secretary-General cannot enter into contracts of service which are not in conformity with the Charter. The Staff Regulations are made a part of the contracts of service and No. 11.2 reads as follows:

> "The United Nations Administrative Tribunal shall, under conditions prescribed in its Statute, hear and pass judgment upon applications from staff members alleging non-observance of their terms of appointment, including all pertinent regulations and rules."

It is contended that the incorporation, in the contracts of service, of the right to rely on the Statute of the Administrative Tribunal would conflict with the powers conferred on the General Assembly and on the Secretary-General by the Charter. In view of the foregoing considerations, the Court cannot accept this contention. There can be no doubt that, by virtue of the terms thus incorporated in the contracts of service, and so long as the Statute of the Administrative Tribunal in its present form is in force, the staff members are entitled to resort to the Tribunal and rely on its judgments.

*

In the third place, the view has been put forward that the Administrative Tribunal is a subsidiary, subordinate, or secondary organ; and that, accordingly, the Tribunal's judgments cannot bind the General Assembly which established it.

This view assumes that, in adopting the Statute of the Administrative Tribunal, the General Assembly was establishing an organ which it deemed necessary for the performance of its own functions. But the Court cannot accept this basic assumption. The Charter does not confer judicial functions on the General Assembly and the relations between staff and Organization come within the scope of Chapter XV of the Charter. In the absence of the establishment of an Administrative Tribunal, the function of resolving disputes between staff and Organization could be discharged by the Secretary-General by virtue of the provisions of Articles 97 and 101. Accordingly, in the three years or more preceding the establishment of the Administrative Tribunal, the Secretary-General coped with this problem by means of joint administrative machinery, leading to ultimate decision by himself. By establishing the Administrative Tribunal, the General Assembly was not delegating the performance of its own functions: it was exercising a power which it had under the Charter to regulate staff relations. In regard to the Secretariat, the General Assembly is given by the Charter a power to make regulations, but not a power to adjudicate upon, or otherwise deal with, particular instances.

It has been argued that an authority exercising a power to make regulations is inherently incapable of creating a subordinate body competent to make decisions binding its creator. There can be no doubt that the Administrative Tribunal is subordinate in the sense that the General Assembly can abolish the Tribunal by repealing the Statute, that it can amend the Statute and provide for review of the future decisions of the Tribunal and that it can amend the Staff Regulations and make new ones. There is no lack of power to deal effectively with any problem that may arise. But the contention that the General Assembly is inherently incapable of creating a tribunal competent to make decisions binding on itself cannot be accepted. It cannot be justified by analogy to national laws, for it is common practice in national legislatures to create courts with the capacity to render decisions legally binding on the legislatures which brought them into being.

The question cannot be determined on the basis of the description of the relationship between the General Assembly and the Tribunal, that is, by considering whether the Tribunal is to be regarded as a subsidiary, a subordinate, or a secondary organ, or on the basis of the fact that it was established by the General Assembly. It depends on the intention of the General Assembly in establishing the Tribunal, and on the nature of the functions conferred upon it by its Statute. An examination of the language of the Statute of the Administrative Tribunal has shown that the General Assembly intended to establish a judicial body; moreover, it had the legal capacity under the Charter to do so.

*

[...]

Certain Expenses of the United Nations (Article 17, Paragraph 2, of the Charter), ICJ Advisory Opinion, 20 July 1962

[*Note:*

Opinion requested by: the UN General Assembly resolution 1731 (XVI) of 20 December 1961

Question before the Court: *The circumstance leading to the request for an advisory opinion was the apportionment of certain expenses relating to the United Nations Emergency Force (UNEF) and United Nations Operation in Congo (ONUC) among UN Member States, many of which refused to pay on the grounds that these were not expenses of the Organization to be borne by the Members within the meaning of Article 17 (2) of the UN Charter.*

The General Assembly asked the following question:
"Do the expenditures authorized in General Assembly resolutions [...] relating to the United Nations operations in the Congo undertaken in pursuance of the Security Council resolutions [...] and General Assembly resolutions [...] and the expenditures authorized in General Assembly resolutions [...] relating to the operations of the United Nations Emergency Force undertaken in pursuance of General Assembly resolutions [...] constitute 'expenses of the Organization' within the meaning of Article 17, paragraph 2, of the Charter of the United Nations?"]

The Opinion:

[...]

Turning to the question which has been posed, the Court observes that it involves an interpretation of Article 17, paragraph 2, of the Charter. On the previous occasions when the Court has had to interpret the Charter of the United Nations, it has followed the principles and rules applicable in general to the interpretation of treaties, since it has recognized that the Charter is a multilateral treaty, albeit a treaty having certain special characteristics. In interpreting Article 4 of the Charter, the Court was led to consider "the structure of the Charter" and "the relations established by it between the General Assembly and the Security Council"; a comparable problem confronts the Court in the instant matter. The Court sustained its interpretation of Article 4 by considering the manner in which the organs concerned "have consistently interpreted the text" in their practice (*Competence of the General Assembly for the Admission of a State to the United Nations, I.C.J. Reports 1950*, pp. 8-9).

The text of Article 17 is in part as follows:

"1. The General Assembly shall consider and approve the budget of the Organization.
2. The expenses of the Organization shall be borne by the Members as apportioned by the General Assembly."

[...]

The text of Article 17, paragraph 2, refers to "the expenses of the Organization" without any further explicit definition of such expenses. It would be possible to begin with a general proposition to the effect that the "expenses" of any organization are the amounts paid out to defray the costs of carrying out its purposes, in this case, the political, economic, social, humanitarian and other purposes of the United Nations. The next step would be to examine, as the Court will, whether the resolutions authorizing the operations here in question were intended to carry out the purposes of the United Nations and whether the expenditures were incurred in furthering these operations. Or, it might simply be said that the "expenses" of an organization are those which are provided for in its budget. But the Court has not been asked to give an abstract definition of the words "expenses of the Organization". It has been asked to answer a specific question related to certain identified expenditures which have actually been made, but the Court would not adequately discharge the obligation incumbent on it unless it examined in some detail various problems raised by the question which the General Assembly has asked.

[...]

Passing from the text of Article 17 to its place in the general structure and scheme of the Charter, the Court will consider whether in that broad context one finds any basis for implying a limitation upon the budgetary authority of the General Assembly which in turn might limit the meaning of "expenses" in paragraph 2 of that Article.

The general purposes of Article 17 are the vesting of control over the finances of the Organization, and the levying of apportioned amounts of the expenses of the Organization in order to enable it to carry out the functions of the Organization as a whole acting through its principal organs and such subsidiary organs as may be established under the authority of Article 22 or Article 29.

Article 17 is the only article in the Charter which refers to budgetary authority or to the power to apportion expenses, or otherwise to raise revenue, except for Articles 33 and 35, paragraph 3, of the Statute of the Court which have no bearing on the point here under discussion. Nevertheless, it has been argued before the Court that one type of expenses, namely those resulting from operations for the maintenance of international peace and security, are not "expenses of the Organization" within the meaning of Article 17, paragraph 2, of the Charter, inasmuch as they fall to be dealt with exclusively by the Security Council, and more especially through agreements negotiated in accordance with Article 43 of the Charter.

The argument rests in part upon the view that when the maintenance of international peace and security is involved, it is only the Security Council which is authorized to decide on any action relative thereto. It is argued further that since the General Assembly's power is limited to discussing, considering, studying and recommending, it cannot impose an obligation to pay the expenses which result from the implementation of its recommendations. This argument leads to an examination of the respective functions of the General Assembly and of the Security Council under the Charter, particularly with respect to the maintenance of international peace and security.

Article 24 of the Charter provides:

> "In order to ensure prompt and effective action by the United Nations, its Members confer on the Security Council primary responsibility for the maintenance of international peace and security..."

The responsibility conferred is "primary", not exclusive. This primary responsibility is conferred upon the Security Council, as stated in Article 24, "in order to ensure prompt and effective action". To this end, it is the Security Council which is given a power to impose an explicit obligation of compliance if for example it issues an order or command to an aggressor under Chapter VII. It is only the Security Council which can require enforcement by coercive action against an aggressor.

The Charter makes it abundantly clear, however, that the General Assembly is also to be concerned with international peace and security. Article 14 authorizes the General Assembly to "recommend measures for the peaceful adjustment of any situation, regardless of origin, which it deems likely to impair the general welfare or friendly relations among nations, including situations resulting from a violation of the provisions of the present Charter setting forth the purposes and principles of the United

Nations". The word "measures" implies some kind of action, and the only limitation which Article 14 imposes on the General Assembly is the restriction found in Article 12, namely, that the Assembly should not recommend measures while the Security Council is dealing with the same matter unless the Council requests it to do so. Thus while it is the Security Council which, exclusively, may order coercive action, the functions and powers conferred by the Charter on the General Assembly are not confined to discussion, consideration, the initiation of studies and the making of recommendations; they are not merely hortatory. Article 18 deals with "*decisions*" of the General Assembly "on important questions". These "decisions" do indeed include certain recommendations, but others have dispositive force and effect. Among these latter decisions, Article 18 includes suspension of rights and privileges of membership, expulsion of Members, "and budgetary questions". In connection with the suspension of rights and privileges of membership and expulsion from membership under Articles 5 and 6, it is the Security Council which has only the power to recommend and it is the General Assembly which decides and whose decision determines status; but there is a close collaboration between the two organs. Moreover, these powers of decision of the General Assembly under articles 5 and 6 are specifically related to preventive or enforcement.

By Article 17, paragraph 1, the General Assembly is given the power not only to "consider" the budget of the Organization, but also to "approve" it. The decision to "approve" the budget has a close connection with paragraph 2 of Article 17, since thereunder the General Assembly is also given the power to apportion the expenses among the Members and the exercise of the power of apportionment creates the obligation, specifically stated in Article 17, paragraph 2, of each Member to bear that part of the expenses which is apportioned to it by the General Assembly. When those expenses include expenditures for the maintenance of peace and security, which are not otherwise provided for, it is the General Assembly which has the authority to apportion the latter amounts among the Members. The provisions of the Charter which distribute functions and powers to the Security Council and to the General Assembly give no support to the view that such distribution excludes from the powers of the General Assembly the power to provide for the financing of measures designed to maintain peace and security.

The argument supporting a limitation on the budgetary authority of the General Assembly with respect to the maintenance of international peace and security relies especially on the reference to "action" in the last sentence of Article 11, paragraph 2. This paragraph reads as follows:

> "The General Assembly may discuss any questions relating to the maintenance of international peace and security brought before it by any Member of the United Nations, or by the Security Council, or by a State which is not a Member of the United Nations in accordance with Article 35, paragraph 2, and, except as provided in Article 12, may make recommendations with regard to any such question to the State or States concerned or to the Security Council, or to both. Any such question on which action is necessary shall be referred to the Security Council by the General Assembly either before or after discussion."

The Court considers that the kind of action referred to in Article 11, paragraph 2, is coercive or enforcement action. This paragraph, which applies not merely to general questions relating to peace and security, but also to specific cases brought before the General Assembly by a State under Article 35, in its first sentence empowers the General Assembly, by means of recommendations to States or to the Security Council, or to both, to organize peace-keeping operations, at the request, or with the consent, of the States concerned. This power of the General Assembly is a special power which in no way derogates from its general powers under Article 10 or Article 14, except as limited by the last sentence of

Article 11, paragraph 2. This last sentence says that when "action" is necessary the General Assembly shall refer the question to the Security Council. The word "action" must mean such action as is solely within the province of the Security Council. It cannot refer to recommendations which the Security Council might make, as for instance under Article 38, because the General Assembly under Article 11 has a comparable power. The "action" which is solely within the province of the Security Council is that which is indicated by the title of Chapter VII of the Charter, namely "Action with respect to threats to the peace, breaches of the peace, and acts of aggression". If the word "action" in Article 11, paragraph 2, were interpreted to mean that the General Assembly could make recommendations only of a general character affecting peace and security in the abstract, and not in relation to specific cases, the paragraph would not have provided that the General Assembly may make recommendations on questions brought before it by States or by the Security Council. Accordingly, the last sentence of Article 11, paragraph 2, has no application where the necessary action is not enforcement action.

The practice of the Organization throughout its history bears out the foregoing elucidation of the term "action" in the last sentence of Article 11, paragraph 2. Whether the General Assembly proceeds under Article 11 or under Article 14, the implementation of its recommendations for setting up commissions or other bodies involves organizational activity – action – in connection with the maintenance of international peace and security. Such implementation is a normal feature of the functioning of the United Nations. Such committees, commissions or other bodies or individuals, constitute, in some cases, subsidiary organs established under the authority of Article 22 of the Charter. The functions of the General Assembly for which it may establish such subsidiary organs include, for example, investigation, observation and supervision, but the way in which such subsidiary organs are utilized depends on the consent of the State or States concerned.

The Court accordingly finds that the argument which seeks, by reference to Article 11, paragraph 2, to limit the budgetary authority of the General Assembly in respect of the maintenance of international peace and security, is unfounded.

[...] The Court has considered the general problem of the interpretation of Article 17, paragraph 2, in the light of the general structure of the Charter and of the respective functions assigned by the Charter to the General Assembly and to the Security Council, with a view to determining the meaning of the phrase "the expenses of the Organization". The Court does not find it necessary to go further in giving a more detailed definition of such expenses. The Court will, therefore, proceed to examine the expenditures enumerated in the request for the advisory opinion. In determining whether the actual expenditures authorized constitute "expenses of the Organization within the meaning of Article 17, paragraph 2, of the Charter", the Court agrees that such expenditures must be tested by their relationship to the purposes of the United Nations in the sense that if an expenditure were made for a purpose which is not one of the purposes of the United Nations, it could not be considered an "expense of the Organization".

The purposes of the United Nations are set forth in Article 1 of the Charter. The first two purposes as stated in paragraphs 1 and 2, may be summarily described as pointing to the goal of international peace and security and friendly relations. The third purpose is the achievement of economic, social, cultural and humanitarian goals and respect for human rights. The fourth and last purpose is: "To be a center for harmonizing the actions of nations in the attainment of these common ends."

The primary place ascribed to international peace and security is natural, since the fulfilment of the other purposes will be dependent upon the attainment of that basic condition. These purposes are broad indeed, but neither they nor the powers conferred to effectuate them are unlimited. Save as they have entrusted the Organization with the attainment of these common ends, the Member States retain their freedom of action. But when the Organization takes action which warrants the assertion that it was appropriate for the fulfilment of one of the stated purposes of the United Nations, the presumption is that such action is not *ultra vires* the Organization.

If it is agreed that the action in question is within the scope of the functions of the Organization but it is alleged that it has been initiated or carried out in a manner not in conformity with the division of functions among the several organs which the Charter prescribes, one moves to the internal plane, to the internal structure of the Organization. If the action was taken by the wrong organ, it was irregular as a matter of that internal structure, but this would not necessarily mean that the expense incurred was not an expense of the Organization. Both national and international law contemplate cases in which the body corporate or politic may be bound, as to third parties, by an *ultra vires* act of an agent.

In the legal systems of States, there is often some procedure for determining the validity of even a legislative or governmental act, but no analogous procedure is to be found in the structure of the United Nations. Proposals made during the drafting of the Charter to place the ultimate authority to interpret the Charter in the International Court of Justice were not accepted; the opinion which the Court is in course of rendering is an *advisory* opinion. As anticipated in 1945, therefore, each organ must, in the first place at least, determine its own jurisdiction. If the Security Council, for example, adopts a resolution purportedly for the maintenance of international peace and security and if, in accordance with a mandate or authorization in such resolution, the Secretary-General incurs financial obligations, these amounts must be presumed to constitute "expenses of the Organization".

Legal Consequences for States of the Continued Presence of South Africa in Namibia (South West Africa) Notwithstanding SC Resolution 276 (1970), ICJ Advisory Opinion, 21 June 1971

[*Note:*

Opinion requested by: the UN Security Council resolution 284 (1970) of 29 July 1970

Question before the Court:
On 30 January 1970 the UN Security Council adopted resolution 276(1970) which, inter alia, strongly condemned the refusal of the Government of South Africa to comply with the resolutions of the General Assembly and Security Council pertaining to Namibia and declared that after the termination of the Mandate (by the UN General Assembly resolution 2145(XXI) of 27 October 1966) the continued presence of the South African authorities in Namibia was illegal and all acts taken by the Government of South Africa on behalf or concerning Namibia were illegal and invalid.

The Court was asked to give an advisory opinion on the following question:

"What are the legal consequences for States of the continued presence of South Africa in Namibia, notwithstanding Security Council resolution 276(1970)?"]

The Opinion:

[...]

25. The question of Namibia was placed on the agenda of the Security Council as a "situation" and not as a "dispute". No member State made any suggestion or proposal that the matter should be examined as a dispute, although due notice was given of the placing of the question on the Security Council's agenda under the title "Situation in Namibia". Had the Government of South Africa considered that the question should have been treated in the Security Council as a dispute, it should have drawn the Council's attention to that aspect of the matter. Having failed to raise the question at the appropriate time in the proper forum, it is not open to it to raise it before the Court at this stage.

26. A similar answer must be given to the related objection based on the proviso to paragraph 3 of Article 27 of the Charter. This proviso also requires for its application the prior determination by the Security Council that a dispute exists and that certain members of the Council are involved as parties to such a dispute.

[...]

89. Undoubtedly, the Court does not possess powers of judicial review or appeal in respect of the decisions taken by the United Nations organs concerned. The question of the validity or conformity with the Charter of General Assembly resolution 2145 (XXI) or of related Security Council resolutions does not form the subject of the request for advisory opinion. However, in the exercise of its judicial function and since objections have been advanced the Court, in the course of its reasoning, will consider these objections before determining any legal consequences arising from those resolutions.

90. As indicated earlier, with the entry into force of the Charter of the United Nations a relationship was established between all Members of the United Nations on the one side, and each mandatory Power on the other. The mandatory Powers while retaining their mandates assumed, under Article 80 of the Charter, vis-à-vis all United Nations Members, the obligation to keep intact and preserve, until trusteeship agreements were executed, the rights of other States and of the peoples of mandated territories, which resulted from the existing mandate agreements and related instruments, such as Article 22 of the Covenant and the League Council's resolution of 31 'January 1923 concerning petitions. The mandatory Powers also bound themselves to exercise their functions of administration in conformity with the relevant obligations emanating from the United Nations Charter, which member States have undertaken to fulfil in good faith in all their international relations.

91. One of the fundamental principles governing the international relationship thus established is that a party which disowns or does not fulfil its own obligations cannot be recognized as retaining the rights which it claims to derive from the relationship.

92. The terms of the preamble and operative part of resolution 2145 (XXI) leave no doubt as to the character of the resolution. In the preamble the General Assembly declares itself "*Convinced* that the administration of the Mandated Territory by South Africa has been conducted in a manner contrary" to the two basic international instruments directly imposing obligations upon South Africa, the Mandate and the Charter of the United Nations, as well as to the Universal Declaration of Human Rights. In another paragraph of the preamble the conclusion is reached that, after having insisted with no avail upon performance for more than twenty years, the moment has arrived for the General Assembly to exercise the right to treat such violation as a ground for termination.

93. In paragraph 3 of the operative part of the resolution the General Assembly "*Declares* that South Africa has failed to fulfil its obligations in respect of the administration of the Mandated Territory and to ensure the moral and material well-being and security of the indigenous inhabitants of South West Africa and has, in fact, disavowed the Mandate". In paragraph 4 the decision is reached, as a consequence of the previous declaration "that the Mandate conferred upon His Britannic Majesty to be exercised on his behalf by the Government of the Union of South Africa is *therefore* terminated . . . ". (Emphasis added.) It is this part of the resolution which is relevant in the present proceedings.

94. In examining this action of the General Assembly it is appropriate to have regard to the general principles of international law regulating termination of a treaty relationship on account of breach. For even if the mandate is viewed as having the character of an institution, as is maintained, it depends on those international agreements which created the system and regulated its application. As the Court indicated in 1962 "this Mandate, like practically all other similar Mandates "was" a special type of instrument composite in nature and instituting a novel international régime. It incorporates a definite agreement . . ." (*I.C.J. Reports 1962*, p. 331). The Court stated conclusively in that Judgment that the Mandate ". . . in fact and in law, is an international agreement having the character of a treaty or convention" (I.C.J. *Reports* 1962. p. *330*). The rules laid down by the Vienna Convention on the Law of Treaties concerning termination of a treaty relationship on account of breach (adopted without a dissenting vote) may in many respects be considered as a codification of existing customary law on the subject. In the light of these rules, only a material breach of a treaty justifies termination, such breach being defined as:

"(a) a repudiation of the treaty not sanctioned by the present Convention; or
(b) the violation of a provision essential to the accomplishment of the object or purpose of the treaty" (Art. *60*, para. *3*).

95. General Assembly resolution 2145 (XXI) determines that both forms of material breach had occurred in this case. By stressing that South Africa "has, in fact, disavowed the Mandate", the General Assembly declared in fact that it had repudiated it. The resolution in question is therefore to be viewed as the exercise of the right to terminate a relationship in case of a deliberate and persistent violation of obligations which destroys the very object and purpose of that relationship.

***

112. It would be an untenable interpretation to maintain that, once such a declaration had been made by the Security Council under Article 24 of the Charter, on behalf of all member States, those Members would be free to act in disregard of such illegality or even to recognize violations of law resulting from it. When confronted with such an internationally unlawful situation, Members of the United Nations would be expected to act in consequence of the declaration made on their behalf. The question therefore arises as to the effect of this decision of the Security Council for States Members of the United Nations in accordance with Article 25 of the Charter.

113. It has been contended that Article 25 of the Charter applies only to enforcement measures adopted under Chapter VII of the Charter. It is not possible to find in the Charter any support for this view. Article 25 is not confined to decisions in regard to enforcement action but applies to "the decisions of the Security Council" adopted in accordance with the Charter. Moreover, that Article is placed, not in Chapter VII, but immediately after Article 24 in that part of the Charter which deals with the functions and powers of the Security Council. If Article 25 had reference solely to decisions of the Security Council concerning enforcement action under Articles 41 and 42 of the Charter, that is to say, if it were only such decisions which had binding effect, then Article 25 would be superfluous, since this effect is secured by Articles 48 and 49 of the Charter.

114. It has also been contended that the relevant Security Council resolutions are couched in exhortatory rather than mandatory language and that, therefore, they do not purport to impose any legal duty on any State nor to affect legally any right of any State. The language of a resolution of the Security Council should be carefully analysed before a conclusion can be made as to its binding effect. In view of the nature of the powers under Article 25, the question whether they have been in fact exercised is to be determined in each case, having regard to the terms of the resolution to be interpreted, the discussions leading to it, the Charter provisions invoked and, in general, all circumstances that might assist in determining the legal consequences of the resolution of the Security Council.

[...]

116. In pronouncing upon the binding nature of the Security Council decisions in question, the Court would recall the following passage in its Advisory Opinion of 11 April 1949 on *Reparation for Injuries Suffered in the Service of the United Nations:*

> "The Charter has not been content to make the Organization created by it merely a centre 'for harmonizing the actions of nations in the attainment of these common ends' (Article 1, para. 4). It has equipped that centre with organs, and has given its special tasks. It has defined the position of the Members in relation to the Organization by requiring them to give it every assistance in any action undertaken by it (Article 2, para. 5), and to accept and carry out the decisions of the Security Council." (*I.C.J. Reports 1949*, p. 178.)

Thus when the Security Council adopts a decision under Article 25 in accordance with the Charter, it is for member States to comply with that decision, including those members of the Security Council which voted against it and those Members of the United Nations who are not members of the Council. To hold otherwise would be to deprive this principal organ of its essential functions and powers under the Charter.

[...]

122. For the reasons given above, and subject to the observations contained in paragraph 125 below, member States are under obligation to abstain from entering into treaty relations with South Africa in all cases in which the Government of South Africa purports to act on behalf of or concerning Namibia. With respect to existing bilateral treaties, member States must abstain from invoking or applying those treaties or provisions of treaties concluded by South Africa on behalf of or concerning Namibia which involve active intergovernmental CO-operation. With respect to multilateral treaties, however, the same rule cannot be applied to certain general conventions such as those of a humanitarian character, the non-performance of which may adversely affect the people of Namibia. It will be for the competent international organs to take specific measures in this respect.

123. Member States, in compliance with the duty of non-recognition imposed by paragraphs 2 and 5 of resolution 276 (1970), are under obligation to abstain from sending diplomatic or special missions to South Africa including in their jurisdiction the Territory of Namibia, to abstain from sending consular agents to Namibia, and to withdraw any such agents already there. They should also make it clear to the South African authorities that the maintenance of diplomatic or consular relations with South Africa does not imply any recognition of its authority with regard to Namibia.

124. The restraints which are implicit in the non-recognition of South Africa's presence in Namibia and the explicit provisions of paragraph 5 of resolution 276 (1970) impose upon member States the obligation to abstain from entering into economic and other forms of relationship or dealings with South Africa on behalf of or concerning Namibia which may entrench its authority over the Territory.

125. In general, the non-recognition of South Africa's administration of the Territory should not result in depriving the people of Namibia of any advantages derived from international CO-operation. In particular, while official acts performed by the Government of South Africa on behalf of or concerning Namibia after the termination of the Mandate are illegal and invalid, this invalidity cannot be extended to those acts, such as, for instance, the registration of births, deaths and marriages, the effects of which can be ignored only to the detriment of the inhabitants of the Territory.

126. As to non-member States, although not bound by Articles 24 and 25 of the Charter, they have been called upon in paragraphs 2 and 5 of resolution 276 (1970) to give assistance in the action which has been taken by the United Nations with regard to Namibia. In the view of the Court, the termination of the Mandate and the declaration of the illegality of South Africa's presence in Namibia are opposable to all States in the sense of barring *erga omnes* the legality of a situation which is maintained in violation of international law: in particular, no State which enters into relations with South Africa concerning Namibia may expect the United Nations or its Members to recognize the validity or effects of such relationship, or of the consequences thereof. The Mandate having been terminated by decision of the international organization in which the supervisory authority over its administration was vested, and South Africa's continued presence in Namibia having been declared illegal, it is for non-member States to act in accordance with those decisions.

127. As to the general consequences resulting from the illegal presence of South Africa in Namibia, all States should bear in mind that the injured entity is a people which must look to the international community for assistance in its progress towards the goals for which the sacred trust was instituted.

Applicability of the Obligation to Arbitrate under Section 21 of the United Nations Headquarters Agreement of 26 June 1947, ICJ Advisory Opinion, 26 April 1988

[*Note:*

Opinion requested by: the UN General Assembly resolution 42/229 B of 2 March 1988.

The question before the Court:
In 1987 the US Congress adopted an Anti-Terrorism Act which, inter alia, declared illegal the establishment or maintenance of an office of the Observer Mission of the Palestine Liberation Organization (PLO) to the United Nations in New York. In the view of the United Nations the United States violated Section 21 of the 1947 Headquarters Agreement when it requested the United Nations in the national court to close the office of the PLO Observer Mission instead of following the dispute settlement procedure as provided for in the Agreement.

The General Assembly asked the Court the following question:
"In the light of facts reflected in the reports of the Secretary-General, is the United States of America, as a party to the Agreement between the United Nations and the United States of America regarding the Headquarters of the United Nations, under an obligation to enter into arbitration in accordance with section 21 of the Agreement?"]

The Opinion:

"

[...]

7. The question upon which the opinion of the Court has been requested is whether the United States of America (hereafter referred to as "the United States"), as a party to the United Nations Headquarters Agreement, is under an obligation to enter into arbitration. The Headquarters Agreement of 26 June 1947 came into, force in accordance with its terms on 21 November 1947 by exchange of letters between the Secretary-General and the United States Permanent Representative. The Agreement was registered the same day with the United Nations Secretariat, in accordance with Article 102 of the Charter. In section 21, paragraph *(a)*, it provides as follows:

> "Any dispute between the United Nations and the United States concerning the interpretation or application of this agreement or of any supplemental agreement, which is not settled by negotiation or other agreed mode of settlement, shall be referred for final decision to a tribunal of three arbitrators, one to be named by the Secretary- General, one to be named by the Secretary of State of the United States, and the third to be chosen by the two, or, if they should fail to agree upon a third, then by the President of the International Court of Justice."

There is no question but that the Headquarters Agreement is a treaty in force binding the parties thereto. What the Court has therefore to determine, in order to answer the question put to it, is whether there exists a dispute between the United Nations and the United States of the kind contemplated by section 21 of the Agreement. For this purpose the Court will first set out the sequence of events, preceding the adoption of resolutions 42/229A and 42/229B, which led first the Secretary-General and subsequently the General Assembly of the United Nations to conclude that such a dispute existed.

8. The events in question centred round the Permanent Observer Mission of the Palestine Liberation Organization (referred to hereafter as "the PLO") to the United Nations in New York. The PLO has enjoyed in relation to the United Nations the status of an observer since 1974; by General Assembly resolution 3237 (XXIX) of 22 November 1974, the Organization was invited to "participate in the sessions and the work of the General Assembly in the capacity of observer". Following this invitation, the PL0 established an Observer Mission in 1974, and maintains an office, entitled office of the PLO Observer Mission, at 11 5 East 65th Street, in New York City, outside the United Nations Headquarters District. Recognized observers are listed as such in officia1 United Nations publications: the PL0 appears in such publications in a category of "organizations which have received a standing invitation from the General Assembly to participate in the sessions and the work of the General Assembly as observers".

9. In May 1987 a bill (S.1203) was introduced into the Senate of the United States, the purpose of which was stated in its title to be "to make unlawful the establishment or maintenance within the United States of an office of the Palestine Liberation Organization".

[...]

10. The text of this bill was repeated in the form of an amendment, presented in the United States Senate in the autumn of 1987, to the "Foreign Relations Authorization Act, Fiscal Years 1988 and 1989". From the terms of this amendment it appeared that the United States Government would, if the bill were passed into law, seek to close the office of the PL0 Observer Mission. The Secretary-General therefore explained his point of view to that Government, by a letter to the United States Permanent Representative dated 13 October 1987. In that letter he emphasized that the legislation contemplated "runs counter to obligations arising from the Headquarters Agreement". On 14 October 1987 the PL0 Observer brought the matter to the attention of the United Nations Committee on Relations with the Host Country.

11. On 22 October 1987, the view of the Secretary-General was summed up in the following statement made by the Spokesman for the Secretary-General (subsequently endorsed by the General Assembly in resolution 42/210 B):

> "The members of the PL0 Observer Mission are, by virtue of resolution 3237 (XXIX), invitees to the United Nations. As such, they are covered by sections 11,12 and 13 of the Headquarters Agreement of 26 June 1947. There is therefore a treaty obligation on the host country to permit PL0 personnel to enter and remain in the United States to carry out their officia1 functions at United Nations Headquarters."

In this respect, it may be noted that section 11 of the Headquarters Agreement provides that

> "The federal, state or local authorities of the United States shall not impose any impediments to transit to or from the headquarters district of:
>
> (1) representatives of Members . . . or the families of such representatives . . . (5) other persons invited to the headquarters district by the United Nations . . . on official business . . ."

Section 12 provides that

> "The provisions of section 11 shall be applicable irrespective of the relations existing between the Governments of the persons referred to in that section and the Government of the United States."

Section 13 provides *(inter alia)* that

> "Laws and regulations in force in the United States regarding the entry of aliens shall not be applied in such manner as to interfere with the privileges referred to in section 11."

12. When the report of the Committee on Relations with the Host Country was placed before the Sixth Committee of the General Assembly on 25 November 1987, the representative of the United States noted:

> "that the United States Secretary of State had stated that the closing of that mission would constitute a violation of United States obligation under the Headquarters Agreement, and that the United States Government was strongly opposed to it ; moreover the United States representative to the United Nations had given the Secretary-General the same assurances" (A/C.6/42/SR.58). When the draft resolution which subsequently became General Assembly resolution 42/210B was put to the vote in the Sixth Committee on 11 December 1987, the United States delegation did not participate in the voting because in its opinion: "it was unnecessary and inappropriate since it addressed a matter still under consideration within the United States Government".

The position taken by the United States Secretary of State, namely:

> "that the United States was under an obligation to permit PL0 Observer Mission personnel to enter and remain in the United States to carry out their official functions at United Nations Headquarters" was cited by another delegate and confirmed by the representative of the United States, who referred to it as "well known" (A/C.6/42/SR.62).

13. The provisions of the amendment referred to above became incorporated into the United States "Foreign Relations Authorization Act, Fiscal Years 1988 and 1989" as Title X, the "Anti-Terrorism Act of 1987". At the beginning of December 1987 the Act had not yet been adopted by the United States Congress. In anticipation of such adoption the Secretary-General addressed a letter, dated 7 December 1987, to the Permanent Representative of the United States, Ambassador Vernon Walters, in which he reiterated to the Permanent Representative the view previously expressed by the United Nations that the members of the PLO Observer Mission are, by virtue of General Assembly resolution 3237 (XXIX), invitees to the United Nations and that the United States is under an obligation to permit PL0 personnel to enter and remain in the United States to carry out their official functions at the United Nations under the Headquarters Agreement. Consequently, it was said, the United States was under a legal obligation to maintain the current arrangements for the PLO Observer Mission, which had by then been in effect for some 13 years. The Secretary-General sought assurances that, in the event that the proposed legislation became law, the present arrangements for the PLO Observer Mission would not be curtailed or otherwise affected.

14. In a subsequent letter, dated 21 December 1987, after the adoption on 15/16 December of the Act by the United States Congress, the Secretary-General informed the Permanent Representative of the adoption on 17 December 1987 of resolution 42/210B by the General Assembly. By that resolution the Assembly

> "*Having been apprised* of the action being considered in the host country, the United States of America, which might impede the maintenance of the facilities of the Permanent Observer Mission of the Palestine Liberation Organization to the United Nations in New York, which enables it to discharge its official functions, . . .
> 1. *Reiterates* that the Permanent Observer Mission of the Palestine Liberation Organization to the United Nations in New York is covered by the provisions of the Agreement between the United Nations and the United States of America regarding the Headquarters of the United Nations and should be enabled to establish and maintain premises and adequate functional facilities, and that the personnel of the Mission should be enabled to enter and remain in the United States to carry out their official functions;
> 2. *Requests* the host country to abide by its treaty obligations under the Headquarters Agreement and in this connection to refrain from taking any action that would prevent the discharge of the official functions of the Permanent Observer Mission of the Palestine Liberation Organization to the United Nations;"

15. On 22 December 1987 the Foreign Relations Authorization Act, Fiscal Years 1988 and 1989, was signed into law by the President of the United States. Title X thereof, the Anti-Terrorism Act of 1987, was, according to its terms, to take effect 90 days after that date. On 5 January 1988 the Acting Permanent Representative of the United States to the United Nations, Ambassador Herbert Okun, in a reply to the Secretary-General's letters of 7 and 21 December 1987, informed the Secretary-General of this. The letter went on to Say that

> "Because the provisions concerning the PL0 Observer Mission may infringe on the President's constitutional authority and, if implemented, would be contrary to our international legal obligations under the United Nations Headquarters Agreement, the Administration intends, during the ninety-day period before this provision is to take effect, to engage in consultations with the Congress in an effort to resolve this matter."

[...]

17. Beginning on 7 January 1988, a series of consultations were held; from the account of these consultations presented to the General Assembly by the Secretary-General in the report referred to in the request for advisory opinion, it appears that the positions of the parties thereto were as follows:

> "the [United Nations] Legal Counsel was informed that the United States was not in a position and not willing to enter formally into the dispute settlement procedure under section 21 of the Headquarters Agreement; the United States was still evaluating the situation and had not yet concluded that a dispute existed between the United Nations and the United States at the present time because the legislation in question had not yet been implemented. The Executive Branch was still examining the possibility of interpreting the law in conformity with the United States obligations under the

Headquarters Agreement regarding the PLO Observer Mission, as reflected in the arrangements currently made for that Mission, or alternatively of providing assurances that would set aside the ninety-day period for the coming into force of the legislation." (A/42/915, para. 6.)

18. The United Nations Legal Counsel stated that for the Organization the question was one of compliance with international law. The Headquarters Agreement was a binding international instrument the obligations of the United States under which were, in the view of the Secretary-General and the General Assembly, being violated by the legislation in question. Section 21 of the Agreement set out the procedure to be followed in the event of a dispute as to the interpretation or application of the Agreement and the United Nations had every intention of defending its righ is under that Agreement. He insisted, therefore, that if the PL0 Observer Mission was not to be exempted from the application of the law, the procedure provided for in section 21 be implemented and also that technical discussions regarding the establishment of an arbitral tribunal take place immediately. The United States agreed to such discussions but only on an informal basis. Technical discussions were commenced on 28 January 1988. Among the matters discussed were the costs of the arbitration, its location, its secretariat, languages, rules of procedure and the form of the *compromis* between the two sides (ibid., paras. 7-8).

19. On 2 February 1988 the Secretary-General once more wrote to Ambassador Walters. The Secretary-General took note that

> "the United States side is still in the process of evaluating the situation which would arise out of the application of the legislation and pending the conclusion of such evaluation takes the position that it cannot enter into the dispute settlement procedure outlined in section 21 of the Headquarters Agreement".

The Secretary-General then went on to Say that

> "The section 21 procedure is the only legal remedy available to the United Nations in this matter and since the United States so far has not been in a position to give appropriate assurances regarding the deferral of the application of the law to the PL0 Observer Mission, the time is rapidly approaching when **1** will have no alternative but to proceed either together with the United States within the framework of section 21 of the Headquarters Agreement or by informing the General Assembly of the impasse that has been reached."

20. On 11 February 1988 the United Nations Legal Counsel, referring to the formal invocation of the dispute settlement procedure on 14 January 1988 (paragraph 16 above), informed the Legal Adviser of the State Department of the United Nations' choice of its arbitrator, in the event of an arbitration under section 21 of the Headquarters Agreement. In view of the time constraints under which both parties found themselves, the Legal Counsel urged the Legal Adviser of the State Department to inform the United Nations as soon as possible of the choice made by the United States. No communication was received in this regard from the United States.

[...]

23. The question put to the Court is expressed, by resolution 42/229 B, to concern a possible obligation of the United States, "In the light of [the] facts reflected in the reports of the Secretary-General [A/42/915 and Add. 1]", that is to say in the light of the facts which had been reported to the General

Assembly at the time at which it took its decision to request an opinion. The Court does not however consider that the General Assembly, in employing this form of words, has requested it to reply to the question put on the basis solely of these facts, and to close its eyes to subsequent events of possible relevance to, or capable of throwing light on, that question. The Court will therefore set out here the developments in the affair subsequent to the adoption of resolution 42/229 B.

[...]

35. As the Court observed in the case concerning *Interpretation of Peace Treaties with Bulgaria, Hungary and Romania*, "whether there exists an international dispute is a matter for objective determination" (*I.C.J. Reports 1950*, p. 74). In this respect the Permanent Court of International Justice, in the case concerning *Mavrommatis Palestine Concessions*, had defined a dispute as "a disagreement on a point of law or fact, a conflict of legal views or of interests between two persons" (*P.C.I.J., Series A, No. 2*, p. 11). This definition has since been applied and clarified on a number of occasions. In the Advisory Opinion of 30 March 1950 the Court, after examining the diplomatic exchanges between the States concerned, noted that "the two sides hold clearly opposite views concerning the question of the performance or non-performance of certain treaty obligations" and concluded that "international disputes have arisen" (*Interpretation of Peace Treaties with Bulgaria, Hungary and Romania, First Phase, I.C.J. Reports 1950*, p. 74). Furthermore, in its Judgment of 21 December 1962 in the *South West Africa* cases, the Court made it clear that in order to prove the existence of a dispute

> "it is not sufficient for one party to a contentious case to assert that a dispute exists with the other party. A mere assertion is not sufficient to prove the existence of a dispute any more than a mere denial of the existence of the dispute proves its non-existence. Nor is it adequate to show that the interests of the two parties to such a case are in conflict. It must be shown that the claim of one party is positively opposed by the other." (*I.C.J. Reports 1962*, p. 328.)

The Court found that the opposing attitudes of the parties clearly established the existence of a dispute (*ibid.*; *see* also *Northern Cameroons, I.C.J. Reports 1963*, p. 27).

36. In the present case, the Secretary-General informed the Court that, in his opinion, a dispute within the meaning of section 21 of the Headquarters Agreement existed between the United Nations and the United States from the moment the Anti-Terrorism Act was signed into law by the President of the United States and in the absence of adequate assurances to the Organization that the Act would not be applied to the PLO Observer Mission to the United Nations. By his letter of 14 January 1988 to the Permanent Representative of the United States, the Secretary-General formally contested the consistency of the Act with the Headquarters Agreement (paragraph 16 above). The Secretary-General confirmed and clarified that point of view in a letter of 15 March 1988 (paragraph 28 above) to the Acting Permanent Representative of the United States in which he told him that the determination made by the Attorney General of the United States on 11 March 1988 was a "clear violation of the Headquarters Agreement". In that same letter he once more asked that the matter be submitted to arbitration.

37. The United States has never expressly contradicted the view expounded by the Secretary-General and endorsed by the General Assembly regarding the sense of the Headquarters Agreement. Certain United States authorities have even expressed the same view, but the United States has nevertheless taken measures against the PLO Mission to the United Nations. It has indicated that those measures were being taken "irrespective of any obligations the United States may have under the [Headquarters] Agreement" (paragraph 24 above).

38. In the view of the Court, where one party to a treaty protests against the behaviour or a decision of another party, and claims that such behaviour or decision constitutes a breach of the treaty, the mere fact that the party accused does not advance any argument to justify its conduct under international law does not prevent the opposing attitudes of the parties from giving rise to a dispute concerning the interpretation or application of the treaty. In the case concerning *United States Diplomatic and Consular Staff in Tehran*, the jurisdiction of the Court was asserted principally on the basis of the Optional Protocols concerning the Compulsory Settlement of Disputes accompanying the Vienna Conventions of 1961 on Diplomatic Relations and of 1963 on Consular Relations, which defined the disputes to which they applied as "Disputes arising out of the interpretation or application of 'the relevant Convention. Iran, which did not appear in the proceedings before the Court, had acted in such a way as, in the view of the United States, to commit breaches of the Conventions, but, so far as the Court was informed, Iran had at no time claimed to justify its actions by advancing an alternative interpretation of the Conventions, on the basis of which such actions would not constitute such a breach. The Court saw no need to enquire into the attitude of Iran in order to establish the existence of a "dispute"; in order to determine whether it had jurisdiction, it stated:

> "The United States' claims here in question concern alleged violations by Iran of its obligations under several articles of the Vienna Conventions of 1961 and 1963 with respect to the privileges and immunities of the personnel, the inviolability of the premises and archives, and the provision of facilities for the performance of the functions of the United States Embassy and Consulates in Iran ... By their very nature all these claims concern the interpretation or application of one or other of the two Vienna Conventions." (I.C.J. *Reports 1980*, pp. 24-25, para. 46.)

39. In the present case, the United States in its public statements has not referred to the matter as a "dispute" (save for a passing reference on 23 March 1988 to "the current dispute over the status of the PL0 Observer Mission" (paragraph 3 1 above)), and it has expressed the view that arbitration would be "premature". According to the report of the Secretary-General to the General Assembly (A/42/915, para. 6), the position taken by the United States during the consultations in January 1988 was that it "had not yet concluded that a dispute existed between the United Nations and the United States" at that time "because the legislation in question had not yet been implemented". Finally, the Government of the United States, in its written statement of 25 March 1988, told the Court that:

> "The United States will take no action to close the Mission pending a decision in that litigation. Since the matter is still pending in our courts, we do not believe arbitration would be appropriate or timely."

40. The Court could not allow considerations as to what might be "appropriate" to prevail over the obligations which derive from section 21 of the Headquarters Agreement, as "the Court, being a Court of justice, cannot disregard rights recognized by it, and base its decision on considerations of pure expediency" (*Free Zones of Upper Savoy and the District of Gex, Order of 6 December 1930, P.C.* I.J., *Series A*, No. *24*, p. 15).

41. The Court must further point out that the alleged dispute relates solely to what the United Nations considers to be its rights under the Headquarters Agreement. The purpose of the arbitration procedure envisaged by that Agreement is precisely the settlement of such disputes as may arise between the Organization and the host country without any prior recourse to municipal courts, and it would be

against both the letter and the spirit of the Agreement for the implementation of that procedure to be subjected to such prior recourse. It is evident that a provision of the nature of section 21 of the Headquarters Agreement cannot require the exhaustion of local remedies as a condition of its implementation.

42. The United States in its written statement might be implying that neither the signing into law of the Anti-Terrorism Act, nor its entry into force, nor the Attorney General's decision to apply it, nor his resort to court proceedings to close the PLO Mission to the United Nations, would have been sufficient to bring about a dispute between the United Nations and the United States, since the case was still pending before an American court and, until the decision of that court, the United States, according to the Acting Permanent Representative's letter of 11 March 1988, "will not take other actions to close" the Mission. The Court cannot accept such an argument. While the existence of a dispute does presuppose a claim arising out of the behaviour of or a decision by one of the parties, it in no way requires that any contested decision must already have been carried into effect. What is more, a dispute may arise even if the party in question gives an assurance that no measure of execution will be taken until ordered by decision of the domestic courts.

43. The Anti-Terrorism Act was signed into law on 22 December 1987. It was automatically to take effect 90 days later. Although the Act extends to every PLO office situated within the jurisdiction of the United States and contains no express reference to the office of the PLO Mission to the United Nations in New York, its chief, if not its sole, objective was the closure of that office. On 11 March 1988, the United States Attorney General considered that he was under an obligation to effect such a closure; he notified the Mission of this, and applied to the United States courts for an injunction prohibiting those concerned "from continuing violations of" the Act. As noted above, the Secretary-General, acting both on his own behalf and on instructions from the General Assembly, has consistently challenged the decisions contemplated and then taken by the United States Congress and the Administration. Under those circumstances, the Court is obliged to find that the opposing attitudes of the United Nations and the United States show the existence of a dispute between the two parties to the Headquarters Agreement.

44. For the purposes of the present advisory opinion there is no need to seek to determine the date at which the dispute came into existence, once the Court has reached the conclusion that there is such a dispute at the date on which its opinion is given.

45. The Court has next to consider whether the dispute is one which concerns the interpretation or application of the Headquarters Agreement. It is not however the task of the Court to say whether the enactment, or the enforcement, of the United States Anti-Terrorism Act would or would not constitute a breach of the provisions of the Headquarters Agreement; that question is reserved for the arbitral tribunal which the Secretary-General seeks to have established under section 21 of the Agreement.

46. In the present case, the Secretary-General and the General Assembly of the United Nations have constantly pointed out that the PLO was invited "to participate in the sessions and the work of the General Assembly in the capacity of Observer" (resolution 3237 (XXIX)). In their view, therefore, the PLO Observer Mission to the United Nations was, as such, covered by the provisions of sections 11,12 and 13 of the Headquarters Agreement; it should therefore "be enabled to establish and maintain premises and adequate functional facilities" (General Assembly resolution 42/229A, para. 2). The Secretary-General and the General Assembly have accordingly concluded that the various measures envisaged and then taken by the United States Congress and Administration would be incompatible with the Agreement if

they were to be applied to that Mission, and that the adoption of those measures gave rise to a dispute between the United Nations Organization and the United States with regard to the interpretation and application of the Headquarters Agreement.

[...]

49. To conclude, the United States has taken a number of measures against the PL0 Observer Mission to the United Nations in New York. The Secretary-General regarded these as contrary to the Headquarters Agreement. Without expressly disputing that point, the United States stated that the measures in question were taken "irrespective of any obligations the United States may have under the Agreement". Such conduct cannot be reconciled with the position of the Secretary-General. There thus exists a dispute between the United Nations and the United States concerning the application of the Headquarters Agreement, falling within the terms of section 21 thereof.

50. The question might of course be raised whether in United States domestic law the decisions taken on 11 and 21 March 1988 by the Attorney General brought about the application of the Anti-Terrorism Act, or whether the Act can only be regarded as having received effective application when or if, on completion of the current judicial proceedings, the PL0 Mission is in fact closed. This is however not decisive as regards section 21 of the Headquarters Agreement, which refers to any dispute "concerning the interpretation or application" of the Agreement, and not concerning the application of the measures taken in the municipal law of the United States. The Court therefore sees no reason not to find that a dispute exists between the United Nations and the United States concerning the "interpretation or application" of the Headquarters Agreement.

[...]

When in the case concerning *United States Diplomatic and Consular Staff in Tehran* the attempts of the United States to negotiate with Iran "had reached a deadlock, owing to the refusal of the Iranian Government to enter into any discussion of the matter", the Court concluded that "In consequence, there existed at that date not only a dispute but, beyond any doubt, a 'dispute . . . not satisfactorily adjusted by diplomacy' within the meaning of" the relevant jurisdictional text (I.C.J. *Reports 1980*, p. 27, para. 5 1). In the present case, the Court regards it as similarly beyond any doubt that the dispute between the United Nations and the United States is one "not settled by negotiation" within the meaning of section 21, paragraph (a), of the Headquarters Agreement.

56. Nor was any "other agreed mode of settlement" of their dispute contemplated by the United Nations and the United States. In this connection the Court should observe that current proceedings brought by the United States Attorney General before the United States courts cannot be an "agreed mode of settlement" within the meaning of section 21 of the Headquarters Agreement. The purpose of these proceedings is to enforce the Anti-Terrorism Act of 1987; it is not directed to settling the dispute, concerning the application of the Headquarters Agreement, which has come into existence between the United Nations and the United States. Furthermore, the United Nations has never agreed to settlement of the dispute in the American courts; it has taken care to make it clear that it wishes to be admitted only as *arnicus curiae* before the District Court for the Southern District of New York.

57. The Court must therefore conclude that the United States is bound to respect the obligation to have recourse to arbitration under section 21 of the Headquarters Agreement. The fact remains however that, as the Court has already observed, the United States has declared (letter from the Permanent Representative, 11 March 1988) that its measures against the PLO Observer Mission were taken "irrespective of any obligations the United States may have under the [Headquarters] Agreement". If it were necessary to interpret that statement as intended to refer not only to the substantive obligations laid down in, for example, sections 11,12 and 13, but also to the obligation to arbitrate provided for in section 21, this conclusion would remain intact. It would be sufficient to recall the fundamental principle of international law that international law prevails over domestic law. This principle was endorsed by judicial decision as long ago as the arbitral award of 14 September 1872 in the *Alabama* case between Great Britain and the United States, and has frequently been recalled since, for example in the case concerning the *Greco-Bulgarian "Communities"* in which the Permanent Court of International Justice laid it down that

> "it is a generally accepted principle of international law that in the relations between Powers who are contracting Parties to a treaty, the provisions of municipal law cannot prevail over those of the treaty" (*P.C.I.J., Series* B, *No. 17*, p. 32).

Applicability of Article VI, Section 22 of the Convention on the Privileges and Immunities of the United Nations, ICJ Advisory Opinion, 13 June 1989

[*Note:*

Opinion requested by: the United Nations Economic and Social Council (ECOSOC) resolution 1989/75 of 24 May 1989.

Question before the Court:
The advisory opinion was requested because of the difference that arose between the United Nations and the Government of Romania concerning the applicability of the 1946 Convention on the Privileges and Immunities of the United Nations to the Romanian national, Mr. Dumitru Mazilu, Special Rapporteur of the Sub-Commission on Prevention of Discrimination and Protection of Minorities. The question was formulated as follows:
"In the light of facts reflected in the reports of the Secretary-General, is the United States of America, as a party to the Agreement between the United Nations and the United States of America regarding the Headquarters of the United Nations, under an obligation to enter into arbitration in accordance with section 21 of the Agreement?"]

The Opinion:

[...]

10. On 13 March 1984 the Commission, upon nomination by Romania, elected Mr. Dumitru Mazilu, a Romanian national, to serve as a member of the Sub-Commission for a three-year term, due to expire on 31 December 1986. Pursuant to the Commission's resolution 1985/13 calling upon the Sub-Commission to pay due attention to the role of youth in the field of human rights, the Sub-Commission at its thirty-eighth session adopted on 29 August 1985 resolution 1985/12 whereby it requested Mr. Mazilu to "prepare a report on human rights and youth analysing the efforts and measures for securing the implementation and enjoyment by youth of human rights, particularly, the right to life, education and work and requested the Secretary-General to provide him with all necessary assistance for the completion of his task. This report was to be submitted under an agenda item entitled "Promotion, protection and restoration of human rights at national, regional and international levels", at the thirtyninth session of the Sub-Commission scheduled for 1986.

11. The thirty-ninth session of the Sub-Commission, at which Mr. Mazilu's report was to be presented, was not convened in 1986 but was rescheduled for 1987. The three-year mandate of its members – originally due to expire on 31 December 1986 – was extended by Council decision 1987/102 for an additional year. When the thirty-ninth session of the Sub-Commission opened in Geneva on 10 August 1987 no report had been received from Mr. Mazilu, nor was he present. By a letter received by the United Nations Office at Geneva on 12 August 1987, the Permanent Mission of Romania to that Office informed it that Mr. Mazilu had suffered a heart attack and was still in hospital. In its written statement to the Court, Romania stated that Mr. Mazilu had fallen seriously il1 in May 1987, and that at that time he had not yet begun to draw up the report entrusted to him. According to the written statement of the Secretary- General, a telegram was received in Geneva on 18 August 1987 signed "D. Mazilu" informing the Sub-Commission of his inability, due to heart illness, to attend the current session.

[...]

13. After the thirty-ninth session of the Sub-Commission, the Centre for Human Rights of the United Nations Secretariat in Geneva made various attempts to contact Mr. Mazilu and to provide him with assistance in the preparation of his report, including arranging a visit to Geneva. Relevant information submitted by Governments, intergovernmental organizations and non-governmental organizations was sent to him on a regular basis. Having received from Mr. Mazilu two letters postmarked 25 and 29 December 1987, whereby he stated that he had not received the previous communications of the Centre, the Under-Secretary-General for Human Rights, in a telegram dated 19 January 1988 and addressed to the Acting Director of the United Nations Information Centre in Bucharest, requested the latter's assistance in facilitating Mr. Mazilu's work on his report by serving as a channel through which a ticket to Geneva would be provided to Mr. Mazilu; the Under-Secretary-General also asked that a formal invitation be communicated to Mr. Mazilu to come to the Centre for Human Rights for consultations.

14. In its written statement submitted to the Court, Romania stated that at Mr. Mazilu's request he had, from 1 December 1987, been put on the retired list as being unfit for service, and that in 1988 a medical commission, acting in accordance with current Romanian legislation, had re-examined Mr. Mazilu's state of health and decided to extend for a further one-year period his retirement on the grounds of continued unfitness for service. In a letter addressed to the Under-Secretary-General for Human Rights, handed on 15 January 1988 to the Acting Director of the United Nations Information Centre in Bucharest, Mr. Mazilu said that he had been twice in hospital, and that he had been forced to retire, as of 1 December 1987, from his various governmental posts. He stated that despite his willingness to come to Geneva for consultations, the Romanian authorities were refusing him a travel permit. In a series of letters dated 5 April, 19 April, 8 May and 17 May 1988, Mr. Mazilu further described his personal situation; in the first of these letters he alleged that he had refused to comply with a request addressed to him on 22 February 1988 by a special commission from the Romanian Ministry of Foreign Affairs voluntarily to decline to submit his report to the Sub-Commission. He consistently complained that strong pressure had been exerted on him and on his family.

[...]

18. At its 10th meeting, held on 15 August 1988, the Sub-Commission adopted decision 1988/102, whereby it requested the Secretary-General

> "to establish contact with the Government of Romania and to bring to the Government's attention the Sub-Commission's urgent need to establish personal contact with its Special Rapporteur Mr. Dumitru Mazilu and to convey the request that the Govemment assist in locating Mr. Mazilu and facilitate a visit to him by a member of the Sub-Commission and the secretariat to help him in the completion of his study on human rights and youth if he so wished".

The Under-Secretary-General for Human Rights informed the Sub-Commission at its 14th meeting, held on 17 August 1988, that in contacts between the Secretary-General's Office and the Chargé d'affaires of the Romanian Permanent Mission to the United Nations in New York, the possibility of establishing contact with Mr. Mazilu was raised.

19. The Under-Secretary-General reported that in these contacts the Chargé d'affaires had stated that any intervention by the United Nations Secretariat and any form of investigation in Bucharest would be considered interference in Romania's internal affairs; the case of Mr. Mazilu was an internal matter between a citizen and his own Government and for that reason no visit to Mr. Mazilu would be allowed.

[...]

24. On the law, Romania expressed the view in that Aide-Mémoire that "the problem of the application of the General Convention does not arise in this case": the Convention "does not equate rapporteurs, whose activities are only occasional, with experts on missions for the United Nations"; and

> "even if rapporteurs are given some of the status of experts, . . . they can enjoy only functional immunities and privileges, that is, privileges connected with their activities for the United Nations, during the period of their mission, and then only in the countries in which they perform the mission and in countries of transit".

For Romania, it was obvious that

> "an expert does not enjoy privileges and immunities in the country in which he has his permanent residence but only in the country in which he is on mission and during the period of his mission. Likewise, the privileges and immunities provided by the Convention begin to apply only at the moment when the expert leaves on a journey connected with the performance of his mission."

Moreover,

> "in the country of which he is a national and in countries other than the country to which he is sent on mission, an expert enjoys privileges and immunities only in respect of actual activities spoken or written which he performs in connection with his mission".

Romania stated expressly that it was opposed to a request for advisory opinion from the Court of any kind in this case. Similar contentions were also put forward in the written statement presented by Romania to the Court in the present proceedings.

[...]

31. The jurisdiction of the Court under Article 96 of the Charter and Article 65 of the Statute, to give advisory opinions on legal questions, enables United Nations entities to seek guidance from the Court in order to conduct their activities in accordance with law. These opinions are advisory, not binding. As the opinions are intended for the guidance of the United Nations, the consent of States is not a condition precedent to the competence of the Court to give them. As the Court observed in 1950,

> "The consent of States, parties to a dispute, is the basis of the Court's jurisdiction in contentious cases. The situation is different in regard to advisory proceedings even where the Request for an Opinion relates to a legal question actually pending between States. The Court's reply is only of an advisory character: as such, it has no binding force. It follows that no State, whether a Member of the United Nations or not, can prevent the giving of an Advisory Opinion which the United Nations considers to be desirable in order to obtain enlightenment as to the course of action it should take.

> The Court's Opinion is given not to the States, but to the organ which is entitled to request it; the reply of the Court, itself an 'organ of the United Nations', represents its participation in the activities of the Organization, and, in principle, should not be refused."
> (*Interpretation of Peace Treaties with Bulgaria, Hungary and Romania, First Phase, Advisory Opinion, 1. C.J. Reports 1950*, p. 71.)

This reasoning is equally valid where it is suggested that a legal question is pending, not between two States, but between the United Nations and a member State.

32. Romania however relies on its reservation to Section 30 of the General Convention; but that Section operates on a different plane and in a different context from that of Article 96 of the Charter. When the provisions of the Section are read in their totality, it is clear that their object is to provide a dispute settlement mechanism. The first sentence of the Section provides for the case where a difference arises out of the interpretation or application of the General Convention between States parties to it, and contains two elements. The first is the treaty obligation to refer the difference to the Court, unless another mode of settlement is decided upon by the parties; the second is the object of the reference to the Court, namely to settle the difference.

33. The United Nations is itself intimately, and for the most part directly, concerned with the operation of the General Convention. Section 30 was therefore so framed as to take in also the settlement of differences between the United Nations and a State party to the General Convention. If such a difference arises,

> "a request shall be made for an advisory opinion on any legal question involved in accordance with Article 96 of the Charter and Article 65 of the Statute of the Court. The opinion given by the Court shall be accepted as decisive by the parties."

This provision pursues the same intent as expressed in the first sentence of Section 30; the particular nature of the proceeding contemplated is attributable to the status as an international organization of one of the parties to the difference.

34. In case of a request for an advisory opinion made under Section 30, the Court would of course have to consider any reservation which a party to the dispute had made to that Section. In the particular case of Romania, the Court would have to consider whether the effect of its reservation could be to act as a bar to the operation of the procedure of request for advisory opinion, or merely to deprive any opinion given of the decisive effect attributed to such opinions by Section 30. But in the present case, the resolution requesting the advisory opinion made no reference to Section 30, and it is evident from the dossier that, in view of the existence of the Romanian reservation, it was not the intention of the Council to invoke Section 30. The request is not made under that Section, and the Court does not therefore need to determine the effect of the Romanian reservation to that provision.

35. Romania however contends that although the Council resolution 1989/75 dated 24 May 1989 does not allude to Section 30 of the General Convention as the basis of its request for advisory opinion, the question which it raises nevertheless relates to the applicability of a substantive provision of the General Convention "to a concrete case considered to be a dispute between a State party to the Convention and the United Nations". It argues that

> "If it were accepted that a State party to the Convention, or the United Nations, might ask for disputes concerning the application or interpretation of the Convention to be brought before the Court on a basis other than the provisions of Section 30 of the Convention, that would disrupt the unity of the Convention, by separating the substantive provisions from those relating to dispute settlement, which would be tantamount to a modification of the content and extent of the obligations entered into by States when they consented to be bound by the Convention."

However, the nature and purpose of the present proceedings are, as explained above, that of a request for advice on the applicability of a part of the General Convention, and not the bringing of a dispute before the Court for determination. Furthermore, the "content and extent of the obligations entered into by States" – and, in particular, by Romania – "when they consented to be bound by the Convention" are not modified by the request and by the present advisory opinion.

36. The Court thus finds that the reservation made by Romania to Section 30 of the General Convention does not affect the Court's jurisdiction to entertain the present request.

37. While, however, the absence of the consent of Romania to the present proceedings can have no effect on the jurisdiction of the Court, it is a matter to be considered when examining the propriety of the Court giving an opinion. It is well settled in the Court's jurisprudence that when a request is made under Article 96 of the Charter by an organ of the United Nations or a specialized agency for an advisory opinion by way of guidance or enlightenment on a question of law, the Court should entertain the request and give its opinion unless there are "compelling reasons" to the contrary. In the *Western Sahara* case the Court adverted to a possible situation in which such a "compelling reason" might be present. In that case, commenting on its observations in the *Interpretation of Peace Treaties* case, to the effect that its competence to give an opinion does not depend on the consent of the interested States, the Court observed:

> "the Court recognized that lack of consent might constitute a ground for declining to give the opinion requested if, in the circumstances of a given case, considerations of judicial propriety should oblige the Court to refuse an opinion. In short, the consent of an interested State continues to be relevant, not for the Court's competence, but for the appreciation of the propriety of giving an opinion.
> 33. In certain circumstances, therefore, the lack of consent of an interested State may render the giving of an advisory opinion incompatible with the Court's judicial character. An instance of this would be when the circumstances disclose that to give a reply would have the effect of circumventing the principle that a State is not obliged to allow its disputes to be submitted to judicial settlement without its consent. If such a situation should arise, the powers of the Court under the discretion given to it by Article 65, paragraph 1, of the Statute, would afford sufficient legal means to ensure respect for the fundamental principle of consent to jurisdiction." (*Western Sahara, Advisory Opinion, I.C.J. Reports 1975*, p. 25, paras. 32-33.)

38. In view of the emphasis placed by Romania on its reservation to Article 30 of the General Convention and the absence of its consent to the present request for advisory opinion, the Court must consider whether in this case "to give a reply would have the effect of circumventing the principle that a State is not obliged to allow its disputes to be submitted to judicial settlement without its consent". The Court

considers that in the present case to give a reply would have no such effect. Certainly the Council, in its resolution requesting the opinion, did conclude that a difference had arisen between the United Nations and the Government of Romania as to the *applicability* of the Convention to Mr. Dumitru Mazilu. But this difference, and the question put to the Court in the light of it, are not to be confused with the dispute between the United Nations and Romania with respect to the *application* of the General Convention in the case of Mr. Mazilu.

39. In the present case, the Court thus does not find any compelling reason to refuse an advisory opinion. The Court will therefore proceed now to reply to the legal question on which such an opinion has been requested.

40. In order to determine the applicability of Article VI, Section 22, of the General Convention, to special rapporteurs of the Sub-Commission, and its applicability in the case of Mr. Dumitru Mazilu, the Court must first ascertain the meaning of that text.

41. According to Article 105, paragraph 1, of the Charter of the United Nations

> "The Organization shall enjoy in the territory of each of its Members such privileges and immunities as are necessary for the fulfilment of its purposes."

Furthermore, according to Article 105, paragraph 2,

> "Representatives of the Members of the United Nations and officials of the Organization shall similarly enjoy such privileges and immunities as are necessary for the independent exercise of their functions in connection with the Organization."

Lastly, Article 105, paragraph 3, States that the General Assembly "may propose conventions to the Members of the United Nations" with a view to determining the details of the application of paragraphs 1 and 2.

42. Acting in conformity with Article 105 of the Charter, the General Assembly approved the General Convention on 13 February 1946 and proposed it for accession by each Member of the United Nations. One hundred and twenty-four States, including Romania, are parties to the Convention.

43. As contemplated by Article 105 of the Charter, the General Convention determines the privileges and immunities enjoyed by the United Nations as such (Arts. II and III), lays down the privileges and immunities of the representatives of Members of the United Nations (Art. IV), and defines those of the officials of the Organization (Art. V). It contains in addition an Article VI entitled "Experts on Missions for the United Nations", divided into two Sections. Section 22 provides as follows:

> "Experts (other than officials coming within the scope of Article V) performing missions for the United Nations shall be accorded such privileges and immunities as are necessary for the independent exercise of their functions during the period of their missions, including the time spent on journeys in connection with their missions. In particular they shall be accorded:

> (a) immunity from personal arrest or detention and from seizure of their personal baggage ;
> (b) in respect of words spoken or written and acts done by them in the course of the performance of their mission, immunity from legal process of every kind. This immunity from legal process shall continue to be accorded notwithstanding that the persons concerned are no longer employed on missions for the United Nations;
> (c) inviolability for all papers and documents;
> (d)for the purpose of their communications with the United Nations, the right to use codes and to receive papers or correspondence by courier or in sealed bags;
> (e) the same facilities in respect of currency or exchange restrictions as are accorded to representatives of foreign governments on temporary official missions;
> (j) the same immunities and facilities in respect of their personal baggage as are accorded to diplomatic envoys."

Section 23 adds :

> "Privileges and immunities are granted to experts in the interests of the United Nations and not for the personal benefit of the individuals themselves. The Secretary-General shall have the right and the duty to waive the immunity of any expert in any case where, in his opinion, the immunity would impede the course of justice and it can be waived without prejudice to the interests of the United Nations."

Finally, Article VII, Section 26, of the General Convention grants certain facilities to experts when travelling on the business of the Organization.

44. The Court will examine the applicability of Section 22 *ratione personae, ratione temporis* and *ratione loci*, that is to Say it will consider first what is meant by "experts on missions" for the purposes of Section 22, and then the meaning to be attached to the expression "period of [the] missions", before considering the position of experts in their relations with the States of which they are nationals or on the territory of which they reside.

45. The General Convention gives no definition of "experts on missions". All it does is to clarify two points, one negative and the other positive. From Section 22 it is clear, first that the officials of the Organization, even if chosen in consideration of their technical expertise in a particular field, are not included in the category of experts within the meaning of that provision; and secondly that only experts performing missions for the United Nations are covered by Section 22. The Section does not, however, furnish any indication of the nature, duration or place of these missions.

46. Nor is there really any guidance in this respect to be found in the *travaux préparatoires* of the General Convention. The Convention was initially drafted and submitted to the General Assembly by the Preparatory Commission set up at San Francisco in June 1945; that initial draft did not contain anything corresponding to the present Article VI. That article was added by the Sub-Commission on Privileges and Immunities established by the Sixth Committee to examine the draft, but the contemporary official records do not make it possible to ascertain the reasons for the addition.

47. The purpose of Section 22 is nevertheless evident, namely, to enable the United Nations to entrust missions to persons who do not have the status of an official of the Organization, and to guarantee them "such privileges and immunities as are necessary for the independent exercise of their functions". The experts thus appointed or elected may or may not be remunerated, may or may not have a contract, may be given a task requiring work over a lengthy period or a short time. The essence of the matter lies not in their administrative position but in the nature of their mission.

48. In practice, according to the information supplied by the Secretary-General, the United Nations has had occasion to entrust missions – increasingly varied in nature – to persons not having the status of United Nations officials. Such persons have been entrusted with mediation, with preparing reports, preparing studies, conducting investigations or finding and establishing facts. They have participated in certain peace-keeping forces, technical assistance work, and a multitude of other activities. In addition, many committees, commissions or similar bodies whose members serve, not as representatives of States, but in a personal capacity, have been set up within the Organization; for example the International Law Commission, the Advisory Committee on Administrative and Budgetary Questions, the International Civil Service Commission, the Human Rights Committee established for the implementation of the International Covenant on Civil and Political Rights, and various other committees of the same nature, such as the Committee on the Elimination of Racial Discrimination or the Committee on the Elimination of All Forms of Discrimination Against Women. In all these cases, the practice of the United Nations shows that the persons so appointed, and in particular the members of these committees and commissions, have been regarded as experts on missions within the meaning of Section 22.

49. According to that Section, experts enjoy the privileges and immunities therein provided for "during the period of their missions, including the time spent on journeys". The question thus arises whether experts are covered by Section 22 only during missions requiring travel or whether they are also covered when there is no such travel or apart from such travel. To answer this question, it is necessary to determine the meaning of the word "*mission*" in French and "mission" in English, the two languages in which the General Convention was adopted. Initially, in keeping with its Latin derivation, the word referred to a task entrusted to a person only if that person was sent somewhere to perform it. It implied a journey. The same connotation is apparent in the words, of the same derivation, "emissary", "missionary" and "missive". The French word "*mission*", and the English word "mission", have however long since acquired a broader meaning and nowadays embrace in general the tasks entrusted to a person, whether or not those tasks involve travel.

50. The Court considers that Section 22, in its reference to experts performing missions for the United Nations, uses the word "mission" in a general sense. While some experts have necessarily to travel in order to perform their tasks, others can perform them without having to travel. In either case, the intent of Section 22 is to ensure the independence of such experts in the interests of the Organization by according them the privileges and immunities necessary for the purpose. In some cases these privileges and immunities are designed to facilitate the travel of experts and their stay abroad, for instance those concerning seizure or searching of personal baggage. In other cases, however, they are of a far more general nature, particularly with respect to communications with the United Nations or the inviolability of papers and documents. Accordingly, Section 22 is applicable to every expert on mission, whether or not he travels.

51. The question whether experts on missions can invoke these privileges and immunities against the States of which they are nationals or on the territory of which they reside has also been raised. In this connection, the Court notes that Section 15 of the General Convention provides that the terms of Article IV, Sections 11,12 and 13, relating to the representatives of Members "are not applicable as between a representative and the authorities of the State of which he is a national or of which he is or has been the representative". Article V, concerning officials of the Organization, and Article VI, concerning experts on missions for the United Nations, do not, however, contain any comparable rule. This difference of approach can readily be explained. The privileges and immunities of Articles V and VI are conferred with a view to ensuring the independence of international officials and experts in the interests of the Organization. This independence must be respected by all States including the State of nationality and the State of residence. Some States parties to the General Convention (Canada, the Lao People's Democratic Republic, Nepal, Thailand, Turkey and the United States of America) have indeed entered reservations to certain provisions of Article V, or of Article VI itself (Mexico and the United States of America), as regards their nationals or persons habitually resident on their territory. The very fact that it was felt necessary to make such reservations confirms the conclusion that, in the absence of such reservations, experts on missions enjoy the privileges and immunities provided for under the Convention in their relations with the States of which they are nationals or on the territory of which they reside.

52. To sum up, the Court takes the view that Section 22 of the General Convention is applicable to persons (other than United Nations officials) to whom a mission has been entrusted by the Organization and who are therefore entitled to enjoy the privileges and immunities provided for in this Section with a view to the independent exercise of their functions. During the whole period of such missions, experts enjoy these functional privileges and immunities whether or not they travel. They may be invoked as against the State of nationality or of residence unless a reservation to Section 22 of the General Convention has been validly made by that State.

***

53. In the light of the foregoing, the Court will now consider the situation of special rapporteurs of the Sub-Commission. This is a question which touches on the legal position of rapporteurs in general, a category of persons whom the United Nations and the specialized agencies find it necessary to engage for the implementation of increasingly varied functions, and is thus one of importance for the whole of the United Nations system.

[...]

55. In accordance with the practice followed by many United Nations bodies, the Sub-Commission has from time to time appointed rapporteurs or special rapporteurs with the task of studying specified subjects. These rapporteurs or special rapporteurs are normally selected from among members of the Sub-Commission. However, over the past ten years, special rapporteurs have, on at least three occasions, been appointed from outside the Sub-Commission. Furthermore, in numerous cases, special rapporteurs appointed from among members of the Sub-Commission have completed their reports only after their membership of the Sub-Commission had expired. In any event, rapporteurs or special rapporteurs are entrusted by the Sub-Commission with a research mission. Their functions are diverse,

since they have to compile, analyse and check the existing documentation on the problem to be studied, prepare a report making appropriate recommendations, and present the report to the Sub-Commission. Since their status is neither that of a representative of a member State nor that of a United Nations official, and since they carry out such research independently for the United Nations, they must be regarded as experts on missions within the meaning of Section 22, even in the event that they are not, or are no longer, members of the Sub-Commission. Consequently they enjoy, in accordance with Section 22, the privileges and immunities necessary for the exercise of their functions, and in particular for the establishment of any contacts which may be useful for the preparation, the drafting and the presentation of their reports to the Sub-Commission.

Case Concerning Questions of Interpretation and Application of the 1971 Montreal Convention Arising from the Aerial Incident at Lockerbie (*Libyan Arab Jamahiriya v. United States Of America*), ICJ Order on Provisional Measures, 14 April 1992

[*Note:*

On 3 March 1992 the Libyan Arab Jamahiriya instituted proceedings before the International Court of Justice against the United States and the United Kingdom in respect of a dispute over the interpretation or application of the 1971 Montreal Convention. The dispute arose from the aerial incident of Pan Am flight 103 that occurred over Lockerbie, Scotland, on 21 December 1988 killing 259 passengers and crew members and 11 people on ground. Following up on a three-year investigation murder warrants were issued by the US authorities against two Libyan nationals who were charged that they "caused a bomb to be placed aboard, which bomb had exploded causing the aeroplane to crash".

On the same day, 3 March 1992, Libya also submitted requests for indication of provisional measures against the United States and the United Kingdom asking the Court to enjoin the two countries from taking any action against Libya calculated to coerce or compel Libya to surrender the accused individuals to any jurisdiction outside of Libya; and (b) to ensure that no steps are taken that would prejudice in any way the rights of Libya with respect to the legal proceedings that are the subject of Libya's Application."

Oral observations of the Parties on the requests for the provisional measures were presented at public hearings held on 26, 27 and 28 March 1992 for the United States and on 26 and 28 March 1992 for the United Kingdom. Three days after the close of the hearing, on 31 March 1992, acting under Chapter VII of the UN Charter, the Security Council adopted resolution 748 (1992).

The findings of the Court in its two Orders of 14 April 1992 are identical.]

The Order:

[...]

34. Whereas on 31 March 1992 (three days after the close of the hearings) the Security Council adopted resolution 748 (1992) stating *inter alia* that the Security Council:

> "....
>
> *Deeply concerned* that the Libyan Government has still not provided a full and effective response to the requests in its resolution 731 (1992) of 21 January 1992,
>
> *Convinced* that the suppression of acts of international terrorism, including those in which States are directly or indirectly involved, is essential for the maintenance of international peace and security,
>
> *Determining*, in this context, that the failure by the Libyan Government to demonstrate by concrete actions its renunciation of terrorism and in particular its continued failure to respond fully and effectively to the requests in resolution 73 1 (1992) constitute a threat to international peace and security,

. . .

to international peace and security,

. . .

Acting under Chapter VI1 of the Charter,

1. *Decides* that the Libyan Government must now comply without any further delay with paragraph 3 of resolution 731 (1992) regarding the requests contained in documents S/23306, S/23308 and S/23309;

2. *Decides also* that the Libyan Government must commit itself definitively to cease all forms of terrorist action and all assistance to terrorist groups and that it must promptly, by concrete actions, demonstrate its renunciation of terrorism;

3. *Decides* that, on 15 April 1992 all States shall adopt the measures set out below, which shall apply until the Security Council decides that the Libyan Government has complied with paragraphs 1 and 2 above;

. . .

7. *Calls* upon all States, including States not members of the United Nations, and all international organizations, to act strictly in accordance with the provisions of the present resolution, notwithstanding the existence of any rights or obligations conferred or imposed by any international agreement or any contract entered into or any licence or permit granted prior to 15 April 1992";

35. Whereas, by a letter of 2 April 1992, a copy of which was transmitted to Libya by the Registrar, the Agent of the United States drew the Court's attention to the adoption of Security Council resolution 748 (1992) the text of which he enclosed; and whereas, in that letter, the Agent stated:

"That resolution, adopted pursuant to Chapter VI1 of the United Nations Charter, 'decides that the Libyan Government must now comply without any further delay with paragraph 3 of resolution 731 (1992) of 21 January 1992 regarding the requests contained in documents S/23306, S/23308 and S/23309'. It will be recalled that the referenced requests include the request that Libya surrender the two Libyan suspects in the bombing of Pan Am flight 103 to the United States or to the United Kingdom. For this additional reason, the United States maintains its submission of 28 March 1992 that the request of the Government of the Great Socialist People's Libyan Arab Jamahiriya for the indication of provisional measures of protection should be denied, and that no such measures should be indicated":

36. Whereas document S/23308, to which reference was made in resolution 748 (1992), included the demands set out in paragraph 30 above;

37. Whereas the Registrar, on the instructions of the Court, informed the Parties, on 4 April 1992, that, in accordance with Article 62 of the Rules of Court, the Court was willing to receive, no later than 7 April1992, any observations the Parties might wish to transmit to it on the possible implications of Security Council resolution 748 (1992) for the proceedings before the Court;

38. Whereas in its observations on Security Council resolution 748 (1992) presented in response to the Court's invitation, Libya contends as follows : first, that that resolution does not prejudice the rights of Libya to request the Court to indicate provisional measures, inasmuch as by deciding, in effect, that Libya must surrender its nationals to the United States and the United Kingdom, the Security Council infringes, or threatens to infringe, the enjoyment and the exercise of the rights conferred on Libya by the Montreal Convention and its economic, commercial and diplomatic rights; whereas Libya therefore claims that the United States and the United Kingdom should so act as not to infringe Libya's rights, for example by seeking a suspension of the relevant part of resolution 748 (1992);

39. Whereas Libya in its observations contends, secondly, that the risk of contradiction between the resolution and the provisional measures requested of the Court by Libya does not render the Libyan request inadmissible, since there is in law no competition or hierarchy between the Court and the Security Council, each exercising its own competence; whereas Libya recalls in this connection that it regards the decision of the Security Council as contrary to international law, and considers that the Council has employed its power to characterize the situation for purposes of Chapter VII simply as a pretext to avoid applying the Montreal Convention.

40. Whereas in its observations on Security Council resolution 748 (1992), presented in response to the Court's invitation, the United States observes that that resolution was adopted under Chapter VII rather than Chapter VI of the Charter and was framed as a "decision" and contended that, given that binding decision, no object would be served by provisional measures; that, irrespective of the right claimed by Libya under the Montreal Convention, Libya has a Charter-based duty to accept and carry out the decisions in the resolution, and other States have a Charter-based duty to seek Libya's compliance; that any indication of provisional measures would run a serious risk of conflicting with the work of the Security Council; that the Council had rejected (*inter alia*) Libya's contention that the matter should be addressed on the basis of the right claimed by Libya under the Montreal Convention, which Libya asks the Court to protect through provisional measures; and that the Court should therefore decline the request;

41. Whereas the Court, in the context of the present proceedings on a request for provisional measures, has, in accordance with Article 41 of the Statute, to consider the circumstances drawn to its attention as requiring the indication of such measures, but cannot make definitive findings either of fact or of law on the issues relating to the merits, and the right of the Parties to contest such issues at the stage of the merits must remain unaffected by the Court's decision;

42. Whereas both Libya and the United Kingdom, as Members of the United Nations, are obliged to accept and carry out the decisions of the Security Council in accordance with Article 25 of the Charter; whereas the Court, which is at the stage of proceedings on provisional measures, considers that prima facie this obligation extends to the decision contained in resolution 748 (1992); and whereas, in accordance with Article 103 of the Charter, the obligations of the Parties in that respect prevail over their obligations under any other international agreement, including the Montreal Convention;

43. Whereas the Court, while thus not at this stage called upon to determine definitively the legal effect of Security Council resolution 748 (1992), considers that, whatever the situation previous to the adoption of that resolution, the rights claimed by Libya under the Montreal Convention cannot now be regarded as appropriate for protection by the indication of provisional measures;

44. Whereas, furthermore, an indication of the measures requested by Libya would be likely to impair the rights which appear prima facie to be enjoyed by the United States by virtue of the Security Council resolution 748 (1992);

45. Whereas, in order to pronounce on the present request for provisional measures, the Court is not called upon to determine any of the other questions which have been raised before it in the present proceedings, including the question of its jurisdiction to entertain the merits of the case; and whereas the decision given in these proceedings in no way prejudices any such question, and leaves unaffected the rights of the Governments of Libya and the Government of the United States to submit arguments in respect of any of these questions.

46. For these reasons,

By eleven votes to five,

The Court

Finds that the circumstances of the case are not such as to require the exercise of its power under Article 41 of the Statute to indicate provisional measures.

Legality of the Threat or Use of Force of Nuclear Weapons in Armed Conflict, ICJ Advisory Opinion, 8 July 1996

[*Note:*

Opinion requested by: the resolution of the Assembly of the World Health Organization resolution WHA46.40 adopted on 14 May 1993.

Question before the Court:

"In view of the health and environmental effects, would the use of nuclear weapons by a State in war or other armed conflict be a breach of its obligations under international law including the WHO Constitution?"]

The Opinion:

[...]

10. The Court has the authority to give advisory opinions by virtue of Article 65 of its Statute, paragraph 1 of which reads as follows:

> "The Court may give an advisory opinion on any legal question at the request of whatever body may be authorized by or in accordance with the Charter of the United Nations to make such a request."

It is also stated, in Article 96, paragraph 2, of the Charter that the

> "specialized agencies, which may at any time be so authorized by the General Assembly, may also request advisory opinions of the Court on legal questions arising within the scope of their activities".

Consequently, three conditions must be satisfied in order to found the jurisdiction of the Court when a request for an advisory opinion is submitted to it by a specialized agency: the agency requesting the opinion must be duly authorized, under the Charter, to request opinions from the Court; the opinion requested must be on a legal question; and this question must be one arising within the scope of the activities of the requesting agency (cf. *Application for Review of Judgment No. 273 of the United Nations Administrative Tribunal, Advisory Opinion, I. C. J. Reports 1982*, pp. 333-334).

11. Where the WHO is concerned, the above-mentioned texts are reflected in two other provisions, to which World Health Assembly resolution WHA46.40 expressly refers in paragraph 1 of its operative part. These are, on the one hand, Article 76 of that Organization's Constitution, under which:

> "Upon authorization by the General Assembly of the United Nations or upon authorization in accordance with any agreement between the Organization and the United Nations, the Organization may request the International Court of Justice for an advisory opinion on any legal question arising within the competence of the Organization."

And on the other hand, paragraph 2 of Article X of the Agreement of 10 July 1948 between the United Nations and the WHO, under which:

> "The General Assembly authorizes the World Health Organization to request advisory opinions of the International Court of Justice on legal questions arising within the scope of its competence other than questions concerning the mutual relationships of the Organization and the United Nations or other specialized agencies."

This agreement was approved by the United Nations General Assembly on 15 November 1947 (resolution 124 (II)) and by the World Health Assembly on 10 July 1948 (resolution [WHAl. 102]).

12. There is thus no doubt that the WHO has been duly authorized, in accordance with Article 96, paragraph 2, of the Charter, to request advisory opinions of the Court. The first condition which must be met in order to found the competence of the Court in this case is thus fulfilled. Moreover, this point has not been disputed; and the Court has in the past agreed to deal with a request for an advisory opinion submitted by the WHO (see *Interpretation of the Agreement of 25 March 1951 between the WHO and Egypt, Advisory Opinion, I. C. J. Reports 1980*, pp. 73 *et seq.*).

[...]

15. The Court must therefore first satisfy itself that the advisory opinion requested does indeed relate to a "legal question" within the meaning of its Statute and the United Nations Charter. The Court has already had occasion to indicate that questions

> "framed in terms of law and rais[ing] problems of international law . . . are by their very nature susceptible of a reply based on law . . . [and] appear . . . to be questions of a legal character" (*Western Sahara, Advisory Opinion, I. C. J. Reports 1975*, p. 18, para. 15).

16. The question put to the Court by the World Health Assembly does in fact constitute a legal question, as the Court is requested to rule on whether,

> "in view of the health and environmental effects, . . . the use of nuclear weapons by a State in war or other armed conflict [would] be a breach of its obligations under international law including the WHO Constitution".

To do this, the Court must identify the obligations of States under the rules of law invoked, and assess whether the behaviour in question conforms to those obligations, thus giving an answer to the question posed based on law.

The fact that this question also has political aspects, as, in the nature of things, is the case with so many questions which arise in international life, does not suffice to deprive it of its character as a "legal question" and to "deprive the Court of a competence expressly conferred on it by its Statute" (*Application for Review of Judgment No. 158 of the United Nations Administrative Tribunal, Advisory Opinion, I. C. J. Reports 1973*, p. 172, para. 14). Whatever its political aspects, the Court cannot refuse to admit the legal character of a question which invites it to discharge an essentially judicial task, namely, an assessment of the legality of the possible conduct of States with regard to the obligations imposed upon them by international law (cf. *Conditions of Admission of a State to Membership in the United Nations (Article 4 of Charter), Advisory Opinion, 1948, I.C.J. Reports 1947-1948,* pp. 61-62; *Competence of the General Assembly for the Admission of a State to the United Nations, Advisory Opinion, I. C. J. Reports 1950,* pp. 6-7; *Certain Expenses of the United Nations (Article 17, paragraph 2, of the Charter), Advisory Opinion, I. C. J. Reports 1962,* p. 155).

[...]

18. The Court will now seek to determine whether the advisory opinion requested by the WHO relates to a question which arises "within the scope of [the] activities" of that Organization, in accordance with Article 96, paragraph 2, of the Charter.

[...]

19. In order to delineate the field of activity or the area of competence of an international organization, one must refer to the relevant rules of the organization and, in the first place, to its constitution. From a formal standpoint, the constituent instruments of international organizations are multilateral treaties, to which the well-established rules of treaty interpretation apply. As the Court has said with respect to the Charter:

> "On the previous occasions when the Court has had to interpret the Charter of the United Nations, it has followed the principles and rules applicable in general to the interpretation of treaties, since it has recognized that the Charter is a multilateral treaty, albeit a treaty having certain special characteristics." (Certain Expenses of the United Nations (Article 17, paragraph 2, of the Charter), Advisory Opinion, I.C.J. Reports 1962, p. 157.)

But the constituent instruments of international organizations are also treaties of a particular type; their object is to create new subjects of law endowed with a certain autonomy, to which the parties entrust the task of realizing common goals. Such treaties can raise specific problems of interpretation owing, inter alia, to their character which is conventional and at the same time institutional; the very nature of the organization created, the objectives which have been assigned to it by its founders, the imperatives associated with the effective performance of its functions, as well as its own practice, are all elements which may deserve special attention when the time comes to interpret these constituent treaties.

According to the customary rule of interpretation as expressed in Article 31 of the 1969 Vienna Convention on the Law of Treaties, the terms of a treaty must be interpreted "in their context and in the light of its object and purpose" and there shall be

> "taken into account, together with the context:
>
> ...
>
> (b) any subsequent practice in the application of the treaty which establishes the agreement of the parties regarding its interpretation".

[...]

20. The WHO Constitution was adopted and opened for signature on 22 July 1946; it entered into force on 7 April 1948 and was amended in 1960, 1975, 1977, 1984 and 1994.

The functions attributed to the Organization are listed in 22 subparagraphs (subparagraphs (a) to (v)) in Article 2 of its Constitution. None of these subparagraphs expressly refers to the legality of any activity hazardous to health; and none of the functions of the WHO is dependent upon the legality of the situations upon which it must act. Moreover, it is stated in the introductory sentence of Article 2 that the Organization discharges its functions "in order to achieve its objective". The objective of the Organization is defined in Article 1 as being "the attainment by all peoples of the highest possible level of health". As for the Preamble to the Constitution, it sets out various principles which the States parties "declare, in conformity with the Charter of the United Nations, ... [to be] basic to the happiness, harmonious relations and security of all peoples": hence, it is stated therein, inter alia, that

> "[t]he enjoyment of the highest attainable standard of health is one of the fundamental rights of every human being" and that "[t]he health of all peoples is fundamental to the attainment of peace and security";

it is further indicated, at the end of the Preamble that,

> "for the purpose of co-operation among themselves and with others to promote and protect the health of all peoples, the Contracting Parties ... establish ... the ... Organization ... as a specialized agency within the terms of Article 57 of the Charter of the United Nations".

21. Interpreted in accordance with their ordinary meaning, in their context and in the light of the object and purpose of the WHO Constitution, as well as of the practice followed by the Organization, the provisions of its Article 2 may be read as authorizing the Organization to deal with the effects on health of the use of nuclear weapons, or of any other hazardous activity, and to take preventive measures aimed at protecting the health of populations in the event of such weapons being used or such activities engaged in.

The question put to the Court in the present case relates, however, not to the effects of the use of nuclear weapons on health, but to the legality of the use of such weapons in view of their health and environmental effects. Whatever those effects might be, the competence of the WHO to deal with them is not dependent on the legality of the acts that caused them. Accordingly, it does not seem to the Court that the provisions of Article 2 of the WHO Constitution, interpreted in accordance with the criteria referred to above, can be understood as conferring upon the Organization a competence to address the legality of the use of nuclear weapons, and thus in turn a competence to ask the Court about that.

22. World Health Assembly resolution WHA46.40, by which the Court has been seized of this request for an opinion, expressly refers, in its Preamble, to the functions indicated under subparagraphs (a), (k), (p) and (v) of Article 2 under consideration. These functions are defined as:

> "(a) to act as the directing and co-ordinating authority on international health work;
>
> ...
>
> (k) to propose conventions, agreements and regulations, and make recommendations with respect to international health matters;
>
> ...

> (p) to study and report on, in co-operation with other specialized agencies where necessary, administrative and social techniques affecting public health and medical care from preventive and curative points of view, including hospital services and social security;
>
> . . .
>
> [and]
>
> (v) generally to take all necessary action to attain the objective of the Organization."

In the view of the Court, none of these functions has a sufficient connection with the question before it for that question to be capable of being considered as arising "within the scope of [the] activities" of the WHO. The causes of the deterioration of human health are numerous and varied; and the legal or illegal character of these causes is essentially immaterial to the measures which the WHO must in any case take in an attempt to remedy their effects. In particular, the legality or illegality of the use of nuclear weapons in no way determines the specific measures, regarding health or otherwise (studies, plans, procedures, etc.), which could be necessary in order to seek to prevent or cure some of their effects. Whether nuclear weapons are used legally or illegally, their effects on health would be the same. Similarly, while it is probable that the use of nuclear weapons might seriously prejudice the WHO's material capability to deliver all the necessary services in such an eventuality, for example, by making the affected areas inaccessible, this does not raise an issue falling within the scope of the Organization's activities within the meaning of Article 96, paragraph 2, of the Charter. The reference in the question put to the Court to the health and environmental effects, which according to the WHO the use of a nuclear weapon will always occasion, does not make the question one that falls within the WHO's functions.

[...]

25. The Court need hardly point out that international organizations are subjects of international law which do not, unlike States, possess a general competence. International organizations are governed by the "principle of speciality", that is to say, they are invested by the States which create them with powers, the limits of which are a function of the common interests whose promotion those States entrust to them. The Permanent Court of International Justice referred to this basic principle in the following terms:

> "As the European Commission is not a State, but an international institution with a special purpose, it only has the functions bestowed upon it by the Definitive Statute with a view to the fulfilment of that purpose, but it has power to exercise those functions to their full extent, in so far as the Statute does not impose restrictions on it." (*Jurisdiction of the European Commission of the Danube, Advisory Opinion, P.C.I.J., Series B, No. 14, p. 64.*)

The powers conferred on international organizations are normally the subject of an express statement in their constituent instruments. Nevertheless, the necessities of international life may point to the need for organizations, in order to achieve their objectives, to possess subsidiary powers which are not expressly provided for in the basic instruments which govern their activities. It is generally accepted that international organizations can exercise such powers, known as "implied" powers. As far as the United Nations is concerned, the Court has expressed itself in the following terms in this respect:

> "Under international law, the Organization must be deemed to have those powers which, though not expressly provided in the Charter, are conferred upon it by necessary implication as being essential to the performance of its duties. This principle of law was applied by the Permanent Court of International Justice to the International Labour Organization in its Advisory Opinion No. 13 of July 23rd, 1926 (Series B, No. 13, p. 18), and must be applied to the United Nations." (*Reparation for Injuries Suffered in the Service of the United Nations, Advisory Opinion, I.C.J. Reports 1949, pp. 182-183*; cf. *Effect of Awards of Compensation Made by the United Nations Administrative Tribunal, I.C.J. Reports 1954, p. 57.*)

In the opinion of the Court, to ascribe to the WHO the competence to address the legality of the use of nuclear weapons – even in view of their health and environmental effects – would be tantamount to disregarding the principle of speciality; for such competence could not be deemed a necessary implication of the Constitution of the Organization in the light of the purposes assigned to it by its member States.

26. The World Health Organization is, moreover, an international organization of a particular kind. As indicated in the Preamble and confirmed by Article 69 of its Constitution, "the Organization shall be brought into relation with the United Nations as one of the specialized agencies referred to in Article 57 of the Charter of the United Nations." Article 57 of the Charter defines "specialized agencies" as follows:

> "1. The various specialized agencies, established by intergovernmental agreement and having wide international responsibilities, as defined in their basic instruments, in economic, social, cultural, educational, health, and related fields, shall be brought into relationship with the United Nations in accordance with the provisions of Article 63.
> 2. Such agencies thus brought into relationship with the United Nations are hereinafter referred to as 'specialized agencies'."

Article 58 of the Charter reads:

> "The Organization shall make recommendations for the co-ordination of the policies and activities of the specialized agencies."

Article 63 of the Charter then provides:

> "1. The Economic and Social Council may enter into agreements with any of the agencies referred to in Article 57, defining the terms on which the agency concerned shall be brought into relationship with the United Nations. Such agreements shall be subject to approval by the General Assembly.
>
> 2. It may co-ordinate the activities of the specialized agencies through consultation with and recommendations to such agencies and through recommendations to the General Assembly and to the Members of the United Nations."

As these provisions demonstrate, the Charter of the United Nations laid the basis of a "system" designed to organize international co-operation in a coherent fashion by bringing the United Nations, invested with powers of general scope, into relationship with various autonomous and complementary organizations, invested with sectorial powers. The exercise of these powers by the organizations belonging to the "United Nations system" is co-ordinated, notably, by the relationship agreements concluded between the United Nations and each of the specialized agencies. In the case of the WHO, the agreement of 10 July 1948 between the United Nations and that Organization actually refers to the WHO Constitution in the following terms in Article I:

> "The United Nations recognizes the World Health Organization as the specialized agency responsible for taking such action as may be appropriate under its Constitution for the accomplishment of the objectives set forth therein."

It follows from the various instruments mentioned above that the WHO Constitution can only be interpreted, as far as the powers conferred upon that Organization are concerned, by taking due account not only of the general principle of speciality, but also of the logic of the overall system contemplated by the Charter. If, according to the rules on which that system is based, the WHO has, by virtue of Article 57 of the Charter, "wide international responsibilities", those responsibilities are necessarily restricted to the sphere of public "health" and cannot encroach on the responsibilities of other parts of the United Nations system. And there is no doubt that questions concerning the use of force, the regulation of armaments and disarmament are within the competence of the United Nations and lie outside that of the specialized agencies. Besides, any other conclusion would render virtually meaningless the notion of a specialized agency; it is difficult to imagine what other meaning that notion could have if such an organization need only show that the use of certain weapons could affect its objectives in order to be empowered to concern itself with the legality of such use. It is therefore difficult to maintain that, by authorizing various specialized agencies to request opinions from the Court under Article 96, paragraph 2, of the Charter, the General Assembly intended to allow them to seize the Court of questions belonging within the competence of the United Nations.

For all these reasons, the Court considers that the question raised in the request for an advisory opinion submitted to it by the WHO does not arise "within the scope of [the] activities" of that Organization as defined by its Constitution.

[...]

28. It remains to be considered whether the insertion of the words "including the WHO Constitution" in the question put to the Court (which essentially seeks an opinion on the legality of the use of nuclear weapons in general) could allow it to offer an opinion on the legality of the use of nuclear weapons by reference to the passage in the question concerning the WHO Constitution. The Court must answer in the negative. Indeed, the WHO is not empowered to seek an opinion on the interpretation of its Constitution in relation to matters outside the scope of its functions.

29. Other arguments have nevertheless been put forward in the proceedings to found the jurisdiction of the Court in the present case. It has thus been argued that World Health Assembly resolution WHA46.40, having been adopted by the requisite majority, "must be presumed to have been validly adopted" (cf. *Legal Consequences for States of the Continued Presence of South Africa in Namibia (South West Africa) notwithstanding Security Council Resolution 276 (1970), Advisory Opinion, I.C.J. Reports 1971*, p. *22*, para. 20). The Court would observe in this respect that the question whether a resolution has been duly adopted from a procedural point of view and the question whether that resolution has been adopted *intra vires* are two separate issues. The mere fact that a majority of States, in voting on a

resolution, have complied with all the relevant rules of form cannot in itself suffice to remedy any fundamental defects, such as acting *ultra vires*, with which the resolution might be afflicted.

As the Court has stated, "each organ must, in the first place at least, determine its own jurisdiction" (*Certain Expenses of the United Nations (Article 17, paragraph 2, of the Charter), Advisory Opinion, I.C.J. Reports 1962*, p. 168). It was therefore certainly a matter for the World Health Assembly to decide on its competence – and, thereby, that of the WHO – to submit a request to the Court for an advisory opinion on the question under consideration, having regard to the terms of the Constitution of the Organization and those of the Agreement of 10 July 1948 bringing it into relationship with the United Nations. But likewise it is incumbent on the Court to satisfy itself that the conditions governing its own competence to give the opinion requested are met; through the reference made, respectively, by Article 96, paragraph 2, of the Charter to the "scope of [the] activities" of the Organization and by Article X, paragraph 2, of the Agreement of 10 July 1948 to its "competence", the Court also finds itself obliged, in the present case, to interpret the Constitution of the WHO.

The exercise of the functions entrusted to the Court under Article 65, paragraph 1, of its Statute requires it to furnish such an interpretation, independently of any operation of the specific recourse mechanism which Article 75 of the WHO Constitution reserves for cases in which a question or dispute arises between States concerning the interpretation or application of that instrument; and in doing so the Court arrives at different conclusions from those reached by the World Health Assembly when it adopted resolution WHA46.40.

[...]

31. Having arrived at the view that the request for an advisory opinion submitted by the WHO does not relate to a question which arises "within the scope of [the] activities" of that Organization in accordance with Article 96, paragraph 2, of the Charter, the Court finds that an essential condition of founding its jurisdiction in the present case is absent and that it cannot, accordingly, give the opinion requested. Consequently, the Court is not called upon to examine the arguments which were laid before it with regard to the exercise of its discretionary power to give an opinion.

Legality of the Threat or Use of Nuclear Weapons, ICJ Advisory Opinion, 8 July 1996

[*Note:*

Opinion requested by: the UN General Assembly resolution 49/75 K adopted on 15 December 1994

Question before the Court:
"Is the threat or use of nuclear weapons in any circumstance permitted under international law?"]

The Opinion:

[...]

70. The Court notes that General Assembly resolutions, even if they are not binding, may sometimes have normative value. They can, in certain circumstances, provide evidence important for establishing the existence of a rule or the emergence of an *opinio juris*. To establish whether this is true of a given General Assembly resolution, it is necessary to look at its content and the conditions of its adoption; it is also necessary to see whether an *opinio juris* exists as to its normative character. Or a series of resolutions may show the gradual evolution of the *opinio juris* required for the establishment of a new rule.

71. Examined in their totality, the General Assembly resolutions put before the Court declare that the use of nuclear weapons would be "a direct violation of the Charter of the United Nations7'; and in certain formulations that such use "should be prohibited". The focus of these resolutions has sometimes shifted to diverse related matters; however, several of the resolutions under consideration in the present case have been adopted with substantial numbers of negative votes and abstentions; thus, although those resolutions are a clear sign of deep concern regarding the problem of nuclear weapons, they still fall short of establishing the existence of an *opinio juvis* on the illegality of the use of such weapons.

72. The Court further notes that the first of the resolutions of the General Assembly expressly proclaiming the illegality of the use of nuclear weapons, resolution 1653 (XVI) of 24 November 1961 (mentioned in subsequent resolutions), after referring to certain international declarations and binding agreements, from the Declaration of St. Petersburg of 1868 to the Geneva Protocol of 1925, proceeded to qualify the legal nature of nuclear weapons, determine their effects, and apply general rules of customary international law to nuclear weapons in particular. That application by the General Assembly of general rules of customary law to the particular case of nuclear weapons indicates that, in its view, there was no specific rule of customary law which prohibited the use of nuclear weapons; if such a rule had existed, the General Assembly could simply have referred to it and would not have needed to undertake such an exercise of legal qualification.

73. Having said this, the Court points out that the adoption each year by the General Assembly, by a large majority, of resolutions recalling the content of resolution 1653 (XVI), and requesting the member States to conclude a convention prohibiting the use of nuclear weapons in any circumstance, reveals the desire of a very large section of the international community to take, by a specific and express prohibition of the use of nuclear weapons, a significant step forward along the road to complete nuclear

disarmament. The emergence, as *lex lata,* of a customary rule specifically prohibiting the use of nuclear weapons as such is hampered by the continuing tensions between the nascent *opinio juris* on the one hand, and the still strong adherence to the practice of deterrence on the other.

Difference Relating to Immunity from Legal Process of a Special Rapporteur of the Commission of Human Rights, ICJ Advisory Opinion, 29 April 1999

[*Note:*

Opinion requested by: the decision 1998/297 of the UN Economic and Social Council (ECOSOC) of 5 August 1998.

Question before the Court:
"on the legal question of the applicability of Article VI, Section 22, of the Convention on the Privileges and Immunities of the United Nations in the case of Dato' Param Cumaraswamy as Special Rapporteur of the Commission on Human Rights on the independence of judges and lawyers . . ."]

The Opinion:

[...]

10. In its decision 19981297, the Council asked the Court to take into account, for purposes of the advisory opinion requested, the "circumstances set out in paragraphs 1 to 15 of the note by the Secretary-General" (E/1998194). Those paragraphs read as follows:

"1. In its resolution 22 A (1) of 13 February 1946, the General Assembly adopted, pursuant to Article 105 (3) of the Charter of the United Nations, the Convention on the Privileges and Immunities of the United Nations (the Convention). Since then, 137 Member States have become parties to the Convention, and its provisions have been incorporated by reference into many hundreds of agreements relating to the headquarters or seats of the United Nations and its organs, and to activities carried out by the Organization in nearly every country of the world.

2. That Convention is, *inter alia*, designed to protect various categories of persons, including 'Experts on Mission for the United Nations', from all types of interference by national authorities. In particular, Section 22 *(b)* of Article VI of the Convention provides:

'*Section 22:* Experts (other than officials coming within the scope of Article V) performing missions for the United Nations shall be accorded such privileges and immunities as are necessary for the independent exercise of their functions during the period of their missions, including time spent on journeys in connection with their missions. In particular they shall be accorded:

. . .

(b) in respect of words spoken or written and acts done by them in the course of the performance of their mission, immunity from legal process of every kind. This immunity from legal process shall continue to be accorded notwithstanding that the persons concerned are no longer employed on missions for the United Nations.'

3. In its Advisory Opinion of 14 December 1989, on the *Applicability of Article VI, Section 22, of the Convention on the Privileges and Immunities of the United Nations* (the so-called '*Mazilu* case'), the International Court of Justice held that a Special Rapporteur of the Subcommission on the Prevention of Discrimination and Protection of Minorities of the Commission on Human Rights was an 'expert on mission' within the meaning of Article VI of the Convention.

4. The Commission on Human Rights, by its resolution 1994/41 of 4 March 1994, endorsed by the Economic and Social Council in its decision 1994125 1 of *22* July 1994, appointed Dato' Param Cumaraswamy, a Malaysian jurist, as the Commission's Special Rapporteur on the Independence of Judges and Lawyers. His mandate consists of tasks including, *infer alia*, to inquire into substantial allegations concerning, and to identify and record attacks on, the independence of the judiciary, lawyers and court officials. Mr. Cumaraswamy has submitted four reports to the Commission on the execution of his mandate : ElCN.411995139, ElCN.411996137, ElCN.411997132 and ElCN.411998139. After the third report containing a section on the litigation pending against him in the Malaysian civil courts, the Commission at its fifty-fourth session, in April 1997, renewed his mandate for an additional three years.

5. In November 1995 the Special Rapporteur gave an interview to *International Commrrcial Litigation*, a magazine published in the United Kingdom of Great Britain and Northern Ireland but circulated also in Malaysia, in which he commented on certain litigations that had been carried out in Malaysian courts. As a result of an article published on the basis of that interview, two commercial companies in Malaysia asserted that the said article contained defamatory words that had 'brought them into public scandal, odium and contempt'. Each Company filed a suit against him for damages amounting to M$30 million (approximately US12 million each), 'including exemplary damages for slander'.

6. Acting on behalf of the Secretary-General, the Legal Counsel considered the circumstances of the interview and of the controverted passages of the article and determined that Dato' Param Cumaraswamy was interviewed in his official capacity as Special Rapporteur on the Independence of Judges and Lawyers, that the article clearly referred to his United Nations capacity and to the Special Rapporteur's United Nations global mandate to investigate allegations concerning the independence of the judiciary and that the quoted passages related to such allegations. On 15 January 1997, the Legal Counsel, in a note verbale addressed to the Permanent Representative of Malaysia to the United Nations, therefore 'requested the competent Malaysian authorities to promptly advise the Malaysian courts of the Special Rapporteur's immunity from legal process' with respect to that particular complaint. On 20 January 1997, the Special Rapporteur filed an application in the High Court of Kuala Lumpur (the trial court in which the said suit had been filed) to set aside and/or strike out the plaintiffs' writ, on the ground that the words that were the subject of the suits had been spoken by him in the course of performing his mission for the United Nations as Special Rapporteur on the Independence of Judges and Lawyers. The Secretary-General issued a note on 7 March 1997 confirming that 'the words which constitute the basis of plaintiffs' complaint in this case were spoken by the Special Rapporteur in the course of his mission' and that the Secretary-General 'therefore maintains that Dato' Param Cumaraswamy is immune from legal process with respect thereto'. The Special Rapporteur filed this note in support of his above-mentioned application.

7. After a draft of a certificate that the Minister for Foreign Affairs proposed to file with the trial court had been discussed with representatives of the Office of Legal Affairs, who had indicated that the draft set out the immunities of the Special Rapporteur incompletely and inadequately, the Minister nevertheless on 12 March 1997 filed the certificate in the form originally proposed: in particular the final sentence of that certificate in effect invited the trial court to determine at its own discretion whether the immunity applied, by stating that this was the case 'only in respect of words spoken or written and acts done by him in the course of the performance of his mission' (emphasis added). In spite of the representations that had been made by the Office of Legal Affairs, the certificate failed to refer in any way to the note that the Secretary-General had issued a few days earlier and that had in the meantime been filed with the court, nor did it indicate that in this respect, i.e. in deciding whether particular words or acts of an expert fell within the scope of his mission, the determination could exclusively be made by the Secretary- General, and that such determination had conclusive effect and therefore had to be accepted as such by the court. In spite of repeated requests by the Legal Counsel, the Minister for Foreign Affairs refused to amend his certificate or to supplement it in the manner urged by the United Nations.

8. On 28 June 1997, the competent judge of the Malaysian High Court for Kuala Lumpur concluded that she was 'unable to hold that the Defendant is absolutely protected by the immunity he claims', in part because she considered that the Secretary-General's note was merely 'an opinion' with scant probative value and no binding force upon the court and that the Minister for Foreign Affairs' certificate 'would appear to be no more than a bland statement as to a state of fact pertaining to the Defendant's status and mandate as a Special Rapporteur and appears to have room for interpretation'. The Court ordered that the Special Rapporteur's motion be dismissed with costs, that costs be taxed and paid forthwith by him and that he file and serve his defence within 14 days. On 8 July, the Court of Appeal dismissed Mr. Cumaraswamy's motion for a stay of execution.

9. On 30 June and 7 July 1997, the Legal Counsel thereupon sent notes verbales to the Permanent Representative of Malaysia, and also held meetings with him and his Deputy. In the latter note, the Legal Counsel, *inter dia*, called on the Malaysian Government to intervene in the current proceedings so that the burden of any further defence, including any expenses and taxed costs resulting therefrom, be assumed by the Government; to hold Mr. Cumaraswamy harmless in respect of the expenses he had already incurred or that were being taxed to him in respect of the proceedings so far; and, so as to prevent the accumulation of additional expenses and costs and the further need to submit a defence until the matter of his immunity was definitively resolved between the United Nations and the Government, to support a motion to have the High Court proceedings stayed until such resolution. The Legal Counsel referred to the provisions for the settlement of differences arising out of the interpretation and application of the 1946 Convention that might arise between the Organization and a Member State, which are set out in Section 30 of the Convention, and indicated that if the Government decided that it cannot or does not wish to protect and to hold harmless the Special Rapporteur in the indicated manner, a difference within the meaning of those provisions might be considered to have arisen between the Organization and the Government of Malaysia.

[...]

11. On 10 July yet another lawsuit was filed against the Special Rapporteur by one of the lawyers mentioned in the magazine article referred to in paragraph 5 above, based on precisely the same passages of the interview and claiming damages in an amount of M$60 million (US24 million). On 11 July, the

Secretary-General issued a note corresponding to the one of 7 March 1997 (see para. 6 above) and also communicated a note verbale with essentially the same text to the Permanent Representative of Malaysia with the request that it be presented formally to the competent Malaysian court by the Government.

12. On 23 October and 21 November 1997, new plaintiffs filed a third and fourth lawsuit against the Special Rapporteur for M$100 million (US$40 million) and M$60 million (US$24 million) respectively. On 27 October and 22 November 1997, the Secretary-General issued identical certificates of the Special Rapporteur's immunity.

13. On 7 November 1997, the Secretary-General advised the Prime Minister of Malaysia that a difference might have arisen between the United Nations and the Government of Malaysia and about the possibility of resorting to the International Court of Justice pursuant to Section 30 of the Convention. Nonetheless on 19 February 1998, the Federal Court of Malaysia denied Mr. Cumaraswamy's application for leave to appeal stating that he is neither a sovereign nor a fullfledged diplomat but merely 'an unpaid, part-time provider of information'.

[...]

14. On 18 December 1995, two commercial firms and their legal counsel addressed letters to Mr. Cumaraswamy in which they maintained that they were defamed by Mr. Cumaraswamy's statements in the article, since it was clear, they claimed, that they were being accused of corruption in the *Ayer Molek* case. They informed Mr. Cumaraswamy that they had "no choice but to issue defamation proceedings against him" and added

> "It is important that all steps are taken for the purpose of mitigating the continuing damage being done to [our] business and commercial reputations which is worldwide, as quickly and effectively as possible."

[...]

50. In the process of determining whether a particular expert on mission is entitled, in the prevailing circumstances, to the immunity provided for in Section 22 *(b)*, the Secretary-General of the United Nations has a pivotal role to play. The Secretary-General, as the chief administrative officer of the Organization, has the authority and the responsibility to exercise the necessary protection where required. This authority has been recognized by the Court when it stated:

> "Upon examination of the character of the functions entrusted to the Organization and of the nature of the missions of its agents, it becomes clear that the capacity of the Organization to exercise a measure of functional protection of its agents arises by necessary intendment out of the Charter." (*Reparation for Injuries Suffered in the Service of the United Nations, Advisory Opinion, I.C.J. Reports 1949*, p. 184.)

51. Article VI, Section 23, of the General Convention provides that "[p]rivileges and immunities are granted to experts in the interests of the United Nations and not for the personal benefit of the individuals themselves". In exercising protection of United Nations experts, the Secretary-General is therefore protecting the mission with which the expert is entrusted. In that respect, the Secretary-General has the primary responsibility and authority to protect the interests of the Organization and its agents, including experts on mission. As the Court held:

"In order that the agent may perform his duties satisfactorily, he must feel that this protection is assured to him by the Organization, and that he may count on it. To ensure the independence of the agent, and, consequently, the independent action of the Organization itself, it is essential that in performing his duties he need not have to rely on any other protection than that of the Organization . . ." (*Ibid*, p. 183.)

52. The determination whether an agent of the Organization has acted in the course of the performance of his mission depends upon the facts of a particular case. In the present case, the Secretary-General, or the Legal Counsel of the United Nations on his behalf, has on numerous occasions informed the Government of Malaysia of his finding that Mr. Cumaraswamy had spoken the words quoted in the article in *International Commercial Litigation* in his capacity as Special Rapporteur of the Commission and that he consequently was entitled to immunity from "every kind" of legal process.

53. As is clear from the written and oral pleadings of the United Nations, the Secretary-General was reinforced in this view by the fact that it has become standard practice of Special Rapporteurs of the Commission to have contact with the media. This practice was confirmed by the High Commissioner for Human Rights who, in a letter dated 2 October 1998, included in the dossier, wrote that: "it is more common than not for Special Rapporteurs to speak to the press about matters pertaining to their investigations, thereby keeping the general public informed of their work".

54. As noted above (see paragraph 13), Mr. Cumaraswamy was explicitly referred to several times in the article "Malaysian Justice on Trial" in *International Commercial Litigation* in his capacity as United Nations Special Rapporteur on the Independence of Judges and Lawyers. In his reports to the Commission (see paragraph 18 above), Mr. Cumaraswamy set out his methods of work, expressed concern about the independence of the Malaysian judiciary, and referred to the civil lawsuits initiated against him. His third report noted that the Legal Counsel of the United Nations had informed the Government of Malaysia that he had spoken in the performance of his mission and was therefore entitled to immunity from legal process.

55. As noted in paragraph 18 above, in its various resolutions the Commission took note of the Special Rapporteur's reports and of his methods of work. In 1997, it extended his mandate for another three years (see paragraphs 18 and 45 above). The Commission presumably would not have so acted if it had been of the opinion that Mr. Cumaraswamy had gone beyond his mandate and had given the interview to *International Commercial Litigation* outside the course of his functions. Thus the Secretary-General was able to find support for his findings in the Commission's position.

56. The Court is not called upon in the present case to pass upon the aptness of the terms used by the Special Rapporteur or his assessment of the situation. In any event, in view of all the circumstances of this case, elements of which are set out in paragraphs 1 to 15 of the note by the Secretary-General, the Court is of the opinion that the Secretary-General correctly found that Mr. Cumaraswamy, in speaking the words quoted in the article in *International Commercial Litigation*, was acting in the course of the performance of his mission as Special Rapporteur of the Commission. Consequently, Article VI, Section 22 (b),of the General Convention is applicable to him in the present case and affords Mr. Cumaraswamy immunity from legal process of every kind.

***

57. The Court will now deal with the second part of the Council's question, namely, "the legal obligations of Malaysia in this case".

58. Malaysia maintains that it is premature to deal with the question of its obligations. It is of the view that the obligation to ensure that the requirements of Section 22 of the Convention are met is an obligation of result and not of means to be employed in achieving that result. It further states that Malaysia has complied with its obligation under Section 34 of the General Convention, which provides that a party to the Convention must be "in a position under its own law to give effect to [its] terms", by enacting the necessary legislation; finally it contends that the Malaysian courts have not yet reached a final decision as to Mr. Cumaraswamy's entitlement to immunity from legal process.

59. The Court wishes to point out that the request for an advisory opinion refers to "the legal obligations of Malaysia in this case". The difference which has arisen between the United Nations and Malaysia originated in the Government of Malaysia not having informed the competent Malaysian judicial authorities of the Secretary-General's finding that Mr. Cumaraswamy had spoken the words at issue in the course of the performance of his mission and was, therefore, entitled to immunity from legal process (see paragraph 17 above). It is as from the time of this omission that the question before the Court must be answered.

60. As the Court has observed, the Secretary-General, as the chief administrative officer of the Organization, has the primary responsibility to safeguard the interests of the Organization; to that end, it is up to him to assess whether its agents acted within the scope of their functions and, where he so concludes, to protect these agents, including experts on mission, by asserting their immunity. This means that the Secretary-General has the authority and responsibility to inform the Government of a member State of his finding and, where appropriate, to request it to act accordingly and, in particular, to request it to bring his finding to the knowledge of the local courts if acts of an agent have given or may give rise to court proceedings.

61. When national courts are seized of a case in which the immunity of a United Nations agent is in issue, they should immediately be notified of any finding by the Secretary-General concerning that immunity. That finding, and its documentary expression, creates a presumption which can only be set aside for the most compelling reasons and is thus to be given the greatest weight by national courts.

The governmental authorities of a party to the General Convention are therefore under an obligation to convey such information to the national courts concerned, since a proper application of the Convention by them is dependent on such information.

Failure to comply with this obligation, among others, could give rise to the institution of proceedings under Article VIII, Section 30, of the General Convention.

62. The Court concludes that the Government of Malaysia had an obligation, under Article 105 of the Charter and under the General Convention, to inform its courts of the position taken by the Secretary-General. According to a well-established rule of international law, the conduct of any organ of a State must be regarded as an act of that State. This rule, which is of a customary character, is reflected in Article 6 of the Draft Articles on State Responsibility adopted provisionally by the International Law Commission on first reading, which provides:

> "The conduct of an organ of the State shall be considered as an act of that State under international law, whether that organ belongs to the constituent, legislative, executive, judicial or other power, whether its functions are of an international or an internal character, and whether it holds a superior or a subordinated position in the organization of the State." (*Yearbook of the International Law Commission*, 1973, Vol. II, p. 193.)

Because the Government did not transmit the Secretary-General's finding to the competent courts, and the Minister for Foreign Affairs did not refer to it in his own certificate, Malaysia did not comply with the above-mentioned obligation.

63. Section 22 (b)of the General Convention explicitly states that experts on mission shall be accorded immunity from legal process of every kind in respect of words spoken or written and acts done by them in the course of the performance of their mission. By necessary implication, questions of immunity are therefore preliminary issues which must be expeditiously decided *in limine litis*. This is a generally recognized principle of procedural law, and Malaysia was under an obligation to respect it. The Malaysian courts did not rule *in limine litis* on the immunity of the Special Rapporteur (see paragraph 17 above), thereby nullifying the essence of the immunity rule contained in Section 22 (b). Moreover, costs were taxed to Mr. Cumaraswamy while the question of immunity was still unresolved. As indicated above, the conduct of an organ of a State – even an organ independent of the executive power – must be regarded as an act of that State. Consequently, Malaysia did not act in accordance with its obligations under international law.

***

64. In addition, the immunity from legal process to which the Court finds Mr. Cumaraswamy entitled entails holding Mr. Cumaraswamy financially harmless for any costs imposed upon him by the Malaysian courts, in particular taxed costs.

65. According to Article VIII, Section 30, of the General Convention, the opinion given by the Court shall be accepted as decisive by the parties to the dispute. Malaysia has acknowledged its obligations under Section 30.

Since the Court holds that Mr. Cumaraswamy is an expert on mission who under Section 22 (b) is entitled to immunity from legal process, the Government of Malaysia is obligated to communicate this advisory opinion to the competent Malaysian courts, in order that Malaysia's international obligations be given effect and Mr. Cumaraswamy's immunity be respected.

66. Finally, the Court wishes to point out that the question of immunity from legal process is distinct from the issue of compensation for any damages incurred as a result of acts performed by the United Nations or by its agents acting in their official capacity.

The United Nations may be required to bear responsibility for the damage arising from such acts.

However, as is clear from Article VIII, Section 29, of the General Convention, any such claims against the United Nations shall not be dealt with by national courts but shall be settled in accordance with the appropriate modes of settlement that "[t]he United Nations shall make provisions for" pursuant to Section 29.

Furthermore, it need hardly be said that all agents of the United Nations, in whatever official capacity they act, must take care not to exceed the scope of their functions, and should so comport themselves as to avoid claims against the United Nations.

Legal Consequences of the Construction of Wall in the Occupied Palestinian Territory, ICJ Advisory Opinion, 9 July 2004

[*Note:*

Opinion requested by: the UN General Assembly resolution ES-10/14 adopted on 8 December 2003

Question before the Court:
In 2002 Israel started building a barrier in and around the West Bank. The wall departed from the Armistice (Green) Line of 1949 by cutting about ten percent of the Palestinian territory and providing a largest illegal settlement to Israeli settlers. Israel justified its action by invoking the right to self-defence from Palestinian suicide bombers. According to the Palestinian Authority Israel was trying to control the Palestinian territory and to divide the Arab population in West Bank.

The General Assembly asked the Court the following question:
"What are the legal consequences arising from the construction of the wall being built by Israel, the occupying Power, in the Occupied Palestinian Territory, including in and around East Jerusalem, as described in the report of the Secretary-General, considering the rules and principles of international law, including the Fourth Geneva Convention of 1949, and relevant Security Council and General Assembly resolutions?"]

The Opinion:

[...]

25. The Court has already indicated that the subject of the present request for an advisory opinion falls within the competence of the General Assembly under the Charter (see paragraphs 15-17 above). However, Article 12, paragraph 1, of the Charter provides that:

> "While the Security Council is exercising in respect of any dispute or situation the functions assigned to it in the present Charter, the General Assembly shall not make any recommendation with regard to that dispute or situation unless the Security Council so requests."

A request for an advisory opinion is not in itself a "recommendation" by the General Assembly "with regard to [a] dispute or situation". It has however been argued in this case that the adoption by the General Assembly of resolution ES-10/14 was *ultra vires* as not in accordance with Article 12. The Court thus considers that it is appropriate for it to examine the significance of that Article, having regard to the relevant texts and the practice of the United Nations.

26. Under Article 24 of the Charter the Security Council has "primary responsibility for the maintenance of international peace and security". In that regard it can impose on States "an explicit obligation of compliance if for example it issues an order or command ... under Chapter VII" and can, to that end, "require enforcement by coercive action" (*Certain Expenses of the United Nations (Article 17, paragraph 2, of the Charter), Advisory Opinion, I.C.J. Reports 1962,* p. 163). However, the Court would emphasize that Article 24 refers to a primary, but not necessarily exclusive, competence. The General Assembly does have the power, *inter alia*, under Article 14 of the Charter, to "recommend measures for the peaceful adjustment" of various situations *(ibid.).*

> "[T]he only limitation which Article 14 imposes on the General Assembly is the restriction found in Article 12, namely, that the Assembly should not recommend measures while the Security Council is dealing with the same matter unless the Council requests it to do so." (*I. C. J. Reports 1962*, p. 163.)

27. As regards the practice of the United Nations, both the General Assembly and the Security Council initially interpreted and applied Article 12 to the effect that the Assembly could not make a recommendation on a question concerning the maintenance of international peace and security while the matter remained on the Council's agenda. Thus the Assembly during its fourth session refused to recommend certain measures on the question of Indonesia, on the ground, *inter alia*, that the Council remained seized of the matter (*Official Records of the General Assembly, Fourth Session,* Ad Hoc *Political Committee, Summary Records of Meetings, 27 September-7 December 1949,* 56th Meeting, 3 December 1949, p. 339, para. 118). As for the Council, on a number of occasions it deleted items from its agenda in order to enable the Assembly to deliberate on them (for example, in respect of the Spanish question (*Official Records of the Security Council, First Year: Second Series, No. 21,* 79th Meeting, 4 November 1946, p. 498), in connection with incidents on the Greek border (*Official Records of the Security Council, Second Year, No. 89,* 202nd Meeting, 15 September 1947, pp. 2404-2405) and in regard to the Island of Taiwan (Formosa) (*Official Records of the Security Council, Fifth Year, No. 48,* 506th Meeting, 29 September 1950, p. 5)). In the case of the Republic of Korea, the Council decided on 31 January 1951 to remove the relevant item from the list of matters of which it was seized in order to enable the Assembly to deliberate on the matter (*Official Records of the Security Council, Sixth Year,* S/PV.531, 53Ist Meeting, 31 January 1951, pp. 11-12, para. 57).

However, this interpretation of Article 12 has evolved subsequently. Thus the General Assembly deemed itself entitled in 1961 to adopt recommendations in the matter of the Congo (resolutions 1955 (XV) and 1600 (XVI)) and in 1963 in respect of the Portuguese colonies (resolution 1913 (XVIII)) while those cases still appeared on the Council's agenda, without the Council having adopted any recent resolution concerning them. In response to a question posed by Peru during the twenty-third session of the General Assembly, the Legal Counsel of the United Nations confirmed that the Assembly interpreted the words "is exercising the functions" in Article 12 of the Charter as meaning "is exercising the functions at this moment" (General Assembly, Twenty-third Session, Third Committee, 1637th meeting, A/C.3/SR.1637, para. 9). Indeed, the Court notes that there has been an increasing tendency over time for the General Assembly and the Security Council to deal in parallel with the same matter concerning the maintenance of international peace and security (see, for example, the matters involving Cyprus, South Africa, Angola, Southern Rhodesia and more recently Bosnia and Herzegovina and Somalia). It is often the case that, while the Security Council has tended to focus on the aspects of such matters related to international peace and security, the General Assembly has taken a broader view, considering also their humanitarian, social and economic aspects.

28. The Court considers that the accepted practice of the General Assembly, as it has evolved, is consistent with Article 12, paragraph 1, of the Charter.

The Court is accordingly of the view that the General Assembly, in adopting resolution ES-10/14, seeking an advisory opinion from the Court, did not contravene the provisions of Article 12, paragraph 1, of the Charter. The Court concludes that by submitting that request the General Assembly did not exceed its competence.

29. It has however been contended before the Court that the present request for an advisory opinion did not fulfil the essential conditions set by résolution 377 A (V), under which the Tenth Emergency Special Session was convened and has continued to act. In this regard, it has been said, first, that "The Security Council was never seised of a draft resolution proposing that the Council itself should request an advisory opinion from the Court on the matters now in contention", and, that specific issue having thus never been brought before the Council, the General Assembly could not rely on any inaction by the Council to make such a request. Secondly, it has been claimed that, in adopting resolution 1515 (2003), which endorsed the "Roadmap", before the adoption by the General Assembly of resolution ES-10/14, the Security Council continued to exercise its responsibility for the maintenance of international peace and security and that, as a result, the General Assembly was not entitled to act in its place. The validity of the procedure followed by the Tenth Emergency Special Session, especially the Session's "rolling character" and the fact that its meeting was convened to deliberate on the request for the advisory opinion at the same time as the General Assembly was meeting in regular session, has also been questioned.

30. The Court would recall that résolution 377 A (V) states that:

> "if the Security Council, because of lack of unanimity of the permanent members, fails to exercise its primary responsibility for the maintenance of international peace and security in any case where there appears to be a threat to the peace, breach of the peace, or act of aggression, the General Assembly shall consider the matter immediately with a view to making appropriate recommendations to Members for collective measures . . ."

The procedure provided for by that resolution is premised on two conditions, namely that the Council has failed to exercise its primary responsibility for the maintenance of international peace and security as a result of a negative vote of one or more permanent members, and that the situation is one in which there appears to be a threat to the peace, breach of the peace, or act of aggression. The Court must accordingly ascertain whether these conditions were fulfilled as regards the convening of the Tenth Emergency Special Session of the General Assembly, in particular at the time when the Assembly decided to request an advisory opinion from the Court.

31. In the light of the sequence of events described in paragraphs 18 to 23 above, the Court observes that, at the time when the Tenth Emergency Special Session was convened in 1997, the Council had been unable to take a decision on the case of certain Israeli settlements in the Occupied Palestinian Territory, due to negative votes of a permanent member; and that, as indicated in resolution ES-10/2 (see paragraph 19 above), there existed a threat to international peace and security.

The Court further notes that, on 20 October 2003, the Tenth Emergency Special Session of the General Assembly was reconvened on the same basis as in 1997 (see the statements by the representatives of Palestine and Israel, A/ES-10/PV.21, pp. 2 and 5), after the rejection by the Security Council, on 14 October 2003, again as a result of the negative vote of a permanent member, of a draft resolution concerning the construction by Israel of the wall in the Occupied Palestinian Territory. The Court considers that the Security Council again failed to act as contemplated in resolution 377 A (V). It does not appear to the Court that the situation in this regard changed between 20 October 2003 and 8 December 2003, since the Council neither discussed the construction of the wall nor adopted any resolution in that connection. Thus, the Court is of the view that, up to 8 December 2003, the Council had not reconsidered the negative vote of 14 October 2003. It follows that, during that period, the Tenth Emergency Special

Session was duly reconvened and could properly be seised, under resolution 377 A (V), of the matter now before the Court.

32. The Court would also emphasize that, in the course of this Emergency Special Session, the General Assembly could adopt any resolution falling within the subject-matter for which the Session had been convened, and otherwise within its powers, including a resolution seeking the Court's opinion. It is irrelevant in that regard that no proposal had been made to the Security Council to request such an opinion.

[...]

41. Furthermore, the Court cannot accept the view, which has also been advanced in the present proceedings, that it has no jurisdiction because of the "political" character of the question posed. As is clear from its long-standing jurisprudence on this point, the Court considers that the fact that a legal question also has political aspects,

> "as, in the nature of things, is the case with so many questions which arise in international life, does not suffice to deprive it of its character as a 'legal question' and to 'deprive the Court of a competence expressly conferred on it by its Statute' (*Application for Review of Judgment No. 158 of the United Nations Administrative Tribunal, Advisory Opinion, I.C.J. Reports 1973*, p. 172, para. 14). Whatever its political aspects, the Court cannot refuse to admit the legal character of a question which invites it to discharge an essentially judicial task, namely, an assessment of the legality of the possible conduct of States with regard to the obligations imposed upon them by international law (cf. *Conditions of Admission of a State to Membership in the United Nations (Article 4 of the Charter), Advisory Opinion, 1948, I.C.J. Reports 1947-1948*, pp. 61-62; *Competence of the General Assembly for the Admission of a State to the United Nations, Advisory Opinion, I.C.J. Reports 1950*, pp. 6-7; *Certain Expenses of the United Nations (Article 17, paragraph 2, of the Charter), Advisory Opinion, I.C.J. Reports 1962*, p. 155)." (*Legality of the Threat or Use of Nuclear Weapons, Advisory Opinion, I.C.J. Reports 1996 (I)*, p. 234, para. 13.)

In its Opinion concerning the *Interpretation of the Agreement of 25 March 1951 between the WHO and Egypt*, the Court indeed emphasized that,

> "in situations in which political considerations are prominent it may be particularly necessary for an international organization to obtain an advisory opinion from the Court as to the legal principles applicable with respect to the matter under debate . . ." (*I.C.J. Reports 1980*, p. 87, para. 33).

Moreover, the Court has affirmed in its Opinion on the *Legality of the Threat or Use of Nuclear Weapons* that

> "the political nature of the motives which may be said to have inspired the request and the political implications that the opinion given might have are of no relevance in the establishment of its jurisdiction to give such an opinion" (*I.C.J. Reports 1996 (I)*, p. 234, para. 13).

The Court is of the view that there is no element in the present proceedings which could lead it to conclude otherwise.

***

42. The Court accordingly has jurisdiction to give the advisory opinion requested by resolution ES-10114 of the General Assembly.

[...]

50. The object of the request before the Court is to obtain from the Court an opinion which the General Assembly deems of assistance to it for the proper exercise of its functions. The opinion is requested on a question which is of particularly acute concern to the United Nations, and one which is located in a much broader frame of reference than a bilateral dispute. In the circumstances, the Court does not consider that to give an opinion would have the effect of circumventing the principle of consent to judicial settlement, and the Court accordingly cannot, in the exercise of its discretion, decline to give an opinion on that ground.

[...]

161. The Court, being concerned to lend its support to the purposes and principles laid down in the United Nations Charter, in particular the maintenance of international peace and security and the peaceful settlement of disputes, would emphasize the urgent necessity for the United Nations as a whole to redouble its efforts to bring the Israeli-Palestinian conflict, which continues to pose a threat to international peace and security, to a speedy conclusion, thereby establishing a just and lasting peace in the region.

Case Concerning Legality of Use of Force (*Serbia and Montenegro v. Belgium*), Preliminary Objections, ICJ Judgment, 15 December 2004

[*Note:*

On 29 April 1999 the Government of the Federal Republic of Yugoslavia (FRY) submitted applications against ten NATO Member States which had taken part in the military intervention against FRY carried out in the period from 23 March-10 June 1999. The countries against which FRY filled in applications were: Belgium, Canada, France, Germany, Italy, the Netherlands, Portugal, Spain, United Kingdom and the United States.

In almost all Judgments on Preliminary Objections the Court gave the same line of reasoning with regard to the question of membership of the Federal Republic of Yugoslavia in the United Nations. In its documents the Court referred to the Serbia and Montenegro which as a loose state union created by the Yugoslav Parliament on 4 February 2003 succeeded the Federal Republic of Yugoslavia.]

The Judgment:

[...]

25. The official title of the Applicant in these proceedings has changed during the period of time relevant to the present proceedings. On 27 April 1992, the Assembly of the Socialist Federal Republic of Yugoslavia adopted and promulgated the Constitution of "the Federal Republic of Yugoslavia". The State so named claimed to be the continuation of the Socialist Federal Republic of Yugoslavia, and as such to be entitled to continued membership in the United Nations. Inasmuch as this latter claim was not recognized by, *inter alia*, the Security Council and the General Assembly of the United Nations, these bodies initially referred to the Federal Republic of Yugoslavia as "the Federal Republic of Yugoslavia (Serbia and Montenegro)", and this term was also used in certain previous decisions of the Court. On 1 November 2000 the Applicant was admitted to membership in the United Nations under the name of "the Federal Republic of Yugoslavia"; and on 4 February 2003, the Federal Republic of Yugoslavia officially changed its name to "Serbia and Montenegro". In the present judgment, the Applicant will be referred to so far as possible as "Serbia and Montenegro", even when reference is made to a procedural step taken before the change of name; in some instances, however, where the term in a historical context might cause confusion, the title in use at the relevant time will be employed.

[...]

29. However, in its Observations on the preliminary objections of each of the respondent States, filed on 20 December 2002, Serbia and Montenegro claimed that "the acceptance of the Federal Republic of Yugoslavia as a new member of the United Nations on 1 November 2000" constituted a "new fact"; and on this basis it stated as follows:

> "As the Federal Republic of Yugoslavia became a *new* member of the United Nations on 1 November 2000, it follows that it was not a member before that date. Accordingly, it became an established fact that before 1 November 2000, the Federal Republic of Yugoslavia was not and could not have been a party to the Statute of the Court by way of UN membership."

In addition, as regards the question of jurisdiction of the Court under the Genocide Convention, Serbia and Montenegro in its Observations drew attention to its own accession to that Convention in March 2001, and stated that

> "[t]he Federal Republic of Yugoslavia did not continue the personality and treaty membership of the former Yugoslavia, and thus specifically, it was not bound by the Genocide Convention until it acceded to that Convention (with a reservation to Article IX) in March 2001".

In its submissions, however, Serbia and Montenegro did not ask the Court to rule that it had no jurisdiction but only requested the Court "to decide on its jurisdiction *considering the pleadings in these Written Observations*" (emphasis added).

30. The question whether Serbia and Montenegro was or was not a party to the Statute of the Court at the time of the institution of the present proceedings is a fundamental one (see paragraph 46 below). However, at this initial stage of its judgment, it is necessary for the Court to decide first on a preliminary question raised by the Respondents, namely whether in the light of the assertions by the Applicant quoted above coupled with the contentions of each of the respondent States, the Court should take a decision to dismiss the case *in limine litis*, without further entering into the examination of the question whether the Court has jurisdiction under the circumstances.

[...]

53. In addressing the question whether Serbia and Montenegro had access to the Court under Article 35, paragraph 1, of the Statute, the Court will consider the arguments put forward in this case and any other legal issue which it deems relevant to consider with a view to arriving at its conclusion on this point, including the issues raised in the other cases referred to in paragraph 3 above.

54. The Court will first recapitulate the sequence of events relating to the legal position of Serbia and Montenegro vis-à-vis the United Nations – events already examined, so far as was necessary to the Court, in the context of another case (see Judgment in the case concerning Application for Revision, I.C.J. Reports 2003, pp. 14-26, paras. 2453).

55. In the early 1990s the Socialist Federal Republic of Yugoslavia, made up of Bosnia and Herzegovina, Croatia, Macedonia, Montenegro, Serbia and Slovenia, began to break up. On 25 June 1991 Croatia and Slovenia both declared independence, followed by Macedonia on 17 September 1991 and Bosnia and Herzegovina on 6 March 1992. On 22 May 1992, Bosnia and Herzegovina, Croatia and Slovenia were admitted as Members to the United Nations; as was the former Yugoslav Republic of Macedonia on 8 April 1993.

56. On 27 April 1992 the "participants of the joint session of the SFRY Assembly, the National Assembly of the Republic of Serbia and the Assembly of the Republic of Montenegro" adopted a declaration, stating in pertinent parts:

> "The representatives of the people of the Republic of Serbia and the Republic of Montenegro,
>
> Expressing the will of the citizens of their respective Republics to stay in the common state of Yugoslavia,

> . . .
> wish to state in this Declaration their views on the basic, immediate and lasting objectives of the policy of their common state, and on its relations with the former Yugoslav Republics.
> . . .
> 1. The Federal Republic of Yugoslavia, continuing the state, international legal and political personality of the Socialist Federal Republic of Yugoslavia, shall strictly abide by all the commitments that the SFR of Yugoslavia assumed internationally,
> . . .
> Remaining bound by all obligations to international organizations and institutions whose member it is . . ." (United Nations doc. A/46/915, Ann. II.)

57. An official Note of the same date from the Permanent Mission of Yugoslavia to the United Nations, addressed to the Secretary-General of the United Nations, stated *inter alia* that:

> "The Assembly of the Socialist Federal Republic of Yugoslavia, at its session held on 27 April 1992, promulgated the Constitution of the Federal Republic of Yugoslavia. Under the Constitution, on the basis of the continuing personality of Yugoslavia and the legitimate decisions by Serbia and Montenegro to continue to live together in Yugoslavia, the Socialist Federal Republic of Yugoslavia is transformed into the Federal Republic of Yugoslavia, consisting of the Republic of Serbia and the Republic of Montenegro.
> Strictly respecting the continuity of the international personality of Yugoslavia, the Federal Republic of Yugoslavia shall continue to fulfil all the rights conferred to, and obligations assumed by, the Socialist Federal Republic of Yugoslavia in international relations, including its membership in all international organizations and participation in international treaties ratified or acceded to by Yugoslavia." (United Nations doc. A/46/915, Ann. I.)

58. On 30 May 1992, the Security Council adopted resolution 757 (1992), in which, *inter alia*, it noted that "the claim by the Federal Republic of Yugoslavia (Serbia and Montenegro) to continue automatically the membership of the former Socialist Federal Republic of Yugoslavia in the United Nations has not been generally accepted".

59. On 19 September 1992, the Security Council adopted resolution 777 (1992) which read as follows:

> "*The Security Council*,
> *Reaffirming* its resolution 713 (1991) of 25 September 1991 and all subsequent relevant resolutions,
> *Considering* that the state formerly known as the Socialist Federal Republic of Yugoslavia has ceased to exist,
> *Recalling* in particular resolution 757 (1992) which notes that 'the claim by the Federal Republic of Yugoslavia (Serbia and Montenegro) to continue automatically the membership of the former Socialist Federal Republic of Yugoslavia in the United Nations has not been generally accepted',
>
> 1. *Considers* that the Federal Republic of Yugoslavia (Serbia and Montenegro) cannot continue automatically the membership of the former Socialist Federal Republic of Yugoslavia in the United Nations; and therefore recommends to the General Assembly that it decide that the Federal Republic of Yugoslavia (Serbia and Montenegro) should apply for membership in the United Nations and that it shall not participate in the work of the General Assembly;

2. *Decides* to consider the matter again before the end of the main part of the forty-seventh session of the General Assembly." (United Nations doc. S/RES/777.)

The resolution was adopted by 12 votes in favour, none against, and 3 abstentions.

60. On 22 September 1992 the General Assembly adopted resolution 47/1, according to which:

"*The General Assembly,*
Having received the recommendation of the Security Council of 19 September 1992 that the Federal Republic of Yugoslavia (Serbia and Montenegro) should apply for membership in the United Nations and that it shall not participate in the work of the General Assembly,
1. *Considers* that the Federal Republic of Yugoslavia (Serbia and Montenegro) cannot continue automatically the membership of the former Socialist Federal Republic of Yugoslavia in the United Nations; and therefore decides that the Federal Republic of Yugoslavia (Serbia and Montenegro) should apply for membership in the United Nations and that it shall not participate in the work of the General Assembly;
2. *Takes note* of the intention of the Security Council to consider the matter again before the end of the main part of the forty-seventh session of the General Assembly." (United Nations doc. A/RES/47/1.)

The resolution was adopted by 127 votes to 6, with 26 abstentions.

61. On 25 September 1992, the Permanent Representatives of Bosnia and Herzegovina and Croatia addressed a letter to the Secretary-General, in which, with reference to Security Council resolution 777 (1992) and General Assembly resolution 47/1, they stated their understanding as follows: "At this moment, there is no doubt that the Socialist Federal Republic of Yugoslavia is not a member of the United Nations any more. At the same time, the Federal Republic of Yugoslavia is clearly not yet a member." They concluded that "[t]he flag flying in front of the United Nations and the name-plaque bearing the name 'Yugoslavia' do not represent anything or anybody any more" and "kindly request[ed] that [the Secretary-General] provide a legal explanatory statement concerning the questions raised" (United Nations doc. A/47/474).

62. In response, on 29 September 1992, the Under-Secretary-General and Legal Counsel of the United Nations addressed a letter to the Permanent Representatives of Bosnia and Herzegovina and Croatia, in which he stated that the "considered view of the United Nations Secretariat regarding the practical consequences of the adoption by the General Assembly of resolution 47/1" was as follows:

"While the General Assembly has stated unequivocally that the Federal Republic of Yugoslavia (Serbia and Montenegro) cannot automatically continue the membership of the former Socialist Federal Republic of Yugoslavia in the United Nations and that the Federal Republic of Yugoslavia (Serbia and Montenegro) should apply for membership in the United Nations, the only practical consequence that the resolution draws is that the Federal Republic of Yugoslavia (Serbia and Montenegro) shall not *participate* in the work of the General Assembly. It is clear, therefore, that representatives of the Federal Republic of Yugoslavia (Serbia and Montenegro) can no longer *participate* in the work of the General Assembly, its subsidiary organs, nor conferences and meetings convened by it.

On the other hand, the resolution neither terminates nor suspends Yugoslavia's *membership* in the Organization. Consequently, the seat and nameplate remain as before, but in Assembly bodies representatives of the Federal Republic of Yugoslavia (Serbia and Montenegro) cannot sit behind the sign 'Yugoslavia'. Yugoslav missions at United Nations Headquarters and offices may continue to function and may receive and circulate documents. At Headquarters, the Secretariat will continue to fly the flag of the old Yugoslavia as it is the last flag of Yugoslavia used by the Secretariat. The resolution does not take away the right of Yugoslavia to participate in the work of organs other than Assembly bodies. The admission to the United Nations of a new Yugoslavia under Article 4 of the Charter will terminate the situation created by resolution 47/1." (United Nations doc. A/47/485; original emphasis.)

63. On 29 April 1993, the General Assembly, upon the recommendation contained in Security Council resolution 821 (1993) (couched in terms similar to those of Security Council resolution 777 (1992)), adopted resolution 47/229 in which it decided that "the Federal Republic of Yugoslavia (Serbia and Montenegro) shall not participate in the work of the Economic and Social Council".

64. As is clear from the sequence of events summarized in the above paragraphs (paragraphs 55-63), the legal position of the Federal Republic of Yugoslavia within the United Nations and vis-à-vis that Organization remained highly complex during the period 1992-2000. In fact, it is the view of the Court that the legal situation that obtained within the United Nations during that eight-year period concerning the status of the Federal Republic of Yugoslavia, after the break-up of the Socialist Federal Republic of Yugoslavia, remained ambiguous and open to different assessments. This was due, *inter alia*, to the absence of an authoritative determination by the competent organs of the United Nations defining clearly the legal status of the Federal Republic of Yugoslavia vis-à-vis the United Nations.

[...]

75. This situation, however, came to an end with a new development in 2000. On 24 September 2000, Mr. Kostunica was elected President of the Federal Republic of Yugoslavia. In that capacity, on 27 October 2000 he sent a letter to the Secretary-General requesting admission of the Federal Republic of Yugoslavia to membership in the United Nations, in the following terms:

> "In the wake of fundamental democratic changes that took place in the Federal Republic of Yugoslavia, in the capacity of President, I have the honour to request the admission of the Federal Republic of Yugoslavia to membership in the United Nations in light of the implementation of Security Council resolution 777 (1992)." (United Nations doc. A/55/528-S/2000/1043; emphasis added.)

76. Acting upon this application by the Federal Republic of Yugoslavia for membership in the United Nations, the Security Council on 31 October 2000 "*recommend[ed]* to the General Assembly that the Federal Republic of Yugoslavia be admitted to membership in the United Nations" (United Nations doc. S/RES/1326). On 1 November 2000, the General Assembly, by resolution 55/12, "*[h]aving received* the recommendation of the Security Council of 31 October 2000" and "*[h]aving considered* the application for membership of the Federal Republic of Yugoslavia", decided to "admit the Federal Republic of Yugoslavia to membership in the United Nations".

77. As the letter of the President of the Federal Republic of Yugoslavia quoted above demonstrates, this action on the part of the Federal Republic of Yugoslavia signified that it had finally decided to act on Security Council resolution 777 (1992) by aligning itself with the position of the Security Council as expressed in that resolution. Furthermore, the Security Council confirmed its own position by taking steps for the admission of the Federal Republic of Yugoslavia as a new Member of the United Nations, which, when followed by corresponding steps taken by the General Assembly, completed the procedure for the admission of a new Member under Article 4 of the Charter, rather than pursuing any course involving recognition of continuing membership of the Federal Republic of Yugoslavia in the United Nations.

78. This new development effectively put an end to the *sui generis* position of the Federal Republic of Yugoslavia within the United Nations, which, as the Court has observed in earlier pronouncements, had been fraught with "legal difficulties" throughout the period between 1992 and 2000 (cf. *Application of the Convention on the Prevention and Punishment of the Crime of Genocide (Bosnia and Herzegovina* v. *Yugoslavia (Serbia and Montenegro)), Provisional Measures, Order of 8 April 1993, I.C.J. Reports 1993*, p. 14, para. 18). The Applicant thus has the status of membership in the United Nations as from 1 November 2000. However, its admission to the United Nations did not have, and could not have had, the effect of dating back to the time when the Socialist Federal Republic of Yugoslavia broke up and disappeared; there was in 2000 no question of restoring the membership rights of the Socialist Federal Republic of Yugoslavia for the benefit of the Federal Republic of Yugoslavia. At the same time, it became clear that the *sui generis* position of the Applicant could not have amounted to its membership in the Organization.

79. In the view of the Court, the significance of this new development in 2000 is that it has clarified the thus far amorphous legal situation concerning the status of the Federal Republic of Yugoslavia vis-à-vis the United Nations. It is in that sense that the situation that the Court now faces in relation to Serbia and Montenegro is manifestly different from that which it faced in 1999. If, at that time, the Court had had to determine definitively the status of the Applicant vis-à-vis the United Nations, its task of giving such a determination would have been complicated by the legal situation, which was shrouded in uncertainties relating to that status. However, from the vantage point from which the Court now looks at the legal situation, and in light of the legal consequences of the new development since 1 November 2000, the Court is led to the conclusion that Serbia and Montenegro was not a Member of the United Nations, and in that capacity a State party to the Statute of the International Court of Justice, at the time of filing its Application to institute the present proceedings before the Court on 29 April 1999.

[...]

91. For all these reasons, the Court concludes that, at the time of filing of its Application to institute the present proceedings before the Court on 29 April 1999, the Applicant in the present case, Serbia and Montenegro, was not a Member of the United Nations, and, consequently, was not, on that basis, a State party to the Statute of the International Court of Justice. It follows that the Court was not open to Serbia and Montenegro under Article 35, paragraph 1, of the Statute.

[...]

Accordance with International Law of the Unilateral Declaration of Independence in Respect of Kosovo, ICJ Advisory Opinion, 22 July 2010

[*Note:*

Opinion requested by: the UN General Assembly resolution 63/3 of 8 October 2008.

Question before the Court:
'Is the unilateral declaration of independence by the Provisional Institutions of Self-Government of Kosovo in accordance with international law?' "]

The Opinion:

[...]

A. Jurisdiction

18. The Court will thus first address the question whether it possesses jurisdiction to give the advisory opinion requested by the General Assembly on 8 October 2008. The power of the Court to give an advisory opinion is based upon Article 65, paragraph 1, of its Statute, which provides that:

> "The Court may give an advisory opinion on any legal question at the request of whatever body may be authorized by or in accordance with the Charter of the United Nations to make such a request."

19. In its application of this provision, the Court has indicated that:

> "It is . . . a precondition of the Court's competence that the advisory opinion be requested by an organ duly authorized to seek it under the Charter, that it be requested on a legal question, and that, except in the case of the General Assembly or the Security Council, that question should be one arising within the scope of the activities of the requesting organ." (*Application for Review of Judgment No. 273 of the United Nations Administrative Tribunal, Advisory Opinion, I.C.J. Reports 1982*, pp. 333-334, para. 21.)

20. It is for the Court to satisfy itself that the request for an advisory opinion comes from an organ of the United Nations or a specialized agency having competence to make it. The General Assembly is authorized to request an advisory opinion by Article 96 of the Charter, which provides that :

> "1. The General Assembly or the Security Council may request the International Court of Justice to give an advisory opinion on any legal question.
> 2. Other organs of the United Nations and specialized agencies, which may at any time be so authorized by the General Assembly, may also request advisory opinions of the Court on legal questions arising within the scope of their activities."

21. While paragraph 1 of Article 96 confers on the General Assembly the competence to request an advisory opinion on "any legal question", the Court has sometimes in the past given certain indications as to the relationship between the question which is the subject of a request for an advisory opinion and the activities of the General Assembly (*Interpretation of Peace Treaties with Bulgaria, Hungary and Romania, First Phase, Advisory Opinion, I.C.J. Reports 1950*, p. 70; *Legality of the Threat or Use of Nuclear Weapons Advisory Opinion, I.C.J. Reports 1996 (I)*, pp. 232-233, paras. 11-12; *Legal Consequences of the Construction of a Wall in the Occupied Palestinian Territory, Advisory Opinion, I.C.J. Reports 2004 (I)*, p. 145, paras. 16-17).

22. The Court observes that Article 10 of the Charter provides that:

> "The General Assembly may discuss any questions or any matters within the scope of the present Charter or relating to the powers and functions of any organs provided for in the present Charter, and, except as provided in Article 12, may make recommendations to the Members of the United Nations or to the Security Council or to both on any such questions or matters."

Moreover, Article 11, paragraph 2, of the Charter has specifically provided the General Assembly with competence to discuss "any questions relating to the maintenance of international peace and security brought before it by any Member of the United Nations" and, subject again to the limitation in Article 12, to make recommendations with respect thereto.

23. Article 12, paragraph 1, of the Charter provides that :

> "While the Security Council is exercising in respect of any dispute or situation the functions assigned to it in the present Charter, the General Assembly shall not make any recommendation with regard to that dispute or situation unless the Security Council so requests."

24. In the present proceedings, it was suggested that, since the Security Council was seized of the situation in Kosovo, the effect of Article 12, paragraph 1, was that the General Assembly's request for an advisory opinion was outside its powers under the Charter and thus did not fall within the authorization conferred by Article 96, paragraph 1. As the Court has stated on an earlier occasion, however, "[a] request for an advisory opinion is not in itself a 'recommendation' by the General Assembly 'with regard to [a] dispute or situation'" (*Legal Consequences of the Construction of a Wall in the Occupied Palestinian Territory, Advisory Opinion, I.C.J. Reports 2004 (I)*, p. 148, para. 25). Accordingly, while Article 12 may limit the scope of the action which the General Assembly may take subsequent to its receipt of the Court's opinion (a matter on which it is unnecessary for the Court to decide in the present context), it does not in itself limit the authorization to request an advisory opinion which is conferred upon the General Assembly by Article 96, paragraph 1. Whether the delimitation of the respective powers of the Security Council and the General Assembly – of which Article 12 is one aspect – should lead the Court, in the circumstances of the present case, to decline to exercise its jurisdiction to render an advisory opinion is another matter (which the Court will consider in paragraphs 29 to 48 below).

25. It is also for the Court to satisfy itself that the question on which it is requested to give its opinion is a "legal question" within the meaning of Article 96 of the Charter and Article 65 of the Statute. In the present case, the question put to the Court by the General Assembly asks whether the declaration of independence to which it refers is "in accordance with international law". A question which expressly

asks the Court whether or not a particular action is compatible with international law certainly appears to be a legal question; as the Court has remarked on a previous occasion, questions "framed in terms of law and rais[ing] problems of international law . . . are by their very nature susceptible of a reply based on law" (*Western Sahara, Advisory Opinion, I.C.J. Reports 1975*, p. 18, para. 15) and therefore appear to be questions of a legal character for the purposes of Article 96 of the Charter and Article 65 of the Statute.

26. Nevertheless, some of the participants in the present proceedings have suggested that the question posed by the General Assembly is not, in reality, a legal question. According to this submission, international law does not regulate the act of making a declaration of independence, which should be regarded as a political act ; only domestic constitutional law governs the act of making such a declaration, while the Court's jurisdiction to give an advisory opinion is confined to questions of international law. In the present case, however, the Court has not been asked to give an opinion on whether the declaration of independence is in accordance with any rule of domestic law but only whether it is in accordance with international law. The Court can respond to that question by reference to international law without the need to enquire into any system of domestic law.

27. Moreover, the Court has repeatedly stated that the fact that a question has political aspects does not suffice to deprive it of its character as a legal question (*Application for Review of Judgment No. 158 of the United Nations Administrative Tribunal, Advisory Opinion, I.C.J. Reports 1973*, p. 172, para. 14). Whatever its political aspects, the Court cannot refuse to respond to the legal elements of a question which invites it to discharge an essentially judicial task, namely, in the present case, an assessment of an act by reference to international law. The Court has also made clear that, in determining the jurisdictional issue of whether it is confronted with a legal question, it is not concerned with the political nature of the motives which may have inspired the request or the political implications which its opinion might have (*Conditions of Admission of a State to Membership in the United Nations (Article 4 of the Charter), Advisory Opinion, 1948, I.C.J. Reports 1947-1948*, p. 61, and *Legality of the Threat or Use of Nuclear Weapons, Advisory Opinion, I.C.J. Reports 1996 (I)*, p. 234, para. 13).

28. The Court therefore considers that it has jurisdiction to give an advisory opinion in response to the request made by the General Assembly.

B. Discretion

29. The fact that the Court has jurisdiction does not mean, however, that it is obliged to exercise it:

> "The Court has recalled many times in the past that Article 65, paragraph 1, of its Statute, which provides that 'The Court *may* give an advisory opinion . . .' (emphasis added), should be interpreted to mean that the Court has a discretionary power to decline to give an advisory opinion even if the conditions of jurisdiction are met." (*Legal Consequences of the Construction of a Wall in the Occupied Palestinian Territory, Advisory Opinion, I.C.J. Reports 2004 (I)*, p. 156, para. 44.)

The discretion whether or not to respond to a request for an advisory opinion exists so as to protect the integrity of the Court's judicial function and its nature as the principal judicial organ of the United Nations (*Status of Eastern Carelia, Advisory Opinion, 1923, P.C.I.J., Series B, No. 5*, p. 29; *Application for Review of Judgment No. 158 of the United Nations Administrative Tribunal, Advisory Opinion, I.C.J.*

Reports 1973, p. 175, para. 24; *Application for Review of Judgment No. 273 of the United Nations Administrative Tribunal, Advisory Opinion, I.C.J. Reports 1982*, p. 334, para. 22; and *Legal Consequences of the Construction of a Wall in the Occupied Palestinian Territory, Advisory Opinion, I.C.J. Reports 2004 (I)*, pp. 156-157, paras. 44-45).

30. The Court is, nevertheless, mindful of the fact that its answer to a request for an advisory opinion "represents its participation in the activities of the Organization, and, in principle, should not be refused" (*Interpretation of Peace Treaties with Bulgaria, Hungary and Romania, First Phase, Advisory Opinion, I.C.J. Reports 1950*, p. 71; *Difference Relating to Immunity from Legal Process of a Special Rapporteur of the Commission on Human Rights, Advisory Opinion, I.C.J. Reports 1999 (I)*, pp. 78-79, para. 29; *Legal Consequences of the Construction of a Wall in the Occupied Palestinian Territory, Advisory Opinion, I.C.J. Reports 2004 (I)*, p. 156, para. 44). Accordingly, the consistent jurisprudence of the Court has determined that only "compelling reasons" should lead the Court to refuse its opinion in response to a request falling within its jurisdiction (*Judgments of the Administrative Tribunal of the ILO upon Complaints Made against UNESCO, I.C.J. Reports 1956*, p. 86; *Legal Consequences of the Construction of a Wall in the Occupied Palestinian Territory, Advisory Opinion, I.C.J. Reports 2004 (I)*, p. 156, para. 44).

31. The Court must satisfy itself as to the propriety of the exercise of its judicial function in the present case. It has therefore given careful consideration as to whether, in the light of its previous jurisprudence, there are compelling reasons for it to refuse to respond to the request from the General Assembly.

32. One argument, advanced by a number of participants in the present proceedings, concerns the motives behind the request. Those participants drew attention to a statement made by the sole sponsor of the resolution by which the General Assembly requested the Court's opinion to the effect that

> "the Court's advisory opinion would provide politically neutral, yet judicially authoritative, guidance to many countries still deliberating how to approach unilateral declarations of independence in line with international law.
> ....
> Supporting this draft resolution would also serve to reaffirm a fundamental principle: the right of any Member State of the United Nations to pose a simple, basic question on a matter it considers vitally important to the Court. To vote against it would be in effect a vote to deny the right of any country to seek – now or in the future – judicial recourse through the United Nations system." (A/63/PV.22, p. 1.)

According to those participants, this statement demonstrated that the opinion of the Court was being sought not in order to assist the General Assembly but rather to serve the interests of one State and that the Court should, therefore, decline to respond.

33. The advisory jurisdiction is not a form of judicial recourse for States but the means by which the General Assembly and the Security Council, as well as other organs of the United Nations and bodies specifically empowered to do so by the General Assembly in accordance with Article 96, paragraph 2, of the Charter, may obtain the Court's opinion in order to assist them in their activities. The Court's opinion is given not to States but to the organ which has requested it (*Interpretation of Peace Treaties with Bulgaria, Hungary and Romania, First Phase, Advisory Opinion, I.C.J. Reports 1950*, p. 71). Nevertheless, precisely for that reason, the motives of individual States which sponsor, or vote in favour

of, a resolution requesting an advisory opinion are not relevant to the Court's exercise of its discretion whether or not to respond. As the Court put it in its Advisory Opinion on *Legality of the Threat or Use of Nuclear Weapons*,

> "once the Assembly has asked, by adopting a resolution, for an advisory opinion on a legal question, the Court, in determining whether there are any compelling reasons for it to refuse to give such an opinion, will not have regard to the origins or to the political history of the request, or to the distribution of votes in respect of the adopted resolution" (*I.C.J. Reports 1996 (I)*, p. 237, para. 16).

34. It was also suggested by some of those participating in the proceedings that resolution 63/3 gave no indication of the purpose for which the General Assembly needed the Court's opinion and that there was nothing to indicate that the opinion would have any useful legal effect. This argument cannot be accepted. The Court has consistently made clear that it is for the organ which requests the opinion, and not for the Court, to determine whether it needs the opinion for the proper performance of its functions. In its Advisory Opinion on *Legality of the Threat or Use of Nuclear Weapons*, the Court rejected an argument that it should refuse to respond to the General Assembly's request on the ground that the General Assembly had not explained to the Court the purposes for which it sought an opinion, stating that

> "it is not for the Court itself to purport to decide whether or not an advisory opinion is needed by the Assembly for the performance of its functions. The General Assembly has the right to decide for itself on the usefulness of an opinion in the light of its own needs." (*I.C.J. Reports 1996 (I)*, p. 237, para. 16.)

Similarly, in the Advisory Opinion on *Legal Consequences of the Construction of a Wall in the Occupied Palestinian Territory*, the Court commented that "[t]he Court cannot substitute its assessment of the usefulness of the opinion requested for that of the organ that seeks such opinion, namely the General Assembly" (*I.C.J. Reports 2004 (I)*, p. 163, para. 62).

35. Nor does the Court consider that it should refuse to respond to the General Assembly's request on the basis of suggestions, advanced by some of those participating in the proceedings, that its opinion might lead to adverse political consequences. Just as the Court cannot substitute its own assessment for that of the requesting organ in respect of whether its opinion will be useful to that organ, it cannot – in particular where there is no basis on which to make such an assessment – substitute its own view as to whether an opinion would be likely to have an adverse effect. As the Court stated in its Advisory Opinion on *Legality of the Threat or Use of Nuclear Weapons*, in response to a submission that a reply from the Court might adversely affect disarmament negotiations, faced with contrary positions on this issue "there are no evident criteria by which it can prefer one assessment to another" (*Legality of the Threat or Use of Nuclear Weapons, Advisory Opinion, I.C.J. Reports 1996 (I)*, p. 237, para. 17; see also *Western Sahara, Advisory Opinion, I.C.J. Reports 1975*, p. 37, para. 73; and *Legal Consequences of the Construction of a Wall in the Occupied Palestinian Territory, Advisory Opinion, I.C.J. Reports 2004 (I)*, pp. 159-160, paras. 51-54).

36. An important issue which the Court must consider is whether, in view of the respective roles of the Security Council and the General Assembly in relation to the situation in Kosovo, the Court, as the principal judicial organ of the United Nations, should decline to answer the question which has been

put to it on the ground that the request for the Court's opinion has been made by the General Assembly rather than the Security Council.

37. The situation in Kosovo had been the subject of action by the Security Council, in the exercise of its responsibility for the maintenance of international peace and security, for more than ten years prior to the present request for an advisory opinion. The Council first took action specifically relating to the situation in Kosovo on 31 March 1998, when it adopted resolution 1160 (1998). That was followed by resolutions 1199 (1998), 1203 (1998) and 1239 (1999). On 10 June 1999, the Council adopted resolution 1244 (1999), which authorized the creation of an international military presence (subsequently known as "KFOR") and an international civil presence (the United Nations Interim Administration Mission in Kosovo, "UNMIK") and laid down a framework for the administration of Kosovo. By resolution 1367 (2001), the Security Council decided to terminate the prohibitions on the sale or supply of arms established by paragraph 8 of resolution 1160 (1998). The Security Council has received periodic reports from the Secretary-General on the activities of UNMIK. The dossier submitted to the Court by the Secretary-General records that the Security Council met to consider the situation in Kosovo on 29 occasions between 2000 and the end of 2008. Although the declaration of independence which is the subject of the present request was discussed by the Security Council, the Council took no action in respect of it (Security Council, provisional verbatim record, 18 February 2008, 3 p.m. (S/PV.5839); Security Council, provisional verbatim record, 11 March 2008, 3 p.m. (S/PV.5850)).

38. The General Assembly has also adopted resolutions relating to the situation in Kosovo. Prior to the adoption by the Security Council of resolution 1244 (1999), the General Assembly adopted five resolutions on the situation of human rights in Kosovo (resolutions 49/204, 50/190, 51/111, 52/139 and 53/164). Following resolution 1244 (1999), the General Assembly adopted one further resolution on the situation of human rights in Kosovo (resolution 54/183 of 17 December 1999) and 15 resolutions concerning the financing of UNMIK (resolutions 53/241, 54/245A, 54/245B, 55/227A, 55/227B, 55/295, 57/326, 58/305, 59/286A, 59/286B, 60/275, 61/285, 62/262, 63/295 and 64/279). However, the broader situation in Kosovo was not part of the agenda of the General Assembly at the time of the declaration of independence and it was therefore necessary in September 2008 to create a new agenda item for the consideration of the proposal to request an opinion from the Court.

39. Against this background, it has been suggested that, given the respective powers of the Security Council and the General Assembly, if the Court's opinion were to be sought regarding whether the declaration of independence was in accordance with international law, the request should rather have been made by the Security Council and that this fact constitutes a compelling reason for the Court not to respond to the request from the General Assembly. That conclusion is said to follow both from the nature of the Security Council's involvement and the fact that, in order to answer the question posed, the Court will necessarily have to interpret and apply Security Council resolution 1244 (1999) in order to determine whether or not the declaration of independence is in accordance with international law.

40. While the request put to the Court concerns one aspect of a situation which the Security Council has characterized as a threat to international peace and security and which continues to feature on the agenda of the Council in that capacity, that does not mean that the General Assembly has no legitimate interest in the question. Articles 10 and 11 of the Charter, to which the Court has already referred, confer upon the General Assembly a very broad power to discuss matters within the scope of the activities of the United Nations, including questions relating to international peace and security. That power is

not limited by the responsibility for the maintenance of international peace and security which is conferred upon the Security Council by Article 24, paragraph 1. As the Court has made clear in its Advisory Opinion on *Legal Consequences of the Construction of a Wall in the Occupied Palestinian Territory*, paragraph 26, "Article 24 refers to a primary, but not necessarily exclusive, competence". The fact that the situation in Kosovo is before the Security Council and the Council has exercised its Chapter VII powers in respect of that situation does not preclude the General Assembly from discussing any aspect of that situation, including the declaration of independence. The limit which the Charter places upon the General Assembly to protect the role of the Security Council is contained in Article 12 and restricts the power of the General Assembly to make recommendations following a discussion, not its power to engage in such a discussion.

41. Moreover, Article 12 does not bar all action by the General Assembly in respect of threats to international peace and security which are before the Security Council. The Court considered this question in some detail in paragraphs 26 to 27 of its Advisory Opinion on *Legal Consequences of the Construction of a Wall in the Occupied Palestinian Territory*, in which the Court noted that there has been an increasing tendency over time for the General Assembly and the Security Council to deal in parallel with the same matter concerning the maintenance of international peace and security and observed that it is often the case that, while the Security Council has tended to focus on the aspects of such matters related to international peace and security, the General Assembly has taken a broader view, considering also their humanitarian, social and economic aspects.

42. The Court's examination of this subject in its Advisory Opinion on *Legal Consequences of the Construction of a Wall in the Occupied Palestinian Territory* was made in connection with an argument relating to whether or not the Court possessed the jurisdiction to give an advisory opinion, rather than whether it should exercise its discretion not to give an opinion. In the present case, the Court has already held that Article 12 of the Charter does not deprive it of the jurisdiction conferred by Article 96, paragraph 1 (paragraphs 23 to 24 above). It considers, however, that the analysis contained in the 2004 Advisory Opinion is also pertinent to the issue of discretion in the present case. That analysis demonstrates that the fact that a matter falls within the primary responsibility of the Security Council for situations which may affect the maintenance of international peace and security and that the Council has been exercising its powers in that respect does not preclude the General Assembly from discussing that situation or, within the limits set by Article 12, making recommendations with regard thereto. In addition, as the Court pointed out in its 2004 Advisory Opinion, General Assembly resolution 377A (V) ("Uniting for Peace") provides for the General Assembly to make recommendations for collective measures to restore international peace and security in any case where there appears to be a threat to the peace, breach of the peace or act of aggression and the Security Council is unable to act because of lack of unanimity of the permanent members (*Legal Consequences of the Construction of a Wall in the Occupied Palestinian Territory, Advisory Opinion, I.C.J. Reports 2004 (I)*, p. 150, para. 30). These considerations are of relevance to the question whether the delimitation of powers between the Security Council and the General Assembly constitutes a compelling reason for the Court to decline to respond to the General Assembly's request for an opinion in the present case.

43. It is true, of course, that the facts of the present case are quite different from those of the Advisory Opinion on *Legal Consequences of the Construction of a Wall in the Occupied Palestinian Territory*. The situation in the occupied Palestinian territory had been under active consideration by the General Assembly for several decades prior to its decision to request an opinion from the Court and the General

Assembly had discussed the precise subject on which the Court's opinion was sought. In the present case, with regard to the situation in Kosovo, it was the Security Council which had been actively seized of the matter. In that context, it discussed the future status of Kosovo and the declaration of independence (see paragraph 37 above).

44. However, the purpose of the advisory jurisdiction is to enable organs of the United Nations and other authorized bodies to obtain opinions from the Court which will assist them in the future exercise of their functions. The Court cannot determine what steps the General Assembly may wish to take after receiving the Court's opinion or what effect that opinion may have in relation to those steps. As the preceding paragraphs demonstrate, the General Assembly is entitled to discuss the declaration of independence and, within the limits considered in paragraph 42, above, to make recommendations in respect of that or other aspects of the situation in Kosovo without trespassing on the powers of the Security Council. That being the case, the fact that, hitherto, the declaration of independence has been discussed only in the Security Council and that the Council has been the organ which has taken action with regard to the situation in Kosovo does not constitute a compelling reason for the Court to refuse to respond to the request from the General Assembly.

45. Moreover, while it is the scope for future discussion and action which is the determining factor in answering this objection to the Court rendering an opinion, the Court also notes that the General Assembly has taken action with regard to the situation in Kosovo in the past. As stated in paragraph 38 above, between 1995 and 1999, the General Assembly adopted six resolutions addressing the human rights situation in Kosovo. The last of these, resolution 54/183, was adopted on 17 December 1999, some six months after the Security Council had adopted resolution 1244 (1999). While the focus of this resolution was on human rights and humanitarian issues, it also addressed (in para. 7) the General Assembly's concern about a possible "cantonization" of Kosovo. In addition, since 1999 the General Assembly has each year approved, in accordance with Article 17, paragraph 1, of the Charter, the budget of UNMIK (see paragraph 38 above). The Court observes therefore that the General Assembly has exercised functions of its own in the situation in Kosovo.

46. Further, in the view of the Court, the fact that it will necessarily have to interpret and apply the provisions of Security Council resolution 1244 (1999) in the course of answering the question put by the General Assembly does not constitute a compelling reason not to respond to that question. While the interpretation and application of a decision of one of the political organs of the United Nations is, in the first place, the responsibility of the organ which took that decision, the Court, as the principal judicial organ of the United Nations, has also frequently been required to consider the interpretation and legal effects of such decisions. It has done so both in the exercise of its advisory jurisdiction (see for example, *Certain Expenses of the United Nations (Article 17, paragraph 2, of the Charter), Advisory Opinion, I.C.J. Reports 1962*, p. 175; and *Legal Consequences for States of the Continued Presence of South Africa in Namibia (South West Africa) notwithstanding Security Council Resolution 276 (1970), Advisory Opinion, I.C.J. Reports 1971*, pp. 51-54, paras. 107-116), and in the exercise of its contentious jurisdiction (see for example, *Questions of Interpretation and Application of the 1971 Montreal Convention arising from the Aerial Incident at Lockerbie (Libyan Arab Jamahiriya* v. *United Kingdom), Provisional Measures, Order of 14 April 1992, I.C.J. Reports 1992*, p. 15, paras. 39-41; *Questions of Interpretation and Application of the 1971 Montreal Convention arising from the Aerial Incident at Lockerbie (Libyan Arab Jamahiriya* v. *United States of America), Provisional Measures, Order of 14 April 1992, I.C.J. Reports 1992*, pp. 126-127, paras. 42-44).

47. There is, therefore, nothing incompatible with the integrity of the judicial function in the Court undertaking such a task. The question is, rather, whether it should decline to undertake that task unless it is the organ which has taken the decision that asks the Court to do so. In its Advisory Opinion on *Certain Expenses of the United Nations*, however, the Court responded to the question posed by the General Assembly, even though this necessarily required it to interpret a number of Security Council resolutions (namely, resolutions 143, 145 and 146 of 1960 and 161 and 169 of 1961) (*Certain Expenses of the United Nations (Article 17, paragraph 2, of the Charter), Advisory Opinion, I.C.J. Reports 1962*, pp. 175-177). The Court also notes that, in its Advisory Opinion on *Conditions of Admission of a State to Membership in the United Nations (Article 4 of the Charter)* (*I.C.J. Reports 1947-1948*, pp. 61-62), it responded to a request from the General Assembly even though that request referred to statements made in a meeting of the Security Council and it had been submitted that the Court should therefore exercise its discretion to decline to reply (*I.C.J. Pleadings, Conditions of Admission of a State to Membership in the United Nations (Article 4 of the Charter)*, p. 90). Where, as here, the General Assembly has a legitimate interest in the answer to a question, the fact that that answer may turn, in part, on a decision of the Security Council is not sufficient to justify the Court in declining to give its opinion to the General Assembly.

48. Accordingly, the Court considers that there are no compelling reasons for it to decline to exercise its jurisdiction in respect of the present request.

[...]

III. FACTUAL BACKGROUND

57. The declaration of independence of 17 February 2008 must be considered within the factual context which led to its adoption. The Court therefore will briefly describe the relevant characteristics of the framework put in place by the Security Council to ensure the interim administration of Kosovo, namely, Security Council resolution 1244 (1999) and the regulations promulgated thereunder by the United Nations Mission in Kosovo. The Court will then proceed with a brief description of the developments relating to the so-called "final status process" in the years preceding the adoption of the declaration of independence, before turning to the events of 17 February 2008.

A. Security Council Resolution 1244 (1999) and the Relevant UNMIK Regulations

58. Resolution 1244 (1999) was adopted by the Security Council, acting under Chapter VII of the United Nations Charter, on 10 June 1999. In this resolution, the Security Council, "determined to resolve the grave humanitarian situation" which it had identified (see the fourth preambular paragraph) and to put an end to the armed conflict in Kosovo, authorized the United Nations Secretary-General to establish an international civil presence in Kosovo in order to provide "an interim administration for Kosovo . . . which will provide transitional administration while establishing and overseeing the development of provisional democratic self-governing institutions" (para. 10).
Paragraph 3 demanded

> "in particular that the Federal Republic of Yugoslavia put an immediate and verifiable end to violence and repression in Kosovo, and begin and complete verifiable phased withdrawal from Kosovo of all military, police and paramilitary forces according to a rapid timetable".

Pursuant to paragraph 5 of the resolution, the Security Council decided on the deployment in Kosovo, under the auspices of the United Nations, of international civil and security presences and welcomed the agreement of the Federal Republic of Yugoslavia to such presences. The powers and responsibilities of the security presence were further clarified in paragraphs 7 and 9. Paragraph 15 of resolution 1244 (1999) demanded that the Kosovo Liberation Army (KLA) and other armed Kosovo Albanian groups end immediately all offensive actions and comply with the requirements for demilitarization. Immediately preceding the adoption of Security Council resolution 1244 (1999), various implementing steps had already been taken through a series of measures, including, *inter alia*, those stipulated in the Military Technical Agreement of 9 June 1999, whose Article I.2 provided for the deployment of KFOR, permitting these to

> "operate without hindrance within Kosovo and with the authority to take all necessary action to establish and maintain a secure environment for all citizens of Kosovo and otherwise carry out its mission".

The Military Technical Agreement also provided for the withdrawal of FRY ground and air forces, save for "an agreed number of Yugoslav and Serb military and police personnel" as foreseen in paragraph 4 of resolution 1244 (1999).

59. Paragraph 11 of the resolution described the principal responsibilities of the international civil presence in Kosovo as follows:

> "*(a)* Promoting the establishment, pending a final settlement, of substantial autonomy and selfgovernment in Kosovo, taking full account of annex 2 and of the Rambouillet accords (S/1999/648);
> *(b)* Performing basic civilian administrative functions where and as long as required;
> *(c)* Organizing and overseeing the development of provisional institutions for democratic and autonomous self-government pending a political settlement, including the holding of elections;
> *(d)* Transferring, as these institutions are established, its administrative responsibilities while overseeing and supporting the consolidation of Kosovo's local provisional institutions and other peace-building activities ;
> *(e)* Facilitating a political process designed to determine Kosovo's future status, taking into account the Rambouillet accords (S/1999/648);
> *(f)* In a final stage, overseeing the transfer of authority from Kosovo's provisional institutions to institutions established under a political settlement . . . ".

60. On 12 June 1999, the Secretary-General presented to the Security Council "a preliminary operational concept for the overall organization of the civil presence, which will be known as the United Nations Interim Administration Mission in Kosovo (UNMIK)", pursuant to paragraph 10 of resolution 1244 (1999), according to which UNMIK would be headed by a Special Representative of the Secretary-General, to be appointed by the Secretary-General in consultation with the Security Council (Report of the Secretary-General of 12 June 1999 (United Nations doc. S/1999/672, 12 June 1999)). The Report of the Secretary-General provided that there would be four Deputy Special Representatives working within UNMIK, each responsible for one of four major components (the so-called "four pillars") of the UNMIK régime (para. 5): *(a)* interim civil administration (with a lead role assigned to the United Nations); *(b)* humanitarian affairs (with a lead role assigned to the Office of the United Nations High Commissioner for Refugees (UNHCR)); *(c)* institution building (with a lead role assigned to the Organization for Security and Co-operation in Europe (OSCE)); and *(d)* reconstruction (with a lead role assigned to the European Union).

61. On 25 July 1999, the first Special Representative of the Secretary-General promulgated UNMIK regulation 1999/1, which provided in its Section 1.1 that "[a]ll legislative and executive authority with respect to Kosovo, including the administration of the judiciary, is vested in UNMIK and is exercised by the Special Representative of the Secretary- General". Under Section 3 of UNMIK regulation 1999/1, the laws applicable in the territory of Kosovo prior to 24 March 1999 were to continue to apply, but only to the extent that these did not conflict with internationally recognized human rights standards and non-discrimination or the fulfilment of the mandate given to UNMIK under resolution 1244 (1999). Section 3 was repealed by UNMIK regulation 1999/25 promulgated by the Special Representative of the Secretary-General on 12 December 1999, with retroactive effect to 10 June 1999. Section 1.1 of UNMIK regulation 1999/24 of 12 December 1999 provides that "[t]he law applicable in Kosovo shall be: *(a)* the regulations promulgated by the Special Representative of the Secretary-General and subsidiary instruments issued thereunder; and *(b)* the law in force in Kosovo on 22 March 1989". Section 4, entitled "Transitional Provision", reads as follows:

> "All legal acts, including judicial decisions, and the legal effects of events which occurred, during the period from 10 June 1999 up to the date of the present regulation, pursuant to the laws in force during that period under section 3 of UNMIK Regulation No. 1999/1 of 25 July 1999, shall remain valid, insofar as they do not conflict with the standards referred to in section 1 of the present regulation or any UNMIK regulation in force at the time of such acts."

62. The powers and responsibilities thus laid out in Security Council resolution 1244 (1999) were set out in more detail in UNMIK regulation 2001/9 of 15 May 2001 on a Constitutional Framework for Provisional Self-Government (hereinafter "Constitutional Framework"), which defined the responsibilities relating to the administration of Kosovo between the Special Representative of the Secretary-General and the Provisional Institutions of Self-Government of Kosovo. With regard to the role entrusted to the Special Representative of the Secretary-General under Chapter 12 of the Constitutional Framework,

> "[t]he exercise of the responsibilities of the Provisional Institutions of Self-Government under this Constitutional Framework shall not affect or diminish the authority of the SRSG to ensure full implementation of UNSCR 1244 (1999), including overseeing the Provisional Institutions of Self-Government, its officials and its agencies, and taking appropriate measures whenever their actions are inconsistent with UNSCR 1244 (1999) or this Constitutional Framework".

Moreover, pursuant to Chapter 2 *(a)*, "[t]he Provisional Institutions of Self-Government and their officials shall . . . [e]xercise their authorities consistent with the provisions of UNSCR 1244 (1999) and the terms set forth in this Constitutional Framework". Similarly, according to the ninth preambular paragraph of the Constitutional Framework,

> "the exercise of the responsibilities of the Provisional Institutions of Self-Government in Kosovo shall not in any way affect or diminish the ultimate authority of the SRSG for the implementation of UNSCR 1244 (1999)".

In his periodical report to the Security Council of 7 June 2001, the Secretary-General stated that the Constitutional Framework contained "broad authority for my Special Representative to intervene and correct any actions of the provisional institutions of self-government that are inconsistent with Security Council resolution 1244 (1999), including the power to veto Assembly legislation, where necessary" (Report of the Secretary-General on the United Nations Interim Administration Mission in Kosovo, United Nations doc. S/2001/ 565, 7 June 2001).

63. Having described the framework put in place by the Security Council to ensure the interim administration of the territory of Kosovo, the Court now turns to the relevant events in the final status process which preceded the declaration of independence of 17 February 2008.

B. The Relevant Events in the Final Status Process Prior to 17 February 2008

64. In June 2005, the Secretary-General appointed Kai Eide, Permanent Representative of Norway to the North Atlantic Treaty Organization, as his Special Envoy to carry out a comprehensive review of Kosovo. In the wake of the Comprehensive Review report he submitted to the Secretary-General (attached to United Nations doc. S/2005/635 (7 October 2005)), there was consensus within the Security Council that the final status process should be commenced:

"The Security Council agrees with Ambassador Eide's overall assessment that, notwithstanding the challenges still facing Kosovo and the wider region, the time has come to move to the next phase of the political process. The Council therefore supports the Secretary- General's intention to start a political process to determine Kosovo's Future Status, as foreseen in Security Council resolution 1244 (1999)." (Statement by the President of the Security Council of 24 October 2005, United Nations doc. S/PRST/2005/51.)

65. In November 2005, the Secretary-General appointed Mr. Martti Ahtisaari, former President of Finland, as his Special Envoy for the future status process for Kosovo. This appointment was endorsed by the Security Council (see Letter dated 10 November 2005 from the President of the Security Council addressed to the Secretary-General, United Nations doc. S/2005/709). Mr. Ahtisaari's Letter of Appointment included, as an annex to it, a document entitled "Terms of Reference" which stated that the Special Envoy "is expected to revert to the Secretary- General at all stages of the process". Furthermore, "[t]he pace and duration of the future status process will be determined by the Special Envoy on the basis of consultations with the Secretary-General, taking into account the co-operation of the parties and the situation on the ground" (Terms of Reference, dated 10 November 2005, as an appendix to the Letter of the Secretary-General to Mr. Martti Ahtisaari of 14 November 2005, United Nations dossier No. 198).

66. The Security Council did not comment on these Terms of Reference. Instead, the members of the Council attached to their approval of Mr. Ahtisaari's appointment the Guiding Principles of the Contact Group (an informal grouping of States formed in 1994 to address the situation in the Balkans and composed of France, Germany, Italy, the Russian Federation, the United Kingdom and the United States). Members of the Security Council further indicated that the Guiding Principles were meant for the Secretary-General's (and therefore also for the Special Envoy's) "reference". These Principles stated, *inter alia*, that

> "[t]he Contact Group . . . welcomes the intention of the Secretary-General to appoint a Special Envoy to lead this process . . . A negotiated solution should be an international priority. Once the process has started, it cannot be blocked and must be brought to a conclusion. The Contact Group calls on the parties to engage in good faith and constructively, to refrain from unilateral steps and to reject any form of violence.
>
> ...
>
> The Security Council will remain actively seized of the matter. The final decision on the status of Kosovo should be endorsed by the Security Council." (Guiding Principles of the Contact Group for a Settlement of the Status of Kosovo, as Annexed to the Letter Dated 10 November 2005 from the President of the Security Council addressed to the Secretary-General, United Nations doc. S/2005/ 709.)

67. Between 20 February and 8 September 2006, several rounds of negotiations were held, at which delegations of Serbia and Kosovo addressed, in particular, the decentralization of Kosovo's governmental and administrative functions, cultural heritage and religious sites, economic issues, and community rights (Reports of the Secretary-General on the United Nations Interim Administration Mission in Kosovo, United Nations docs. S/2006/361, S/2006/707 and S/2006/906). According to the Reports of the Secretary-General, "the parties remain[ed] far apart on most issues" (Reports of the Secretary-General on the United Nations Interim Administration Mission in Kosovo, S/2006/707; S/2006/906).

68. On 2 February 2007, the Special Envoy of the Secretary-General submitted a draft comprehensive proposal for the Kosovo status settlement to the parties and invited them to engage in a consultative process (recalled in the Report of the Secretary-General on the United Nations Interim Administration Mission in Kosovo, United Nations doc. S/2007/ 134, 9 March 2007). On 10 March 2007, a final round of negotiations was held in Vienna to discuss the settlement proposal. As reported by the Secretary-General, "the parties were unable to make any additional progress" at those negotiations (Report of the Secretary-General on the United Nations Interim Administration Mission in Kosovo, United Nations doc. S/2007/395, 29 June 2007, p. 1).

69. On 26 March 2007, the Secretary-General submitted the report of his Special Envoy to the Security Council. The Special Envoy stated that "after more than one year of direct talks, bilateral negotiations and expert consultations, it [had] become clear to [him] that the parties [were] not able to reach an agreement on Kosovo's future status" (Letter dated 26 March 2007 from the Secretary-General addressed to the President of the Security Council attaching the Report of the Special Envoy of the Secretary-General on Kosovo's future status, United Nations doc. S/2007/ 168, 26 March 2007). After emphasizing that his

> "mandate explicitly provides that [he] determine the pace and duration of the future status process on the basis of consultations with the Secretary-General, taking into account the co-operation of the parties and the situation on the ground" (*ibid.*, para. 3),

the Special Envoy concluded:

> "It is my firm view that the negotiations' potential to produce any mutually agreeable outcome on Kosovo's status is exhausted. No amount of additional talks, whatever the format, will overcome this impasse.

> …
>
> The time has come to resolve Kosovo's status. Upon careful consideration of Kosovo's recent history, the realities of Kosovo today and taking into account the negotiations with the parties, I have come to the conclusion that the only viable option for Kosovo is independence, to be supervised for an initial period by the international community." (*Ibid.*, paras. 3 and 5.)

70. The Special Envoy's conclusions were accompanied by his finalized Comprehensive Proposal for the Kosovo Status Settlement (United Nations doc. S/2007/168/Add. 1, 26 March 2007), which, in his words, set forth "international supervisory structures, [and] provide[d] the foundations for a future independent Kosovo" (United Nations doc. S/2007/168, para. 5). The Comprehensive Proposal called for the immediate convening of a Constitutional Commission to draft a Constitution for Kosovo (*ibid.*, Add. 1, 26 March 2007, Art. 10.1), established guidelines concerning the membership of that Commission (*ibid.*, Art. 10.2), set numerous requirements concerning principles and provisions to be contained in that Constitution (*ibid.*, Art. 1.3 and Ann. I), and required that the Assembly of Kosovo approve the Constitution by a two-thirds vote within 120 days (*ibid.*, Art. 10.4). Moreover, it called for the expiry of the UNMIK mandate after a 120-day transition period, after which "all legislative and executive authority vested in UNMIK shall be transferred *en bloc* to the governing authorities of Kosovo, unless otherwise provided for in this Settlement" (*ibid.*, Art. 15.1). It mandated the holding of general and municipal elections no later than nine months from the entry into force of the Constitution (UN doc. S/2007/168/Add. 1, 26 March 2007, Art. 11.1). The Court further notes that the Comprehensive Proposal for the Kosovo Status Settlement provided for the appointment of an International Civilian Representative (ICR), who would have the final authority in Kosovo regarding interpretation of the Settlement (*ibid.*, Art. 12). The Comprehensive Proposal also specified that the mandate of the ICR would be reviewed "no later than two years after the entry into force of [the] Settlement, with a view to gradually reducing the scope of the powers of the ICR and the frequency of intervention" (*ibid.*, Ann. IX, Art. 5.1) and that

> "[t]he mandate of the ICR shall be terminated when the International Steering Group [a body composed of France, Germany, Italy, the Russian Federation, the United Kingdom, the United States, the European Union, the European Commission and NATO] determine[d] that Kosovo ha[d] implemented the terms of [the] Settlement" (*ibid.*, Art. 5.2).

71. The Secretary-General "fully support[ed] both the recommendation made by [his] Special Envoy in his report on Kosovo's future status and the Comprehensive Proposal for the Kosovo Status Settlement" (letter dated 26 March 2007 from the Secretary-General addressed to the President of the Security Council, United Nations doc. S/2007/168). The Security Council, for its part, decided to undertake a mission to Kosovo (see Report of the Security Council mission on the Kosovo issue, United Nations doc. S/2007/256, 4 May 2007), but was not able to reach a decision regarding the final status of Kosovo. A draft resolution was circulated among the Council's members (see draft resolution sponsored by Belgium, France, Germany, Italy, the United Kingdom and the United States, United Nations doc. S/2007/437 Prov., 17 July 2007) but was withdrawn after some weeks when it had become clear that it would not be adopted by the Security Council.

72. Between 9 August and 3 December 2007, further negotiations on the future status of Kosovo were held under the auspices of a Troika comprising representatives of the European Union, the Russian Federation and the United States. On 4 December 2007, the Troika submitted its report to the

Secretary-General, which came to the conclusion that, despite intensive negotiations, "the parties were unable to reach an agreement on Kosovo's status" and "[n]either side was willing to yield on the basic question of sovereignty" (Report of the European Union/United States/Russian Federation Troika on Kosovo, 4 December 2007, annexed to S/2007/723).

73. On 17 November 2007, elections were held for the Assembly of Kosovo, 30 municipal assemblies and their respective mayors (Report of the Secretary-General on the United Nations Interim Administration Mission in Kosovo, United Nations doc. S/2007/768). The Assembly of Kosovo held its inaugural session on 4 and 9 January 2008 (Report of the Secretary-General on the United Nations Interim Administration Mission in Kosovo, United Nations doc. S/2008/211).

C. The Events of 17 February 2008 and Thereafter

74. It is against this background that the declaration of independence was adopted on 17 February 2008. The Court observes that the original language of the declaration is Albanian. For the purposes of the present Opinion, when quoting from the text of the declaration, the Court has used the translations into English and French included in the dossier submitted on behalf of the Secretary-General.

In its relevant passages, the declaration of independence states that its authors were "*[c]onvened* in an extraordinary meeting on 17 February 2008, in Pristina, the capital of Kosovo" (first preambular paragraph); it "*[r]ecall[ed]* the years of internationally-sponsored negotiations between Belgrade and Pristina over the question of [Kosovo's] future political status" and "*[r]egrett[ed]* that no mutually acceptable status outcome was possible" (tenth and eleventh preambular paragraphs). It further declared that the authors were "*[d]etermin[ed]* to see [Kosovo's] status resolved in order to give [its] people clarity about their future, move beyond the conflicts of the past and realise the full democratic potential of [its] society" (thirteenth preambular paragraph).

75. In its operative part, the declaration of independence of 17 February 2008 states :

> "1. We, the democratically-elected leaders of our people, hereby declare Kosovo to be an independent and sovereign state. This declaration reflects the will of our people and it is in full accordance with the recommendations of UN Special Envoy Martti Ahtisaari and his Comprehensive Proposal for the Kosovo Status Settlement.
> 2. We declare Kosovo to be a democratic, secular and multiethnic republic, guided by the principles of non-discrimination and equal protection under the law. We shall protect and promote the rights of all communities in Kosovo and create the conditions necessary for their effective participation in political and decision-making processes.
> ...
> 5. We welcome the international community's continued support of our democratic development through international presences established in Kosovo on the basis of UN Security Council resolution 1244 (1999). We invite and welcome an international civilian presence to supervise our implementation of the Ahtisaari Plan, and a European Union-led rule of law mission.
> ...
> 9. We hereby undertake the international obligations of Kosovo, including those concluded on our behalf by the United Nations Interim Administration Mission in Kosovo (UNMIK) . . .
> ...

12. We hereby affirm, clearly, specifically, and irrevocably, that Kosovo shall be legally bound to comply with the provisions contained in this Declaration, including, especially, the obligations for it under the Ahtisaari Plan . . . We declare publicly that all States are entitled to rely upon this declaration . . ."

76. The declaration of independence was adopted at a meeting held on 17 February 2008 by 109 out of the 120 members of the Assembly of Kosovo, including the Prime Minister of Kosovo and by the President of Kosovo (who was not a member of the Assembly). The ten members of the Assembly representing the Kosovo Serb community and one member representing the Kosovo Gorani community decided not to attend this meeting. The declaration was written down on two sheets of papyrus and read out, voted upon and then signed by all representatives present. It was not transmitted to the Special Representative of the Secretary- General and was not published in the Official Gazette of the Provisional Institutions of Self-Government of Kosovo.

77. After the declaration of independence was issued, the Republic of Serbia informed the Secretary-General that it had adopted a decision stating that that declaration represented a forceful and unilateral secession of a part of the territory of Serbia, and did not produce legal effects either in Serbia or in the international legal order (United Nations doc. S/PV.5839; Report of the Secretary-General on the United Nations Interim Administration Mission in Kosovo, United Nations doc. S/2008/ 211). Further to a request from Serbia, an emergency public meeting of the Security Council took place on 18 February 2008, in which Mr. Boris Tadic′, the President of the Republic of Serbia, participated and denounced the declaration of independence as an unlawful act which had been declared null and void by the National Assembly of Serbia (United Nations doc. S/PV.5839).

IV. THE QUESTION WHETHER THE DECLARATION OF INDEPENDENCE IS IN ACCORDANCE WITH INTERNATIONAL LAW

78. The Court now turns to the substance of the request submitted by the General Assembly. The Court recalls that it has been asked by the General Assembly to assess the accordance of the declaration of independence of 17 February 2008 with "international law" (resolution 63/3 of the General Assembly, 8 October 2008). The Court will first turn its attention to certain questions concerning the lawfulness of declarations of independence under general international law, against the background of which the question posed falls to be considered, and Security Council resolution 1244 (1999) is to be understood and applied. Once this general framework has been determined, the Court will turn to the legal relevance of Security Council resolution 1244 (1999), and determine whether the resolution creates special rules, and ensuing obligations, under international law applicable to the issues raised by the present request and having a bearing on the lawfulness of the declaration of independence of 17 February 2008.

A. General International Law

79. During the eighteenth, nineteenth and early twentieth centuries, there were numerous instances of declarations of independence, often strenuously opposed by the State from which independence was being declared. Sometimes a declaration resulted in the creation of a new State, at others it did not. In no case, however, does the practice of States as a whole suggest that the act of promulgating the declaration was regarded as contrary to international law. On the contrary, State practice during this period points clearly to the conclusion that international law contained no prohibition of declarations

of independence. During the second half of the twentieth century, the international law of self-determination developed in such a way as to create a right to independence for the peoples of non-self-governing territories and peoples subject to alien subjugation, domination and exploitation (cf. *Legal Consequences for States of the Continued Presence of South Africa in Namibia (South West Africa) notwithstanding Security Council Resolution 276 (1970), Advisory Opinion, I.C.J. Reports 1971*, pp. 31-32, paras. 52-53; *East Timor (Portugal* v. *Australia), Judgment, I.C.J. Reports 1995*, p. 102, para. 29; *Legal Consequences of the Construction of a Wall in the Occupied Palestinian Territory, Advisory Opinion, I.C.J. Reports 2004 (I)*, pp. 171-172, para. 88). A great many new States have come into existence as a result of the exercise of this right. There were, however, also instances of declarations of independence outside this context. The practice of States in these latter cases does not point to the emergence in international law of a new rule prohibiting the making of a declaration of independence in such cases.

80. Several participants in the proceedings before the Court have contended that a prohibition of unilateral declarations of independence is implicit in the principle of territorial integrity. The Court recalls that the principle of territorial integrity is an important part of the international legal order and is enshrined in the Charter of the United Nations, in particular in Article 2, paragraph 4, which provides that :

> "All Members shall refrain in their international relations from the threat or use of force against the territorial integrity or political independence of any State, or in any other manner inconsistent with the Purposes of the United Nations."

In General Assembly resolution 2625 (XXV), entitled "Declaration on Principles of International Law concerning Friendly Relations and Co-operation among States in Accordance with the Charter of the United Nations", which reflects customary international law (*Military and Paramilitary Activities in and against Nicaragua (Nicaragua* v. *United States of America), Merits, Judgment, I.C.J. Reports 1986*, pp. 101-103, paras. 191-193), the General Assembly reiterated "[t]he principle that States shall refrain in their international relations from the threat or use of force against the territorial integrity or political independence of any State". This resolution then enumerated various obligations incumbent upon States to refrain from violating the territorial integrity of other sovereign States. In the same vein, the Final Act of the Helsinki Conference on Security and Co-operation in Europe of 1 August 1975 (the Helsinki Conference) stipulated that "[t]he participating States will respect the territorial integrity of each of the participating States" (Art. IV). Thus, the scope of the principle of territorial integrity is confined to the sphere of relations between States.

81. Several participants have invoked resolutions of the Security Council condemning particular declarations of independence: see, *inter alia*, Security Council resolutions 216 (1965) and 217 (1965), concerning Southern Rhodesia; Security Council resolution 541 (1983), concerning northern Cyprus; and Security Council resolution 787 (1992), concerning the Republika Srpska.

The Court notes, however, that in all of those instances the Security Council was making a determination as regards the concrete situation existing at the time that those declarations of independence were made; the illegality attached to the declarations of independence thus stemmed not from the unilateral character of these declarations as such, but from the fact that they were, or would have been, connected with the unlawful use of force or other egregious violations of norms of general international law, in particular those of a peremptory character *(jus cogens)*. In the context of Kosovo, the Security Council has never taken this position. The exceptional character of the resolutions enumerated above appears to the Court to confirm that no general prohibition against unilateral declarations of independence may be inferred from the practice of the Security Council.

[...]

84. For the reasons already given, the Court considers that general international law contains no applicable prohibition of declarations of independence. Accordingly, it concludes that the declaration of independence of 17 February 2008 did not violate general international law. Having arrived at that conclusion, the Court now turns to the legal relevance of Security Council resolution 1244, adopted on 10 June 1999.

B. Security Council Resolution 1244 (1999) and the UNMIK Constitutional Framework Created Thereunder

85. Within the legal framework of the United Nations Charter, notably on the basis of Articles 24, 25 and Chapter VII thereof, the Security Council may adopt resolutions imposing obligations under international law. The Court has had the occasion to interpret and apply such Security Council resolutions on a number of occasions and has consistently treated them as part of the framework of obligations under international law (*Legal Consequences for States of the Continued Presence of South Africa in Namibia (South West Africa) notwithstanding Security Council Resolution 276 (1970), Advisory Opinion, I.C.J. Reports 1971*, p. 16; *Questions of Interpretation and Application of the 1971 Montreal Convention arising from the Aerial Incident at Lockerbie (Libyan Arab Jamahiriya* v. *United Kingdom), Provisional Measures, Order of 14 April 1992, I.C.J. Reports 1992*, p. 15, paras. 39-41; *Questions of Interpretation and Application of the 1971 Montreal Convention arising from the Aerial Incident at Lockerbie (Libyan Arab Jamahiriya* v. *United States of America), Provisional Measures, Order of 14 April 1992, I.C.J. Reports 1992*, pp. 126-127, paras. 42-44). Resolution 1244 (1999) was expressly adopted by the Security Council on the basis of Chapter VII of the United Nations Charter, and therefore clearly imposes international legal obligations. The Court notes that none of the participants has questioned the fact that resolution 1244 (1999), which specifically deals with the situation in Kosovo, is part of the law relevant in the present situation.

86. The Court notes that there are a number of other Security Council resolutions adopted on the question of Kosovo, notably Security Council resolutions 1160 (1998), 1199 (1998), 1203 (1998) and 1239 (1999); however, the Court sees no need to pronounce specifically on resolutions of the Security Council adopted prior to resolution 1244 (1999), which are, in any case, recalled in the second preambular paragraph of the latter.

*

87. A certain number of participants have dealt with the question whether regulations adopted on behalf of UNMIK by the Special Representative of the Secretary-General, notably the Constitutional Framework (see paragraph 62 above), also form part of the applicable international law within the meaning of the General Assembly's request.

88. In particular, it has been argued before the Court that the Constitutional Framework is an act of an internal law rather than an international law character. According to that argument, the Constitutional Framework would not be part of the international law applicable in the present instance and the question of the compatibility of the declaration of independence therewith would thus fall outside the scope of the General Assembly's request.

The Court observes that UNMIK regulations, including regulation 2001/9, which promulgated the Constitutional Framework, are adopted by the Special Representative of the Secretary-General on the basis of the authority derived from Security Council resolution 1244 (1999), notably its paragraphs 6, 10, and 11, and thus ultimately from the United Nations Charter. The Constitutional Framework derives its binding force from the binding character of resolution 1244 (1999) and thus from international law. In that sense it therefore possesses an international legal character.

89. At the same time, the Court observes that the Constitutional Framework functions as part of a specific legal order, created pursuant to resolution 1244 (1999), which is applicable only in Kosovo and the purpose of which is to regulate, during the interim phase established by resolution 1244 (1999), matters which would ordinarily be the subject of internal, rather than international, law. Regulation 2001/9 opens with the statement that the Constitutional Framework was promulgated

> "[f]or the purposes of developing meaningful self-government in Kosovo pending a final settlement, and establishing provisional institutions of self-government in the legislative, executive and judicial fields through the participation of the people of Kosovo in free and fair elections".

The Constitutional Framework therefore took effect as part of the body of law adopted for the administration of Kosovo during the interim phase. The institutions which it created were empowered by the Constitutional Framework to take decisions which took effect within that body of law. In particular, the Assembly of Kosovo was empowered to adopt legislation which would have the force of law within that legal order, subject always to the overriding authority of the Special Representative of the Secretary-General.

90. The Court notes that both Security Council resolution 1244 (1999) and the Constitutional Framework entrust the Special Representative of the Secretary-General with considerable supervisory powers with regard to the Provisional Institutions of Self-Government established under the authority of the United Nations Interim Administration Mission in Kosovo. As noted above (see paragraph 58), Security Council resolution 1244 (1999) envisages "an interim administration for Kosovo . . . which will provide transitional administration while establishing and overseeing the development of provisional democratic self-governing institutions" (para. 10). Resolution 1244 (1999) further states that "the main responsibilities of the international civil presence will include . . . [o]rganizing and overseeing the development of provisional institutions for democratic and autonomous self-government pending a political settlement, including the holding of elections" (paragraph 11 *(c)*). Similarly, as described above (see paragraph 62), under the Constitutional Framework, the Provisional Institutions of Self-Government were to function in conjunction with and subject to the direction of the Special Representative of the Secretary-General in the implementation of Security Council resolution 1244 (1999).

91. The Court notes that Security Council resolution 1244 (1999) and the Constitutional Framework were still in force and applicable as at 17 February 2008. Paragraph 19 of Security Council resolution 1244 (1999) expressly provides that "the international civil and security presences are established for an initial period of 12 months, to continue thereafter unless the Security Council decides otherwise". No decision amending resolution 1244 (1999) was taken by the Security Council at its meeting held on 18 February 2008, when the declaration of independence was discussed for the first time, or at any subsequent meeting. The Presidential Statement of 26 November 2008 (S/PRST/2008/44) merely "welcom[ed] the co-operation between the UN and other international actors, *within* the framework of Security Council resolution 1244 (1999)" (emphasis added). In addition, pursuant to paragraph 21 of Security Council resolution 1244 (1999), the Security Council decided "to remain actively seized of the matter" and maintained the item "Security Council resolutions 1160 (1998), 1199 (1998), 1203 (1998), 1239 (1999) and 1244 (1999)" on its agenda (see, most recently, Report of the Security Council, 1 August 2008-31 July 2009, General Assembly, Official Records, 64th session, Supplement No. 2, pp. 39 ff. and 132 ff.). Furthermore, Chapter 14.3 of the Constitutional Framework sets forth that "[t]he SRSG . . . may effect amendments to this Constitutional Framework". Minor amendments were effected by virtue of UNMIK regulations UNMIK/REG/2002/9 of 3 May 2002, UNMIK/REG/2007/29 of 4 October 2007, UNMIK/REG/ 2008/1 of 8 January 2008 and UNMIK/REG/2008/9 of 8 February 2008. Finally, neither Security Council resolution 1244 (1999) nor the Constitutional Framework contains a clause providing for its termination and neither has been repealed; they therefore constituted the international law applicable to the situation prevailing in Kosovo on 17 February 2008.

92. In addition, the Special Representative of the Secretary-General continues to exercise his functions in Kosovo. Moreover, the Secretary-General has continued to submit periodic reports to the Security Council, as required by paragraph 20 of Security Council resolution 1244 (1999) (see the most recent quarterly Report of the Secretary-General on the United Nations Interim Administration Mission in Kosovo, S/2010/169, 6 April 2010, as well as the preceding Reports S/2008/692 of 24 November 2008, S/2009/149 of 17 March 2009, S/2009/300 of 10 June 2009, S/2009/497 of 30 September 2009 and S/2010/5 of 5 January 2010).

93. From the foregoing, the Court concludes that Security Council resolution 1244 (1999) and the Constitutional Framework form part of the international law which is to be considered in replying to the question posed by the General Assembly in its request for the advisory opinion.

International Criminal Tribunal for the Former Yugoslavia (ICTY)

Prosecutor v. Dusko Tadic, Decision on the Defence Motion for Interlocutory Appeal on Jurisdiction, ICTY Appeals Chamber, 2 October 1995

[*Note:*

The ad hoc International Criminal Tribunal for the former Yugoslavia (ICTY) was created by the UN Security Council resolution 827(1993) of 25 May 1993. It based its resolution on Chapter VII and Article 29 of the UN Charter. On the same basis the Security Council created the ad hoc International Criminal Tribunal on Rwanda (Security Council resolution 955(1994) of 8 November 1994). In the first case considered by the ICTY, the accused Duško Tadić, claimed that as a political body of the United Nations, the Security Council had no power to create the ICTY].

The Decision:

I. INTRODUCTION

A. The Judgement Under Appeal

1. The Appeals Chamber of the International Tribunal for the Prosecution of Persons Responsible for Serious Violations of International Humanitarian Law Committed in the Territory of Former Yugoslavia since 1991 (hereinafter "International Tribunal") is seized of an appeal lodged by Appellant the Defence against a judgement rendered by the Trial Chamber II on 10 August 1995. By that judgement, Appellant's motion challenging the jurisdiction of the International Tribunal was denied.

2. Before the Trial Chamber, Appellant had launched a three-pronged attack:

a) illegal foundation of the International Tribunal;
b) wrongful primacy of the International Tribunal over national courts;
c) lack of jurisdiction *ratione materiae.*

[…]

15. To assume that the jurisdiction of the International Tribunal is absolutely limited to what the Security Council "intended" to entrust it with, is to envisage the International Tribunal exclusively as a "subsidiary organ" of the Security Council (see United Nations Charter, Arts. 7(2) & 29), a "creation" totally fashioned to the smallest detail by its "creator" and remaining totally in its power and at its mercy. But the Security Council not only decided to establish a subsidiary organ (the only legal means available to it for setting up such a body), it also clearly intended to establish a special kind of "subsidiary organ": a tribunal.

[...]

17. Earlier, the Court had derived the judicial nature of the United Nations Administrative Tribunal ("UNAT") from the use of certain terms and language in the Statute and its possession of certain attributes. Prominent among these attributes of the judicial function figures the power provided for in Article 2, paragraph 3, of the Statute of UNAT:

> "In the event of a dispute as to whether the Tribunal has competence, the matter shall be settled by the decision of the Tribunal." (Id. at 51-2, quoting Statute of the United Nations Administrative Tribunal, art. 2, para. 3.)

18. This power, known as the principle of "*Kompetenz-Kompetenz*" in German or "*la compétence de la compétence*" in French, is part, and indeed a major part, of the incidental or inherent jurisdiction of any judicial or arbitral tribunal, consisting of its "jurisdiction to determine its own jurisdiction." It is a necessary component in the exercise of the judicial function and does not need to be expressly provided for in the constitutive documents of those tribunals, although this is often done (see, e.g., Statute of the International Court of Justice, Art. 36, para. 6). But in the words of the International Court of Justice:

> "[T]his principle, which is accepted by the general international law in the matter of arbitration, assumes particular force when the international tribunal is no longer an arbitral tribunal [...] but is an institution which has been pre-established by an international instrument defining its jurisdiction and regulating its operation." (Nottebohm Case (Liech. v. Guat.), 1953 I.C.J. Reports 7, 119 (21 March).)

This is not merely a power in the hands of the tribunal. In international law, where there is no integrated judicial system and where every judicial or arbitral organ needs a specific constitutive instrument defining its jurisdiction, "the first obligation of the Court – as of any other judicial body – is to ascertain its own competence." (Judge Cordova, dissenting opinion, advisory opinion on Judgements of the Administrative Tribunal of the I.L.O. upon complaints made against the U.N.E.S.C.O., 1956 I.C.J. Reports, 77, 163 (Advisory Opinion of 23 October)(Cordova, J., dissenting).)
[...]

22. In conclusion, the Appeals Chamber finds that the International Tribunal has jurisdiction to examine the plea against its jurisdiction based on the invalidity of its establishment by the Security Council.

[...]

1. The Power Of The Security Council To Invoke Chapter VII

28. Article 39 opens Chapter VII of the Charter of the United Nations and determines the conditions of application of this Chapter. It provides:

> "The Security Council shall determine the existence of any threat to the peace, breach of the peace, or act of aggression and shall make recommendations, or decide what measures shall be taken in accordance with Articles 41 and 42, to maintain or restore international peace and security." (United Nations Charter, 26 June 1945, Art. 39.)

It is clear from this text that the Security Council plays a pivotal role and exercises a very wide discretion under this Article. But this does not mean that its powers are unlimited. The Security Council is an organ of an international organization, established by a treaty which serves as a constitutional framework for that organization. The Security Council is thus subjected to certain constitutional limitations, however broad its powers under the constitution may be. Those powers cannot, in any case, go beyond the limits of the jurisdiction of the Organization at large, not to mention other specific limitations or those which may derive from the internal division of power within the Organization. In any case, neither the text nor the spirit of the Charter conceives of the Security Council as *legibus solutus* (unbound by law).

In particular, Article 24, after declaring, in paragraph 1, that the Members of the United Nations "confer on the Security Council primary responsibility for the maintenance of international peace and security", imposes on it, in paragraph 3, the obligation to report annually (or more frequently) to the General Assembly, and provides, more importantly, in paragraph 2, that:

> "In discharging these duties the Security Council shall act in accordance with the Purposes and Principles of the United Nations. The specific powers granted to the Security Council for the discharge of these duties are laid down in Chapters VI, VII, VIII, and XII." (Id., Art. 24(2).)

The Charter thus speaks the language of specific powers, not of absolute fiat.

29. What is the extent of the powers of the Security Council under Article 39 and the limits thereon, if any?

The Security Council plays the central role in the application of both parts of the Article. It is the Security Council that makes the **determination** that there exists one of the situations justifying the use of the "exceptional powers" of Chapter VII. And it is also the Security Council that chooses the reaction to such a situation: it either makes **recommendations** (*i.e.* opts not to use the exceptional powers but to continue to operate under Chapter VI) or decides to use the exceptional powers by ordering measures to be taken in accordance with Articles 41 and 42 with a view to maintaining or restoring international peace and security.

The situations justifying resort to the powers provided for in Chapter VII are a "threat to the peace", a "breach of the peace" or an "act of aggression." While the "act of aggression" is more amenable to a legal determination, the "threat to the peace" is more of a political concept. But the determination that there exists such a threat is not a totally unfettered discretion, as it has to remain, at the very least, within the limits of the Purposes and Principles of the Charter.

30. It is not necessary for the purposes of the present decision to examine any further the question of the limits of the discretion of the Security Council in determining the existence of a "threat to the peace", for two reasons.

The first is that an armed conflict (or a series of armed conflicts) has been taking place in the territory of the former Yugoslavia since long before the decision of the Security Council to establish this International Tribunal. If it is considered an international armed conflict, there is no doubt that it falls within the literal sense of the words "breach of the peace" (between the parties or, at the very least, would be a as a "threat to the peace" of others).

But even if it were considered merely as an "internal armed conflict", it would still constitute a "threat to the peace" according to the settled practice of the Security Council and the common understanding of the United Nations membership in general. Indeed, the practice of the Security Council is rich with cases of civil war or internal strife which it classified as a "threat to the peace" and dealt with under Chapter VII, with the encouragement or even at the behest of the General Assembly, such as the Congo crisis at the beginning of the 1960s and, more recently, Liberia and Somalia. It can thus be said that there is a common understanding, manifested by the "subsequent practice" of the membership of the United Nations at large, that the "threat to the peace" of Article 39 may include, as one of its species, internal armed conflicts.

The second reason, which is more particular to the case at hand, is that Appellant has amended his position from that contained in the Brief submitted to the Trial Chamber. Appellant no longer contests the Security Council's power to determine whether the situation in the former Yugoslavia constituted a threat to the peace, nor the determination itself. He further acknowledges that the Security Council "has the power to address to such threats [...] by appropriate measures." [Defence] Brief to Support the Notice of (Interlocutory) Appeal, 25 August 1995 (Case No. IT-94-1-AR72), at para. 5.4 (hereinafter Defence Appeal Brief).) But he continues to contest the legality and appropriateness of the measures chosen by the Security Council to that end.

2. The Range of Measures Envisaged Under Chapter VII

31. Once the Security Council determines that a particular situation poses a threat to the peace or that there exists a breach of the peace or an act of aggression, it enjoys a wide margin of discretion in choosing the course of action: as noted above (see para. 29) it can either continue, in spite of its determination, to act via recommendations, i.e., as if it were still within Chapter VI ("Pacific Settlement of Disputes") or it can exercise its exceptional powers under Chapter VII. In the words of Article 39, it would then "decide what measures shall be taken in accordance with Articles 41 and 42, to maintain or restore international peace and security." (United Nations Charter, art. 39.)

A question arises in this respect as to whether the choice of the Security Council is limited to the measures provided for in Articles 41 and 42 of the Charter (as the language of Article 39 suggests), or whether it has even larger discretion in the form of general powers to maintain and restore international peace and security under Chapter VII at large. In the latter case, one of course does not have to locate every measure decided by the Security Council under Chapter VII within the confines of Articles 41 and 42, or possibly Article 40. In any case, under both interpretations, the Security Council has a broad discretion in deciding on the course of action and evaluating the appropriateness of the measures to be taken. The language of Article 39 is quite clear as to the channelling of the very broad and exceptional powers of the Security Council under Chapter VII through Articles 41 and 42. These two Articles leave to the Security Council such a wide choice as not to warrant searching, on functional or other grounds, for even wider and more general powers than those already expressly provided for in the Charter.

These powers are **coercive** *vis-a-vis* the culprit State or entity. But they are also **mandatory** vis-à-vis the other Member States, who are under an obligation to cooperate with the Organization (Article 2, paragraph 5, Articles 25, 48) and with one another (Articles 49), in the implementation of the action or measures decided by the Security Council.

3. The Establishment Of The International Tribunal As A Measure Under Chapter VII

32. As with the determination of the existence of a threat to the peace, a breach of the peace or an act of aggression, the Security Council has a very wide margin of discretion under Article 39 to choose the appropriate course of action and to evaluate the suitability of the measures chosen, as well as their

potential contribution to the restoration or maintenance of peace. But here again, this discretion is not unfettered; moreover, it is limited to the measures provided for in Articles 41 and 42. Indeed, in the case at hand, this last point serves as a basis for the Appellant's contention of invalidity of the establishment of the International Tribunal.

In its resolution 827, the Security Council considers that "in the particular circumstances of the former Yugoslavia", the establishment of the International Tribunal "would contribute to the restoration and maintenance of peace" and indicates that, in establishing it, the Security Council was acting under Chapter VII (S.C. Res. 827, U.N. Doc. S/RES/827 (1993)). However, it did not specify a particular Article as a basis for this action.

Appellant has attacked the legality of this decision at different stages before the Trial Chamber as well as before this Chamber on at least three grounds:

a) that the establishment of such a tribunal was never contemplated by the framers of the Charter as one of the measures to be taken under Chapter VII; as witnessed by the fact that it figures nowhere in the provisions of that Chapter, and more particularly in Articles 41 and 42 which detail these measures;
b) that the Security Council is constitutionally or inherently incapable of creating a judicial organ, as it is conceived in the Charter as an executive organ, hence not possessed of judicial powers which can be exercised through a subsidiary organ;
c) that the establishment of the International Tribunal has neither promoted, nor was capable of promoting, international peace, as demonstrated by the current situation in the former Yugoslavia.

(a) What Article of Chapter VII Serves As A Basis For The Establishment Of A Tribunal?

33. The establishment of an international criminal tribunal is not expressly mentioned among the enforcement measures provided for in Chapter VII, and more particularly in Articles 41 and 42.

Obviously, the establishment of the International Tribunal is not a measure under Article 42, as these are measures of a military nature, implying the use of armed force. Nor can it be considered a "provisional measure" under Article 40. These measures, as their denomination indicates, are intended to act as a "holding operation", producing a "stand-still" or a "cooling-off" effect, "without prejudice to the rights, claims or position of the parties concerned." (United Nations Charter, art. 40.)

They are akin to emergency police action rather than to the activity of a judicial organ dispensing justice according to law. Moreover, not being enforcement action, according to the language of Article 40 itself ("before making the recommendations or deciding upon the measures provided for in Article 39"), such provisional measures are subject to the Charter limitation of Article 2, paragraph 7, and the question of their mandatory or recommendatory character is subject to great controversy; all of which renders inappropriate the classification of the International Tribunal under these measures.

34. *Prima facie*, the International Tribunal matches perfectly the description in Article 41 of "measures not involving the use of force." Appellant, however, has argued before both the Trial Chamber and this Appeals Chamber, that:"

> . . . [I]t is clear that the establishment of a war crimes tribunal was not intended. The examples mentioned in this article focus upon economic and political measures and do not in any way suggest judicial measures." (Brief to Support the Motion [of the Defence] on the Jurisdiction of the Tribunal before the Trial Chamber of the International Tribunal, 23 June 1995 (Case No. IT-94-1-T), at para. 3.2.1 (hereinafter Defence Trial Brief).)

It has also been argued that the measures contemplated under Article 41 are all measures to be undertaken by Member States, which is not the case with the establishment of the International Tribunal.

35. The first argument does not stand by its own language. Article 41 reads as follows:"

> "The Security Council may decide what measures not involving the use of armed force are to be employed to give effect to its decisions, and it may call upon the Members of the United Nations to apply such measures. These may include complete or partial interruption of economic relations and of rail, sea, air, postal, telegraphic, radio, and other means of communication, and the severance of diplomatic relations." (United Nations Charter, art. 41.)

It is evident that the measures set out in Article 41 are merely illustrative examples which obviously do not exclude other measures. All the Article requires is that they do not involve "the use of force." It is a negative definition.

That the examples do not suggest judicial measures goes some way towards the other argument that the Article does not contemplate institutional measures implemented directly by the United Nations through one of its organs but, as the given examples suggest, only action by Member States, such as economic sanctions (though possibly coordinated through an organ of the Organization). However, as mentioned above, nothing in the Article suggests the limitation of the measures to those implemented by States. The Article only prescribes what these measures cannot be. Beyond that it does not say or suggest what they have to be.

Moreover, even a simple literal analysis of the Article shows that the first phrase of the first sentence carries a very general prescription which can accommodate both institutional and Member State action. The second phrase can be read as referring particularly to one species of this very large category of measures referred to in the first phrase, but not necessarily the only one, namely, measures undertaken directly by States. It is also clear that the second sentence, starting with "These [measures]" not "Those [measures]", refers to the species mentioned in the second phrase rather than to the "ge nus" referred to in the first phrase of this sentence.

36. Logically, if the Organization can undertake measures which have to be implemented through the intermediary of its Members, it can a fortiori undertake measures which it can implement directly via its organs, if it happens to have the resources to do so. It is only for want of such resources that the United Nations has to act through its Members. But it is of the essence of "collective measures" that they are collectively undertaken. Action by Member States on behalf of the Organization is but a poor substitute *faute de mieux*, or a "second best" for want of the first. This is also the pattern of Article 42 on measures involving the use of armed force.

In sum, the establishment of the International Tribunal falls squarely within the powers of the Security Council under Article 41.

(b) Can The Security Council Establish A Subsidiary Organ With Judicial Powers?

37. The argument that the Security Council, not being endowed with judicial powers, cannot establish a subsidiary organ possessed of such powers is untenable: it results from a fundamental misunderstanding of the constitutional set-up of the Charter.

Plainly, the Security Council is not a judicial organ and is not provided with judicial powers (though it may incidentally perform certain quasi-judicial activities such as effecting determinations or findings). The principal function of the Security Council is the maintenance of international peace and security, in the discharge of which the Security Council exercises both decision-making and executive powers.

38. The establishment of the International Tribunal by the Security Council does not signify, however, that the Security Council has delegated to it some of its own functions or the exercise of some of its own powers. Nor does it mean, in reverse, that the Security Council was usurping for itself part of a judicial function which does not belong to it but to other organs of the United Nations according to the Charter. The Security Council has resorted to the establishment of a judicial organ in the form of an international criminal tribunal as an instrument for the exercise of its own principal function of maintenance of peace and security, i.e., as a measure contributing to the restoration and maintenance of peace in the former Yugoslavia.

The General Assembly did not need to have military and police functions and powers in order to be able to establish the United Nations Emergency Force in the Middle East ("UNEF") in 1956. Nor did the General Assembly have to be a judicial organ possessed of judicial functions and powers in order to be able to establish UNAT. In its advisory opinion in the Effect of Awards, the International Court of Justice, in addressing practically the same objection, declared:

> "[T]he Charter does not confer judicial functions on the General Assembly [...] By establishing the Administrative Tribunal, the General Assembly was not delegating the performance of its own functions: it was exercising a power which it had under the Charter to regulate staff relations."
> (Effect of Awards, at 61.)

(c) Was The Establishment Of The International Tribunal An Appropriate Measure?

39. The third argument is directed against the discretionary power of the Security Council in evaluating the appropriateness of the chosen measure and its effectiveness in achieving its objective, the restoration of peace.

Article 39 leaves the choice of means and their evaluation to the Security Council, which enjoys wide discretionary powers in this regard; and it could not have been otherwise, as such a choice involves political evaluation of highly complex and dynamic situations.

It would be a total misconception of what are the criteria of legality and validity in law to test the legality of such measures ex post facto by their success or failure to achieve their ends (in the present case, the restoration of peace in the former Yugoslavia, in quest of which the establishment of the International Tribunal is but one of many measures adopted by the Security Council).

40. For the aforementioned reasons, the Appeals Chamber considers that the International Tribunal has been lawfully established as a measure under Chapter VII of the Charter.

II. Regional Courts

European Court of Human Rights

Behrami v. France and Saramati v. France, Germany and Norway, Decision of the Grand Chamber of the European Court of Human Rights, 2 May 2007(Applications No. 78166/01 and No. 71412/01)

[*Note:*

The Application by Behrami was lodged on 28 September 2000 and by Saramati on 28 September 2001. On 13 June 2006 the Chamber of the Second Section relinquished its jurisdiction in favour of the Grand Chamber of the European Court which decided to join its examination of both Applications.]

The Decision:

THE FACTS

1. Mr Agim Behrami, was born in 1962 and his son, Mr Bekir Behrami, was born in 1990. Both are of Albanian origin. Mr Agim Behrami complained on his own behalf, and on behalf of his deceased son, Gadaf Behrami born in 1988. These applicants live in the municipality of Mitrovica in Kosovo, Republic of Serbia. They were represented by Mr Gazmend Nushi, a lawyer with the Council for the Defence of Human Rights and Freedoms, an organisation based in Pristina, Kosovo. Mr Saramati was born in 1950. He is also of Albanian origin living in Kosovo.

[...]

I. RELEVANT BACKGROUND TO THE CASES

2. The conflict between Serbian and Kosovar Albanian forces during 1998 and 1999 is well documented. On 30 January 1999, and following a decision of the North Atlantic Council ("NAC") of the North Atlantic Treaty Organisation ("NATO"), NATO announced air strikes on the territory of the then Federal Republic of Yugoslavia ("FRY") should the FRY not comply with the demands of the international community. Negotiations took place between the parties to the conflict in February and March 1999. The resulting proposed peace agreement was signed by the Kosovar Albanian delegation but not by the Serbian delegation. The NAC decided on, and on 23 March 1999 the Secretary General of NATO announced, the beginning of air strikes against the FRY. The air strikes began on 24 March 1999 and ended on 8 June 1999 when the FRY troops agreed to withdraw from Kosovo. On 9 June 1999 "KFOR", the FRY and the Republic of Serbia signed a "Military Technical Agreement" ("MTA") by

which they agreed on FRY withdrawal and the presence of an international security force following an appropriate UN Security Council Resolution ("UNSC Resolution").

3. UNSC Resolution 1244 of 10 June 1999 provided for the establishment of a security presence (KFOR) by "Member States and relevant international institutions", "under UN auspices", with "substantial NATO participation" but under "unified command and control". NATO pre-deployment to The Former Yugoslav Republic of Macedonia allowed deployment of significant forces to Kosovo by 12 June 1999 (in accordance with OPLAN 10413, NATO's operational plan for the UNSC Resolution 1244 mission called "Operation Joint Guardian"). By 20 June FRY withdrawal was complete. KFOR contingents were grouped into four multinational brigades ("MNBs") each of which was responsible for a specific sector of operations with a lead country. They included MNB Northeast (Mitrovica) and MNB Southeast (Prizren), led by France and Germany, respectively. Given the deployment of Russian forces after the arrival of KFOR, a further agreement on 18 June 1999 (between Russia and the United States) allocated various areas and roles to the Russian forces.

4. UNSC Resolution 1244 also decided on the deployment, under UN auspices, of an interim administration for Kosovo (UNMIK) and requested the Secretary General ("SG"), with the assistance of relevant international organisations, to establish it and to appoint a Special Representative to the SG ("SRSG") to control its implementation. UNMIK was to coordinate closely with KFOR. UNMIK comprised four pillars corresponding to the tasks assigned to it. Each pillar was placed under the authority of the SRSG and was headed by a Deputy SRSG. Pillar I (as it was at the relevant time) concerned humanitarian assistance and was led by UNHCR before it was phased out in June 2000. A new Pillar I (police and justice administration) was established in May 2001 and was led directly by the UN, as was Pillar II (civil administration). Pillar III, concerning democratisation and institution building, was led by the Organisation for Security and Co-operation in Europe ("OSCE") and Pillar IV (reconstruction and economic development) was led by the European Union.

II. THE CIRCUMSTANCES OF THE BEHRAMI CASE

5. On 11 March 2000 eight boys were playing in the hills in the municipality of Mitrovica. The group included two of Agim Behrami's sons, Gadaf and Bekim Behrami. At around midday, the group came upon a number of undetonated cluster bomb units ("CBUs") which had been dropped during the bombardment by NATO in 1999 and the children began playing with the CBUs. Believing it was safe, one of the children threw a CBU in the air: it detonated and killed Gadaf Behrami. Bekim Behrami was also seriously injured and taken to hospital in Pristina (where he later had eye surgery and was released on 4 April 2000). Medical reports submitted indicate that he underwent two further eye operations (on 7 April and 22 May 2000) in a hospital in Bern, Switzerland. It is not disputed that Bekim Behrami was disfigured and is now blind.

6. UNMIK police investigated. They took witness statements from, *inter alia*, the boys involved in the incident and completed an initial report. Further investigation reports dated 11, 12 and 13 March 2000 indicated, *inter alia*, that UNMIK police could not access the site without KFOR agreement; reported that a French KFOR officer had accepted that KFOR had been aware of the unexploded CBUs for months but that they were not a high priority; and pointed out that the detonation site had been marked out by KFOR the day after the detonation. The autopsy report confirmed Gadaf Behrami's death from multiple injuries resulting from the CBU explosion. The UNMIK Police report of 18 March 2000 concluded that the incident amounted to "unintentional homicide committed by imprudence".

7. By letter dated 22 May 2000 the District Public Prosecutor wrote to Agim Behrami to the effect that the evidence was that the CBU detonation was an accident, that criminal charges would not be pursued but that Mr Behrami had the right to pursue a criminal prosecution within eight days of the date of that letter. On 25 October 2001 Agim Behrami complained to the Kosovo Claims Office ("KCO") that France had not respected UNSC Resolution 1244. The KCO forwarded the complaint to the French Troop Contributing Nation Claims Office (TCNCO"). By letter of 5 February 2003 that TCNCO rejected the complaint stating, *inter alia*, that the UNSC Resolution 1244 had required KFOR to supervise mine clearing operations until UNMIK could take over and that such operations had been the responsibility of the UN since 5 July 1999.

III. THE CIRCUMSTANCES OF THE SARAMATI CASE

8. On 24 April 2001 Mr Saramati was arrested by UNMIK police and brought before an investigating judge on suspicion of attempted murder and illegal possession of a weapon. On 25 April 2001 that judge ordered his pre-trial detention and an investigation into those and additional charges. On 23 May 2001 a prosecutor filed an indictment and on 24 May 2001 the District Court ordered his detention to be extended. On 4 June 2001 the Supreme Court allowed Mr Saramati's appeal and he was released.

9. In early July 2001 UNMIK police informed him by telephone that he had to report to the police station to collect his money and belongings. The station was located in Prizren in the sector assigned to MNB Southeast, of which the lead nation was Germany. On 13 July 2001 he so reported and was arrested by UNMIK police officers by order of the Commander of KFOR ("COMKFOR"), who was a Norwegian officer at the time. 10. On 14 July 2001 detention was extended by COMKFOR for 30 days.

11. On 26 July 2001, and in response to a letter from Mr Saramati's representatives taking issue with the legality of his detention, KFOR Legal Adviser advised that KFOR had the authority to detain under the UNSC Resolution 1244 as it was necessary "to maintain a safe and secure environment" and to protect KFOR troops. KFOR had information concerning Mr Saramati's alleged involvement with armed groups operating in the border region between Kosovo and the Former Yugoslav Republic of Macedonia and was satisfied that Mr Saramati represented a threat to the security of KFOR and to those residing in Kosovo.

12. On 26 July 2001 the Russian representative in the UNSC referred to "the arrest of Major Saramati, the Commander of a Kosovo Protection Corps Brigade, accused of undertaking activities threatening the international presence in Kosovo".

13. On 11 August 2001 Mr Saramati's detention was again extended by order of COMKFOR. On 6 September 2001 his case was transferred to the District Court for trial, the indictment retaining charges of, *inter alia*, attempted murder and the illegal possession of weapons and explosives. By letter dated 20 September 2001, the decision of COMKFOR to prolong his detention was communicated to his representatives.

14. During each trial hearing from 17 September 2001 to 23 January 2002 Mr Saramati's representatives requested his release and the trial court responded that, although the Supreme Court had so ruled in June 2001, his detention was entirely the responsibility of KFOR.

15. On 3 October 2001 a French General was appointed to the position of COMKFOR.

16. On 23 January 2002 Mr Saramati was convicted of attempted murder under Article 30 § 2(6) of the Criminal Code of Kosovo in conjunction with Article 19 of the Criminal Code of the FRY. He was acquitted on certain charges and certain charges were either rejected or dropped. Mr Saramati was transferred by KFOR to the UNMIK detention facilities in Prishtina.

17. On 9 October 2002 the Supreme Court of Kosovo quashed Mr Saramati's conviction and his case was sent for re-trial. His release from detention was ordered. A re-trial has yet to be fixed.

IV. RELEVANT LAW AND PRACTICE

A. The prohibition on the unilateral use of force and its collective security counterpart

18. The prohibition on the unilateral use of force by States, together with its counterpart principle of collective security, mark the dividing line between the classic concept of international law, characterised by the right to have recourse to war (*ius ad bellum*) as an indivisible part of State sovereignty, and modern international law which recognises the prohibition on the use of force as a fundamental legal norm (*ius contra bellum*).

19. More particularly, the *ius contra bellum* era of public international law is accepted to have begun (at the latest, having regard, inter alia, to the Kellog-Briand Pact signed in 1928) with the end of the First World War and with the constitution of the League of Nations. The aim of this organisation of universal vocation was maintaining peace through an obligation not to resort to war (First recital and Article 11 of the Covenant of the League of Nations) as well as through universal systems of peaceful settlement of disputes (Articles 12-15 of the Covenant) and of collective security (Article 16 of the Covenant). It is argued by commentators that, by that stage, customary international law prohibited unilateral recourse to the use of force unless in self-defence or as a collective security measure (for example, R. Kolb, "*Ius Contra Bellum* – Le Droit international relatif au maintien de la paix", Helbing and Lichtenhahn, Bruylant, 2003, pp. 60-68).

20. The UN succeeded the League of Nations in 1946. The primary objective of the UN was to maintain international peace and security (First recital and Article 1 § 1 of the Charter) and this was to be achieved through two complimentary actions. The first, often described as "positive peace" (the Preamble to the Charter as well as Article 2 § 3, Chapter VI, Chapter IX-X and certain measures under Article 41 of Chapter VII), aimed at the suppression of the causes of dispute and the building of sustainable peace. The second type of action, "negative peace", was founded on the Preamble, Article 2 § 4 and most of the Chapter VII measures and amounted to the prohibition of the unilateral use of force (Article 2 § 4) in favour of collective security implemented by a central UN organ (the UNSC) with the monopoly on the right to use force in conflicts identified as threatening peace. Two matters were essential to this peace and security mechanism: its "collective" nature (States had to act together against an aggressor identified by the UNSC) as well as its "universality" (competing alliances were considered to undermine the mechanism so that coercive action by regional organisations was subjected to the universal system by Article 53 of the Charter).

B. The Charter of the UN, 1945

21. The Preamble as well as Articles 1 and 2, in so far as relevant, provide as follows:

"WE THE PEOPLES OF THE UNITED NATIONS DETERMINED
- to save succeeding generations from the scourge of war, which twice in our lifetime has brought untold sorrow to mankind, and
- to reaffirm faith in fundamental human rights, in the dignity and worth of the human person, in the equal rights of men and women and of nations large and small, and
- to establish conditions under which justice and respect for the obligations arising from treaties and other sources of international law can be maintained, and
- to promote social progress and better standards of life in larger freedom,

AND FOR THESE ENDS
- to practice tolerance and live together in peace with one another as good neighbours, and
- to unite our strength to maintain international peace and security, and
- to ensure, by the acceptance of principles and the institution of methods, that armed force shall not be used, save in the common interest, and
- to employ international machinery for the promotion of the economic and social advancement of all peoples,

HAVE RESOLVED TO COMBINE OUR EFFORTS TO ACCOMPLISH THESE AIMS
Accordingly, our respective Governments, . . ., have agreed to the present Charter of the United Nations and do hereby establish an international organisation to be known as the United Nations.

Article 1

The Purposes of the United Nations are:
1. To maintain international peace and security, and to that end: to take effective collective measures for the prevention and removal of threats to the peace, and for the suppression of acts of aggression or other breaches of the peace, and to bring about by peaceful means, and in conformity with the principles of justice and international law, adjustment or settlement of international disputes or situations which might lead to a breach of the peace;
. . .

Article 2
. . .
5. All Members shall give the United Nations every assistance in any action it takes in accordance with the present Charter, and shall refrain from giving assistance to any state against which the United Nations is taking preventive or enforcement action.
. . .
7. Nothing contained in the present Charter shall authorize the United Nations to intervene in matters which are essentially within the domestic jurisdiction of any state or shall require the Members to submit such matters to settlement under the present Charter; but this principle shall not prejudice the application of enforcement measures under Chapter VII."

22. Chapter V deals with the UNSC and Article 24 outlines its "Functions and Powers" as follows:

> "1. In order to ensure prompt and effective action by the [UN], its Members confer on the [UNSC] primary responsibility for the maintenance of international peace and security, and agree that in carrying out its duties under this responsibility the [UNSC] acts on their behalf.
> 2. In discharging these duties the [UNSC] shall act in accordance with the Purposes and Principles of the [UN]. The specific powers granted to the [UNSC] for the discharge of these duties are laid down in Chapters VI, VII, VIII, and XII. . . ."

Article 25 provides:

> "The Members of the United Nations agree to accept and carry out the decisions of the [UNSC] in accordance with the present Charter."

23. Chapter VII is entitled "Action with respect to threats to the peace, breaches of the peace and acts of aggression". Article 39 provides:

> "The Security Council shall determine the existence of any threat to the peace, breach of the peace, or act of aggression and shall make recommendations, or decide what measures shall be taken in accordance with Articles 41 and 42, to maintain or restore international peace and security."

The notion of a "threat to the peace" within the meaning of Article 39 has evolved to include internal conflicts which threaten to "spill over" or concern serious violations of fundamental international (often humanitarian) norms. Large scale cross border displacement of refugees can also render a threat international (Article 2(7) of the UN Charter; and, for example, R. Kolb, "*Ius Contra Bellum* – Le Droit international relatif au maintien de la paix", Helbing and Lichtenhahn, Bruylant, 2003, pp. 60-68; and "Yugoslav Territory, United Nations Trusteeship or Sovereign State? Reflections on the current and Future Legal Status of Kosovo", Zimmermann and Stahn, NJIL 70, 2001, p. 437).

Articles 41 and 42 read as follows:

> "41. The Security Council may decide what measures not involving the use of armed force are to be employed to give effect to its decisions, and it may call upon the Members of the United Nations to apply such measures. These may include complete or partial interruption of economic relations and of rail, sea, air, postal, telegraphic, radio, and other means of communication, and the severance of diplomatic relations."
> 42. Should the Security Council consider that measures provided for in Article 41 would be inadequate or have proved to be inadequate, it may take such action by air, sea, or land forces as may be necessary to maintain or restore international peace and security. Such action may include demonstrations, blockade, and other operations by air, sea, or land forces of Members of the United Nations."

24. Articles 43-45 provide for the conclusion of agreements between member states and the UNSC for the former to contribute to the latter land and air forces necessary for the purpose of maintaining international peace and security. No such agreements have been concluded. There is, consequently, no basis

in the Charter for the UN to oblige Member States to contribute resources to Chapter VII missions. Articles 46-47 provide for the UNSC to be advised by a Military Staff Committee (comprising military representatives of the permanent members of the UNSC) on, inter alia, military requirements for the maintenance of international peace and security and on the employment and command of forces placed at the UNSC's disposal. The MSC has had very limited activity due to the absence of Article 43 agreements.

25. Chapter VII continues:

> Article 48
> The action required to carry out the decisions of the Security Council for the maintenance of international peace and security shall be taken by all the Members of the United Nations or by some of them, as the Security Council may determine.
> Such decisions shall be carried out by the Members of the United Nations directly and through their action in the appropriate international agencies of which they are members.
>
> Article 49
> The Members of the United Nations shall join in affording mutual assistance in carrying out the measures decided upon by the Security Council."

C. Article 103 of the Charter

26. This Article reads as follows:

> "In the event of a conflict between the obligations of the Members of the United Nations under the present Charter and their obligations under any other international agreement, their obligations under the present Charter shall prevail."

27. The ICJ considers Article 103 to mean that the Charter obligations of UN member states prevail over conflicting obligations from another international treaty, regardless of whether the latter treaty was concluded before or after the UN Charter or was only a regional arrangement (Nicaragua v. United States of America, ICJ Reports, 1984, p. 392, at § 107. See also *Kadi* v. *Council and Commission*, § 183, judgment of the Court of First Instance of the European Communities ("CFI") of 21 September 2005 (under appeal) and two more recent judgments of the CFI in the same vein: Yusuf and Al Barakaat v. Council and Commission, 21 September 2005, §§ 231, 234, 242-243 and 254 as well as Ayadi v. Council, 12 July 2006, § 116). The ICJ has also found Article 25 to mean that UN member states' obligations under a UNSC Resolution prevail over obligations arising under any other international agreement (Orders of 14 April 1992 (provisional measures), Questions of Interpretation and Application of the 1971 Montreal Convention arising from the Aerial Incident at Lockerbie (Libyan Arab Jamahiriya v United States of America and Libyan Arab Jamahiriya v United Kingdom), ICJ Reports, 1992, p. 16, § 42 and p. 113, § 39, respectively).

[...]

G. The UNSC Resolution 1244 of 10 June 1999

41. The Resolution reads, in so far as relevant, as follows:

> "Bearing in mind the purposes and principles of the Charter of the United Nations, and the primary responsibility of the Security Council for the maintenance of international peace and security,
> Recalling its [previous relevant] resolutions . . .,
> Regretting that there has not been full compliance with the requirements of these resolutions,
> Determined to resolve the grave humanitarian situation in Kosovo . . . and to provide for the safe and free return of all refugees and displaced persons to their homes,
> . . .
> Welcoming the general principles on a political solution to the Kosovo crisis adopted on 6 May 1999 (S/1999/516, annex 1 to this resolution) and welcoming also the acceptance by the [FRY] of the principles set forth in points 1 to 9 of the paper presented in Belgrade on 2 June 1999 (S/1999/649, annex 2 to this resolution), and the [FRY's] agreement to that paper,
> . . .
> Determining that the situation in the region continues to constitute a threat to international peace and security,
> Determined to ensure the safety and security of international personnel and the implementation by all concerned of their responsibilities under the present resolution, and acting for these purposes under Chapter VII of the Charter of the United Nations,
> . . .
> 5. Decides on the deployment in Kosovo, under United Nations auspices, of international civil and security presences, with appropriate equipment and personnel as required, and welcomes the agreement of the [FRY] to such presences;
> 6. Requests the Secretary-General to appoint, in consultation with the Security Council, a Special Representative to control the implementation of the international civil presence, and further requests the Secretary-General to instruct his Special Representative to coordinate closely with the international security presence to ensure that both presences operate towards the same goals and in a mutually supportive manner;
> 7. Authorizes Member States and relevant international organizations to establish the international security presence in Kosovo as set out in point 4 of annex 2 with all necessary means to fulfil its responsibilities under paragraph 9 below;
> . . .
> 9. Decides that the responsibilities of the international security presence to be deployed and acting in Kosovo will include:
> . . .
> (e) Supervising de-mining until the international civil presence can, as appropriate, take over responsibility for this task;
> (f) Supporting, as appropriate, and coordinating closely with the work of the international civil presence;
> (g) Conducting border monitoring duties as required;
> . . .
> 10. Authorizes the Secretary-General, with the assistance of relevant international organizations, to establish an international civil presence in Kosovo in order to provide an interim administration for Kosovo under which the people of Kosovo can enjoy substantial autonomy within the [FRY],

> and which will provide transitional administration while establishing and overseeing the development of provisional democratic self-governing institutions to ensure conditions for a peaceful and normal life for all inhabitants of Kosovo;
> 11. Decides that the main responsibilities of the international civil presence will include: . . .
> (b) Performing basic civilian administrative functions where and as long as required;
> (c) Organizing and overseeing the development of provisional institutions for democratic and autonomous self-government pending a political settlement, including the holding of elections;
> (d) Transferring, as these institutions are established, its administrative responsibilities while overseeing and supporting the consolidation of Kosovo's local provisional institutions and other peace-building activities;
> . . .
> (i) Maintaining civil law and order, including establishing local police forces and meanwhile through the deployment of international police personnel to serve in Kosovo;
> (j) Protecting and promoting human rights;
> (k) Assuring the safe and unimpeded return of all refugees and displaced persons to their homes in Kosovo;
> . . .
> 19. Decides that the international civil and security presences are established for an initial period of 12 months, to continue thereafter unless the Security Council decides otherwise;
> 20. Requests the Secretary-General to report to the Council at regular intervals on the implementation of this resolution, including reports from the leaderships of the international civil and security presences, the first reports to be submitted within 30 days of the adoption of this resolution;
> 21. Decides to remain actively seized of the matter."

42. Annex 1 listed the general principles on a political solution to the Kosovo crisis adopted by the G-8 Foreign Ministers on 6 May 1999. Annex 2 comprised nine principles (guiding the resolution of the crisis presented in Belgrade on 2 June 1999 to which the FRY had agreed) including:

> ". . . 3. Deployment in Kosovo under [UN] auspices of effective international civil and security presences, acting as may be decided under Chapter VII of the Charter, capable of guaranteeing the achievement of common objectives.
> 4. The international security presence with substantial [NATO] participation must be deployed under unified command and control and authorized to establish a safe environment for all people in Kosovo and to facilitate the safe return to their homes of all displaced persons and refugees.
> 5. Establishment of an interim administration for Kosovo as a part of the international civil presence . . ., to be decided by the Security Council of the [UN]. The interim administration to provide transitional administration while establishing and overseeing the development of provisional democratic self-governing institutions to ensure conditions for a peaceful and normal life for all inhabitants in Kosovo. . . ."

43. While this Resolution used the term "authorise", that term and the term "delegation" are used interchangeably. Use of the term "delegation" in the present decision refers to the empowering by the UNSC of another entity to exercise its function as opposed to "authorising" an entity to carry out functions which it could not itself perform.

L. Detention and De-mining in Kosovo

1. Detention

51. A letter from COMKFOR to the OSCE of 6 September 2001 described how COMKFOR authorised detention: each case was reviewed by KFOR staff, the MNB commander and by a review panel at KFOR HQ, before being authorised by COMKFOR based on KFOR/OPS/FRAGO997 (superseded by COMKFOR Detention Directive 42 in October 2001).

2. De-mining

52. Landmines and unexploded ordinance (from the NATO bombardment of early 1999) posed a significant problem in post-conflict Kosovo, a problem exacerbated by the relative absence of local knowledge given the large scale displacement of the population during the conflict. The UN Mine Action Service (UNMAS) was the primary UN body charged with monitoring de-mining developments in general.

53. On 12 June 1999 the SG delivered his operational plan for the civil mission in Kosovo to the UNSC (Doc. No. S/1999/672). In outlining the structure of UNMIK, he noted that mine action was dealt with under humanitarian affairs (the former Pillar I of UNMIK) and that UNMIK had been tasked to establish, as soon as possible, a mine action centre. The UN Mine Action Coordination Centre ("UNMACC": used interchangeably with "UNMIK MACC") opened its office in Kosovo on 17 June 1999 and it was placed under the direction of the Deputy SRSG of Pillar I. Pending the transfer of responsibility for mine action to UNMACC, in accordance with the UNSC Resolution 1244, KFOR acted as the de facto coordination centre. The SG's detailed report on UNMIK of 12 July 1999 (Doc No. S/1999/779) confirmed that UNMACC would plan mine action activities and act as the point of coordination between the mine action partners including KFOR, UN agencies, NGOs and commercial companies".

54. On 24 August 1999 the Concept Plan for UNMIK Mine Action Programme ("MAP") was published in a document entitled "UNMIK MACC, Office of the Deputy SRSG (Humanitarian Affairs)". It confirmed that the UN, through UNMAS, the SRSG and the Deputy SRSG of Pillar I of UNMIK retained "overall responsibility" for the MAP in terms of providing policy guidance, identifying needs and priorities, coordinating with UN and non-UN partners as well as member states, and defining the overall operational plan and structure. The MAP was an "integral component of UNMIK". As to the role of UNMIK MACC, it was underlined that, since the UN did not intend to implement the mine action activities in Kosovo itself, it would rely on a variety of operators including UN agencies, KFOR contingents, NGOs and commercial companies. Those operators had to be accredited, supported and co-ordinated to ensure they worked in a coherent and integrated manner. Accordingly, a key factor in the execution of the MAP was the integration and coordination of all de-mining activities through an appropriately structured UNMIK MACC which would, inter alia, act as the "focal point and coordination mechanism for all mine activities in Kosovo". The Concept Plan went on to define the nature of the problem and the consequent phases and priorities for mine clearance.

55. Accordingly, on 24 August 1999 a memorandum was sent by the Deputy SRSG of Pillar I to the SRSG, requesting that, since the Concept Plan had been approved, it should also be forwarded to KFOR "along with an appropriate annotation that UNMIK have now assumed the responsibility for humanitarian mine action in Kosovo".

[...]

56. KFOR Directive on CBU Marking (KFOR/OPS/FRAGO 300) was adopted on 29 August 1999 and provided:

> "...KFOR will only clear mines/CBUs when deemed essential to the conduct of the mission and to maintain freedom of movement. KFOR does not wish to undertake de-mining, which is the responsibility of UNMACC and the NGOs. However, there is growing pressure for KFOR to dispose of NATO munitions. Therefore it has been decided that KFOR will do more to reduce the threat without amending its policy by marking the perimeter of each of the CBU footprints . . . MNBs are to conduct these tasks against a priority list co-ordinated with UNMACC and UNMIK regional offices. The intent is to mark all known areas by 10 October 1999".

57. On 5 October 1999 that Deputy SRSG wrote to COMKFOR noting paragraph 9(e) of UNSC Resolution 1244, attaching the Concept Plan, confirming that "we are now in a position to officially assume responsibility for mine action in Kosovo" and underlining the critical need for UNMIK and KFOR to co-operate and to work closely together.

58. The report of KFOR for July 1999 (submitted to the UNSC by the SG's letter of 10 August 1999) explained that KFOR worked closely with UNMAS and had "jointly established" UNMACC. The report continued:

> "Upon entry into Kosovo and prior to establishment of UNMACC, KFOR organized a Mines Action Centre, which has since been augmented by [UN] personnel and has now become UNMACC. This is now . . . charged by the [UN] with de-mining the region. It accomplishes this task using civilian contracted de-mining teams. KFOR is principally conducting mission-essential mine and unexploded ordnance clearance, including clearance of essential civilian infrastructure and public buildings."

KFOR's report for August 1999 (submitted to the UNSC by the SG's letter of 15 September 1999) confirmed that KFOR worked closely with UNMACC which had been "set up jointly" by KFOR and the UN. KFOR's subsequent monthly reports (submitted to the UNSC by the SG) noted that KFOR worked closely with UNMAS and UNMACC and emphasised that the eradication of the CBU threat was a priority for MNBs, the aim being to mark and clear as many areas as possible before the first snow (report Nos. S/1999/868, S/1999/982, S/1999/1062, S/1999/1185 and S/1999/1266).

59. By letter dated 6 April 2000 to COMKFOR, the Deputy SRSG drew the latter's attention to recent CBU explosions involving deaths and asked for the latter's personal support to ensure KFOR continued to support the mine clearance project by marking CBU sites as a matter of urgency and providing any further information they had.

60. In 2001 UNMAS commissioned an external evaluation of its mine action programme in Kosovo for the period mid-1999–2001. The report, entitled "An evaluation of the United Nations Mine Action Programme in Kosovo 1999-2001", commented as follows:

> "At the beginning of August 1999, the MACC had de facto taken full control of the mine action programme, although formally it still fell under KFOR's responsibility. . . . This was followed, on 24 August, by UNMIK's approval of the [Concept Plan]. . . . [which] coincided with a Memo being

sent by . . . DSRSG (24 August) to . . . SRSG . . . [T]hat request was followed up with a letter dated 5 October 1999 from [Deputy SRSG] to General Jackson, [COMKFOR], ... Through this letter the formal handing over from the military to the civilian sector of the mine action programme for Kosovo took place, as mandated in [UNSC Resolution] 1244; although, in reality, this had already taken place towards the end of August."

COMPLAINTS

61. Agim Behami complained under Article 2, on his own behalf and on behalf of his son Gadaf Behrami, about the latter's death and Bekir Behrami complained about his serious injury. They submitted that the incident took place because of the failure of French KFOR troops to mark and/or defuse the un-detonated CBUs which those troops knew to be present on that site.

62. Mr Saramati complained under Article 5 alone, and in conjunction with Article 13 of the Convention, about his extra-judicial detention by KFOR between 13 July 2001 and 26 January 2002. He also complained under Article 6 § 1 that he did not have access to court and about a breach of the respondent States' positive obligation to guarantee the Convention rights of those residing in Kosovo.

THE LAW

63. Messrs Behrami invoked Article 2 of the Convention as regards the impugned inaction of KFOR troops. Mr Saramati relied on Articles 5, 6 and 13 as regards his detention by, and on the orders of, KFOR. The President of the Court agreed that the parties' submissions to the Grand Chamber could be limited to the admissibility of the cases.

[...]

118. The UN outlined the respective mandates and responsibilities of UNMIK and KFOR as set out in UNSC Resolution 1244. The mandate adopted by the UNSC was an expression of the will of the member states to grant a UN organ authority, as opposed to a duty, to act: it was not an obligation of result. In executing the mandate, the UN operation retained, unless otherwise specified, discretion to determine implementation including timing and priorities. The UN recalled the relevant provisions of UNSC Resolution 1244 which outlined the main responsibilities of the civil and security presences, noting that the general and at time "imprecise" mandate was, for the most part, left to be concretised and agreed upon in the realities of their daily operations.

In addition, it was important to understand the legal status of UNMIK and its relationship to KFOR. UNMIK was a subsidiary organ of the UN endowed with all-inclusive legislative and administrative powers in Kosovo including the administration of justice (UNMIK Regulation 1999/1, at paragraph 70 above), it was headed by a SRSG and reported directing to the UNSC via the SG. KFOR was established as an equal presence but with a separate mandate and control structure: it was a NATO led operation authorised by the UNSC under unified command and control. There was no formal or hierarchical relationship between the two presences nor was the military in any way accountable to the civil presence. However, both were required to co-ordinate and operate in a mutually supportive manner towards the same goals.

119. As to de-mining in particular, paragraph 9(e) of UNSC Resolution 1244 (according responsibility for de-mining to KFOR but expressly leaving for determination by the two presences how that task would be transferred to UNMIK) and paragraph 11(k) (entrusting UNMIK with ensuring the safe and unimpeded return of persons to their homes) constituted the mandate for the UNMIK MAP. On 17 June 1999 UNMACC was established as the focal point and co-ordination mechanism for all mine action activities in Kosovo (the Concept Plan, paragraph 54 above). To fulfil these functions it depended largely on close co-operation with all de-mining partners and, notably, KFOR. Responsibility for de-mining was de facto assumed by UNMACC in August 1999 although it was not until October 1999 that UNMIK officially informed KFOR (letter from the Deputy SRSG at paragraph 57 above). However, this did not relieve KFOR of its residual and continuous responsibility to support de-mining activities and, in particular, to identify, mark and report on the location of CBU sites. KFOR's continuing responsibilities for de-mining activities were set out in the Concept Plan and, more particularly, in the NATO OPLAN 10413 (paragraph 3 above). One of KFOR's most important tasks was information sharing and marking strike sites. Indeed, according to FRAGO300 (paragraph 56 above), KFOR had decided to increase its commitment to CBU site marking. Accordingly, UNMIK's responsibility for demining was dependant on accurate information being available on locations and, since UNMACC was unaware of the location of the unmarked CBUs relevant to the present case, it took no action to de-mine.

120. In sum, while the de-mining operation would have fallen within UNMACCs mandate, in the absence of the necessary location information from KFOR, the impugned inaction could not be attributed to UNMIK.

121. The Court has adopted the following structure in its decision set out below. It has, in the first instance, established which entity, KFOR or UNMIK, had a mandate to detain and de-mine, the parties having disputed the latter point. Secondly, it has ascertained whether the impugned action of KFOR (detention in *Saramati*) and inaction of UNMIK (failure to de-mine in *Behrami*) could be attributed to the UN: in so doing, it has examined whether there was a Chapter VII framework for KFOR and UNMIK and, if so, whether their impugned action and omission could be attributed, in principle, to the UN. The Court has used the term "attribution" in the same way as the ILC in Article 3 of its draft Articles on the Responsibility of International Organisations (see paragraph 29 above). Thirdly, the Court has then examined whether it is competent *ratione personae* to review any such action or omission found to be attributable to the UN.

122. In so doing, the Court has borne in mind that it is not its role to seek to define authoritatively the meaning of provisions of the UN Charter and other international instruments: it must nevertheless examine whether there was a plausible basis in such instruments for the matters impugned before it (*mutatis mutandis*, *Brannigan and McBride v. the United Kingdom*, judgment of 26 May 1993, Series A no. 258-B, § 72).

It also recalls that the principles underlying the Convention cannot be interpreted and applied in a vacuum. It must also take into account relevant rules of international law when examining questions concerning its jurisdiction and, consequently, determine State responsibility in conformity and harmony with the governing principles of international law of which it forms part, although it must remain mindful of the Convention's special character as a human rights treaty (Article 31 § 3 (c) of the Vienna Convention on the Law of Treaties of 23 May 1969; *Al-Adsani v. the United Kingdom* [GC], no. 35763/97, § 55, ECHR 2001-XI; and the above-cited decision of *Banković and Others*, at § 57).

1. The entity with the mandate to detain and to de-mine
123. The respondent and third party States argued that it made no difference whether it was KFOR or UNMIK which had the mandate to detain (the *Saramati* case) and to de-mine (the *Behrami* case) since both were international structures established by, and answerable to, the UNSC. The applicants maintained that KFOR had the mandate to both detain and de-mine and that the nature and structure of KFOR was sufficiently different to UNMIK as to engage the respondent States individually.

124. Having regard to the MTA (notably paragraph 2 of Article 1), UNSC Resolution 1244 (paragraph 9 as well as paragraph 4 of Annex 2 to the Resolution) as confirmed by FRAGO997 and later COMKFOR Detention Directive 42 (see paragraph 51 above), the Court considers it evident that KFOR's security mandate included issuing detention orders.

125. As regards de-mining, the Court notes that Article 9(e) of UNSC Resolution 1244 provided that KFOR retained responsibility for supervising de-mining until UNMIK could take over, a provision supplemented by, as pointed out by the UN to the Court, Article 11(k) of the Resolution. The report of the SG to the UNSC of 12 June 1999 (paragraph 53 above) confirmed that this activity was a humanitarian one (former Pillar I of UNMIK) so UNMIK was to establish UNMACC pending which KFOR continued to act as the *de facto* coordination centre. When UNMACC began operations, it was therefore placed under the direction of the Deputy SRSG of Pillar I. The UN submissions to this Court, the above-cited Evaluation Report, the Concept Plan, FRAGO 300 and the letters of the Deputy SRSG of August and October 1999 to KFOR (paragraphs 55 and 57 above) confirm, in the first place, that the mandate for supervising demining was *de facto* and *de jure* taken over by UNMACC, created by UNMIK, at the very latest, by October 1999 and therefore prior to the detonation date in the *Behrami* case and, secondly, that KFOR remained involved in de-mining as a service provider whose personnel therefore acted on UNMIK's behalf.

126. The Court does not find persuasive the parties' arguments to the contrary. Whether, as noted by the applicants and the UN respectively, NATO had dropped the CBUs or KFOR had failed to secure the site and provide information thereon to UNMIK, this would not alter the mandate of UNMIK. The reports of the SG to the UNSC (53 above) cited by the applicants may have referred to UNMACC as having been set up jointly by KFOR and the UN, but this described the provision of assistance to UNMIK by the previous *de facto* co-ordination centre (KFOR): it was therefore transitional assistance which accorded with KFOR's general obligation to support UNMIK (paragraphs 6 and 9(f) of UNSC Resolution 1244) and such assistance in the field did not change UNMIK's mandate. The report of the International Committee of the Red Cross relied upon by the applicants, indicated (at p. 23) that mine clearance in Kosovo was coordinated by UNMACC which in turn fell under the aegis of UNMIK. Finally, even if KFOR support was, as a matter of fact, essential to the continued presence of UNMIK (the applicants' submission), this did not alter the fact that the Resolution created separate and distinct presences, with different mandates and responsibilities and, importantly, without any hierarchical relationship or accountability between them (UN submissions, paragraph 118 above).

127. Accordingly, the Court considers that issuing detention orders fell within the security mandate of KFOR and that the supervision of de-mining fell within UNMIK's mandate.

2. Can the impugned action and inaction be attributed to the UN?

(a) The Chapter VII foundation for KFOR and UNMIK

128. As the first step in the application of Chapter VII, the UNSC Resolution 1244 referred expressly to Chapter VII and made the necessary identification of a "threat to international peace and security" within the meaning of Article 39 of the Charter (paragraph 23 above). The UNSC Resolution 1244, *inter alia*, recalled the UNSC's "primary responsibility" for the "maintenance of international peace and security". Being "determined to resolve the grave humanitarian situation in Kosovo" and to "provide for the safe and free return of all refugees and displaced persons to their homes", it determined that the "situation in the region continues to constitute a threat to international peace and security" and, having expressly noted that it was acting under Chapter VII, it went on to set out the solutions found to the identified threat to peace and security.

129. The solution adopted by UNSC Resolution 1244 to this identified threat was, as noted above, the deployment of an international security force (KFOR) and the establishment of a civil administration (UNMIK).

In particular, that Resolution authorised "Member States and relevant international organisations" to establish the international security presence in Kosovo as set out in point 4 of Annex 2 to the Resolution with all necessary means to fulfil its responsibilities listed in Article 9. Point 4 of Annex 2 added that the security presence would have "substantial [NATO] participation" and had to be deployed under "unified command and control". The UNSC was thereby delegating to willing organisations and members states (see paragraph 43 as regards the meaning of the term "delegation" and paragraph 24 as regards the voluntary nature of this State contribution) the power to establish an international security presence as well as its operational command. Troops in that force would operate therefore on the basis of UN delegated, and not direct, command. In addition, the SG was authorised (Article 10) to establish UNMIK with the assistance of "relevant international organisations" and to appoint, in consultation with the UNSC, a SRSG to control its implementation (Articles 6 and 10 of the UNSC Resolution). The UNSC was thereby delegating civil administration powers to a UN subsidiary organ (UNMIK) established by the SG. Its broad mandate (an interim administration while establishing and overseeing the development of provisional self-government) was outlined in Article 11 of the Resolution.

130. While the Resolution referred to Chapter VII of the Charter, it did not identify the precise Articles of that Chapter under which the UNSC was acting and the Court notes that there are a number of possible bases in Chapter VII for this delegation by the UNSC: the non-exhaustive Article 42 (read in conjunction with the widely formulated Article 48), the non-exhaustive nature of Article 41 under which territorial administrations could be authorised as a necessary instrument for sustainable peace; or implied powers under the Charter for the UNSC to so act in both respects based on an effective interpretation of the Charter. In any event, the Court considers that Chapter VII provided a framework for the above-described delegation of the UNSC's security powers to KFOR and of its civil administration powers to UNMIK (see generally and *inter alia*, White and Ulgen, "*The Security Council and the Decentralised Military Option: Constitutionality and Function*", Netherlands Law Review 44, 1997, 386; Sarooshi, "*The United Nations and the Development of Collective Security: The Delegation by the UN Security Council of its Chapter VII powers*", Oxford University (1999); Chesterman, "*Just War or Just Peace: Humanitarian Intervention and International Law*", (2002) Oxford University Press, pp. 167-169 and 172); *Zimmermann and Stahn*, cited above; De Wet, "*The Chapter VII Powers of the United*

Nations Security Council", 2004, pp. 260-265; Wolfrum "*International Administration in Post-Conflict Situations by the United Nations and other International Actors*", Max Planck UNYB Vol. 9 (2005), pp. 667-672; Friedrich, "*UNMIK in Kosovo: struggling with Uncertainty*", Max Planck UNYB 9 (2005) and the references cited therein; and *Prosecutor v. Duško Tadić*, Decision of 2.10.95, Appeals Chamber of ICTY, §§ 35-36).

131. Whether or not the FRY was a UN member state at the relevant time (following the dissolution of the former Socialist Federal Republic of Yugoslavia), the FRY had agreed in the MTA to these presences. It is true that the MTA was signed by "KFOR" the day before the UNSC Resolution creating that force was adopted. However, the MTA was completed on the express basis of a security presence "under UN auspices" and with UN approval and the Resolution had already been introduced before the UNSC. The Resolution was adopted the following day, annexing the MTA and no international forces were deployed until the Resolution was adopted.

(b) Can the impugned action be attributed to KFOR?

132. While Chapter VII constituted the foundation for the above-described delegation of UNSC security powers, that delegation must be sufficiently limited so as to remain compatible with the degree of centralisation of UNSC collective security constitutionally necessary under the Charter and, more specifically, for the acts of the delegate entity to be attributable to the UN (as well as Chesterman, de Wet, Friedrich, Kolb and Sarooshi all cited above, see Gowlland-Debbas "*The Limits of Unilateral Enforcement of Community Objectives in the Framework of UN Peace Maintenance*" EIL (2000) Vol 11, No. 2 369-370; Niels Blokker, "*Is the authorisation Authorised? Powers and Practice of the UN Security Council to Authorise the Use of Force by "Coalition of the Able and Willing*", EJIL (2000), Vol. 11 No. 3; pp. 95-104 and *Meroni v. High Authority* Case 9/56, [1958] ECR 133).

Those limits strike a balance between the central security role of the UNSC and two realities of its implementation. In the first place, the absence of Article 43 agreements which means that the UNSC relies on States (notably its permanent members) and groups of States to provide the necessary military means to fulfil its collective security role. Secondly, the multilateral and complex nature of such security missions renders necessary some delegation of command.

133. The Court considers that the key question is whether the UNSC retained ultimate authority and control so that operational command only was delegated. This delegation model is now an established substitute for the Article 43 agreements never concluded.

134. That the UNSC retained such ultimate authority and control, in delegating its security powers by UNSC Resolution 1244, is borne out by the following factors.

In the first place, and as noted above, Chapter VII allowed the UNSC to delegate to "Member States and relevant international organisations". Secondly, the relevant power was a delegable power. Thirdly, that delegation was neither presumed nor implicit, but rather prior and explicit in the Resolution itself. Fourthly, the Resolution put sufficiently defined limits on the delegation by fixing the mandate with adequate precision as it set out the objectives to be attained, the roles and responsibilities accorded as well as the means to be employed. The broad nature of certain provisions (see the UN submissions, paragraph 118 above) could not be eliminated altogether given the constituent nature of such an instrument whose role was to fix broad objectives and goals and not to describe or interfere with the detail of operational implementation and choices. Fifthly, the leadership of the military presence

was required by the Resolution to report to the UNSC so as to allow the UNSC to exercise its overall authority and control (consistently, the UNSC was to remain actively seized of the matter, Article 21 of the Resolution). The requirement that the SG present the KFOR report to the UNSC was an added safeguard since the SG is considered to represent the general interests of the UN.
While the text of Article 19 of UNSC Resolution 1244 meant that a veto by one permanent member of the UNSC could prevent termination of the relevant delegation, the Court does not consider this factor alone sufficient to conclude that the UNSC did not retain ultimate authority and control.

135. Accordingly, UNSC Resolution 1244 gave rise to the following chain of command in the present cases. The UNSC was to retain ultimate authority and control over the security mission and it delegated to NATO (in consultation with non-NATO member states) the power to establish, as well as the operational command of, the international presence, KFOR. NATO fulfilled its command mission *via* a chain of command (from the NAC, to SHAPE, to SACEUR, to CIC South) to COMKFOR, the commander of KFOR. While the MNBs were commanded by an officer from a lead TCN, the latter was under the direct command of COMKFOR. MNB action was to be taken according to an operational plan devised by NATO and operated by COMKFOR in the name of KFOR.

[...]

140. Accordingly, even if the UN itself would accept that there is room for progress in cooperation and command structures between the UNSC, TCNs and contributing international organisations (see, for example, Supplement to an Agenda for Peace: Position paper of the SG on the Occasion of the 50th Anniversary of the UN, A/50/60 - S/1995/1; the *Brahami* report, cited above; UNSC Resolutions 1327 (2000) and 1353 (2001); and Reports of the SG of 1 June and 21 December 2001 on the Implementation of the Recommendations of the Special Committee on Peacekeeping Operations and the Panel on UN Peace Operations (A/55/977, A/56/732)), the Court finds that the UNSC retained ultimate authority and control and that effective command of the relevant operational matters was retained by NATO.

141. In such circumstances, the Court observes that KFOR was exercising lawfully delegated Chapter VII powers of the UNSC so that the impugned action was, in principle, "attributable" to the UN within the meaning of the word outlined at paragraphs 29 and 121 above.

(c) Can the impugned inaction be attributed to UNMIK?

142. In contrast to KFOR, UNMIK was a subsidiary organ of the UN. Whether it was a subsidiary organ of the SG or of the UNSC, whether it had a legal personality separate to the UN, whether the delegation of power by the UNSC to the SG and/or UNMIK also respected the role of the UNSC for which Article 24 of the Charter provided, UNMIK was a subsidiary organ of the UN institutionally directly and fully answerable to the UNSC (see ILC report at paragraph 33 above). While UNMIK comprised four pillars (three of which were at the time led by UNHCR, the OSCE and the EU), each pillar was under the authority of a Deputy SRSG, who reported to the SRSG who in turn reported to the UNSC (Article 20 of UNSC Resolution 1244).

143. Accordingly, the Court notes that UNMIK was a subsidiary organ of the UN created under Chapter VII of the Charter so that the impugned inaction was, in principle, "attributable" to the UN in the same sense.

3. Is the Court competent ratione personae?

144. It is therefore the case that the impugned action and inaction are, in principle, attributable to the UN. It is, moreover, clear that the UN has a legal personality separate from that of its member states (*The Reparations case*, ICJ Reports 1949) and that that organisation is not a Contracting Party to the Convention.

145. In its *Bosphorus* judgment (cited above, §§152-153), the Court held that, while a State was not prohibited by the Convention from transferring sovereign power to an international organisation in order to pursue cooperation in certain fields of activity, the State remained responsible under Article 1 of the Convention for all acts and omissions of its organs, regardless of whether they were a consequence of the necessity to comply with international legal obligations, Article 1 making no distinction as to the rule or measure concerned and not excluding any part of a State's "jurisdiction" from scrutiny under the Convention. The Court went on, however, to hold that where such State action was taken in compliance with international legal obligations flowing from its membership of an international organisation and where the relevant organisation protected fundamental rights in a manner which could be considered at least equivalent to that which the Convention provides, a presumption arose that the State had not departed from the requirements of the Convention. Such presumption could be rebutted, if in the circumstances of a particular case, it was considered that the protection of Convention rights was manifestly deficient: in such a case, the interest of international cooperation would be outweighed by the Convention's role as a "constitutional instrument of European public order" in the field of human rights (*ibid.*, §§ 155-156).

146. The question arises in the present case whether the Court is competent *ratione personae* to review the acts of the respondent States carried out on behalf of the UN and, more generally, as to the relationship between the Convention and the UN acting under Chapter VII of its Charter.

147. The Court first observes that nine of the twelve original signatory parties to the Convention in 1950 had been members of the UN since 1945 (including the two Respondent States), that the great majority of the current Contracting Parties joined the UN before they signed the Convention and that currently all Contracting Parties are members of the UN. Indeed, one of the aims of this Convention (see its preamble) is the collective enforcement of rights in the Universal Declaration of Human Rights of the General Assembly of the UN. More generally, it is further recalled, as noted at paragraph 122 above, that the Convention has to be interpreted in the light of any relevant rules and principles of international law applicable in relations between its Contracting Parties. The Court has therefore had regard to two complementary provisions of the Charter, Articles 25 and 103, as interpreted by the International Court of Justice (see paragraph 27 above).

148. Of even greater significance is the imperative nature of the principle aim of the UN and, consequently, of the powers accorded to the UNSC under Chapter VII to fulfil that aim. In particular, it is evident from the Preamble, Articles 1, 2 and 24 as well as Chapter VII of the Charter that the primary objective of the UN is the maintenance of international peace and security. While it is equally clear that ensuring respect for human rights represents an important contribution to achieving international peace (see the Preamble to the Convention), the fact remains that the UNSC has primary responsibility, as well as extensive means under Chapter VII, to fulfil this objective, notably through the use of coercive measures. The responsibility of the UNSC in this respect is unique and has evolved as a counterpart

to the prohibition, now customary international law, on the unilateral use of force (see paragraphs 18-20 above).

149. In the present case, Chapter VII allowed the UNSC to adopt coercive measures in reaction to an identified conflict considered to threaten peace, namely UNSC Resolution 1244 establishing UNMIK and KFOR.

Since operations established by UNSC Resolutions under Chapter VII of the UN Charter are fundamental to the mission of the UN to secure international peace and security and since they rely for their effectiveness on support from member states, the Convention cannot be interpreted in a manner which would subject the acts and omissions of Contracting Parties which are covered by UNSC Resolutions and occur prior to or in the course of such missions, to the scrutiny of the Court. To do so would be to interfere with the fulfilment of the UN's key mission in this field including, as argued by certain parties, with the effective conduct of its operations. It would also be tantamount to imposing conditions on the implementation of a UNSC Resolution which were not provided for in the text of the Resolution itself. This reasoning equally applies to voluntary acts of the respondent States such as the vote of a permanent member of the UNSC in favour of the relevant Chapter VII Resolution and the contribution of troops to the security mission: such acts may not have amounted to obligations flowing from membership of the UN but they remained crucial to the effective fulfilment by the UNSC of its Chapter VII mandate and, consequently, by the UN of its imperative peace and security aim.

150. The applicants argued that the substantive and procedural protection of fundamental rights provided by KFOR was in any event not "equivalent" to that under the Convention within the meaning of the Court's *Bosphorus* judgment, with the consequence that the presumption of Convention compliance on the part of the respondent States was rebutted.

151. The Court, however, considers that the circumstances of the present cases are essentially different from those with which the Court was concerned in the *Bosphorus* case. In its judgment in that case, the Court noted that the impugned act (seizure of the applicant's leased aircraft) had been carried out by the respondent State authorities, on its territory and following a decision by one of its Ministers (§ 135 of that judgment). The Court did not therefore consider that any question arose as to its competence, notably *ratione personae*, vis-a-vis the respondent State despite the fact that the source of the impugned seizure was an EC Council Regulation which, in turn, applied a UNSC Resolution. In the present cases, the impugned acts and omissions of KFOR and UNMIK cannot be attributed to the respondent States and, moreover, did not take place on the territory of those States or by virtue of a decision of their authorities. The present cases are therefore clearly distinguishable from the *Bosphorus* case in terms both of the responsibility of the respondent States under Article 1 and of the Court's competence *ratione personae*.

There exists, in any event, a fundamental distinction between the nature of the international organisation and of the international cooperation with which the Court was there concerned and those in the present cases. As the Court has found above, UNMIK was a subsidiary organ of the UN created under Chapter VII and KFOR was exercising powers lawfully delegated under Chapter VII of the Charter by the UNSC. As such, their actions were directly attributable to the UN, an organisation of universal jurisdiction fulfilling its imperative collective security objective.

152. In these circumstances, the Court concludes that the applicants' complaints must be declared incompatible *ratione personae* with the provisions of the Convention.

Al-Jedda v. The United Kingdom, Judgment of the Grand Chamber of the European Court of Human Rights, 7 July 2011 (Application No. 27021/08)

[*Note:*

The application was lodged to the European Court of Human Rights by a joint Iraqi/British national, Mr. Hilal Abdul-Razzaq Alli Al-Jedda, in June 2008. He complained that his detention by British troops in Iraq in the period from 2004-2007 was in violation of Article 5 (1) of the European Convention on Human Rights.]

11. The applicant was held on the basis that his internment was necessary for imperative reasons of security in Iraq. He was believed by the British authorities to have been personally responsible for recruiting terrorists outside Iraq with a view to the commission of atrocities there; for facilitating the travel into Iraq of an identified terrorist explosives expert; for conspiring with that explosives expert to conduct attacks with improvised explosive devices against coalition forces in the areas around Fallujah and Baghdad; and for conspiring with the explosives expert and members of an Islamist terrorist cell in the Gulf to smuggle high tech detonation equipment into Iraq for use in attacks against coalition forces. No criminal charges were brought against him.

12. The applicant's internment was initially authorised by the senior officer in the detention facility. Reviews were conducted seven days and twenty-eight days later by the Divisional Internment Review Committee ("the DIRC"). This comprised the senior officer in the detention facility and Army legal and military personnel. Owing to the sensitivity of the intelligence material upon which the applicant's arrest and detention had been based, only two members of the DIRC were permitted to examine it. Their recommendations were passed to the Commander of the Coalition's Multinational Division (South East) ("the Commander"), who himself examined the intelligence file on the applicant and took the decision to continue the internment. Between January and July 2005 a monthly review was carried out by the Commander, on the basis of the recommendations of the DIRC. Between July 2005 and December 2007 the decision to intern was taken by the DIRC itself, which during this period included as members the Commander together with members of the legal, intelligence and other staffs. There was no procedure for disclosure of evidence nor for an oral hearing, but representations could be made by the internee in writing which were considered by the legal branch and put before the DIRC for consideration. The two Commanders who authorised the applicant's internment in 2005 and 2006 gave evidence to the domestic courts that there was a substantial weight of intelligence material indicating that there were reasonable grounds for suspecting the applicant of the matters alleged against him.

13. When the applicant had been detained 18 months, the internment fell to be reviewed by the Joint Detention Committee (JDC). This body included senior representatives of the Multi-National Force, the Iraqi Interim Government and the Ambassador for the United Kingdom. It met once and thereafter delegated powers to a Joint Detention Review Committee, which comprised Iraqi representatives and officers from the Multi-National Force.

14. On 14 December 2007 the Secretary of State signed an order depriving the applicant of British citizenship, on the ground that it was conducive to the public good. The Secretary of State claimed, *inter alia*, that the applicant had connections with violent Islamist groups, in Iraq and elsewhere, and had been responsible for recruiting terrorists outside Iraq and facilitating their travel and the smuggling of bomb parts into Iraq.

15. The applicant was released from internment on 30 December 2007 and travelled to Turkey. He appealed against the deprivation of British citizenship. On 7 April 2009 the Special Immigration Appeals Commission dismissed the appeal, having heard both open and closed evidence, during a hearing where the applicant was represented by special advocates (see further *A. and Others v. the United Kingdom* [GC], no. 3455/05, §§ 91-93, ECHR 2009-...). The Special Immigration Appeals Commission held that, for reasons set out in detail in a closed judgment, it was satisfied on the balance of probabilities that the Secretary of State had proved that the applicant had facilitated the travel to Iraq of a terrorist explosives expert and conspired with him to smuggle explosives into Iraq and to conduct improvised explosives device attacks against coalition forces around Fallujah and Baghdad. The applicant did not appeal against the judgment.

4 AL-JEDDA v. THE UNITED KINGDOM JUDGMENT

[...]

THE LAW

I. ALLEGED VIOLATION OF ARTICLE 5 § 1 OF THE CONVENTION

59. The applicant complained that he was held in internment by United Kingdom armed forces in Iraq between 10 October 2004 and 30 December 2007, in breach of Article 5 § 1 of the Convention. He did not pursue before the Court his complaint under Article 5 § 4 of the Convention, concerning the lack of judicial review of the detention, since proceedings on this issue were still pending before the domestic courts at the time the application was lodged (see paragraphs 23-24 above).

60. The Government contended that the internment was attributable to the United Nations and not to the United Kingdom, and that the applicant was not, therefore, within United Kingdom jurisdiction under Article 1 of the Convention. Further and in the alternative they submitted that the internment was carried out pursuant to United Nations Security Council Resolution 1546, which created an obligation on the United Kingdom to detain the applicant which, pursuant to Article 103 of the United Nations Charter, overrode obligations under the Convention.

[...]

(b) The Court's assessment

74. Article 1 of the Convention reads as follows:

> "The High Contracting Parties shall secure to everyone within their jurisdiction the rights and freedoms defined in Section I of [the] Convention."

As provided by this Article, the engagement undertaken by a Contracting State is confined to "securing" ("*reconnaître*" in the French text) the listed rights and freedoms to persons within its own "jurisdiction" (see *Soering v. the United Kingdom*, 7 July 1989, § 89, Series A no. 161; *Banković*, cited above, § 66). "Jurisdiction" under Article 1 is a threshold criterion. The exercise of jurisdiction is a necessary condition for a Contracting State to be able to be held responsible for acts or omissions imputable to it which give rise to an allegation of the infringement of rights and freedoms set forth in the Convention (see *Ilaşcu and Others v. Moldova and Russia* [GC], no. 48787/99, § 311, ECHR 2004-VII).

75. The Court notes that, before the Divisional Court and the Court of Appeal in the first set of domestic proceedings brought by the applicant, the Government accepted that he fell within United Kingdom jurisdiction under Article 1 of the Convention during his detention in a British-run military prison in Basrah, South East Iraq. It was only before the House of Lords that the Government argued, for the first time, that the applicant did not fall within United Kingdom jurisdiction because his detention was attributable to the United Nations rather than to the United Kingdom. The majority of the House of Lords rejected the Government's argument and held that the internment was attributable to British forces (see paragraphs 16-18 above).

76. When examining whether the applicant's detention was attributable to the United Kingdom or, as the Government submit, the United Nations, it is necessary to examine the particular facts of the case. These include the terms of the United Nations Security Council Resolutions which formed the framework for the security regime in Iraq during the period in question. In performing this exercise, the Court is mindful of the fact that it is not its role to seek to define authoritatively the meaning of provisions of the United Nations Charter and other international instruments. It must, nevertheless, examine whether there was a plausible basis in such instruments for the matters impugned before it (see *Behrami and Saramati*, cited above, § 122). The principles underlying the Convention cannot be interpreted and applied in a vacuum and the Court must take into account relevant rules of international law (ibid.). It relies for guidance in this exercise on the statement of the International Court of Justice in § 114 of its advisory opinion "*Legal consequences for States of the continued presence of South Africa in Namibia*" (see paragraph 49 above), indicating that a Security Council resolution should be interpreted in the light not only of the language used but also the context in which it was adopted.

77. The Court takes as its starting point that, on 20 March 2003, the United Kingdom together with the United States of America and their coalition partners, through their armed forces, entered Iraq with the aim of displacing the Ba'ath regime then in power. At the time of the invasion, there was no United Nations Security Council resolution providing for the allocation of roles in Iraq in the event that the existing regime was displaced. Major combat operations were declared to be complete by 1 May 2003 and the United States and the United Kingdom became Occupying Powers within the meaning of Article 42 of the Hague Regulations (see paragraph 42 above). As explained in the letter dated 8 May 2003 sent jointly by the Permanent Representatives of the United Kingdom and the United States to the President of the United Nations Security Council (see paragraph 27 above), the United States and the United Kingdom, having displaced the previous regime, created the Coalition Provisional Authority "to exercise powers of government temporarily". One of the powers of government specifically referred to in the letter of 8 May 2003 to be exercised by the United States and the United Kingdom through the Coalition Provisional Authority was the provision of security in Iraq.

The letter further stated that "The United States, the United Kingdom and Coalition partners, working through the Coalition Provisional Authority, shall *inter alia*, provide for security in and for the provisional administration of Iraq, including by ... assuming immediate control of Iraqi institutions responsible for military and security matters". The letter acknowledged that the United Nations had "a vital role to play in providing humanitarian relief, in supporting the reconstruction of Iraq, and in helping in the formation of an Iraqi interim authority" and stated that the United States, the United Kingdom and Coalition partners were ready to work closely with representatives of the United Nations and its specialized agencies and would also welcome the support and contributions of Member States, international and regional organizations, and other entities, "under appropriate coordination arrangements with the Coalition Provisional Authority". In its first legislative act, CPA Regulation No. 1 of 16 May 2003, the Coalition Provisional Authority declared that it would "exercise powers of government temporarily in order to provide for the effective administration of Iraq during the period of transitional administration, to restore conditions of security and stability..." (see paragraph 28 above).

78. The first Security Council resolution after the invasion was Resolution 1483, adopted on 22 May 2003 (see paragraph 29 above). In the preamble, the Security Council noted the letter of 8 May 2003 from the Permanent Representatives of the United States and the United Kingdom and recognised that the United States and the United Kingdom were Occupying Powers in Iraq, under unified command (the Coalition Provisional Authority), and that specific authorities, responsibilities, and obligations applied to them under international humanitarian law. The Security Council noted further that other States that were not Occupying Powers were working or might in the future work under the Coalition Provisional Authority, and welcomed the willingness of Member States to contribute to stability and security in Iraq by contributing personnel, equipment, and other resources "under the Authority". Acting under Chapter VII of the United Nations Charter, the Security Council called upon the Occupying Powers, through the Coalition Provisional Authority, "to promote the welfare of the Iraqi people through the effective administration of the territory, including in particular working towards the restoration of conditions of security and stability ...". The United Kingdom and United States were encouraged "to inform the Council at regular intervals of their efforts under this resolution". The preamble to Resolution 1483 recognised that the United Nations was to "play a vital role in humanitarian relief, the reconstruction of Iraq and the restoration and establishment of national and local institutions for representative governance". The Secretary-General was requested to appoint a Special Representative for Iraq, whose independent responsibilities were to include, *inter alia*, reporting regularly to the Security Council on his activities under this resolution, coordinating activities of the United Nations in post-conflict processes in Iraq and coordinating among United Nations and international agencies engaged in humanitarian assistance and reconstruction activities in Iraq. Resolution 1483 did not assign any security role to the United Nations. The Government does not contend that, at this stage in the invasion and occupation, the acts of its armed forces were in any way attributable to the United Nations.

79. In Resolution 1511, adopted on 16 October 2003, the United Nations Security Council, again acting under Chapter VII, underscored the temporary nature of the exercise by the Coalition Provisional Authority of the authorities and responsibilities set out in Resolution 1483, which would cease as soon as an internationally recognised, representative Iraqi government could be sworn in. In paragraphs 13 and 14, the Security Council authorised "a multinational force under unified command to take all necessary measures to contribute to the maintenance of security and stability in Iraq" and urged Member States "to contribute assistance under this United Nations mandate, including military forces, to the multinational force referred to in paragraph 13" (see paragraph 31 above). The United States, on behalf of the multinational force, was requested periodically to report on the efforts and progress of the force.

The Security Council also resolved that the United Nations, acting through the Secretary General, his Special Representative, and the United Nations Assistance Mission in Iraq, should strengthen its role in Iraq, including by providing humanitarian relief, promoting the economic reconstruction of and conditions for sustainable development in Iraq, and advancing efforts to restore and establish national and local institutions for representative government.

80. The Court does not consider that, as a result of the authorisation contained in Resolution 1511, the acts of soldiers within the Multi-National Force became attributable to the United Nations or – more importantly, for the purposes of this case – ceased to be attributable to the troop-contributing nations. The Multi- National Force had been present in Iraq since the invasion and had been recognised already in Resolution 1483, which welcomed the willingness of Member States to contribute personnel. The unified command structure over the force, established from the start of the invasion by the United States and United Kingdom, was not changed as a result of Resolution 1511. Moreover, the United States and the United Kingdom, through the Coalition Provisional Authority which they had established at the start of the occupation, continued to exercise the powers of government in Iraq. Although the United States was requested to report periodically to the Security Council about the activities of the Multi-National Force, the United Nations did not, thereby, assume any degree of control over either the force or any other of the executive functions of the Coalition Provisional Authority.

81. The final resolution of relevance to the present issue was no. 1546 (see paragraph 35 above). It was adopted on 8 June 2004, twenty days before the transfer of power from the Coalition Provisional Authority to Interim Government and some four months before the applicant was taken into detention. Annexed to the resolution was a letter from the Prime Minister of the Interim Government of Iraq, seeking from the Security Council a new resolution on the Multi-National Force mandate. There was also annexed a letter from the United States Secretary of State to the President of the United Nations Security Council, confirming that "the Multi-National Force [under unified command] is prepared to continue to contribute to the maintenance of security in Iraq" and informing the President of the Security Council of the goals of the Multi-National Force and the steps which its Commander intended to take to achieve those goals. It does not appear from the terms of this letter that the Secretary of State considered that the United Nations controlled the deployment or conduct of the Multi-National Force. In Resolution 1546 the Security Council, acting under Chapter VII, reaffirmed the authorisation for the Multi-National Force established under Resolution 1511. There is no indication in Resolution 1546 that the Security Council intended to assume any greater degree of control or command over the Multi-National Force than it had exercised previously.

82. The Security Council in Resolution 1546 also decided that, in implementing their mandates in Iraq, the Special Representative of the Secretary General and the United Nations Assistance Mission for Iraq (UNAMI) should play leading roles in assisting in the establishment of democratic institutions, economic development and humanitarian assistance. The Court notes that the Secretary General and UNAMI, both clearly organs of the United Nations, in their quarterly and bi-monthly reports to the Security Council for the period during which the applicant was detained, repeatedly protested about the extent to which security internment was being used by the Multi-National Force (see paragraphs 40 and 41 above). It is difficult to conceive that the applicant's detention was attributable to the United Nations and not to the United Kingdom when United Nations organs, operating under the mandate of Resolution 1546, did not appear to approve of the practice of indefinite internment without trial and, in the case of UNAMI, entered into correspondence with the United States Embassy in an attempt to persuade the Multi-National Force under American command to modify the internment procedure.

83. In the light of the foregoing, the Court agrees with the majority of the House of Lords that the United Nations' role as regards security in Iraq in 2004 was quite different from its role as regards security in Kosovo in 1999. The comparison is relevant, since in the decision in *Behrami and Saramati* (cited above) the Court concluded, *inter alia*, that Mr Saramati's detention was attributable to the United Nations and not to any of the respondent States. It is to be recalled that the international security presence in Kosovo was established by United Nations Security Council Resolution 1244 (10 June 1999) in which, "determined to resolve the grave humanitarian situation in Kosovo", the Security Council "decide[d] on the deployment in Kosovo, under United Nations auspices, of international civil and security presences". The Security Council therefore authorised "Member States and relevant international organizations to establish the international security presence in Kosovo" and directed that there should be "substantial North Atlantic Treaty Organization participation" in the force, which "must be deployed under unified command and control". In addition, United Nations Security Council Resolution 1244 authorised the Secretary General of the United Nations to establish an international civil presence in Kosovo in order to provide an interim administration for Kosovo. The United Nations, through a Special Representative appointed by the Secretary General in consultation with the Security Council, was to control the implementation of the international civil presence and coordinate closely with the international security presence (see Behrami and Saramati, cited above, §§ 3, 4 and 41). On 12 June 1999, two days after the Resolution was adopted, the first elements of the NATO-led Kosovo Force (KFOR) entered Kosovo.

84. It would appear from the opinion of Lord Bingham in the first set of proceedings brought by the applicant that it was common ground between the parties before the House of Lords that the test to be applied in order to establish attribution was that set out by the International Law Commission, in Article 5 of its draft Articles on the Responsibility of International Organisations and in its commentary thereon, namely that the conduct of an organ of a State placed at the disposal of an international organisation should be attributable under international law to that organisation if the organisation exercises effective control over that conduct (see paragraphs 18 and 56 above). For the reasons set out above, the Court considers that the United Nations Security Council had neither effective control nor ultimate authority and control over the acts and omissions of troops within the Multi-National Force and that the applicant's detention was not, therefore, attributable to the United Nations.

85. The internment took place within a detention facility in Basrah City, controlled exclusively by British forces, and the applicant was therefore within the authority and control of the United Kingdom throughout (see paragraph 10 above; see also *Al-Skeini and Others v. the United Kingdom* [GC], no. 55721/07, § 136 and *Al-Saadoon and Mufdhi v. the United Kingdom* (dec.), no. 61498/08, § 88, ECHR 2010-...; see also the judgment of the United States Supreme Court in *Munaf v. Geren*, paragraph 54 above). The decision to hold the applicant in internment was made by the British officer in command of the detention facility. Although the decision to continue holding the applicant in internment was, at various points, reviewed by committees including Iraqi officials and non-United Kingdom representatives from the Multi-National Force, the Court does not consider that the existence of these reviews operated to prevent the detention from being attributable to the United Kingdom.

86. In conclusion, the Court agrees with the majority of the House of Lords that the internment of the applicant was attributable to the United Kingdom and that during his internment the applicant fell within the jurisdiction of the United Kingdom for the purposes of Article 1 of the Convention.

European Court of Justice

Yassin Abdullah Kadi and Al Barakaat International Foundation v. Council, Judgment of the European Court of Justice (Grand Chamber), 18 July 2013

[*Note:*

Yassin Abdullah Kadi and Al Barakaat International Foundation appealed against the judgments of the Court of First Instance of the European Communities by which the Court rejected the actions brought by the appellants against Council Regulation (EC) No. 881/2002 of 27 May 2002 "imposing certain specific restrictive measures directed against certain persons and entities associated with Usama bin-Laden, the Al-Qaeda network and the Taliban.]

1 JUDGMENT OF THE COURT (Grand Chamber)

18 July 2013 (*)

[...]

THE COURT (Grand Chamber),

composed of V. Skouris, President, K. Lenaerts (Rapporteur), Vice-President, M. Ilešič, L. Bay Larsen, T. von Danwitz and M. Berger, Presidents of Chambers, U. Lohmus, E. Levits, A. Arabadjiev, C. Toader, J.-J. Kasel, M. Safjan and D. Švaby, Judges,

Advocate General: Y. Bot,

Registrar: A. Impellizzeri, Administrator,

having regard to the written procedure and further to the hearing on 16 October 2012, after hearing the Opinion of the Advocate General at the sitting on 19 March 2013, gives the following

Judgment

1 By their appeals, the European Commission, the Council of the European Union and the United Kingdom of Great Britain and Northern Ireland seek to have set aside the judgment of the General Court of the European Union of 30 September 2010 in Case T-85/09 *Kadi v Commission* [2010] ECR II-5177 ('the judgment under appeal'), by which that Court annulled Commission Regulation (EC) No 1190/2008 of 28 November 2008 amending for the 101st time Council Regulation (EC) No 881/2002 imposing certain specific restrictive measures directed against certain persons and entities associated with Usama bin Laden, the Al-Qaeda network and the Taliban (OJ 2008 L 322, p. 25; 'the contested regulation'), in so far as that measure concerns Mr Kadi.

[...]

Background to the proceedings

The case which gave rise to the Kadi judgment

16. On 17 October 2001 Mr Kadi, identified as being an individual associated with Usama bin Laden and the Al-Qaeda network, was listed on the Sanctions Committee Consolidated List.

17. Mr Kadi's name was subsequently added to the list in Annex I to Council Regulation (EC) No 467/2001 of 6 March 2001 prohibiting the export of certain goods and services to Afghanistan, strengthening the flight ban and extending the freeze of funds and other financial resources in respect of the Taliban of Afghanistan, and repealing Regulation No 337/2000 (OJ 2001 L 67, p. 1), by Commission Regulation (EC) No 2062/2001 of 19 October 2001 amending, for the third time, Regulation No 467/2001 (OJ 2001 L 277, p. 25). He was subsequently listed in Annex I to Council Regulation (EC) No 881/2002 of 27 May 2002 imposing certain specific restrictive measures directed against certain persons and entities associated with Usama bin Laden, the Al-Qaeda network and the Taliban, and repealing Regulation No 467/2001 (OJ 2002 L 139, p. 9).

18. On 18 December 2001 Mr Kadi brought before the General Court an action seeking the annulment, initially, of Regulations No 467/2001 and No 2062/2001, then of Regulation No 881/2002, in so far as those regulations concerned him. The grounds for annulment were, respectively, infringement of the right to be heard, the right to respect for property and the principle of proportionality, and also of the right to effective judicial review.

19. By judgment of 21 September 2005 in Case T-315/01 *Kadi v Council and Commission* [2005] ECR II-3649, the General Court dismissed that action. In essence, the General Court held that it followed from the principles governing the relationship between the international legal order under the United Nations and the European Union legal order that Regulation No 881/2002, being designed to implement a Security Council resolution leaving no latitude in that regard, could not be the subject of judicial review of its internal lawfulness and thus enjoyed immunity from jurisdiction, except as regards its compatibility with rules falling within the ambit of *jus cogens*, understood as a body of rules of public international law binding on all subjects of international law, including the bodies of the UN, and from which no derogation is possible.

20. Accordingly, the General Court, applying the standard of universal protection of the fundamental rights of the human person covered by *jus cogens*, ruled out, in the given case, any infringement of the rights relied on by Mr Kadi. As regards, in particular, the right to effective judicial review, the General Court stated that it was not for it to review indirectly whether Security Council Resolutions are compatible with such fundamental rights as are protected by the European Union legal order, nor to verify that there had been no error of assessment of the facts and evidence relied on by the Security Council in support of the measures it had taken, nor, again, to review indirectly the appropriateness and proportionality of those measures. The General Court added that any such lacuna in the judicial protection available to Mr Kadi is not in itself contrary to *jus cogens*.

21. By its judgment of 3 September 2008 in Joined Cases C-402/05 P and C-415/05 P *Kadi and Al Barakaat International Foundation v Council and Commission* [2008] ECR I-6351 ('the Kadi judgment'), the Court set aside the judgment of the General Court in Case T-315/01 *Kadi v Council and Commission* and annulled Regulation No 881/2002 in so far as it concerned Mr Kadi.

22. In essence, the Court held that the obligations imposed by an international agreement cannot have the effect of prejudicing the constitutional principles of the EC Treaty, which include the principle that all European Union acts must respect fundamental rights, that respect constituting a condition of their lawfulness which it is for the Court to review in the framework of the complete system of legal remedies established by that treaty. The Court held further that, notwithstanding the fact that undertakings given in the UN context must be observed when implementing Security Council resolutions, it does not follow from the principles governing the international legal order under the United Nations that an act adopted by the European Union such as Regulation No 881/2002 thereby enjoys immunity from jurisdiction. The Court added that there is no basis for such immunity in the EC Treaty.

23. In those circumstances the Court held, in paragraphs 326 and 327 of the *Kadi* judgment, that the Courts of the European Union must ensure the review, in principle the full review, of the lawfulness of all European Union acts in the light of fundamental rights, including where such acts are designed to implement Security Council resolutions, and that the General Court's reasoning was consequently vitiated by an error of law.

24. Ruling on the action brought by Mr Kadi before the General Court, the Court held, in paragraphs 336 to 341 of the Kadi judgment, that the effectiveness of judicial review means that the competent European Union authority is bound to communicate the grounds for the contested listing decision to the person concerned and to provide that person with the opportunity to be heard in that regard. The Court stated that, as regards a decision that a person's name should be listed for the first time, for reasons connected with the effectiveness of the restrictive measures at issue and with the objective of the regulation concerned, it was necessary that that disclosure and that hearing should occur not prior to the adoption of that decision but when that decision was adopted or as swiftly as possible thereafter.

25. In paragraphs 345 to 349 of the *Kadi* judgment, the Court added that, since the Council had neither communicated to Mr Kadi the evidence relied on against him to justify the restrictive measures imposed on him nor afforded him the right to be informed of that evidence within a reasonable period after those measures were enacted, Mr Kadi had not been in a position effectively to make known his point of view in that regard, with the consequence that the rights of defence and the right to effective judicial review had been infringed. The Court also stated, in paragraph 350 of that judgment, that that infringement had not been remedied before the Courts of the European Union, given that the Council had not adduced before them any such evidence. In paragraphs 369 to 371 of that judgment, the Court concluded, on the same grounds, that Mr Kadi's fundamental right to respect for property had been infringed.

26. The effects of the annulled regulation in so far as it concerned Mr Kadi were maintained for a maximum period of three months in order to allow the Council to remedy the infringements found.

The response of the European Union institutions to the Kadi judgment and the contested regulation

27. On 21 October 2008 the Chairman of the Sanctions Committee communicated the narrative summary of reasons for Mr Kadi's listing on that committee's Consolidated List to France's Permanent Representative to the UN, and authorised its transmission to Mr Kadi.

28. That summary of reasons is worded as follows:

> 'The individual Yasin Abdullah Ezzedine Qadi ... satisfies the standard for listing by the [Sanctions Committee] because of his actions in (a) participating in the financing, planning, facilitating, preparing, or perpetrating of acts or activities by, in conjunction with, under the name of, on behalf of, or in support of; (b) supplying, selling, or transferring arms and related material to; (c) recruiting for; or (d) otherwise supporting acts or activities of; Al-Qaeda, Usama bin Laden or the Taliban, or any cell, affiliate, splinter group or derivative thereof (see United Nations Security Council Resolution 1822 (2008), paragraph 2).

Mr Qadi has acknowledged that he is a founding trustee and directed the actions of the Muwafaq Foundation. The Muwafaq Foundation historically operated under the umbrella of Makhtab Al-Khidamat/Al Kifah (QE.M.12.01), an organisation founded by Mr Abdullah Azzam and Mr Usama Muhammed Awad bin Laden (QI.B.8.01), and the predecessor to Al-Qaeda (QE.A.4.01). Following the dissolution of Makhtab Al-Khidamat/Al Kifah in early June 2001 and its absorption into Al-Qaeda, a number of NGOs formerly associated with Makhtab Al-Khidamat/Al Kifah, including the Muwafaq Foundation, also joined with Al-Qaeda.

In 1992, Mr Qadi hired Mr Shafiq Ben Mohamed Ben Mohamed Al-Ayadi (QI.A.25.01) to head the European offices of the Muwafaq Foundation. During the mid-1990s, Mr Al-Ayadi also headed the Muwafaq Foundation branch in Bosnia and Herzegovina. Mr Qadi hired Mr Al-Ayadi on the recommendation of known Al-Qaeda financier Mr Wa'el Hamza Abd Al-Fatah Julaidan (QI.J.79.02), who fought with Mr bin Laden in Afghanistan in the 1980s. At the time of his appointment by Mr Qadi as the Muwafaq Foundation's European director, Mr Al-Ayadi was operating under agreements with Mr bin Laden. Mr Al-Ayadi was one of the principal leaders of the Tunisian Islamic Front, went to Afghanistan in the early 1990s to receive paramilitary training, and then went to Sudan with others to meet Mr bin Laden, with whom they concluded a formal agreement regarding the reception and training of Tunisians. They later met with Mr bin Laden a second time, securing an agreement for bin Laden collaborators in Bosnia and Herzegovina to receive Tunisian mujahidin from Italy.

In 1995, the leader of Al-Gama'at Al-Islamiya, Mr Talad Fuad Kassem, said that the Muwafaq Foundation had provided logistical and financial support for a mujahidin battalion in Bosnia and Herzegovina. In the mid-1990s, the Muwafaq Foundation was involved in providing financial support for terrorist activities of the mujahidin, as well as arms trafficking from Albania to Bosnia and Herzegovina. Some involvement in the financing of these activities was provided by Mr bin Laden.

Mr Qadi was also a major shareholder in the now closed Sarajevo-based Depositna Banka, in which Mr Al-Ayadi also held a position and acted as nominee for Mr Qadi's shares. Planning sessions for an attack against a United States facility in Saudi Arabia may have taken place at this bank.

Mr Qadi further owned several firms in Albania which funnelled money to extremists or employed extremists in positions where they controlled the firm's funds. Mr Bin Laden provided the working capital for four or five of Mr Qadi's companies in Albania.'

29. That summary of reasons was also published on the website of the Sanctions Committee.

30. On 22 October 2008 France's Permanent Representative to the European Union transmitted that summary of reasons to the Commission, which sent it to Mr Kadi on the same day, informing him that, for the reasons set out in that summary, it envisaged maintaining his listing in Annex I to Regulation No 881/2002. The Commission gave Mr Kadi until 10 November 2008 to comment on those reasons and to provide it with any information that he might consider relevant before it took its final decision.

31. On 10 November 2008 Mr Kadi sent his comments to the Commission. He argued, on the basis of documents certifying that the Swiss, Turkish and Albanian authorities had decided not to pursue criminal investigations against him concerning his alleged support of terrorist organisations or involvement in financial crime, that, whenever he had been given the opportunity to express his point of view on the evidence said to inculpate him, he had been able to demonstrate that the allegations made against him were unfounded, and he requested the production of the evidence in support of the claims and assertions made in the summary of reasons relating to his being listed on the Sanctions Committee Consolidated List and the relevant documents in the Commission's file, and asked that he be allowed to submit comments on that evidence. While drawing attention to the vagueness and generality of a number of the allegations contained in that summary of reasons, he disputed, with supporting evidence, that any of the reasons relied on against him were well founded.

32. On 28 November 2008 the Commission adopted the contested regulation.

33. According to recitals 3 to 6, 8 and 9 of the preamble to that regulation:

> '(3) In order to comply with [the *Kadi* judgment], the Commission has communicated the … [summary] of reasons provided by the … Sanctions Committee, to Mr Kadi … and given [him] the opportunity to comment on these grounds in order to make [his] point of view known.
> (4) The Commission has received comments by Mr Kadi … and examined these comments.
> (5) The list of persons, groups and entities to whom the freezing of funds and economic resources should apply, drawn up by the … Sanctions Committee, includes Mr Kadi …
> (6) After having carefully considered the comments received from Mr Kadi in a letter dated 10 November 2008, and given the preventive nature of the freezing of funds and economic resources, the Commission considers that the listing of Mr Kadi is justified for reasons of his association with the Al-Qaida network.
> …
> (8) In view of this, Mr Kadi … should be added to Annex I.
> (9) This Regulation should apply from 30 May 2002, given the preventive nature and objectives of the freezing of funds and economic resources under Regulation … No 881/2002 and the need to protect legitimate interests of the economic operators, who have been relying on the legality of [the regulation annulled by the *Kadi* judgment].'

[…]

The appeals

59. The Commission, the Council and the United Kingdom put forward various grounds in support of their respective appeals. There are, in essence, three. The first ground, raised by the Council, alleges an error of law in that the contested regulation was not recognised as having immunity from jurisdiction.

The second ground, raised by the Commission, the Council and the United Kingdom, alleges errors of law with regard to the level of intensity of judicial review determined in the judgment under appeal. The third ground, again raised by those three appellants, alleges that the General Court erred in its examination of Mr Kadi's pleas in respect of infringement of his rights of defence and his right to effective judicial protection, and in respect of infringement of the principle of proportionality.

The first ground of appeal: error of law in that the contested regulation was not recognised as having immunity from jurisdiction
[...]

Findings of the Court

65. In paragraph 126 of the judgment under appeal, the General Court held that, in accordance with paragraphs 326 and 327 of the *Kadi* judgment, the contested regulation could not be afforded any immunity from jurisdiction on the ground that its objective is to implement resolutions adopted by the Security Council under Chapter VII of the Charter of the United Nations.

66. Various factors, set out in paragraphs 291 to 327 of the *Kadi* judgment, were advanced in support of the position stated by the Court in that judgment, and there has been no change in those factors which could justify reconsideration of that position, those factors being, essentially, bound up with the constitutional guarantee which is exercised, in a Union based on the rule of law (see Case C-550/09 *E and F* [2010] ECR I-6213, paragraph 44, and the judgment of 26 June 2012 in Case C-335/09 P *Poland v Commission* [2012] ECR I-0000, paragraph 48), by judicial review of the lawfulness of all European Union measures, including those which, as in the present case, implement an international law measure, in the light of the fundamental rights guaranteed by the European Union.

67. That European Union measures implementing restrictive measures decided at international level enjoy no immunity from jurisdiction has moreover been confirmed in Joined Cases C-399/06 P and C-403/06 P *Hassan and Ayadi v Council and Commission* [2009] ECR I-11393, paragraphs 69 to 75, and, more recently, in the judgment of 16 November 2011 in Case C-548/09 P *Bank Melli Iran v Council* [2011] ECR I-0000, where it is stated, in paragraph 105, with reference to the *Kadi* judgment, that, without the primacy of a Security Council resolution at the international level thereby being called into question, the requirement that the European Union institutions should pay due regard to the institutions of the United Nations must not result in there being no review of the lawfulness of such European Union measures, in the light of the fundamental rights which are an integral part of the general principles of European Union law.

68. It follows that the judgment under appeal, in particular paragraph 126 thereof, is not vitiated by any error of law with regard to the General Court's refusal, in accordance with the *Kadi* judgment, to afford the contested regulation immunity from jurisdiction.

69. The first ground of appeal must therefore be rejected.

The second and third grounds of appeal: respectively, errors of law relating to the level of intensity of judicial review defined in the judgment under appeal and errors committed by the General Court in the examination of the pleas for annulment based on infringement of the rights of the defence, the right to effective judicial protection and the principle of proportionality

70. The second and third grounds of appeal should be examined together, since the subject of both is, in essence, a criticism of errors of law vitiating the interpretation of the rights of the defence and the right to effective judicial protection adopted by the General Court in the judgment under appeal.

Arguments of the parties

[...]

Findings of the Court

- The extent of the rights of the defence and of the right to effective judicial protection

109. In the particular case of Mr Kadi, it is apparent from the file that the initial listing of his name, on 17 October 2001 in the Sanctions Committee Consolidated List followed a request by the United States on the basis of the adoption on 12 October 2001 of a decision in which the Office of Foreign Asset Control identified Mr Kadi as a 'Specially Designated Global Terrorist'.

110. As is apparent from recital 3 of the preamble to the contested regulation [Regulation No 1190/2008], following the *Kadi* judgment the Commission, by means of that regulation, decided to maintain the name of Mr Kadi on the list in Annex I to Regulation No 81/2002 on the basis of the narrative summaries of reasons which had been transmitted by the Sanctions Committee. As the General Court recorded in paragraph 95 of the judgment under appeal, and as the Commission confirmed at the hearing before the Court, the Commission was not, for that purpose, put in possession of evidence other than such a summary of reasons.

111. In proceedings relating to the adoption of the decision to list or maintain the listing of the name of an individual in Annex I to Regulation No 881/2002, respect for the rights of the defence and the right to effective judicial protection requires that the competent Union authority disclose to the individual concerned the evidence against that person available to that authority and relied on as the basis of its decision, that is to say, at the very least, the summary of reasons provided by the Sanctions Committee (see, to that effect, the *Kadi* judgment, paragraphs 336 and 337), so that that individual is in a position to defend his rights in the best possible conditions and to decide, with full knowledge of the relevant facts, whether there is any point in bringing an action before the Courts of the European Union.

112. When that disclosure takes place, the competent Union authority must ensure that that individual is placed in a position in which he may effectively make known his views on the grounds advanced against him (see, to that effect, Case C-32/95 P *Commission v Lisrestal and Others* [1996] ECR I-5373, paragraph 21; Case C-462/98 P *Mediocurso v Commission* [2000] ECR I-7183, paragraph 36, and the judgment of 22 November 2012 in Case C-277/11 *M.* [2012] ECR I-0000, paragraph 87 and case-law cited).

113. As regards a decision whereby, as in this case, the name of the individual concerned is to be maintained on the list in Annex I to Regulation No 881/2002, compliance with that dual procedural obligation must, contrary to the position in respect of an initial listing (see, in that regard, the *Kadi* judgment, paragraphs 336 to 341 and 345 to 349, and *France v People's Mojahedin Organization of Iran*, paragraph 61), precede the adoption of that decision (see France v People's Mojahedin *Organization of*

Iran, paragraph 62). It is not disputed that, in the present case, the Commission, the author of the contested regulation, complied with that obligation.

114. When comments are made by the individual concerned on the summary of reasons, the competent European Union authority is under an obligation to examine, carefully and impartially, whether the alleged reasons are well founded, in the light of those comments and any exculpatory evidence provided with those comments (see, by analogy, Case C-269/90 *Technische Universität München* [1991] ECR I-5469, paragraph 14; Case C-525/04 P *Spain v Lenzing* [2007] ECR I-9947, paragraph 58, and *M.*, paragraph 88).

115. In that context, it is for that authority to assess, having regard, inter alia, to the content of any such comments, whether it is necessary to seek the assistance of the Sanctions Committee and, through that committee, the Member of the UN which proposed the listing of the individual concerned on that committee's Consolidated List, in order to obtain, in that spirit of effective cooperation which, under Article 220(1) TFEU, must govern relations between the Union and the organs of the United Nations in the fight against international terrorism, the disclosure of information or evidence, confidential or not, to enable it to discharge its duty of careful and impartial examination.

116. Lastly, without going so far as to require a detailed response to the comments made by the individual concerned (see, to that effect, *Al-Aqsa v Council* and *Netherlands v Al-Aqsa*, paragraph 141), the obligation to state reasons laid down in Article 296 TFEU entails in all circumstances, not least when the reasons stated for the European Union measure represent reasons stated by an international body, that that statement of reasons identifies the individual, specific and concrete reasons why the competent authorities consider that the individual concerned must be subject to restrictive measures (see, to that effect, *Al-Aqsa v Council* and *Netherlands v Al-Aqsa*, paragraphs 140 and 142, and *Council v Bamba*, paragraphs 49 to 53).

117. As regards court proceedings, in the event that the person concerned challenges the lawfulness of the decision to list or maintain the listing of his name in Annex I to Regulation No 881/2002, the review by the Courts of the European Union must extend to whether rules as to procedure and rules as to competence, including whether or not the legal basis is adequate, are observed (see, to that effect, the *Kadi* judgment, paragraphs 121 to 236; see also, by analogy, the judgment of 13 March 2012 in Case C-376/10 P *Tay Za v Council* [2012] ECR I-0000, paragraphs 46 to 72).

118. The Courts of the European Union must, further, determine whether the competent European Union authority has complied with the procedural safeguards set out in paragraphs 111 to 114 of this judgment and the obligation to state reasons laid down in Article 296 TFEU, as mentioned in paragraph 116 of this judgment, and, in particular, whether the reasons relied on are sufficiently detailed and specific.

119. The effectiveness of the judicial review guaranteed by Article 47 of the Charter also requires that, as part of the review of the lawfulness of the grounds which are the basis of the decision to list or to maintain the listing of a given person in Annex I to Regulation No 881/2002 (the *Kadi* judgment, paragraph 336), the Courts of the European Union are to ensure that that decision, which affects that person individually (see, to that effect, the judgment of 23 April 2013 in Joined Cases C-478/11 P to C-482/11 P *Gbagbo and Others v Council* [2013] ECR I-0000, paragraph 56), is taken on a sufficiently solid factual

basis (see, to that effect, *Al-Aqsa v Council* and *Netherlands v Al-Aqsa*, paragraph 68). That entails a verification of the allegations factored in the summary of reasons underpinning that decision (see to that effect, *E and F*, paragraph 57), with the consequence that judicial review cannot be restricted to an assessment of the cogency in the abstract of the reasons relied on, but must concern whether those reasons, or, at the very least, one of those reasons, deemed sufficient in itself to support that decision, is substantiated.

120. To that end, it is for the Courts of the European Union, in order to carry out that examination, to request the competent European Union authority, when necessary, to produce information or evidence, confidential or not, relevant to such an examination (see, by analogy, *ZZ*, paragraph 59).

121. That is because it is the task of the competent European Union authority to establish, in the event of challenge, that the reasons relied on against the person concerned are well founded, and not the task of that person to adduce evidence of the negative, that those reasons are not well founded.

122. For that purpose, there is no requirement that that authority produce before the Courts of the European Union all the information and evidence underlying the reasons alleged in the summary provided by the Sanctions Committee. It is however necessary that the information or evidence produced should support the reasons relied on against the person concerned.

123. If the competent European Union authority finds itself unable to comply with the request by the Courts of the European Union, it is then the duty of those Courts to base their decision solely on the material which has been disclosed to them, namely, in this case, the indications contained in the narrative summary of reasons provided by the Sanctions Committee, the observations and exculpatory evidence that may have been produced by the person concerned and the response of the competent European Union authority to those observations. If that material is insufficient to allow a finding that a reason is well founded, the Courts of the European Union shall disregard that reason as a possible basis for the contested decision to list or maintain a listing.

124. If, on the other hand, the competent European Union authority provides relevant information or evidence, the Courts of the European Union must then determine whether the facts alleged are made out in the light of that information or evidence and assess the probative value of that information or evidence in the circumstances of the particular case and in the light of any observations submitted in relation to them by, among others, the person concerned.

125. Admittedly, overriding considerations to do with the security of the European Union or of its Member States or with the conduct of their international relations may preclude the disclosure of some information or some evidence to the person concerned. In such circumstances, it is none the less the task of the Courts of the European Union, before whom the secrecy or confidentiality of that information or evidence is no valid objection, to apply, in the course of the judicial review to be carried out, techniques which accommodate, on the one hand, legitimate security considerations about the nature and sources of information taken into account in the adoption of the act concerned and, on the other, the need sufficiently to guarantee to an individual respect for his procedural rights, such as the right to be heard and the requirement for an adversarial process (see, to that effect, the *Kadi* judgment, paragraphs 342 and 344; see also, by analogy, *ZZ*, paragraphs 54, 57 and 59).

126. To that end, it is for the Courts of the European Union, when carrying out an examination of all the matters of fact or law produced by the competent European Union authority, to determine whether the reasons relied on by that authority as grounds to preclude that disclosure are well founded (see, by analogy, *ZZ*, paragraphs 61 and 62).

127. If the Courts of the European Union conclude that those reasons do not preclude disclosure, at the very least partial disclosure, of the information or evidence concerned, it shall give the competent European Union authority the opportunity to make such disclosure to the person concerned. If that authority does not permit the disclosure of that information or evidence, in whole or in part, the Courts of the European Union shall then undertake an examination of the lawfulness of the contested measure solely on the basis of the material which has been disclosed (see, by analogy, *ZZ*, paragraph 63).

128. On the other hand, if it turns out that the reasons relied on by the competent European Union authority do indeed preclude the disclosure to the person concerned of information or evidence produced before the Courts of the European Union, it is necessary to strike an appropriate balance between the requirements attached to the right to effective judicial protection, in particular respect for the principle of an adversarial process, and those flowing from the security of the European Union or its Member States or the conduct of their international relations (see, by analogy, ZZ, paragraph 64).

129. In order to strike such a balance, it is legitimate to consider possibilities such as the disclosure of a summary outlining the information's content or that of the evidence in question. Irrespective of whether such possibilities are taken, it is for the Courts of the European Union to assess whether and to what the extent the failure to disclose confidential information or evidence to the person concerned and his consequential inability to submit his observations on them are such as to affect the probative value of the confidential evidence (see, by analogy, *ZZ*, paragraph 67).

130. Having regard to the preventive nature of the restrictive measures at issue, if, in the course of its review of the lawfulness of the contested decision, as defined in paragraphs 117 to 129 of this judgment, the Courts of the European Union consider that, at the very least, one of the reasons mentioned in the summary provided by the Sanctions Committee is sufficiently detailed and specific, that it is substantiated and that it constitutes in itself sufficient basis to support that decision, the fact that the same cannot be said of other such reasons cannot justify the annulment of that decision. In the absence of one such reason, the Courts of the European Union will annul the contested decision.

131. Such a judicial review is indispensable to ensure a fair balance between the maintenance of international peace and security and the protection of the fundamental rights and freedoms of the person concerned (see, to that effect, *E and F*, paragraph 57), those being shared values of the UN and the European Union.

132. Notwithstanding their preventive nature, the restrictive measures at issue have, as regards those rights and freedoms, a substantial negative impact related, first, to the serious disruption of the working and family life of the person concerned due to the restrictions on the exercise of his right to property which stem from their general scope combined, as in this case, with the actual duration of their application, and, on the other, the public opprobrium and suspicion of that person which those measures provoke (see, to that effect, the *Kadi* judgment, paragraphs 358, 369 and 375; *France v People's Mojahedin Organization of Iran*, paragraph 64; *Al-Aqsa v Council* and *Netherlands v Al-Aqsa*, paragraph 120, and

the judgment of 28 May 2013 in Case C-239/12 P *Abdulrahim v Council and Commission* [2013] ECR I-0000, paragraph 70 and case- law cited).

133. Such a review is all the more essential since, despite the improvements added, in particular after the adoption of the contested regulation, the procedure for delisting and *ex officio* re- examination at UN level they do not provide to the person whose name is listed on the Sanctions Committee Consolidated List and, subsequently, in Annex I to Regulation No 881/2002, the guarantee of effective judicial protection, as the European Court of Human Rights, endorsing the assessment of the Federal Supreme Court of Switzerland, has recently stated in paragraph 211 of its judgment of 12 September 2012, *Nada v. Switzerland* (No 10593/08, not yet published in the *Reports of Judgments and Decisions*).

134. The essence of effective judicial protection must be that it should enable the person concerned to obtain a declaration from a court, by means of a judgment ordering annulment whereby the contested measure is retroactively erased from the legal order and is deemed never to have existed, that the listing of his name, or the continued listing of his name, on the list concerned was vitiated by illegality, the recognition of which may re-establish the reputation of that person or constitute for him a form of reparation for the non-material harm he has suffered (see, to that effect, *Abdulrahim v Council and Commission*, paragraphs 67 to 84).

[…]

III. National Courts

Branno v. Ministry of War, Italian Court of Cassation, 1955

[*Note:*

In the case the Italian Court of Cessation considered the question whether the Italian courts had jurisdiction to hear an action for the enforcement of a commercial contract entered by the NATO Headquarters for Southern Europe with a private individual providing canteen facilities for its staff.
The Court of Cassation considered a difference between private (jure gestionis) and official (jure imperii) activities of NATO and decided that in the concrete case the organization "was not performing an act f sovereignty connected with its public activity". For this reason it decided that the Italian law was applicable and Italian courts were competent.]

Obiter dictum:

"The North Atlantic Treaty Organization – which is a union of various States adhering to the North Atlantic Treaty, one organ of which is the General Headquarters for Southern Europe – was established by a Treaty signed in Washington on April 4, 1949, which was ratified and brought into operation in Italy by Law No. 465 of August 1, 1949. It is an international organization, its main purpose being the mutual defence of its members. The North Atlantic Treaty Organization is, therefore, a subject of international law, and it is autonomous with respect to each and all of the member countries. Therefore none of the members – one of which is Italy – may interfere with the activities of the North Atlantic Treaty Organization; the member States cannot exercise judicial functions with regard to any public law activity of the North Atlantic Treaty Organization connected with its organization or with regard to acts performed on the basis of its sovereignty.
The Italian courts will not exercise jurisdiction with respect to cases arising out of public law activities of a subject of international law possessing both *jus imperii* and a legal system of its own."

MacLaine Watson & Co. Ltd v. Department of Trade and Industry, High Court, Chancery Division, Decision of 29 July 1987

[*Note:*

International Tin Council (ITC) was established in 1956 with the purpose of maintaining the price of tin at a steady level by buying surplus and establishing a buffer stock of tin. However, at the beginning of 1980s the demand for tin decreased which led to the situation that the Organization could no longer maintain the price and eventually ran out of money. On 24 October 1985 the Council decided to cease trading which caused a major upheaval in commodity regulation and created financial problems to 16 creditor banks and financial trading houses and threatened some brokers with bankruptcy. This led to diverse legal actions. (Below only excerpts from two decisions were reproduced).

The proceedings were held in the United kingdom which had a threefold relationship with International Tin Council: it was a member of the Organization, a consumer country and a host State under the Headquarters Agreement of 1972.]

The Decision:

I turn then to the terms of para. 5 the 1972 order. It is commendably brief. It provides simply that the ITC is to have "the legal capacities of a body corporate". Two things are immediately noticeable. First, the capacities in question are conferred directly on the ITC itself, not on its members or officials. Thus, for example, the members are not (like partners) given the right to sue and be sued in the name of the ITC. The ITC itself has the legal capacity to sue and be sued. Secondly, the ITC is given, not legal capacity, or full legal capacity *tout court*, but specifically the legal capacities of a body corporate. The first of these is significant but not, I think, decisive; the second, in my judgment, is decisive and puts the meaning of the paragraph beyond argument.

The ITC has been granted "the legal capacities of a body corporate". What is a body corporate? It is an artificial legal entity distinct from its members. So the ITC has been granted specifically the legal capacities of a body which is separate and distinct from its members. It follows, in my judgment, that it has the capacity of such a body to acquire and hold property of its own, with the result that such property is distinct from that of its members. It has the capacity of such a body to act through agents and to be their principal; to enter into contracts with its own members as well as with others; and to incur liabilities on its own account which are not liabilities of its members. It is no objection that a body corporate can do all these things only because it is a separate legal entity distinct from its members. It would be equally true, and probably more accurate, to say that it is such an entity because it can do them. If the ITC could not do them, it would not have the characteristic legal capacities of a body corporate.

To assist me to reach this conclusion, I have been taken through a large number of international treaties together with the corresponding domestic legislation, but I prefer to base my decision simply on the language of para. 5 of the 1972 order, which in my judgment is plain and unambiguous, and on the absence of any indication in the order to the contrary. It is to be observed that, unlike the registered trade union in *Bonsor* v. *Musicians'Union* the ITC cannot don or doff at will the attributes with which it has been endowed by Parliament. It required an Order in Council to be made and laid before Parliament to confer them, and it will require another to revoke them.

The result, in my judgment, is that the ITC has full juridical personality in the sense that it exists as a separate legal entity distinct from its members; though it is sufficient to dispose of this case to say that it has the characteristic attribute of a body corporate which excludes the liability of the members, that is to say the ability to incur liabilities on its own account which are not the liabilities of the members.

The plaintiffs submit that this cannot be right, or the ITC would be indistinguishable from a body corporate, and would thus be a body corporate in all but name, despite the clear intention of Parliament that it should not be. But there were obvious reasons for not incorporating the ITC or granting it the status of a body corporate. That would at least have run the risk of subjecting the ITC to those provisions of our domestic law, such as R.S.C., O. 48, which apply in terms to bodies corporate, and this may have been considered undesirable. But, as the authorities show, Parliament can create an artificial legal entity with all the characteristics and attributes of a body corporate, and thus a body corporate in all but name, without making it one.

In my judgment, this is what Parliament has done by the 1972 order, which confers on the ITC the legal capacities of a body corporate, but does not incorporate it nor require it to be deemed to be or treated as a body corporate. *Staughton* J. has held ((1987) 3 BCC 413, at p. 434) that,

> "whilst the ITC is not a corporation or body corporate for the internal regulation of its affairs under the Companies Acts, in its dealings with others, and in particular when considering the effect of contracts that it may make, it is to be treated as if it were a body corporate."

I would prefer simply to say that, by conferring on the ITC the legal capacities of a body corporate, Parliament has granted it sufficient legal personality to enable it to incur liabilities on its own account which are not the liabilities of its members.

Arab Monetary Fund v. Hashim and Others, Decision of the House of Lords of 21 February 1991

[*Note:*

Arab Monetary Fund (AMF) was created by an agreement between 20 Arab States and Palestine concluded in 1976. It is based in the United Arab Emirates (UAE) with the headquarters in Abu Dhabi. According to Article 2 the Fund has an independent juridical personality and has, in particular, the right to own, contract and litigate.

In the period from 1977-1982 Jawad Hashim was President and Director General of the Arab Monetary Fund. While already emigrated to Canada he was prosecuted in absentia by the courts of the United Arab Emirates for illegal appropriation of funds of the Arab Monetary Fund. In 1988 the Arab Monetary Fund initiated proceedings also in England against Hashim, his wife, sons and other individuals involved.]

The Decision:

By its terms, the agreement conferred on the Fund an "independent juridical personality and . . . in particular the right to own, contract and litigate" and required ratification by the signatory States in accordance with their particular constitutional arrangements. By a federal decree promulgated in 1977, the United Arab Emirates ("UAE"), including Abu Dhabi, complied with that requirement. In 1985, the Fund brought criminal proceedings in Switzerland against H., its former director-general, claiming that large sums belonging to it had been paid into the personal accounts of H. and his wife at the Geneva branch of its bankers. In 1988, the proceedings were dismissed for lack of jurisdiction, H. no longer having assets in Switzerland. In proceedings begun in England against, *inter alios*, H., members of his family and a number of banks, the Fund sought recovery of the sums allegedly misappropriated by H. and damages for the alleged negligence of the bankers. Certain of the defendants applied to strike out the action on the ground that the Fund was not an entity recognized under English law. The judge concluded that, ignoring the 1976 agreement, the Fund was to be regarded as a foreign juridical personality constituted as a *persona ficta* under the law of the UAE and as such recognized under the common law conflict rules. He accordingly held that the Fund had capacity to sue in the English courts and dismissed the applications. The Court of Appeal by a majority allowed appeals by the defendants.

On appeal by the Fund:

Held, allowing the appeal (Lord Lowry dissenting), that by the comity of nations the courts of the United Kingdom recognized a corporate body created by the laws of a foreign State recognized by the Crown, as the UAE was; that the UAE federal decree had conferred legal personality on the Fund and created a corporate body that the English courts could and should recognize as entitled to sue; and that the fact that the Fund had been incorporated not only in the UAE but also in the other signatory States did not prevent that result (post, pp. 158E-F, 160D-G, 161B, 162B-F, 167F-<J).

[...]

The United Arab Emirates . . . is an independent sovereign federal State. By the constitution of the UAE dated 18 July 1971, a treaty entered into by the UAE becomes binding on and within the UAE after confirmation of the treaty by the council of ministers and ratification by decree of the supreme council, followed by signature and promulgation of the decree by the president, and publication of the decree in the official gazette. The AMF agreement was duly confirmed and ratified by decree. The decree was duly signed and promulgated and was published on 16 April 1977 in the official gazette as Federal Decree No. 35 for 1977 with the articles of agreement of the AMF agreement attached. All these matters were the subject of uncontradicted expert evidence given in an affirmation by Mr. Hamza, legal adviser to the Ministry of Foreign Affairs of the UAE He concluded that the Fund "had conferred on it by publication of Federal Decree No. 35 independent legal personality and the capacity to sue and be sued in UAE law."

Thus the Fund was created a corporate body by the UAE and corresponds roughly to an English company limited by shares with the member States as the shareholders, a board of governors which represents the shareholders, a board of executive directors and a director-general corresponding to a managing director.

The AMF agreement came into force on 13 February 1977 and the headquarters of the Fund were duly established at Abu Dhabi in the UAE. The first respondent to this appeal, Dr. Hashim, was appointed director-general of the Fund and occupied that position between 1977 and 1982. For the purposes of this appeal it must be assumed, as the Fund alleges, that while acting as Director-General of the Fund, Dr. Hashim stole about U.S.$50m. from the Fund and that the respondent "banks enabled him to launder a substantial part of the money through numbered accounts. By a statement of claim served on 25 January 1989, the Fund sought to recover from the respondents the sums embezzled by Dr. Hashim or the assets representing those sums. Dr. Hashim, his wife and two sons, a Liechtenstein Anstalt which is the alter ego of Dr. Hashim, and the respondent banks applied to strike out the statement of claim. On 14 November 1989, Hoffmann J., ante, pp. 118c et seq. dismissed the applications. On 9 April 1990, the Court of Appeal (Lord Donaldson of Lymington M.R. and Nourse L.J., Bingham L.J. dissenting) struck out the statement of claim "on the ground that the plaintiff lacked capacity to sue." The Fund now appeals. Although a treaty cannot become part of the law of the United Kingdom without the intervention of Parliament, the recognition of foreign States is a matter for the Crown to decide and by comity the courts of the United Kingdom recognise a corporate body created by the law of a foreign State recognised by the Crown.

As early as 1728 in an action begun by the Dutch West India Company, the defendants argued unsuccessfully in this House:

> "that no recognisance in England could be given to this generalis privilegiata Societas Belgica ad Indos Occidentales negotians, for that the law of England does not take notice of any foreign corporation, nor can any foreign corporation in their corporate name and capacity maintain any action at common law in this kingdom, and that therefore the recognisance was void in law:" Henriques v. Dutch West India Co. (1728) 2 Ld.Raym. 1532, 1534-1535.

In that case judgment was recovered by the Dutch company by producing in evidence the proper instrument whereby according to the law of Holland they were effectually created a corporation there. In the present case the federal decree with the articles of agreement annexed suffices to prove incorporation of the Fund in the UAE.

In Lazard Brothers & Co. v. Midland Bank Ltd. [1933] A.C. 289, 297, Lord Wright said:

> "English courts have long since recognised as juristic persons corporations established by foreign law in virtue of the fact of their F creation and continuance under and by that law. Such recognition is said to be by the comity of nations."

In Gasque v. Inland Revenue Commissioners [1940] 2 K.B. 80, Macnaghten J. held that a limited company was capable of having a domicile. Its domicile is the place of its registration and that domicile clings to it throughout its existence. In the present case the domicile G and residence of the Fund were clearly in the UAE at the headquarters of the Fund from which the Fund operated. In Kuenigl v. Donnersmarck [1955] 1 Q.B. 515, 535, McNair J. accepted that the domicile of a limited company was the place of registration or the country in which it was incorporated and that:

> "in so far as nationality can by analogy be applied to a juristic H person, its nationality is determined in an inalienable manner by the laws of the country from which it derives its personality: . . ."

In Chaff and Hay Acquisition Committee v. J. A. Hemphill and Sons Pty. Ltd. (1947) 74 C.L.R. 375, a committee of four persons created under a statute of South Australia to acquire property in its collective A name and to sue and be sued in its collective name was held by the High Court of Australia not to be a corporation but though unincorporated it was a legal entity in South Australia and as such was entitled to recognition outside the State in accordance with the principle of the comity of nations. McTiernan J. said succinctly, at p. 390:

> "The courts of one country give recognition, by a comity of nations, to a legal personality created by the law of another country."

The courts of the United Kingdom can therefore recognise the Fund as a legal personality created by the law of the UAE.

It was submitted on behalf of the respondent banks that the Fund was created a legal personality not only by the UAE but also by the other 20 States who were parties to the AMF agreement. Therefore, it is said, there are 21 legal personalities and it is not clear whether Dr. Q Hashim embezzled the money of the UAE fund or the money of a fund established by some other Arab State. My Lords, though the Fund was incorporated by 21 States and has multiple incorporation and multiple nationality there is only one Fund with its head office in Abu Dhabi, one board of governors, one executive board of directors and one director-general. The domicile and residence of the Fund are in the UAE and nowhere else. Dr. Hashim was appointed by the board of governors of the Fund as Director-General of the Fund and stole the money belonging to the Fund. It was argued that the Fund as incorporated in Iraq, for example, might be different from the Fund as incorporated in the UAE and that the Iraqi Fund might even sue the UAE Fund. But there is only one Fund to which each of the member States accorded legal personality. No one can bring an action to recover the money of the Fund in any part of the world except the one duly authorised director-general. The articles of agreement which were annexed to the federal decree of the UAE and which thus became part of the law of the UAE are no different from the memorandum and articles of a limited liability company established under the law of England.

It is beyond dispute that if the Fund had been incorporated in the UAE and nowhere else, the Fund would have been recognised in this country as a legal personality. If the Fund has been incorporated not only in the UAE but also in a number of friendly foreign States recognised by the government of this country, it still has legal personality and is capable of suing in this country.

Mothers of Srebrenica v. The State of the Netherlands and the United Nations, Judgment of the Dutch District Court, in The Hague 16 July 2014

[*Note:*

The Judgment concerns the responsibility of the Dutch State and the United Nations for the crimes committed against the civilian population in Srebrenica (Muslim enclave in Bosnia and Herzegovina), in July 1995. In the massacre up to 8,000 Bosnian man and boys were killed. In several suits brought before the Dutch courts relatives of the victims and the association "Mothers of Srebrenica" sought to hold the Dutch State and the United Nations responsible for failing to prevent the massacre.]

[...]

2.11. On May 15th 1993 the UN and Bosnia-Herzegovina signed the *Agreement on the status of the United Nations Protection Force in Bosnia and Herzegovina* (known also as the *Status of Forces Agreement* hereinafter to be referred to as: SOFA).

2.12. Under Resolution 836 of June 4th 1993 the Security Council decided *inter alia* the following:

> "Reaffirming in particular its resolutions 819 (…) and 824 (…)
> (…)
> 4. Decides to ensure full respect for the safe areas referred to in resolution 824 (1993)
> 5. Decides to extend to that end the mandate of UNPROFOR in order to enable it, in the safe areas referred to in resolution 824 (1993), to deter attacks against the safe areas, to monitor the cease-fire, to promote the withdrawal of paramilitary units other than those of the Government of the Republic of Bosnia and Herzegovina and to occupy some key points on the ground, in addition to participating in the delivery of humanitarian relief to the population as provided for in resolution 776 (1992) of 14 September 1992; (…)
> (…)
> 9. Authorizes UNPROFOR, in addition to the mandate defined in resolutions 770 (1992) of 13 August 1992 and 776 (1992), in carrying out the mandate defined in paragraph 5 above, acting in self-defence, to take the necessary measures, including the use of force, in reply to bombardments against the safe areas by any of the parties or to armed incursion into them or in the event of any deliberate obstruction in or around those areas to the freedom of movement of UNPROFOR or of protected humanitarian convoys;
> 10. Decides that, notwithstanding paragraph 1 of resolution 816 (1993), Member States, acting nationally or through regional organizations or arrangements, may take, under the authority of the Security Council and subject to close coordination with the Secretary-General and UNPROFOR, all necessary measures, through the use of air power, in and around the safe areas in the Republic of Bosnia and Herzegovina, to support UNPROFOR in the performance of its mandate set out in paragraphs 5 and 9 above; (…)"

[...]

2.14. On September 3rd 1993 the Permanent Representative of The Netherlands to the UN offered to put at the disposal of the military advisor to the Secretary-General of the UN a battalion of the Air-mobile Brigade (hereinafter referred to as: Dutchbat) to implement in particular Resolution 836 across the *safe areas* it cited. The Dutch Minister of Defence repeated the offer to the Secretary-General of the UN on September 7th 1993 who accepted it on October 21st 1993. On November 12th 1993 the government of The Netherlands approved posting Dutchbat abroad.

[...]

2.16. The headquarters of Dutchbat were located at an abandoned factory site in Potočari (hereinafter to be referred to as: the compound). Potočari lay within the *safe area* about five kilometres from the town of Srebrenica where a company of Dutchbat was encamped in addition to which it manned a number of observation posts (hereinafter to be referred to as: OPs).

[...]

2.31. On July 10th 1995 Dutchbat made three requests for close air support none of which led to actual air support being given on that day.

2.32. On July 11th 1995 at about 08:00 hours Dutchbat requested close air support. The request was denied. A following request for air support at about 10:00 hours was approved at about 12:00 hours by the UN and roughly half an hour after that by NATO. At about 14:45 hours bombs were dropped in the direction of the VRS tanks. At about 15:30 hours airplanes once again took off that dropped no bombs. After that close air support came to an end.

2.33. On July 11th 1995 at about 16:00 hours Dutchbat took up a new *blocking position* to the south of the compound that they abandoned a few hours later.

2.34. On July 11th 1995 at about 16:30 hours the town of Srebrenica fell and was captured by the Bosnian Serbs.

2.35. Earlier that afternoon at about 14:30 hours Bosnian Muslim refugees began to stream out of the town of Srebrenica and head towards the compound. A *mini safe area* was set up there consisting of the compound and the area of Potočari that lay close by with factory premises and a bus depot.

About 20,000 to 25,000 refugees sought refuge in the *mini safe area*. About 5,000 of them were housed in the compound.

2.36. Around 10,000 to 15,000 men from the *safe area* did not flee to the *mini safe area* with factory but to the woods in the vicinity of the town of Srebrenica (hereinafter to be referred to as: the woods). About 6,000 of these men fell into Bosnian Serb hands.

[...]

2.39. In the evening of July 11th 1995 Karremans spoke with Mladić on two separate occasions about evacuating the refugees from the *mini safe area* and in the morning of July 12th 1995 for a third time.

2.40. In the early afternoon of July 12th 1995 on the orders of the Bosnian Serbs buses arrived and lorries (hereinafter to be referred to jointly as: the buses) at the *mini safe area*. At about 14:00 hours the evacuation of the refugees from the mini safe area began. The Bosnian Serbs who had announced they would be screening able-bodied men for war crimes pulled out men from the rows of refugees who were heading towards the buses. In the afternoon of July 12th 1995 the Bosnian Serbs began to carry off the men in separate buses. After the evacuation of the refugees had been stopped in the evening of July 12th 1995 it was resumed in the morning of July 13th 1995. At the end of the afternoon the last of the refugees remaining in the compound were carried off.

[...]

2.43. After the fall of Srebrenica the Bosnian Serbs killed more than 7,000 men from the safe area most of them in mass executions in the period from 14th up to and including 17th July 1995.

2.44. Dutchbat left the compound on July 21st 1995.

2.45. As regards [Claimant 1] et al, where relevant here, the following facts have been established:

2.45.1. Before the war Claimant [Claimant 1] lived with her husband and son in the town of Srebrenica. On July 11th 1995 the husband of [Claimant 1] fled into the woods and was never found again. [Claimant 1] and her son sought refuge in the part of the *mini safe area* that lay outside the compound. On July 13th 1995 she and her son became separated. She has not seen him again since.

[...]

4 THE JUDGMENT

I General considerations

[...]

(i) The scope of the dispute

4.3. In this case the first question for discussion is whether the UN enjoys immunity. The District Court answered this question affirmatively in its interim judgment of July 10th 2008 and declared it was not competent to take cognizance of the claim against the UN. This judgment was confirmed right up to the court of last resort in The Netherlands. Claimants then submitted a complaint to the European Court of Human Rights (hereinafter referred to as: ECHR) that on June 11th 2013 declared their complaint to be without merit.

4.4. Since the District Court is not competent to take cognizance of the claim against the UN it only remains to assess the claim against the State. The District Court is not going to assess the substance of Claimants' accusations against the UN. For these reasons therefore representation of the facts and the dispute is limited to the case against the State.

[...]

4.5.6. Claimants hold the State responsible for the fall of Srebrenica and the consequences this brought with it. Besides the arguments reproduced in 3.2 they also formulate arguments about the decision-making process that led to the participation of The Netherlands in the UN mission and about the preparations for the mission especially the training and equipping of Dutchbat and what in Claimant's eyes was insufficient *intelligence* gathering. According to Claimants these arguments do not contain any substantive accusation but "this is about the State not being able to advance the circumstances as being in any way exculpatory since Claimants can show after all that preparations and the equipping of Dutchbat were an integral part of the State's responsibility and that the State acted irresponsibly in that regard or at least took the wrong decisions." In accordance with Claimants' intentions the District Court is not going to handle as being in any way substantive the accusation concerning the decision-making process and/or the preparations for the mission.

[...]

II Attributable failure

4.22. Claimants argue that failure to meet its obligations to them to protect the populace in the *safe area* is attributable to the State. According to Claimants said obligations arise from the agreement between the State and the UN to put at its disposal troops to protect the populace in the *safe area* and this is to be deemed as a third-party clause in the sense of Section 6:253 BW. They argue that the populace accepted this clause thereby becoming a party to said agreement.

[...]

4.30. Since this dispute relates to a UN peacekeeping operation for which purpose the State sent troops the question arises as to whether in as much as they took place under the flag of the UN the unlawful acts of which it is accused may indeed be attributed to the State. Together with parties the District Court is of the opinion that first and foremost this question must be answered according to the norms of international public law.

4.31. In doing so the District Court distinguishes as between (A) Dutchbat's acts (B) other acts related to Claimants' accusations for example the decision-making process surrounding the provision of close air support [= CAS] to Dutchbat. Under (C) the conclusion on the acts attributable to the State.

(A) Attributing Dutchbat's actions to the State

4.32. The District Court handles *seriatim* the following points:

(a) The attribution criterion: *effective control*
(b) Transfer of *command and control* over Dutchbat to the UN
(c) *Effective control* of Dutchbat's actions in general
(d) Claimants' additional arguments about attributing Dutchbat's actions in the period prior to the fall of Srebrenica
(e) The conclusion as to the *effective control* of the State over Dutchbat's actions in the period prior to the fall of Srebrenica
(f) *Effective control* by the State over Dutchbat's actions after the fall of Srebrenica

(g) *Effective control* by the State over Dutchbat's specific actions after the fall of Srebrenica and
(h) The conclusion as to the State's *effective control* over Dutchbat's actions after the fall of Srebrenica.

(a) The attribution criterion: effective control

4.33. In the Nuhanović and Mustafić cases the Supreme Court ruled that the criterion for attributing Dutchbat's actions to the State is whether the State exercised *effective control* over said actions. The Supreme Court derives this criterion from Section 7 of the *Draft Articles on Responsibility of International Organisations* (hereinafter to be referred to as: DARIO) that the *International Law Organisation* (ILO) has drawn up. In the cases referred to the Appeals Court considered that though this provision of *effective control* is only mentioned in relation to attribution to the UN the same criterion holds when answering the question whether actions of troops must be attributed to the state that placed them at the disposal of others. The Supreme Court considered that the ILO's DARIO recommendations and the *Draft Articles on Responsibility of States for Internationally Wrongful Acts* (hereinafter to be referred to as: DARS) may generally be accepted as a reflection of current, unwritten international law and were apparently accepted as such even in 1995.

4.34. *Effective control* means the actual say or '*factual control*' of the State over Dutchbat's specific actions. Whether or not this is a point of discussion must be assessed in terms of the circumstances surrounding the case. When doing so it should be remembered that under Clause 48 DARIO the same act and/or acts might be attributed to both the State and the UN under what is called '*dual attribution*'.

4.35. Other than Claimants argue the way in which the UN enjoys immunity is not relevant. International law of custom offers no support for Claimants' position that given immunity the "broadest possible" measures of attribution for Dutchbat's actions must be applied, as otherwise Dutchbat would be placed "above the law". The opinion of the Supreme Court in the judgment referred to under 1.1 that according to current international law the absence of an alternative judicial process is not prejudicial to the immunity of the UN (confirmed by the ECHR see: 4.3) underlines the fact that the UN's immunity is not patient of the formulation of an argument that Dutchbat's actions beyond the framework of current international law are attributable to the State.

(b) Transfer of command and control over Dutchbat to the UN

4.36. Since the dispute is related to a UN peacekeeping operation to implement a UN mandate when attributing Dutchbat's actions to the State it is important to know what powers the State still had and what powers it had transferred to the UN. This is why it merits discussion as to whether and if so to what extent the State had handed over *command and control* of Dutchbat to the UN.

4.37. Just like the State the District Court is of the opinion that the State did hand over *command and control* of Dutchbat to the UN. This was not recorded in any written agreement as frequently does occur in a so-called '*transfer of authority*'. Nor is that necessary since in order for the transfer of command and control to take place no procedural requirements have to be observed. After the agreement referred to under 2.14 in which the State put troops at the disposal of the UN Dutchbat was indeed placed under UN orders and operated as a contingent of UNPROFOR.

4.38. The transfer of *command and control* over Dutchbat took place for the purpose of a UN peacekeeping operation based on Chapter VII of the UN Charter to implement the mandate (see 2.12). The Security Council is solely responsible for implementing international peace and security and is primarily responsible for implementing the mandate. The command and control the State transferred to the UN is *inter alia* cited and described in the Operations order of December 14th 1994 that aims at Dutchbat III replacing Dutchbat II. The substance of said order is *inter alia* as follows:

> "*(2) Upon arrival in YU* [District Court's addition: Yugoslavia] *Dutchbat is oob [NAVO: operational control(1) (opcon)] of UNPROFOR*".

[...]

Voorhoeve worded this as follows:

> "When The Netherlands puts its troops at the disposal of an international organisation in the form of a peacekeeping operation it transfers operational orders over its troops to that organisation or coalition of countries. In this case therefore Dutch troops were placed under United Nations' orders and their own commanders Lieutenant Colonel Karremans and the other commanding officers of Dutchbat reported to the North-East Sector of Unprofor in Tuzla and in Sarajevo. (...) The next successive level is General Janvier in Zagreb and on the civilian side Mr Akashi the special representative of the United Nations."(Proceedings TK 1994/95, p. 5987).

4.39. In part in the light of the above the District Court regards as insufficient Claimants' argument that transfer of *command and control* over Dutchbat to the UN was due only to a lack of knowledge.

4.40. It has now been established that the State attached no conditions to the transfer of *command and control* over Dutchbat to the UN. Given the substance of the operation order the primary responsibility of the Security Council for the operational implementation of the mandate and what is usual in peacekeeping operations that the UN carries out included in the command and control the State transferred to the UN the say over Dutchbat's operational implementation of the mandate. In this regard the UN chain of command at UNPROFOR directed Dutchbat in this giving orders and instructions to the commander of Dutchbat. During implementation of the UN mission therefore the State had no formal competence *vis-a-vis* Dutchbat's operational implementation of the mandate and was thus not competent to exercise its say about Dutchbat whether via the Dutch officers in the UN chain of command or directly.

4.41. After transferring *command and control* states supplying troops at all times retain the right to withdraw them and to cease taking part in the operation ('*full command*'). As usual during a transfer of *command and control* over the operational implementation of the mandate to the UN the State retained further say about personal matters of the military personnel put at the disposal of the UN who remained in service of the State and Dutchbat's material logistics. The State also retained the authority to punish said military personnel by disciplining them and subjecting them to criminal law. Finally the State had a say over the preparations for the mission e.g. in selecting and training the troops. Nor is any of this disputed as between parties.

4.42. Transfer of *command and control* over Dutchbat's operational implementation of the mandate was a normal situation in which a state puts its troops at the disposal of others during a peacekeeping operation working under the orders of the UN and that is described in a report of the Secretary-General of the UN of 1994 as follows:

> "In general, United Nations command is not a full command and closer in meaning to the generally recognized concept of "operational command". It involves the full authority to issue operational directives within the limits of (1) a specific mandate of the Security Council; (2) an agreed period of time, with the stipulation that an earlier withdrawal requires adequate prior notification; and (3) a specific geographical range (the mission area as a whole)." (UN Doc. A/49/681 of November 21st. 1994, paragraph 6).

4.43. The situation as described in the above held in any case till the fall of Srebrenica.

(c) Effective control of Dutchbat's actions in general by the State

4.44. Claimants formulate a number of general positions that according to them lead to all of Dutchbat's actions that form part of the accusations being attributed to the State. Based in part on these positions the District Court fills in the details about the criterion for *effective control* over said actions on the part of Dutchbat.

4.45. Given the option of *dual attribution* available we do not need to examine whether the UN also had *effective control* over Dutchbat's actions that form part of the accusations.

4.46. First and foremost the District Court hereby pronounces that in order to accept *effective control* there would be no requirement for the State in giving instructions to Dutchbat to have broken the structure of the chain of command at the UN or exercised independent operational authority to give orders. It comes down to the actual say over specific actions whereby all of the actual circumstances and the particular context of the case must be examined. In the Nuhanović and Mustafić cases the Appeals Court considered that there not only is the question significant as to whether the actions constituted implementation of a specific instruction the State had given but also whether in the absence of any such specific instruction the State had it in its powers to prevent the actions concerned. These considerations remained undisputed on cassation.

[...]

4.49. As summarised above in 2.18 there were within UNPROFOR Dutch officers appointed to various high levels of command. Claimants argue that this "Dutch line" within UNPROFOR maintained close links with "The Hague" (read: the Dutch Government hereinafter also referred to as: The Hague) crossing the UN's *command and control* meaning The Hague exercised continuous influence by passing formal lines and responsibilities.

4.50. The State correctly points out that the mere fact that Dutch military personnel were appointed to UNPROFOR does not mean *per se* that the State exercised *effective control*. Dutch officers worked in the UN chain of command whence operational implementation of the mandate was directed. It is usual for military personnel from countries that supply troops form part of the UN chain of command for UN peacekeeping operations.

[...]

4.54. The fact has become established that in the period leading up to the fall of Srebrenica contact between The Hague on the one hand and the Dutch UNPROFOR officers and Dutchbat on the other hand was intensified, though on its own this would not constitute *effective control*. Claimants argue with reference to page 2276 of the NIOD Report that the DCBC in this period concerned itself more with operational matters. On this page under the heading "*verhoudingen tussen DCBC en KL Crisisstaf*" [= "relations between DCBC and KL Crisis Staff] the relations between these two units are described *inter alia* as follows:

> "As matters in Srebrenica became more and more tense under the political pressure of the moment DCBC began to get more and more involved with implementation of the operation and the dividing line between DCBC's tasks and those of KL Crisis Staff became vague."

That DCBC in relation to KL Crisis Staff "concerned" itself more with operational matters again does not result in *effective control*; even leaving aside the fact that this concern can consist of heightened interest and need for information here above all as the State has sufficiently explained we are dealing with the relationship and division of tasks between two organisational units within The Netherlands.

4.55. Claimants further argue that in conflict with express orders of the UN there was "an invariable line of conduct" at Dutchbat to allow its own interest to prevail. This is why according to them it has become established that Dutchbat's actions are the result of *effective control* being exercised by the State "since military personnel hardly ever act on their own initiative". Quite apart from the question whether the latter remark is true or is true in all circumstances these generalisations on the part of Claimants provide insufficient basis to be able to conclude that such actions were always preceded by instructions from the State.

[...]

(f) Effective control by the State over Dutchbat's actions after the fall of Srebrenica

4.80. The previously normal situation in which a state puts its troops to work at the disposal of and under the orders of the UN during a peacekeeping operation changed substantially when Srebrenica fell at the end of the afternoon of July 11th 1995. After that a period of transition was entered into in which the State had a say in the actions of Dutchbat when providing humanitarian assistance to and preparing the evacuation of the refugees from the *mini safe area*. As to this the District Court deliberates as follows.

4.81. In the morning of July 11th1995 when the Bosnian Serbs approached the town of Srebrenica the situation was discussed within the DCBC. Those present included *inter alia* Voorhoeve, Van Baal and Van den Breemen. After that Van Baal and Van den Breemen travelled to Sarajevo to speak with Janvier. They had received the instruction from Voorhoeve to conduct the talk with Janvier in the context of the meeting held that same morning. Van Baal had stated before the Parliamentary committee of inquiry the following:

"*We agreed amongst ourselves that we would stick to the position that the implementation of the task should be directed towards protecting the populace and that we should do so for as long as possible in addition taking into account that fighting at that point was not or was hardly worthwhile. Allowing casualties to fall unnecessarily would then no longer be a point of discussion. The third point was that we had to take into account that we could find ourselves in a situation in which Dutchbat would have to evacuate along with the populace to MKF* territory [District Court's addition: Muslim Croat Federation]. *Those were the conclusions of the meeting that we took to general Janvier in Zagreb. That is the basis on which we conducted talks with him.*" (PE hearings, p. 344).

4.82. In the meantime when Van Baal and Van den Breemen arrived in Sarajevo Srebrenica had fallen and the mission to protect the *safe area* had failed. The talks that Van Baal and Van den Breemen conducted that evening with Janvier were about the situation that had come about after the fall of Srebrenica. In Van Baal's own words in his statement about the talks with Janvier to the Parliamentary committee of inquiry:

"*The accent then shifted in fact from UNPROFOR's military operation to the problem of the refugees.*" and:

"*We said: Dutchbat and the populace will evacuate together or after each other. That was agreed as such with General Janvier. (...)*" (PE hearings, pp. 344 to 345).

4.83. In the cases of Nuhanović and Mustafić the Appeals Court decided that what was discussed between Janvier, Van den Breemen and Van Baal could not be understood in any other way than that the UN in the person of Janvier and the Government of The Netherlands in the person of Van den Breemen and Van Baal decided in mutual consultation that in the new situation in which Srebrenica had fallen and the UN mission had in fact failed Dutchbat should direct its efforts towards its humanitarian task and the preparations for the evacuation of Dutchbat and the refugees from *the mini safe area*. In doing so the Government of The Netherlands took part in this decision-making process at the highest level. This decision was accompanied by a transitional period in which matters in Potočari were settled.

[...]

4.85. Dutchbat's withdrawal was prepared during the transitional period and the State had independent powers to withdraw it (see 4.41). With the joint decision with the UN not to evacuate Dutchbat any earlier than at the same time as the refugees or after the refugees the State tied implementation of these powers to the provision of humanitarian assistance to preparations for the evacuation of the refugees in the *mini safe area* during the transitional period. This too was discussed in contacts between Voorhoeve and Nicolai on July 11th 1995. [...]

4.87. The foregoing facts and circumstances lead the District Court to conclude that during the transitional period the State did have *effective control* over providing humanitarian assistance to and preparation of Dutchbat's evacuation of the refugees in the *mini safe area*. This action therefore on the part of Dutchbat may be attributed to the State. Such *effective control* was limited to this and did not spread to Dutchbat's involvement with the stream of refugees that prior to commencement of the transitional period moved during the course of the afternoon from the town of Srebrenica to the *mini safe area*. Such *effective control* was also not related to refugees outside the *mini safe area* or to Dutchbat's actions outside the *mini safe area* e.g. the abandonment of observation posts after the fall of Srebrenica.

4.88. Such *effective control* by the State over Dutchbat's actions during the transitional period continued until Dutchbat withdrew on July 21st1995 after the refugees had been evacuated from the *mini safe area*. Resolution 1004 (see 2.42) did not lead to any other actual situation during the transitional period: the Bosnian Serbs did not give heed to the call it contained to discontinue their offensive and to withdraw from the *safe area* forthwith. Nor did it appear that said resolution led to any order to Dutchbat to take positions in and around Srebrenica or in any other way to attempt to retake Srebrenica by military intervention.

4.89. For this reason too if and inasmuch as Dutchbat acted contrary to Gobilliard's order (see: 2.37) this *ultra vires* action must be attributed to the State.

4.90. The District Court considers that inasmuch as it was related to the refugees Gobilliard's order was limited to those refugees in the *mini safe area* that Dutchbat had demarcated and where the refugees were staying when the order was given. On July 11th 1995 Karremans had informed the Bosnian Serbs that he regarded the compound and the surroundings as a safe area (NIOD, p. 2,604). In this actual situation with due regard for the text of Gobilliard's order in which the task of protecting the refugees "*in your care*" follows on immediately after that of withdrawal of Dutchbat in Potočari we are unable to understand the order as reasonably relating to anything other than just the refugees in the *mini safe area*.

[...]

4.262. Claimants argue that in the period from 11th July up to and including 13th July 1995 Dutchbat observed many war crimes being committed by the Bosnian Serbs, but failed to file reports about them to superiors in the UN chain of command. Claimants argue that this failure to report led to the international community becoming informed about these war crimes too late, namely after (most of) the genocide following the fall of Srebrenica had taken place. Claimants also argue that if an alarm about said war crimes of 12th or 13th July 1995 had been raised, the lives of many could have been saved as this could have prompted the UN, NATO or individual states to launch a direct military intervention.

4.263. Parties agree that Dutchbat did not report all observed war crimes to the UN chain of command. Dutchbat did not submit any written notification of war crimes at all. Karremans orally passed on information about Rutten's discovery of nine dead bodies in civilian clothes (see 4.228) in the morning of 13th July 1995 to *Bosnia Herzegovina Command* in Sarajevo and also brought it to the attention of Nicolai. Although Karremans stated during the debriefing in Assen that he also orally reported Groenewegen's observation in the afternoon of 12th or 13th July 1995 of an execution of a refugee at about 200 meters from the compound to the UN chain of command, the District Court is unable to establish with a sufficient degree of certainty – since confirmation from another (Dutchbat) source is not available – that the notification of Groenewegen's observation actually left the compound. The District Court takes into consideration that the NIOD raised the question whether Karremans may have made a mistake regarding this aspect, as he had stated during the debriefing in Zagreb on 22th July 1995 that he had no knowledge of any eyewitness accounts of actual executions (NIOD, p. 2720, middle). It has not been asserted, nor is there any evidence that Dutchbat made any other notifications.

4.264. In the opinion of the District Court Dutchbat's failure to report war crimes observed during the transition period constitutes a violation of generally accepted standards in accordance with law of custom, in connection with which special reference is made to 4.175-4.177 for the interpretation of the standard of care. It is indisputable that during the transition period Dutchbat could not protect the refugees inside and around the *mini safe area* located outside the compound on its own, i.e. without outside help, due to its limited manpower and due to the superior military strength of the Bosnian Serbs. Furthermore, Dutchbat at most had a clear view of the men selected by the Bosnian Serbs who were being held in various buildings outside the *mini safe area*. In these circumstances Dutchbat had the obligation to report the war crimes it had directly and indirectly witnessed up to that point as well as from that moment onwards to the UN chain of command.

4.265. The District Court finds that the argument put forward by the State, namely that reporting war crimes did not have the highest priority in Dutchbat as it lacked the manpower to maintain order on site does not constitute a justification defence, not even when it is taken into consideration that decisions were made under great pressure in a war situation.

[...]

4.276. Following on from the above, the District Court is of the opinion that a military intervention would not have been launched if Dutchbat had met its duty to report. In this regard the District Court refers to the fact that on July 16th 1995 Janvier informed the UN Secretary-General that he agreed with Van Kappen's analysis and that the recapture of the *safe area* lay outside the capabilities of UNPROFOR, all the more so because a possibly military action would have to be undertaken out of sight of a hostile population and in all probability would have led to an overt war with Bosnian Serbs and possible even Yugoslavia, as NATO would have had to attack the integrated air defence system. This was the last word on the French ideas discussed in 4.138 and elsewhere about recapturing the *safe area* (NIOD, p. 2429). Van Kappen analysis applied in full to the situation on July 12th and 13th 1995.

4.277. The conclusion therefore is that the question whether Dutchbat's (proper) compliance with its duty to report would have led to a direct military intervention of the UN, NATO or individual states is answered in the negative. In a situation such as this, the follow-up question remains unanswered whether direct military intervention would have resulted in the lives of Claimants' family members being saved with a sufficient degree of certainty.

4.278. The conclusion is that Dutchbat wrongfully failed to report observed war crimes to the UN chain of command. However, the State is not liable for this unlawful failure, as the causal connection, required for liability, with Claimants' damages is lacking.

4.279. The foregoing includes the opinion that compliance with the duty to report could not have prevented in any way the Bosnian Serbs from committing (more) war crimes in Potočari on July 12th and 13th 1995, including the rape from Claimant [Claimant 10]'s statement (see 2.45.10).

[...]

(d) Upholding the decision throughout the transition period not to allow refugees entry to the compound

4.284. In order to answer the question whether or not Dutchbat should have allowed all refugees entry to the compound during the transition period, particularly after strong suspicions had arisen in the evening of July 12th 1995 that the men selected and carried off by the Bosnian Serbs ran a real risk of being killed or inhumanely treated, it is important to take account of the circumstances in which the decision to allow the refugees entry to the compound was taken and implemented as well as the considerations on which that decision was based.

4.285. The decision to allow refugees entry to the compound was taken when the city of Srebrenica nearly fell and refugees were expected to come to Potočari who would have to be received there. The Bosnian Serbs had made it known on July 11th 1995 that refugees were not allowed to enter the compound. They had also set an ultimatum which was accompanied by the threat to kill the Dutchbat soldiers who had been taken hostage and to use all weapon systems in an attack on the compound and the city of Srebrenica (NIOD, pp. 2603 to 2604). It was unclear how the situation would develop, both in terms of what would (have to) happen with the refugees and the response/further actions of the Bosnian Serbs.

[...]

4.288. Even if the compound had been large enough, as according to Claimants it was as large as the *Malieveld* where crowds of about 20,000 to 25,000 people convene for demonstrations, a large part of the refugees would have been housed outdoors, in sight and in the field of fire of the Bosnian Serbs, who had threatened to open fire at the compound if Dutchbat received refugees there. Furthermore, maintaining freedom of movement at the compound for Dutchbat, which was also included in Franken's consideration, was in the interest of the reception of and assistance to the refugees. When also considering the very precarious living conditions at the compound, admitting all refugees after all (about 25,000) at the compound during the transition period was not a realistic option.

4.289. When in the evening of July 12th 1995 suspicions had arisen that the men selected and carried off by the Bosnian Serbs ran a real risk of being killed or inhumanely treated, admitting all refugees to the compound who were in the mini safe area at the time still was not a viable option. Although it concerned less refugees than the day before, following the evacuation of 4,000 to 5,000 refugees, Franken's consideration still applied and also to the remaining refugees, while the refugees' circumstances were also visibly deteriorating.

4.290. Since the reception of all refugees at the compound was not a realistic option either during the transition period, failure not to make use of that opportunity cannot successfully alleged against Dutchbat.

4.291. Similarly it was not a realistic option for Dutchbat to admit only the male refugees to the compound after suspicions had arisen in the evening of July 12th 1995 that the men selected and carried off by the Bosnian Serbs ran a real risk of being killed or inhumanely treated. This would have entailed Dutchbat removing the men from the crowd of refugees who were in the part of the *mini safe area* that lay just outside the compound and bringing them to the compound. Aside from the fact whether or not the circumstances would have permitted the reception of these men, there are no indications that this would have been practicable, also in view of the limited manpower available to Dutchbat and the risk of endangering the evacuation of the other refugees, whose interests were best served with evacuation. The District Court therefore also finds the decision not to allow the male refugees entry to the compound during the transition period not unlawful.

(e) Separating the male refugees from the other refugees during the evacuation

4.292. Claimants argue that the State should not have cooperated with "the deportation" of the refugees, which they argue the State wrongly qualifies as "evacuation". The State, in turn, objects to Claimants' accusation to have cooperated with the "deportation". So far, the District Court consistently used the term *evacuation* regarding Dutchbat's decisions about all refugees after the fall, the removal of the refugees other than the male refugees by the Bosnian Serbs and in assessing the attributability of Dutchbat's actions during the transition period. The District Court did not use this term when it concerned the removal of the male refugees selected by the Bosnian Serbs. Like Claimants, the District Court is of the opinion that the designation evacuation does not do justice to the actual situation of the removal of the male refugees, which was a deportation. The term evacuation does apply to the removal of the other refugees from the mini safe area, for which the District Court takes into consideration that a safe haven had to be found for the refugees after the fall of Srebrenica and that there was no reason to have concerns about the fate of these refugees. The fact that the men were removed from the queues for the buses, is not reason enough to also designate the removal of the other refugees as deportation.

4.293. Claimants' accusation essentially does not concern the evacuation of the other refugees, but Dutchbat's cooperation with the separation of the men from the other refugees prior to their deportation.

4.294. In so far as Claimants also wish to argue that Dutchbat should not have cooperated at all with the evacuation of the refugees, the District Court considers that there is no reason to regard Dutchbat's cooperation with the evacuation of the other refugees who as a result were brought to safety, which is not in dispute.

4.295. The District Court proceeds to discuss Claimants' accusation about the separation of the men from the rest of the refugees in chronological order, namely supervising the evacuation of the refugees on July 12th 1995 (1), the decision not to stop the evacuation in the evening of July 12th 1995 (2), continuing the supervision of the evacuation on July 13th 1995 (3), and Claimants' asserted active involvement of Dutchbat in separating the men from the other refugees (4).

(1) Supervision of refugees on July 12th 1995

4.296. The State contests that Dutchbat was actively involved in separating the men from the other refugees. It argues that due to the run on the buses, which can be explained by the miserable conditions in which the refugees had been staying at and around the compound, Dutchbat only wanted to channel and guide the evacuation of refugees.

[...]

4.298. As concluded above in 4.247 Dutchbat could initially reasonably assume on July 12th 1995 that the Bosnian Serbs would screen the male refugees who were removed from the queues for war crimes and had no reason to fear for the fate of these men. In part against this background Dutchbat could in all reasonableness decide to supervise the evacuation in the manner described above.

(2) the decision not to stop the evacuation in the evening of July 12th 1995

4.299. In the evening of July 12th 1995 Dutchbat could suspect, and did suspect, that the men selected and carried off by the Bosnian Serbs ran a real risk of being killed or inhumanely treated. It was then also considered to stop the evacuation and it was decided not to do so.

[...]

4.303. The statement cited above shows that Franken acknowledged the consequences of not stopping the evacuation. As has been considered above, it was not a realistic option to admit all refugees to the compound at that point, nor removing the men from the *mini safe area* outside the compound and admit them to the compound. Dutchbat did not have a viable alternative under the given circumstances to bring the refugees to safety and to take them out of the quickly deteriorating situation in the mini safe area. Furthermore, it is not proven – and Claimants do not argue this – that the other refugees who were being evacuated and taken to Kaldanj as agreed ran the risk of being killed or inhumanely treated. Continuing the evacuation was in fact in the interest of this large group of other refugees, who had been brought to safety and taken out of the miserable conditions of the *mini safe area*. In this regard the District Court takes into consideration that as a result of this situation in the *mini safe area* several people had already been killed and that on July 11th 1995 the assessment was made that the refugees – depending on the circumstances – could stay in the *mini safe area* for another three to five days. So on July 12th 1995 another two to four days. It is the District Court's opinion that, in the given circumstances and in view of what it knew at the time, Dutchbat was able to take a reasonable decision to continue the evacuation, which brought the majority of the refugees to safety and out of a situation that was becoming increasingly untenable. The District Court therefore does not accept Claimants' argument that an unjustifiable assessment.

[...]

(4) The asserted active involvement of Dutchbat in separating the men from the other refugees on July 13th 1995

4.312. In the given circumstances, Dutchbat could have been expected to only supervise on July 13th 1995 and to refrain from any active actions that could lead or contribute to Bosnian Serbs taking able-bodied men from the queues of refugees heading towards to the buses. According to the District Court active actions include any acts beyond the mere assistance of refugees to the buses via the lock through which they walked in turns. This includes, for example, pointing out men, removing men from the queues with the Bosnian Serbs and guarding the men who had been removed from the queues. Such actions cannot stand up to the test of reasonableness and must be deemed unlawful.

4.313. Most written statements of [Claimant 1] et al., mention supervision of the evacuation by Dutchbat as described above.

[...]

4.316. If these statements are true, these are unlawful acts by Dutchbat attributable to the State. The truth of these statements disputed by the State by arguing that there is no supporting evidence however does not need to be investigated because in the opinion of the District Court, the required causal relationship for liability of the State is lacking. The District Court considers as follows:

4.317. It cannot be established with a sufficient degree of certainty that the husbands of [Claimant 4] and [Claimant 9] would have survived in the absence of the more active actions of Dutchbat as described in their statements. After all, the Bosnian Serbs systematically selected men from the queues of refugees heading to the buses. Rutten's statement before the Dutch parliamentary committee of inquiry describing the process of the assistance also reveals that the refugees had to walk several hundreds of meters before reaching the buses:

[...]

Finally, it has been established that nearly all men from the *mini safe area* taken prisoner by the Bosnian Serbs were killed.

(f) Cooperating in the evacuation of refugees who had sought refuge at the compound

4.318. In view of Claimants' standpoints, this accusation focuses on the men who had sought refuge at the compound. Apart from that, it applies here too that it has not been proven that the actions of Dutchbat during the evacuation of the other refugees who had sought their refuge at the compound are unlawful.

4.319. Dutchbat assisted with the evacuation of the compound in the same manner it had done up to that point. The Nuhanović and Mustafić cases prove that – in any case by the end of this part of the evacuation, when nearly all refugees had left the compound – Dutchbat urged refugees who did not want to leave the compound to leave and/or sent them away from the compound.

4.320. In order to protect the able-bodied men, Franken faxed the list he had ordered to be drawn up to various national and international authorities, among which the Royal Netherlands Army. According to his interpreter, Franken told the Bosnian Serbs that they had to take into account that Dutchbat had this list and that copies had been sent to the International Red Cross in Geneva and the UN in New York (NIOD, p. 2747). Franken stated before the Dutch parliamentary committee of inquiry that he saw the drawing up of this list as the only way to protect the men: "*I explained to you before why I did not physically protect the men. This does not mean that I regard the drawing up of a list as being equivalent to the physical protection of the men. But in the given situation, it was one of the possibilities to at least offer them some protection.*" (PE hearings, p. 77).

4.321. In the opinion of the District Court, Dutchbat should have reassessed its actions regarding the evacuation of the refugees when the evacuation of the compound started in the afternoon of July 13th 1995, and it was unable to take the decision in reasonableness to let the able-bodied men leave the compound, especially with the knowledge it had at that time, namely that if the men were carried off by the Bosnian Serbs they would face death or inhumane treatment. The District Court therefore considers as follows.

4.322. The compound took up a separate position within the mini safe area. Dutchbat was fully in control of the enclosed compound. The Bosnian Serbs who were present in the mini safe area outside the compound and did not shy away from committing war crimes there, never interfered with the compound and respected Dutchbat's authority over the compound. As has been assessed above, the State had jurisdiction in the compound, as stipulated in Article 1 ECHR and Article 1 ICCPR, in contrast with the part of the mini safe area that lay outside the compound.

4.323. At the start of the evacuation of foreign nationals at the compound, the group of refugees to be evacuated had decreased to approximately 5,000, about a fifth of the original number previously present in the *mini safe area*. This puts the argument of the State in perspective regarding the minor number of Dutchbat soldiers in the *mini safe area* in relation to the number of refugees. In addition, Dutchbat had an overall insight into the number of able-bodied men within the compound, of whom the majority were on the list Franken had had drawn up, and did not have insight into the number of men among the refugees in the part of the *mini safe area* outside the compound.

4.324. Because of the events that took place on July 13th 1995, especially the discovery of the burning pile of identity papers at the White House, Dutchbat knew when the evacuation of the refugees of the compound became relevant that the men selected and carried off by the Bosnian Serbs faced death or inhumane treatment. It has therefore also been considered that by the end of the afternoon of July 13th 1995, Dutchbat must have been aware of the serious danger (serious risk) of genocide if the men residing at the compound were to be carried off by the Bosnian Serbs.

4.325. The District Court acknowledges that the situation at the compound was miserable and that accommodating all refugees for a longer period was not a realistic option due to the lack of food and other provisions, and due to the risks that are inherent to a large group of people living in the sweltering heat and under unsanitary conditions.

However, it has not been proven that it was impossible to accommodate the orderly group of ablebodied men who were present at the compound for some time longer. Nor has it been proven that by allowing the other refugees from the factory hall at the compound to depart and letting the able-bodied men remain there would have presented practical problems. The situation in the compound differed in this sense as well from the situation of the evacuation of refugees from the part of the *mini safe area* outside the compound, which would have entailed Dutchbat picking men out of the crown of refugees.

4.326. The foregoing proves that the evacuation of the refugees from the compound differed substantially in a number of ways from the evacuation of the refugees from the part of the *mini safe area* outside the compound. In all reasonableness, Dutchbat could have been required to reassess the situation and all interests concerned prior to the evacuation of the refugees from the compound and that it should have decided to let the male refugees stay at the compound.

4.327. In that reassessment, Dutchbat should not and could not have reasonably relied on the fact that the list of able-bodied men at the compound drawn up by order of Franken would have offered the assumed protection against the fate faced by these men, known to Dutchbat. Dutchbat could and should have taken into account the possibility that the Bosnian Serbs would not respect this list. The Bosnian Serbs had already demonstrated during the evacuation of the refugees that they did not keep agreements to that effect, for example when it took over control of the evacuation on July 12th 1995 and apparently had already arranged buses. Furthermore, they did not shy away from selecting men from the queues of waiting refugees and from abusing refugees, literally under the gaze of Dutchbat soldiers. The Bosnian Serbs' remarks about the pile of identity papers as referred to in the statement of Van Duijn (see 4.251) does not correspond with the purpose of screening the men, which was still being claimed by them, nor does the taking away and burning of these documents correspond with such a screening. These remarks and the conduct of the Bosnian Serbs showed that they were unreliable in their statements about the able-bodied men.

4.328. The District Court's opinion given above, namely that Dutchbat was unable to take the decision in reasonableness to let the able-bodied men leave the compound is in accordance with the ruling of the Appeals Court in the Nuhanović and Mustafić cases relating to the actions of Dutchbat in the final phase of the evacuation of the refugees from the compound. The Appeals Court considered that it cannot be assumed that a possible order from the UN or the Dutch government to cooperate with the evacuation of the refugees by the Bosnian Serbs would have entailed that the evacuation should have been supported if there had been a real risk for the able-bodied men at the compound to be killed or inhumanely treated by the Bosnian Serbs. The Appeals Court held that it would not have constituted a violation of any order given by the UN or the Dutch government if Dutchbat had decided no later than by the end of the afternoon of July 13th 1995 to no longer cooperate with the evacuation because of this risk. In accordance with the Gobilliard's *order "to take all reasonable measures to protect refugees and civilians in your care"*, Dutchbat should have terminated its cooperation with the evacuation from that moment, in any case with regard to the able-bodied men, according to the Appeals Court. As is apparent from the foregoing, it is the opinion of the District Court that this applies from the moment the evacuation of refugees from the compound started, in which the necessity to terminate its cooperation became all the more pressing as, other than on July 12th 1995 and in the morning of July 13th 1995, Dutchbat must have been aware of a *serious risk* of the male refugees being killed in a genocide.

4.329. The actions of Dutchbat can be qualified as a violation of Article 2 ECHR and Article 6 ICCPR and as actions contrary to the standard of care under Book 6, Section 162 of the Dutch Civil Code. This standard of care is in this case exemplified by the principles of law that constitute the basis for the conventions mentioned above and the State's obligations under international law to prevent genocide. Dutchbat's acts are unlawful with respect to the male refugees who left the compound late in the afternoon on July 13th 1995.

4.330. In the opinion of the District Court, the required causal relationship regarding liability of the State is proven, as it is determined with a sufficient degree of certainty that the able-bodied men staying at the compound would have survived if Dutchbat had not cooperated with their deportation. The District Court therefore considers as follows.

4.331. Not cooperating with the deportation of the able-bodied men at the compound would in practice have meant that these men would have remained at the compound, together with Dutchbat and the local personnel and MSF personnel who were going to be evacuated along with Dutchbat. The Bosnian Serbs would have been unable to carry these men off and subsequently kill them. The fate of the men would have been tied in with that of Dutchbat. Under these circumstances, the Bosnian Serbs would have had no other option than to use force against Dutchbat and the compound in order to be able to transport the remaining men. The District Court holds beyond doubt that the Bosnian Serbs would not have proceeded to do so, even in the face of, in the words of the ICTY, *"a concerted effort (...) to capture all Muslim men of military age*" and was "*the operation to capture and detain the Bosnian men (...) well organized and comprehensive*" (Krstić, legal ground no. 85). The District Court takes into account the fact that the Bosnian Serbs up to that moment had not interfered with the compound and that their earlier threats to use force against the compound had proven to be empty. It was already clear to Franken when the enclave fell that Mladić would not allow UN soldiers to be killed (NIOD, p. 2241) and on July 12th 1995, Voorhoeve had already concluded that sparing peacekeeping forces was part of the Bosnian Serbs' attack strategy (NIOD, p. 2439). It is also taken into account that the Bosnian Serbs must have been aware of the presence of an orderly number of able-bodied men at the compound, contrary to the rest of the *mini safe area*: during the Dutch parliamentary committee of inquiry, Franken stated that he had let two or three Bosnian Serbs onto the compound shortly after the fall of the enclave "*because they wanted to make sure that the entire 28th division was not there with me at the compound*" (PE hearings, p. 74). Finally, the Bosnian Serbs had found out on July 11th 1995 that the UN and NATO were willing to deploy air weapons and the District Court considers it impossible that no air support would have been provided if the compound had been attacked.

4.332. It follows on from the foregoing that the State is liable for the deportation of the able-bodied men who had been staying at the compound in the late afternoon on July 13th 1995 on account of unlawful acts.

[...]

4.336. In a ground included for the sake of completeness, the District Court has held that even if it is established that Dutchbat advised the male refugees to flee to the woods, this advice – as well as the failure to raise the alarm about their fleeing – are not be deemed as unlawful. Whether or not this advice was indeed given does therefore not require further investigation.

4.337. The District Court holds that Dutchbat wrongly failed to report the observed war crimes to the UN chain of command. Since the causal connection required for liability of the State between this failure and Claimants' damages is lacking, the declaration claimed under 3.1 sub II cannot be granted regarding this failure. Even if it is established that the cooperation of Dutchbat with evacuation of refugees on July 13th 1995 also consisted of an active separation of the male refugees, this will not lead to allowing this declaration in this respect due to the lack of a causal connection between these acts and Claimants' damages. Further investigation into the facts is therefore not required.

4.338. The District Court deems Dutchbat's cooperation with the deportation in the late afternoon of July 13th 1995 of the able-bodied male refugees who had sought refuge at the compound an unlawful act for which the State is liable. It concerns about 320 men, among whom were Mustafić and Nuhanović's father and brother, to who the Nuhanović and Mustafić cases related. The majority of these men were never seen alive again. A small number of them ended up in the Batkovici prison camp near Bijelina and were released in December 1995 under the Daytona Agreement, along with another group of men from Srebrenica (NIOD, p. 2659).

4.339. The liability of the State extends to the family members of the men who were carried off from the compound and then killed by the Bosnian Serbs in the late afternoon of July 13th 1995, the starting point for which are the spouses and children of the adult men and the parents of the underage men. It should be noted that men who have reached the age of eighteen are deemed adults.

[...]

4.342. In so far as the *Stichting* represents their interests, the State is liable towards the family members referred to under 4.339 of the men who in the late afternoon of July 13th 1995 were deported from the compound and subsequently killed by the Bosnian Serbs. Further possibly relevant questions fall outside the scope of these proceedings and therefore remain undiscussed.

4.343. The foregoing entails that the declaration referred to under 3.1 sub II shall be awarded in the sense that the ruling is that on account of an unlawful act the State is liable for damages incurred by the persons referred to under 4.339 and represented by the *Stichting*, resulting from the cooperation extended by Dutchbat to the deportation of the male refugees who in the late afternoon of July 13th 1995 were deported from the compound in Potočari by the Bosnian Serbs and subsequently killed.

[...]

5 THE DECISION

The District Court

5.1. Rules that on account of an unlawful act the State is liable for damages incurred by the persons referred to under 4.339 and represented by the Stichting, resulting from the cooperation extended by Dutchbat to the deportation of the male refugees who in the late afternoon of July 13th 1995 were deported from the compound in Potočari by the Bosnian Serbs and subsequently killed

5.2. Orders the State to pay the costs of these proceedings on the part of Claimants so far estimated at €6,060.85

5.3. Declares the cost order provisionally enforceable

5.4. Dismisses all other applications.